The Early Mongols

Indiana University Uralic and Altaic Series

Denis Sinor, Editor

Volume 173

Igor de Rachewiltz

The Early Mongols:
Language, Culture and History

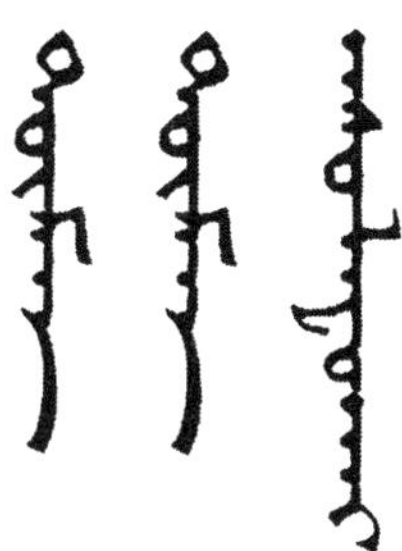

Tümen tümen nasulatuγai

STUDIES IN HONOR OF

Igor de Rachewiltz

ON THE OCCASION OF HIS 80TH BIRTHDAY

Edited by

Volker Rybatzki, Alessandra Pozzi
Peter W. Geier and John R. Krueger

Indiana University
The Denis Sinor Institute for Inner Asian Studies
Bloomington, Indiana
2009

Library of Congress Control Number 2008941597
ISBN 978-0-933070-57-8

Printed in the United States of America

LIST OF CONTENTS

Preface

Igor de Rachewiltz was born on April 11, 1929 in Rome as the second of three children. His mother was Russian, born in St. Petersburg, his father Italian, from Rome. He attended primary, middle and high school in Rome and, in 1948, started to read Law, Asian History, Chinese and Mongolian at the University 'La Sapienza' of Rome. After finishing his juridical studies in 1951, he continued to read Chinese, Japanese and other subjects at the *Istituto Universitario Orientale*, Naples, while working at the same time in the Archives Section of the FAO administration in Rome. In 1955 he won a Ph.D. scholarship at the Australian National University (ANU) in Canberra. What he probably did not imagine at that time was that ANU was to remain his home university for the rest of his academic career. Between 1956 and 1960 de Rachewiltz completed his Ph.D. degree course in Asian History in the *Department of Far Eastern History*, ANU, and thus obtained in 1961 the Ph.D. degree with a thesis entitled *Sino-Mongol Culture Contacts in the Thirteenth Century – A Study of Yeh-lü Ch'u-ts'ai.*

Already in September 1960, de Rachewiltz was appointed Lecturer in Asian Civilisations at the *School of General Studies* (SGS), ANU. This was followed in July 1963 by the appointment as Senior Lecturer in Asian Civilisations at the same institution. In August 1965, de Rachewiltz became a Fellow at the *Department of Far Eastern History*, ANU, followed by the position of Senior Fellow at the *Division of Pacific and Asian History*, ANU, in July 1967. Igor de Rachewiltz remained in this position, including not only research duties, but also supervision of Ph.D. students, administrative duties, as well as giving regular seminars, until 1994, when he retired. After his retirement de Rachewiltz became a Visiting Fellow at the same institution, this title being changed to Emeritus Fellow at the *Division of Pacific and Asian History, Research School of Pacific and Asian Studies*, ANU, in 2004.

Although Canberra and the Australian National University in remote Australia became the home of Igor de Rachewiltz, this did not prevent him from taking actively part in scholary activities all around the world. Since 1965, he has not only been participating in numerous conferences worldwide, but he has also been Guest Speaker and Lecturer at various universities and institutes. The most important of these activities are: Research Scholar at the *Tōyō Bunka Kenkyūjo*, Tokyo, and *Jimbun*

Kagaku Kenkyūjo, Kyoto (1962/October-1963/March), Visiting Professor and Guest Speaker at the *Oriental Institute, Czechoslovak Academy of Sciences*, Prague, Czechoslovakia (1970/November-December), Visiting Professor, *East Asian Institute*, Copenhagen University, Denmark (1971/January), Visiting Professor in the *Seminar für Sprach- und Kulturwissenschaft Zentralasiens*, Bonn University, on a Deutscher Akademischer Austauschdienst Fellowship (1979/September-December), Visiting Professor at *ILCAA*, Tōkyō Gaikokugo Daigaku, on a Japan Society for the Promotion of Science Fellowship (1986/April-June), and lastly Visiting Professor, *Dipartimento di Studi Orientali*, University of Rome 'La Sapienza' (1996/March-May, 1999/April-May, 2001/April-May).

Additionally, Igor de Rachewiltz has been a member of the *Editorial Board of East Asian History* (formerly *Papers on Far Eastern History*) since 1970, a member of the *Faculty of Asian Studies Publication Committee*, ANU, since 1977, a member of the *Sonderforschungsbereich 12* ('Orientalistik unter besonderer Berücksichtigung Zentralasiens'), Bonn University since 1979, a member of the *Executive Committee of the International Association for Mongol Studies* since 1987, and Vice-President of the *International Association for Mongol Studies* since 1992.

For these various activities as well as for his outstanding scientific contributions Igor de Rachewiltz has been honoured several times. He was nominated Fellow of the Australian Academy of the Humanities in 1972, he became a Honourable Member (and Medal) of the International Association for Mongol Studies, Ulaanbaator, in 1992, a Knight of the Order of Merit of the Italian Republic in 1998, and he was awarded Honorary Doctor in Letters and Philosophy, Faculty of Letters and Philosophy, University of Rome 'La Sapienza', in 2001. In addition, he received the Centenary Medal for Service to Australian Society and the Humanities in Asian Studies in 2003, the Gold Medal of the Permanent International Altaistic Conference (PIAC) in 2004, the Polar Star Medal of the Mongolian Republic in 2007, and the Denis Sinor Medal of the Royal Asiatic Society, London, in 2007.

As Igor de Rachewiltz states himself, three are his main research interests: 'Political and cultural history of China and Mongolia in the 13th and 14th centuries', 'East-West political and cultural contacts, especially in the 13th and 14th centuries', and 'Sino-Mongolian philology'.

These are the three big frames of Igor de Rachewiltz scientific works, but, as a look at the biography shows, inside every frame falls a lot of different works, and some very important do not fit at all. It is not our aim to give a full overview over de Rachewiltz' scientific publications, but what we would like to point out are the highlights. From the very beginning, biographies of various persons active in the Mongol and Yüan empire have been the special interest of de Rachewiltz. Besides several articles, this interest resulted in the publication of two voluminous publications: the *Repertory of Proper Names in Yüan Sources* (3 vols, plus supplement; A.6-7), compiled with M. Wang, and *In the Service of the Khan. Eminent Personalities of the Early Mongol-Yüan Period* (A.10). In the last one de Rachewiltz is both an editor (together with H. L. Chan, C. C. Hsiao and P. W. Geier) and contributor. Another project of similar dimensions was his *Index to Bibliographical Material in Chin and Yüan Literary Works* (First to Third Series; bibliography A.3-5), compiled together with N. Nakano and M. Wang. Once de Rachewiltz told that some colleagues were remarking, especially in connection with the *Index* and the *Repertory* that he was wasting time that could be better used. However, it seems more probable that scientifically these two will have a very long-lasting value.

Another big love of de Rachewiltz, and properly the one for which he is best known, is connected with the *Secret History of the Mongols*. Work on the *Secret History* has accompanied him throughout his scientific career. It started with an article on the dating of the *Secret History* (C.3), followed by a transcription of and an index to the text (A.2) and, since 1970, a series of annotated translations of the *Secret History* (A.8-10, 13-14, 18-20, 22-23, 32-33, 35). The life-long research on the *Secret History*, Mongolian history, culture and language(s), culminated in a new annotated translation of the *Secret History* in 2004; a second (paperback) edition with additions and corrections of this *opus magnum* appeared in 2006 (A.13). This, however, did not mean the end of the research, as a *Supplement to the Secret History*, an updating of the translation and commentary, will appear in 2010 (G.2), as de Rachewiltz is also coming back to the very beginning of his studies on the *Secret History* with a new article on *The Dating of the Secret History*, which will appear at the end of 2008 (G.3).

Igor de Rachewiltz has been dealing with various problems connected with the Mongols of the 13th and 14th centuries: historical, philological, religious, and ideological ones, just to number a few. Mention has to be made also of the various transcriptions (and translations as well as commentaries) of various Middle and Classical Mongolian texts produced by de Rachewiltz, f.ex. his works on the *Erdeni-yin tobci* (A.8-9; together with M. Gō, J. R. Krueger, B. Ulaan), the *Bodhicaryāvatāra* (A12, C.39), the *Hua-yi yi-yü* (A.11, C.66, D.1), a poem of Mu□ammad al-Samarqandī (C.7), the stele of Yisüngge (C.15), Töregene's edict (C.21), the *Hsiao-ching* (C.26, 36, 72), two *pai-tzu* (C.28), as well as on a Chinese inscription of 1279 (C.37). Also his efforts in editing (and revising) the posthumous works of four other great Mongolists, A. Mostaert (A.11; D.1, 8), F. W. Cleaves (D.11-13) and P. Pelliot & L. Hambis (10) should not be forgotten.

Finishing, we would like to mention one work of Igor de Rachewiltz, done in cooperation with J. R. Krueger, that falls outside the frame of what has been stated before, but shows de Rachewiltz' wide sphere of interests. We mean the translation (de Rachewitz & Krueger) and commentary (de Rachewiltz) of Čeveng [C. Ž. Žamcarano]'s *Essay on the Origin and State of the Darqad, the Uriyangqai of Lake Köbsögöl, the Dörbed, the Qotong, the Bayad, the Ögöled, the Mingyad, the Jaqačin, Turyut, the Qošud, the Čaqar, the Dariyanya, the Uriyangqai of the Altai, and the Qamniyan* (C.45, 54, 60, 63, 69). This essay, published in 1934 in Ulaanbaatar, gives detailed informations on various aspects of ethnic groups of Mongolia, excluding the Khalkha, at the beginning of the 20th century, not found anywhere else.

It is our pleasure to thank Y.-C. R. Lam, R. Meserve, Y. Saitô and B. Ulaan for their help in getting in contact with colleagues we would have otherwise not been able to contact. Despite all our efforts, we could not reach all of those we would have liked to contact. For this we apologize. We are also in debt with D. Sinor, who from the very beginning supported our project and was willing to include the volume into the *Uralic and Altaic Series* of Indiana University. Lastly, we thank all the contributors for their willingness to contribute to this volume, and for their patience with us. It is due to them that we could produce this volume.

In the name of the contributors and the persons included in the *Tabula gratulatoria*, we wish you, Igor

Tümen tümen nasulatuyai

October 26, 2008

Volker Rybatzki, Alessandra Pozzi, Peter W. Geier, and John R. Krueger

Tabula gratulatoria

Thomas T. Allsen	Eugene
Reuven Amitai	Jerusalem
Ákos Bertalan Apatóczky	Budapest
Christopher I. Beckwith	Bloomington
Marie-Lise Beffa	Paris
Giampiero Bellingeri	Venice
Shagdar Bira	Ulaanbaatar
Michal Biran	Jerusalem
Ágnes Birtalan	Budapest
Elena V. Boykova	Moscow
Paul D. Buell	Seattle
Uradyn E. Bulag	Cambridge
Hok-lam Chan	Seattle
Chinggeltei	Huhhot
Sharav Choimaa	Ulaanbaatar
Pamela Crossley	Norwich, Vermont
Dang Bao-hai	Beijing
Nicola Di Cosmo	Princeton
Ruth W. Dunnell	Mt. Vernon, Ohio
Vera Duran degli Arodij	Roma
Elizabeth Endicott	Middlebury
Marcel Erdal	Frankfurt a.M.
Marie-Dominique Even	Nanterre
Herbert Franke	Gauting
David Gedalecia	Wooster
Peter W. Geier	Cisterna di Latina
Geng Shimin	Beijing
Peter B. Golden	West Windsor
Liliya M. Gorelova	Moscow · Auckland
Stéphane Grivelet	Hanoï · Schœlcher, Martinique

Harry Halén	Helsinki
Charles J. Halperin	Bloomington
Roberte N. Hamayon	Paris
Ho Peng Yoke	Kenmore, Queensland
Hsiao Ch'i-ch'ing	Taipei
Hugjiltu	Huhhot
Caroline Humphrey	Cambridge
Hung Chin-fu	Taipei
Peter Jackson	Keele, United Kingdom
Juha Janhunen	Helsinki
Junast	Beijing
Daniel Kane	Sydney
György Kara	Bloomington
Rudolf Kaschewsky	Bonn
Barbara Kellner-Heinkele	Berlin
Sergei Klyashtornyj	Saint Petersburg
John R. Krueger	Bloomington
Yuan-Chu Ruby Lam	Wellesley
Jens Peter Laut	Göttingen
Colin Mackerras	Brisbane
Victor H. Mair	Philadelphia
Romano Mastromattei	Rome
Koichi Matsuda	Osaka
Dai Matsui	Hirosaki
Takashi Matsukawa	Kyoto
Charles P. Melville	Cambridge
Erling von Mende	Berlin
Ruth I. Meserve	Bloomington
David Morgan	Madison
Mari Nakami	Tokyo
Tatsuo Nakami	Tokyo
Jun Nakamura	Tokyo

Mehmet Ölmez	Istanbul
Mariya N. Orlovskaya	Moscow
Shigeo Ozawa	Saitama-ken
Luciano Petech	Rome
Rodica Pop	Bucharest
Alessandra Pozzi	Helsinki
Purevjav	Ulaanbaatar
Johannes Reckel	Göttingen
Morris Rossabi	New York
Jean Richard	Dijon
William Rozycki	Aizuwakamatsu
Volker Rybatzki	Helsinki
Klaus Sagaster	Bonn
Yoshio Saitô	Tokyo
Alice Sárközi	Budapest
Claus Schönig	Berlin
Henry G. Schwarz	Bellingham
Denis Sinor	Bloomington
Elena Skribnik	Munich
Marek Stachowski	Kraków
Giovanni Stary	Venezia
John C. Street	Madison
Masa'aki Sugiyama	Kyoto
Erika Taube	Markleeberg
Manfred Taube	Markleeberg
Aloïs van Tongerloo	Wavre
Domiin Tumurtogoo	Ulaanbaatar
Helga Uebach	München
Borjigijin Ulaan	Beijing
Nobuhiro Uno	Hiroshima
Käthe Uray-Kőhalmi	Budapest
István Vásáry	Budapest

Veronika Veit	Bonn
Alexander Vovin	Bochum · Manoa, Hawai'i
Hartmut Walravens	Berlin
Wang Gungwu	Singapore · Canberra
Michael Weiers	Königswinter
David C. Wright	Calgary
Natalia S. Yakhontova	St. Petersburg
Yao Dali	Shanghai
Zhang Fan	Beijing
Peter Zieme	Berlin

IGOR: MIO FRATELLO
(ricordi della sorella Vera)

Vera Duran degli Arodij

Alla nascita di Igor la nostra famiglia era composta da mamma, nata in Russia a S. Pietroburgo; da papà, nato a Roma, ma le cui origini risalgono ai Longobardi, con capostipite Rotari; da due nonne, la mamma di papà, italiana, gentile signora molto tradizionale e la mamma di mamma, la nonna russa, anche lei molto gentile, ma un po' meno tradizionale, con una personalità forte e abbastanza originale. Sin dalla nascita Igor è divenuto il suo nipote prediletto e lo è rimasto finchè lei è vissuta.

Poi c'era Boris, il primogenito, di tre anni più grande di Igor.

Io sono arrivata solo cinque anni dopo la nascita di Igor.

I miei due fratelli erano molto legati tra loro e dividevano insieme i loro interessi, molteplici e originali e a volte anche un po' pericolosi (come quando sparavano con un fucile ad aria compressa sui vetri dei vicini!!)

Mi volevano molto bene, ma essendo piccola e femmina venivo un po' trascurata da loro, però ero sempre molto curiosa delle loro attività, per cui li seguivo come un cagnolino e li spiavo ogni volta che potevo.

Igor in particolare era un ragazzino dai mille interessi e infinitamente curioso. Sin da piccolo ha cominciato ad avere grande interesse per gli alfabeti particolari e, a nove anni, si mise a studiare da solo il greco antico, gli piaceva l'alfabeto.

Comunque i suoi interessi e le sue curiosità spaziavano in vari settori. Sempre intorno ai 10 anni cominciò ad interessarsi al funzionamento degli orologi (quelli veri). Vicino a casa nostra c'era un negozio che riparava orologi e Igor, un giorno, entrò per chiedere all'orologiaio se poteva guardarlo lavorare. Naturalmente l'orologiaio disse di sì e si affezionò ad Igor vedendolo tanto interessato al suo lavoro; non solo lo faceva guardare, ma cominciò ad insegnargli i segreti del mestiere e cioè il funzionamento degli orologi e come ripararli.

L'amicizia con questo orologiaio è poi durata finchè lui è vissuto, e Igor è diventato un bravissimo conoscitore e riparatore di orologi, soprattutto quelli antichi.

Un altro hobby di Igor era il lancio dei coltelli. Avevamo in casa una bellissima collezione di coltelli antichi e Igor cominciò ad utilizzarli lanciandoli e, non essendoci in casa un vero bersaglio, li lanciava su tutti gli infissi di legno delle porte e delle finestre (mamma non era molto contenta). Era bravissimo e lo è tuttora. Infatti nella sua casa a Canberra ha un grande bersaglio che ogni tanto sistema nel giardino e si diletta a lanciare i coltelli. Ha insegnato anche a me, ma non sono mai stata alla sua altezza.

Sempre tra gli hobby, Igor ha sempre amato molto le antiche penne stilografiche e viaggiando ne trovava sempre qualcuna, per cui adesso, oltre agli orologi antichi, ha anche una bellissima collezione di vecchie penne stilografiche tutte funzionanti.

Comunque l'interesse maggiore che Igor aveva rimanevano gli alfabeti.

Sempre intorno ai 10-12 anni riuscì a diventare amico della famiglia dell'Attaché Navale dell'Ambasciata Giapponese a Roma. Avevano due bambini, Minoru e Mamoru, molto carini, Igor divenne amico con loro e ogni tanto li portava a casa a fare merenda e loro poi cantavano l'inno giapponese, erano proprio simpatici. Tramite loro lui cominciò a fare domande alla loro madre sulla lingua giapponese, era molto interessato agli ideogrammi. Un giorno mamma si vide arrivare a casa la signora giapponese con un grande mazzo di fiori. Voleva conoscere la madre di Igor "quel bambino tanto intelligente".

Alla sua visita ne seguirono altre di studenti cinesi del Collegio Urbano de Propaganda Fide al Gianicolo, dove Igor andava ogni domenica a imparare il cinese e in cambio delle lezioni di cinese lui dava a loro lezioni di italiano. Questo scambio durò molti anni per cui Igor conosceva già abbastanza bene il cinese ancor prima di andare all'Università. Andava anche a visitare spesso il noto Prof. Giovanni Vacca per leggere con lui antichi testi classici cinesi, e passava parecchio tempo con vecchi missionari italiani che avevano trascorso quasi tutta la loro vita in Cina.

In particolare mi ricordo che veniva a trovarci un frate con una lunga barba bianca anche lui veterano della Cina, si chiamava Padre Bonardi e veniva dalle Missioni Estere di Parma. Era letteralmente affascinato da Igor. Si fermava a parlare con mamma di questo "ragazzo particolare" al quale lui pronosticava un futuro molto brillante. Veniva anche a trovarci un giovane prete cinese, si chiamava Padre Hsu, e ci portava sempre del pane bianco, (alimento molto prezioso per quei tempi). Anche lui amava molto Igor e ammirava la sua viva intelligenza e gli piaceva parlarne con mamma. Sentii dire da Igor che questo religioso, rientrato in Cina, abbia fatto una brutta fine.

Ma la vera svolta che determinò il futuro di tutti e due i miei fratelli fu quando trovarono, sopra un banco di libri usati, un piccolo libro sulla

"Storia dell'Alfabeto" ed uno sulla vita e gesta di Genghis Khan, il conquistatore mongolo.

Li comprarono e ci si immersero.

Boris, che era molto bravo a disegnare, rimase incantato dai geroglifici egiziani e subito dopo si comprò, sempre tra i libri usati, una piccola grammatica egiziana e cominciò a studiarla. Da questi primi studi nacque la sua professione di vita che lo fece diventare uno dei più famosi egittologi del secolo scorso.

Purtroppo ora lui non c'è più, ma i suoi studi, i suoi scritti, le sue scoperte ed il suo nome continuano a vivere.

Igor invece si innamorò dell'alfabeto mongolo e decise di farne il suo studio primario, senza abbandonare però le altre lingue che lo interessavano: cinese e giapponese, nonché le lingue europee.

Finito il liceo cominciò i suoi studi universitari a Roma nella Facoltà di Legge (con la laurea in legge avrebbe fatto il Concorso per entrare al Ministero degli Esteri sperando di essere poi inviato in Cina grazie alla sua conoscenza della lingua), continuando allo stesso tempo a studiare il cinese nella Facoltà di Lettere con il Prof. Pasquale D'Elia. Però quando l'Italia non riconobbe la Cina di Mao, Igor abbandonò lo studio della Legge e si iscrisse subito all'Istituto Universitario Orientale di Napoli per dedicarsi interamente allo studio del cinese e del giapponese. Da solo continuava lo studio del mongolo.

Nel 1955 concorse per una Borsa di Studio al Dipartimento di Storia dell'Estremo Oriente dell'Università Nazionale Australiana di Canberra. La vinse e partì.

Completò i suoi studi in Australia (nel 1960) dove poi decise di rimanere divenendo il grande sino-mongolista che oggi è.

Tales of "Prince Igor"

John R. Krueger

As it happens, I can pinpoint almost to the minute the exact time and place when I first met dear Igor, though I knew not then how close our association would prove to be. It was during April 13-15, at the 1966 annual meeting of the American Oriental Society, held in the Conference Center at University of Chicago, USA. My main work that week was continuing my catalogue of the Laufer Mongolian holdings (published in *Journal of the American Oriental Society* 86/2.156-183, 1966). It was about 8:30 AM on Wednesday, 14 April, 1966, as I stood in the breakfast cafeteria line, when a nice fellow in my age range spoke to me and introduced himself. We each were aware of the writings of the other, and for years Dr de Rachewiltz sent me the ongoing parts of his preliminary translation of the "Secret History", appearing in the *Papers on Far Eastern History* (issues 4-17, 1971-1985) which I then used in my own courses at Indiana University about early Mongolian writings, history, literature and chronicles.

We use the affectionate and friendly term, "Prince Igor", not from any vain or aristocratic ways of his behaviour, but in memory of the famed "Lay of Prince Igor's Host," the opera and dramas of Russian history — all the office staff in Canberra call our hero "Igor" in a cheery manner, as I saw during my two terms in DownUnderLand (Februar to August 1987, and November 2003 to Februar 2004).

For the development of Igor's scientific career, it is best to survey the list of publications presented in this volume of honour, culminating in that grand huge two-volume edition of the "Secret History", he is even now preparing a Supplement to it.

Even as a teen-age lad, Igor had learned quite a lot of Chinese and yearned to know the flowing Mongolian script. He got acquainted with Giuseppe Tucci, who was well-to-do: he had even bought the house next door just to contain his large library. Terry Wylie was at Tucci's during his Italian stay, and he and Igor met; later Terry and I were co-workers in Seattle in the mid-1950s. Latin was another early love of Igor's life; he retains a good knowledge, and likes to call Italian "Modern Latin." As a student of Asia, he chose the Australian National University as his venue of specialization, taking his doctoral degree there, and later also having a study tour in Japan.

A wonderful sidelight on Igor's early years comes from his "e=mail" to me of 20 August 2005. He had learned English well and during 1950-1952 worked for various American film companies, who were filming in Italy, Ischia and Sicily, with many of the stars famous during those years. Igor was running a kind of General Office (postal, mimeograph, stationery supplies, interpreting and translation). As a result, he was in close contact with such film celebrities as Robert Taylor, Buddy Baer, Gregory Peck, Burt Lancaster, Gloria Swanson (then still married to Taylor), Peter Ustinov and others. They came in every day to get their mail and filming schedules, and to gossip and have fun. He found Burt Lancaster and Peter Ustinov to be really nice fellows. These stars appeared in "Quo Vadis, Roman Holiday, The Crimson Pirate" and many other films. He was likewise on the spot when Gloria Swanson's valuable jewels were stolen from the Hotel Regina in Ischia, and still has a suspect in mind for the deed.

Later I met Igor often in Mongolia at the Ulaan Baator conferences, and we remained in touch; after departing Australia in year 1987, even our airmail letters would take 10-12 days for delivery, but as "e=mail" developed, we could readily exchange scholarly information several times a week.

Verily, Dr Igor is an outstanding person, and well-deserving of his honours (membership in Italian orders, and scientific societies in Australia, Mongolia and other countries); I'm proud of our long association, and send him every good wish and greeting.

BIBLIOGRAPHY OF IGOR DE RACHEWILTZ

Volker Rybatzki

A. *Books and Monographs*

1. *Papal Envoys to the Great Khans*. London 1971.
2. *Index to the Secret History of the Mongols*. Part I: Mongolian Text in Transcription; Part II: Word Index. (Indiana University, Uralic & Altaic Series 121.) Bloomington 1972.
3. *Index to Biographical Material in Chin and Yüan Literary Works. First Series*. Compiled by I. de Rachewiltz and M. Nakano. Canberra 1970.
4. *Index to Biographical Material in Chin and Yüan Literary Works. Second Series*. Compiled by I. de Rachewiltz and May Wang. Canberra 1972.
5. *Index to Biographical Material in Chin and Yüan Literary Works. Third Series*. Compiled by I. de Rachewiltz and May Wang. Canberra, 1979.
6. *Repertory of Proper Names in Yüan Literary Sources*, 3 vols., compiled by I. de Rachewiltz and May Wang. Taipei 1988.
7. *Repertory of Proper Names in Yüan Literary Sources*, Vol. IV: *Supplement*, compiled by I. de Rachewiltz and M. Wang, with the collaboration of C. C. Hsiao and with the assistance of S. Rivers. Taipei 1996.
8. Sa'ang Secen: *Erdeni-yin Tobci* (*'Precious Summary'*). *A Mongolian Chronicle of 1662*. The Urga text transcribed and edited by M. Gō, I. de Rachewiltz, J. R. Krueger and B. Ulaan. (Faculty of Asian Studies Monographs, New Series, No. 15.) Canberra 1990.
9. Sa'ang Secen: *Erdeni-yin Tobci* (*'Precious Summary'*). *A Mongolian Chronicle of 1662*, II: Word-index to the Urga text prepared by I. de Rachewiltz and J. R. Krueger. (Faculty of Asian Studies Monographs: New Series, No. 18.) Canberra 1991.
10. I. de Rachewiltz, H. L. Chan, C. C. Hsiao and P. W. Geier (eds) with the assistance of M. Wang. *In the Service of the Khan. Eminent*

Personalities of the Early Mongol-Yüan Period (1200-1300). (Asiatische Forschungen 121.) Wiesbaden 1993. (I. de Rachewiltz is both an editor of, and contributor to, this publication.)

11. A. Mostaert et I. de Rachewiltz. *Le matériel mongol du Houa i i iu de Houng-ou (1389)*, II: *Commentaires*. (Mélanges Chinois et Bouddhiques XXVII.) Bruxelles 1995.
12. *The Mongolian Tanǰur Version of the Bodhicaryāvatāra*. Edited and transcribed, with a word-index and a photo-reproduction of the original text (1748). (Asiatische Forschungen 129.) Wiesbaden 1996.
13. *The Secret History of the Mongols. A Mongolian Epic Chronicle of the Thirteenth Century*. Translated with a historical and philological commentary by Igor de Rachewiltz, 2 vols. (Brill's Inner Asian Library 7/1-2.) Leiden · Boston 2004. [2nd (paperback) edition with additions and corrections, 2006.]

B. *Pamphlets*

1. *Prester John and Europe's Discovery of East Asia*. (The 32nd G. E. Morrison Lecture in Ethnology.) Canberra 1972.

C. *Articles*

1. 'Yeh-lü Ch'u-ts'ai (1189-1243): Buddhist Idealist and Confucian Statesman'. In: A. R. Wright & D. Twitchett (eds), *Confucian Personalities*. Stanford 1962, 189-216, 359-367.
2. 'The *Hsi-yu lu* by Yeh-lü Ch'u-ts'ai'. *Monumenta Serica* 21 (1962), 1-128.
3. 'Some Remarks on the Dating of the *Secret History of the Mongols*'. *Monumenta Serica* 24 (1965), 185-206.
4. 'Personnel and Personalities in North China in the Early Mongol Period'. *Journal of the Economic and Social History of the Orient* 9 (1966), 88-144.
5. 'Some Remarks on the Language Problem in Yüan China'. *The Journal of the Oriental Society of Australia* 5:1&2 (December 1967), 65-80.
6. 'Chingis Khan and the A.N.U. Computer'. *Hemisphere* 12:4 (April 1968), 9-15.

7. 'The Mongolian Poem of Muḥammad al-Samarqandī'. *Central Asiatic Journal* 12 (1968), 280-285.

8. '*The Secret History of the Mongols*: Annotated Translation of Chapter I'. *Bulletin of the Mongolia Society* 9:1 (1970), 55-69.

9. '*The Secret History of the Mongols*: Chapters I and II'. *Papers on Far Eastern History* 4 (September 1971), 155-164. (Supersedes No. 8.)

10. '*The Secret History of the Mongols*: Chapter III'. *Papers on Far Eastern History* 5 (March 1972), 149-175.

11. 'The Ideological Foundations of Chingis Khan's Empire'. *Papers on Far Eastern History* 7 (March 1973), 21-36. (Paper read at the Second International Congress of Mongolists, Ulan-Bator, September 1970, and since reprinted also in the *Transactions* of the Congress, Vol. II, Ulan-Bator, 1973, 56-64.)

12. 'Some Remarks on the Khitan Clan Name Yeh-lü ~ I-la'. *Papers on Far Eastern History* 9 (March 1974), 187-204.

13. '*The Secret History of the Mongols*: Chapter IV'. *Papers on Far Eastern History* 10 (September 1974), 55-82.

14. '*The Secret History of the Mongols*: Chapter V'. *Papers on Far Eastern History* 13 (March 1976), 41-75.

15. 'Some Remarks on the Stele of Yisüngge'. In: W. Heissig *et al.* (eds), *Tractata Altaica* (D. Sinor Festschrift). Wiesbaden 1976, 487-508.

16. Biographies of Fang Hui and Liu Yü. In: H. Franke (ed.), *Sung Biographies*. Wiesbaden 1976, Vol. I, 349-355; Vol. II, 656-660.

17. 'Muqali, Bōl, Tas and An-t'ung'. *Papers on Far Eastern History* 15 (March 1977), 45-62.

18. '*The Secret History of the Mongols:* Chapter VI'. *Papers on Far Eastern History* 16 (September 1977), 27-65.

19. '*The Secret History of the Mongols:* Chapter VII'. *Papers on Far Eastern History* 18 (September 1978), 43-80.

20. '*The Secret History of the Mongols:* Chapter VIII'. *Papers on Far Eastern History* 21 (March 1980), 17-57.

21. 'Some Remarks on Töregene's Edict of 1240'. *Papers on Far Eastern History* 23 (March 1981), 38-63.

22. '*The Secret History of the Mongols:* Chapter IX'. *Papers on Far Eastern History* 23 (March 1981), 111-146.
23. '*The Secret History of the Mongols:* Chapter X'. *Papers on Far Eastern History* 26 (September 1982), 39-84.
24. 'On a Recently Discovered MS. of Činggis Qa'an's Precepts to His Younger Brothers and Sons'. In: L. A. Hercus *et al.* (eds), *Indological and Buddhist Studies. Volume in Honour of Professor J. W. de Jong on His Sixtieth Birthday.* Canberra 1982, 427-439.
25. 'More About the Story of Činggis-qan and the Peace-Loving Rhinoceros'. In: A. R. Davis and A. D. Stefanowska (eds), *Austrina · Essays in Commemoration of the 25th Anniversary of the Founding of the Oriental Society of Australia.* Sydney 1982, 13-29.
26. 'The Preclassical Mongolian Version of the *Hsiao-ching*'. *Zentralasiatische Studien* 16 (1982), 7-109.
27. 'Turks in China Under the Mongols: A Preliminary Investigation of Turco-Mongol Relations in the 13th and 14th Centuries'. In: M. Rossabi (ed.), *China Among Equals. The Middle Kingdom and its Neighbors, 10th-14th Centuries.* Berkeley · Los Angeles · London 1983, 281-310.
28. 'Two Recently Published *Pai-tzu* Discovered in *China'. Acta Orientalia Hungarica* 36 (1983), 413-417.
29. '*Qan, Qa'an* and the Seal of Güyüg'. In: K. Sagaster & M. Weiers (eds), *Documenta Barbarorum. Festschrift für Walther Heissig zum 70. Geburtstag.* Wiesbaden 1983, 272-281.
30. 'On a Recent Translation of the *Meng-Ta pei-lu* and *Hei-Ta shih-lüeh*: A Review-Article'. *Monumenta Serica* 35 (1981-83), 571-582.
31. with T. Russell. 'Ch'iu Ch'u-chi (1148-1227)'. *Papers on Far Eastern History* 29 (March 1984), 1-26.
32. '*The Secret History of the Mongols:* Chapter XI'. *Papers on Far Eastern History* 30 (September 1984), 81-160.
33. '*The Secret History of the Mongols:* Chapter XII'. *Papers on Far Eastern History* 31 (March 1985), 21-93.
34. 'On the Expression *Čul Ulǰa'ur* (? = *Čöl Olǰa'ur*) in Paragraph 254 of *The Secret History of the Mongols*'. In: J. Fletcher *et al.* (eds), *Niğuča Bičig · Pi Wên Shu · An Anniversary Volume in Honor of Francis Woodman Cleaves.* (Journal of Turkish Studies 9.) Harvard 1985, 213-217.

35. '*The Secret History of the Mongols*: Additions and Corrections'. *Papers on Far Eastern History* 33 (March 1986), 129-138.

36. 'More About the Preclassical Version of the *Hsiao-ching*'. *Zentralasiatische Studien* 19 (1986), 27-37.

37. 'The Chinese Inscription of 1279 on the Establishment of the Hsüan-wei Commandery'. *Rocznik Orientalistyczny* 45:2 (1987), 5-13.

38. 'Ou, Mei, Ao ti Meng-ku hsüeh yen-chiu–mu-ch'ien ch'ing-k'uang chi yen-chiu ch'ü-hsiang' ('Mongolian Studies in Europe, America and Australasia: Achievements and Perspectives'). *Minzu Yicong* 1988:2, 59-62.

39. 'The Third Chapter of Chos-kyi 'od-zer's · Translation of the *Bodhicaryāvatāra*: A Tentative Reconstruction'. In: G. Gnoli & L. Lanciotti (eds), *Orientalia Iosephi Tucci Memoriae Dicata.* (Serie Orientale Roma LVI:3.) Roma 1988, 1173-1200.

40. 'The Title Činggis Qan/Qa'an Re-examined'. In: W. Heissig & K. Sagaster (eds), *Gedanke und Wirkung. Festschrift zum 90. Geburtstag von Nikolaus Poppe.* (Asiatische Forschungen 108.) Wiesbaden 1989, 281-98. (Translated into Chinese)

41. 'Dante's *Aleppe*: A Tartar Word in Tartarus?'. In: G. Stary (ed.), *Proceedings of the XXVIII Permanent International Altaistic Conference Venice 8-14 July 1985*. Wiesbaden 1989, 57-71.

42. 'Some Remarks on the Manuscript Copies, Printed Editions and Transcriptions of the *Altan Tobči* of Blo-bzaṅ bstan-'jin'. *Studia Historica Mongolica* 3 (1989), 198-205. (Translated into Chinese)

43. 'Brief Comments on Professor Yü Ta-chün's Article «On the Dating of the *Secret History of the Mongols*»'. *Monumenta Serica* 37 (1986-87), 305-309 (actual date of publication 1989).

44. 'The expression *Qaǰaru Inerü* in Paragraph 70 of *The Secret History of the Mongols*'. In: P. Daffinà (ed.), *Indo-Sino-Tibetica. Studi in onore di Luciano Petech*. (*Studi Orientali* IX.) Rome 1990, 283-290.

45. Čeveng, 'The Darqad and the Uriyangqai of Lake Köbsögöl', translated by I. de Rachewiltz and J. R. Krueger, commentary by I. de Rachewiltz. *East Asian History* 1 (June 1991), 55-80.

46. G. di Pian di Carpine, *Storia dei Mongoli*, a cura di P. Daffinà, C. Leonardi, M. C. Lungarotti, E. Menestò, L. Petech. Spoleto 1989. Review-Article in *Rivista degli Studi Orientali* 64 (1990), 420-429.

47. 'Some Reflections on Paragraph One of the *The Secret History of the Mongols*'. *Fifth International Congress of Mongolists*. Collected papers published by the International Association for Mongol Studies II, Ulan-Bator 1992, 337-343.
48. 'Three Mongolian Chronicles'. *Mongolica* 1 [22] (1990), 71-79.
49. 'Some Reflections on Činggis Qan's *J̌asay*'. *East Asian History* 6 (December 1993), 91-104.
50. 'Some Remarks on Written Mongolian'. In: Chang Chün-i (ed.), *International Symposium on Mongolian Culture*. Taipei 1993, 123-136.
51. '*The Secret History of the Mongols*: Some Fundamental Problems'. *Bulletin of the International Association for Mongol Studies* 1993 (2)-1994 (1), 3-10.
52. 'The Mongols Rethink Their Early History'. In: *The East and the Meaning of History*. Dip. di Studi Orientali, Universita di Roma 'La Sapienza'. Rome 1994, 357-380. (Translated into Mongolian)
53. 'Genghis Khan – Profile of a Man'. In: B. Huldorj (ed.), *Mongolia and the Mongols. Proceedings of the First Mongolian Seminar 24-25 November 1995*. Canberra 1996, 2-6.
54. Čeveng, 'The Dörbed', translated by I. de Rachewiltz and J. R. Krueger, commentary by I. de Rachewiltz. *East Asian History* 10 (Dec. 1995), 53-78.
55. 'Some Puzzling Words in *The Secret History of the Mongols*'. *Mongolica* 6 [27] (1995), 278-286.
56. 'The Name of the Mongols in Asia and Europe'. *Etudes mongoles et sibériennes* 27 (1996), 199-210.
57. 'Hybrid Chinese of the Mongol Period (13th-14th c.)'. In: S. A. Wurm, P. Mühlhäuser, D. T. Tryon (eds), *Atlas of Languages of Intercultural Communication in the Pacific, Asia and the Americas*. Berlin · New York 1996, 905-906.
58. S. A. Wurm with I. de Rachewiltz. 'Contact Languages and Language Influences in Mongolia'. In: S. A. Wurm, P. Mühlhäuser, D. T. Tryon (eds), *Atlas of Languages of Intercultural Communication in the Pacific, Asia and the Americas*. Berlin · New York 1996, 909-912.

59. 'Prester John and Europe's Discovery of East Asia'. *East Asian History* 11 (June 1996), 59-74. (A revised version of the 32nd G. E. Morrison Lecture in Ethnology. See above B.1)

60. Čeveng, 'The Qotong, the Bayad and the Ögeled', translated by I. de Rachewiltz and J. R. Krueger, commentary by I. de Rachewiltz. *East Asian History* 12 (December 1996), 105-120.

61. 'Marco Polo Went to China'. *Zentralasiatische Studien* 27 (1997), 34-92.

62. 'Searching for Čingis Qan: Notes and Comments on Historic Sites in Xentiĭ Aĭmag, Northern Mongolia'. *Rivista degli Studi Orientali* 71 (1997), 239-256 (with 4 ills.).

63. Čeveng, 'The Mingγad, the J̌aqačin, the Torγud, the Qošud and the Čaqar', translated by I. de Rachewiltz and J. R. Krueger, commentary by I. de Rachewiltz. *East Asian History* 13/14 (June-Dec. 1997), 119-132.

64. 'A Note on the Word *Börte* in the *Secret History of the Mongols*'. *East Asian History* 13/14 (June-December 1997), 153-155.

65. 'On a Puzzling Word in the Sino-Mongolian Inscription of 1335 in Memory of Chang Ying-jui'. *Ural-Altaische Jahrbücher*, N.F. 15 (1997/98), 255-259.

66. 'Father Antoine Mostaert's Contribution to the Study of the *Secret History of the Mongols* and the *Hua-i i-yü*'. In: K. Sagaster (ed.), *Antoine Mostaert (1881-1971), C.I.C.M. Missionary and Scholar*, Vol. I: Papers. Leuven 1999, 93-109.

67. 'Some Reflections on So-Called Written Mongolian'. In: H. Eimer, M. Hahn, M. Schetelich, P. Wyzlic (eds), *Studia Tibetica et Mongolica (Festschrift Manfred Taube)*. Swisttal-Odendorf 1999, 235-246. (A revised version of C.50)

68. 'Was Töregene Qatun Ögödei's "Sixth Empress"?'. *East Asian History* 17/18 (June-Dec. 1999), 71-76.

69. Čeveng, 'The Dariγangγa, the State of the Uriγangqai of the Altai, the Qasaγ and the Qamniγan', translated by I. de Rachewiltz and J. R. Krueger, commentary by I. de Rachewiltz. *East Asian History* 19 (June 2000), 53-86.

70. 'The Identification of Geographical Names in *The Secret History of the Mongols* §§ 1-202'. In: *Sino-Asiatica*, 73-85 (see below D.9)

71. ‘A Note on Hu Ssu-hui’s Name’. In: Kong Yun-cheung & Hu Shiu-ying (eds & ann.), *Yin-shan cheng-yao hsin-pien*. Hong Kong 2004, xix-xxi.
72. ‘The Missing First Page of the Preclassical Mongolian Version of the *Hsiao-ching*: A Tentative Reconstruction’. *East Asian History* 27 (June 2004), 51-56.
73. ‘On the *Sheng-wu ch’in-cheng lu* 聖武親征錄’. *East Asian History* 28 (December 2004), 35-44.
74. ‘A Faulty Reading in the Safe Conduct of Abaγa’. *Journal of Asian History* 39 (2005), 177-180.
75. ‘Some Remarks on the *Chih-yüan i-yü* 至元譯語 alias *Meng-ku i-yü* 蒙古譯語, the First Known Sino-Mongol Glossary’. *Acta Orientalia Hungarica* 59 (2006), 11-28.
76. ‘Notes on F. W. Cleaves: An Early Mongolian Version of the *Hsiao Ching*. Chapters One to Eighteen’. *Acta Orientalia Hungarica* 60 (2007), 247-271.
77. ‘The Genesis of the Name “Yeke Mongγol Ulus”’. *East Asian History* 31 (2006), 53-56.
78. ‘Confucius in Mongolian. Some Remarks on the Mongol Exegesis of the *Analects*’. *East Asian History* 31 (2006), 57-64.
79. ‘A Note on Yelü Zhu 耶律鋳 and His Family’. *East Asian History* 31 (2006), 65-74.
80. ‘Heaven, Earth and the Mongols in the Time of Činggis Qan and His Immediate Successors (*ca.* 1160-1260) – A Preliminary Investigation’. In: N. Golvers & S. Lievens (eds), *A Lifelong Dedication to the China Mission. Essays Presented in Honor of Father Jeroom Heyndrickx, CICM, on the Occasion of His 75th Birthday and the 25th Anniversary of the F. Verbiest Institute K.U. Leuven*. (Leuven Chinese Studies 17.) Leuven 2007, 107-139.

D. *Books and Articles edited by Igor de Rachewiltz*

1. A. Mostaert, *Le matériel mongol du Houa i i iu de Houng-ou (1389)*, I. (Mélanges Chinois et Bouddhiques XVIII.) Bruxelles 1977. (Introduction by I. de Rachewiltz)
2. H. H. Chan, ‘Wang O (1190-1273)’. *Papers on Far Eastern History* 12 (September 1975), 43-70.

3. H. L. Chan, 'Yang Huan (1186-1255)'. *Papers on Far Eastern History* 14 (September 1976), 37-59.

4. 'Der Blockdruck des Xiàojìng aus dem Palastmuseum in chinesischer und mongolischer Sprache'. *Zentralasiatische Studien* 12 (1978), 159-235.

5. H. L. Chan, 'Yao Shu (1201-1278)'. *Papers on Far Eastern History* 22 (September 1980), 17-50.

6. H. L. Chan, 'Yang Wei-chung (1206-1260)'. *Papers on Far Eastern History* 29 (March 1984), 27-44.

7. C. C. Hsiao, 'Yen Shih (1182-1240)'. *Papers on Far Eastern History* 33 (March 1986), 113-28.

8. A. Mostaert, 'Quelques problèmes phonétiques dans la transcription en caractères chinois du texte mongol du *Iuen tch'ao pi cheu*', edited by I. de Rachewiltz and P. W. Geier. In: K. Sagaster (ed.), *Antoine Mostaert (1881-1971), C.I.C.M. Missionary and Scholar*, Vol. I: Papers. Leuven 1999, 225-271.

9. *Sino-Asiatica. Papers Dedicated to Professor Liu Ts'un-yan on the Occasion of His Eighty-fifth Birthday*, edited by Wang Gungwu, Rafe de Crespigny and Igor de Rachewiltz. Canberra 2002.

10. 'Index of Mongol and Chinese Proper and Geographical Names in the *Sheng-wu ch'in-cheng lu* 聖武親征錄', by P. Pelliot and L. Hambis, edited by I. de Rachewiltz. *East Asian History* 28 (December 2004), 45-52.

11. F. W. Cleaves, 'An Early Mongolian Version of the *Hsiao Ching*. 1. Facsimile of the Bilingual Text', with an introduction by I. de Rachewiltz. *Acta Orientalia Hungarica* 59 (2006), 241-282.

12. F. W. Cleaves, 'An Early Mongolian Version of the *Hsiao Ching*. 2. Chapters Ten to Thirteen', revised and edited by I. de Rachewiltz. *Acta Orientalia Hungarica* 59 (2006), 393-406.

13. F. W. Cleaves, 'An Early Mongolian Version of the *Hsiao Ching*. 3. Chapters Fourteen to Seventeen', revised and edited by I. de Rachewiltz. *Acta Orientalia Hungarica* 60 (2007), 145-160.

E. *Book Reviews*

1. P. Filippani-Ronconi, *Storia del pensiero cinese*, Torino 1964. In: *Monumenta Serica* 22 (1963), 537-539.

2. P. Ratchnevsky, *Historisch-terminologisches Wörterbuch der Yüan-Zeit, Medizinwesen*, Berlin 1967. In: *Asia Major* 14 (1968), 122-123.
3. W. Chapman, *Kublai Khan: Lord of Xanadu*, New York · Indianapolis 1966. In: *Pacific Affairs* 42.2 (Summer 1969), 229-230.
4. R. Grousset, *Conqueror of the World*, tr. D. Sinor & M. MacKellar, Edinburgh · London 1967. In: *Pacific Affairs* 43:2 (Summer 1970), 284-285.
5. D. Sinor, *Inner Asia: A Syllabus*, Bloomington 1969. In: *Journal of the American Oriental Society* 92 (1972), 162-163.
6. G. Kara, *Chants d'un barde mongol*, Budapest 1970. In: *Asia Major* 18 (1973), 227-228.
7. L. Ligeti (ed.), *Histoire secrète des Mongols*, Budapest 1971; Idem, *Monuments préclassiques* I · (Indices verborum linguae Mongolicae monumentis traditorum I,) Budapest 1970. In: *Asia Major* 18 (1973), 229-232.
8. W. Heissig assisted by Ch. Bawden, *Catalogue of Mongol books · Manuscripts and Xylographs*, Copenhagen 1971. In: *Asia Major* 19 (1975), 264-265.
9. L. Ligeti, *Monuments en écriture 'phags-pa · Pièces de chancellerie en transcription chinoise* · (Indices verborum linguae Mongolicae monumentis traditorum III,) Budapest 1973; Idem, *Trésor des sentences*. (Monumenta linguae Mongolicae collecta IV,) Budapest 1973; Idem, *Trésor des sentences*. (Indices verborum linguae Mongolicae monumentis traditorum IV,) Budapest 1973. In: *Monumenta Serica* 33 (1977-78), 493-497.
10. W. Heissig, *Die mongolischen Handschriften-Reste aus Olon süme, Innere Mongolei (16.-17. Jhdt.)*, Wiesbaden 1976. In: *Ural-altaische Jahrbücher*, N.F. 1 (1981), 297-299.
11. with D. D. Leslie. Jacob d'Ancona, *The City of Light*, tr. and ed. by D. Selbourne, London 1997. In: *Journal of Asian History* 32 (1998), 180-185.

F. *Other Minor Contributions*

1. Items 204 and 221 in the *Revue Bibliographique de Sinologie* No. 2 (1956), 86 and 91.
2. Obituary for Otto B. van der Sprenkel in the *Proceedings 1979 of The Australian Academy of the Humanities*, Sydney 1979, 49-51.

3. Items on pp. 26, 38, 46 and 92 of V. Gómez i Oliver, *XLIX Sonets d'amor, I: Contracant amoros*, Barcelona 1997.
4. Several footnotes in Hung Chin-fu, *Documents on the Censorial System of Yüan China* (in Chinese), Taipei 2003.
5. The 'Introduction' to 'Fourth Supplement to the *Ku-shu i-i chü-li*' by P'ei Hsüeh-hai, tr. by Archilles Fang, repr. in *Monumenta Serica* 50 (2002), 549-550.

G. *In Preparation*

1. *Introduction to Altaic Philology* (= *Linguistics in Culture*), with V. Rybatzki (Helsinki) and C. F. Hung (Taipei), a volume of about 300 pages, nearly completed, to be published by Brill, Leiden · Boston, in 2010.
2. *A Supplement to the Secret History of the Mongols. A Mongolian Epic Chronicle of the Thirteenth Century*. An updating of the translation and commentary (see A.13) to 2009, to be published by Brill, Leiden · Boston, in 2010.
3. 'The Dating of the *Secret History of Mongols* – A Re-interpretation', 42 pages, to appear in *Ural-Altaische Jahrbücher* at the end of 2008.

(15 October 2008)

The Early Mongols

A Note on Mongol Imperial Ideology

Thomas T. Allsen

One of the more striking features of the explosive Mongolian expansion, resulting in the largest contiguous land empire in world history, is that their ideological justification was extremely terse; little effort was made to elaborate these ideas or provide them with intellectual underpinnings. But brevity was an asset, since the entire message could be accommodated on a coin: "By the Might of God/By the Good Fortune of the Emperor/of the World, Munkū Qā'ān."[1] This inscription in Persian, appearing on a dirham struck in Tbilisi in 1252 during the reign of Möngke Qaghan (1251-59), accurately and fully expresses their concepts of authority and legitimacy.

Among his many signal contributions to the field, Igor de Rachewiltz was the first to lay out clearly the basic contours of this political ideology. He showed that in their world view Eternal Heaven (*möngke tengri*) conferred upon Chinggis Qan and his descendants the right to rule over a universal empire through a dispensation of special good fortune (*su* or *suu*) that preordained the success of their imperial venture. The origins of this ideological package, he further argued, were complex and pre-Mongol. The notion of a heavenly mandate points to Chinese influence and Chinggisid claims of universalism had antecedents in the Chinese concept of "all-under-heaven," as well as in the universalist political-religious doctrines of the Near East.[2]

The facet of the Mongols' ideology examined here is the bestowal and subsequent employment of special good fortune, or royal charisma. Perhaps the closest analogue to that of the Mongols is the Iranian *khvarənah*, "royal glory," a concept that passed to the Turkic nomads through the agency of the Soghdians.[3] In the Türk Qaghanate (6th-8th centuries) and among its successor states, *qut*, "royal good fortune," was a central element in the quest for legitimacy.[4] In this regard, as we shall see, the Mongols closely followed the precedents of their Turkic predecessors.

---

[1] Pakhomov 1970, 133.

[2] de Rachewiltz 1973, 21-36.

[3] Gnoli 1990, 83-92; Litvinski 1972, 266-282.

[4] Golden 1982, 44-49, 58-61, 72.

This leads to the issue of the properties of royal charisma, at least as understood in the steppe world. In Weber's formulation, charisma is a quality characterized by superhuman or supernatural attributes, divine in origin, that legitimize individuals' assumption of leadership roles, guide their actions and ensure their success. Moreover, such attributes, once manifest in an inspired founder, can usually be inherited within a dynastic line.[5]

To some extent, this accurately describes the situation in the early Mongolian Empire. There is no doubt, for example, that Ögödei (r. 1229-41), Chinggis Qan's designated successor, wielded the very same kind of charismatic authority enjoyed by his father. This is made abundantly clear in the *Secret History* when Batu reports to Ögödei that he overcame all opposition in the western steppe "by the strength of Eternal Heaven and the good fortune [*su*] of my uncle the Qa'an."[6] It seems quite reasonable to assume, following Weber, that some or most of his luck came to him as a legacy from his "fortunate [*sutu*] father."[7] The fact that a Chinese source states that Qubilai (r. 1260-94), "succeeded to the fortune [*yun*]," certainly affirms this conclusion.[8] But while family inheritance played an important role, it is hardly the whole story; there were in fact other means of acquiring this most precious commodity.

One alternative source was the good fortune of previous dynasties. That the Mongols actively sought to capture this spiritual residue is evidenced by the siting of their imperial capitol, Qara Qorum. Built largely under Ögödei, this "sitting city," as the Mongols called it, was placed in the Orkhon river valley; this was not a matter of chance since it was in the general area of the "Ötüken domain [*il-ötüken*]" where the Türk and Uighur rulers situated their capitals, and from which it was deemed proper to govern a steppe empire. The Mongols, most revealingly, engaged in considerable historical and archaeological research in order to ensure they correctly located their new capital. They went to such trouble because, in steppe tradition and historical memory, this region was a major repository of spiritual power; and to reactivate its latent energy, the Mongols needed to build there a proper political center. Only in this way could they tap into and appropriate the primordial *qut* that inhered in the region, the good fortune that was the fount of the success of earlier steppe polities.[9]

---

[5] Weber 1978, vol. I, 241-242, 248.
[6] *SH* 206 (§ 275); *ISH* 165.
[7] *SH* 203 (§ 272); *ISH* 164.
[8] *YWL*, ch. 24, 11a.
[9] For details and documentation, see Allsen 1996, 116-135.

So far, we have focused on "vertical" transfers of royal charisma, those accomplished through direct inheritance down a single dynastic line or by the more complex process of *translatio imperii*, the transference across time and space of the right to rule from one ethnic group or dynasty to another. But equally important, and as yet little noticed, there were also consequential "horizontal" transfers of good fortune within the Mongolian Empire.

Lateral flows are most apparent between the ruler and his closest associates. In the *Secret History*, Chinggis Qan refers frequently to his "lucky, blessed [*öljeitü qutuqtu*]" sworn friends, *anda*, and companions, *nököd*, and more generally speaks of his "blessed night guard [*öljeitü kebte'ül*]" and of his ten thousand-man guard as his "beneficent spirits [*nendü'üt qutuq*]."[10] Obviously, Chinggis Qan had no monopoly on good fortune; it was a transferable commodity that was exchanged between ruler and retinue. This was possible because according to Mongolian notions of the period, most members of society possessed, as Skrynnikova points out, a measure of *suu*, particularly talented individuals.[11] The systematic collection and display of skilled or creative people at court is of course a common phenomenon, one designed to increase prestige and project majesty. But it was something more than this: it was a way of accumulating, concentrating and sharing good fortune.[12]

In the Mongolian case, the spiritual bonding of ruler and retinue was accomplished through continual gift exchange. Indeed, this was so in many pre-modern societies; such bonding rests on the conviction that physical objects in the form of gifts were animated, containing some of the essence of the giver. A gift was especially so charged and potent when it came from a sacral ruler who endowed his possessions with his spiritual force, his good luck and success. Consequently, a qan's gift of a piece of clothing he had once worn — a common practice among the Chinggisids — had greatly enhanced value, and became in Gurevich's phrase, "a transcendent treasure" whose spiritual worth far surpassed its material worth.[13]

A closer examination of the structure and functions of the imperial guard, *kešik*, will help establish the centrality of the sharing of good fortune. In the early empire the guard, the emperor's household, the court,

---

[10] *SH* I, 130 (§ 200), 136 (§ 206), 143 (§ 211), 159 (§ 230), 160 (§ 231); *SH* II, 784-86; *ISH* 111, 116, 121, 133.

[11] Skrynnikova 1997, 196-199, 215.

[12] Helms 1993, 13-27, 69-87.

[13] Gurevich 1992, 104-107, 178-189.

and the central government were virtually identical. In other words, the same set of officials watched over the ruler's security, tended his personal needs and oversaw the administration of the realm. As a result, the ruler and his subordinates lived and worked together in a patrimonial setting; here his officials/servants/protectors received as a basic component of their remuneration food, drink and clothing from the hand of their sovereign and did so on a regular, often daily basis.[14]

In the steppe world, a leader had to be generous, redistribute his wealth and material possessions to his retinue; and a truly generous, successful qan redistributed his special good fortune as well. He did so because his bestowals of this commodity upon subordinates made certain their loyalty and their success in carrying out his commands. In the Chinggisid era, the ruler's sharing of his spiritual wealth became so identified with the guard that *kešik* also came to mean "blessing" or "good fortune" and the term for its members, *kešikten*, "imperial guardsmen," acquired the secondary meaning of "blessed" or "fortunate ones."

The precepts and practices described above had a long history among the nomads, and the similarities in the political doctrines of the Turks and Mongols make it likely that the Chinggisids' ideological message fell on receptive ears in the steppe. Their success in subduing and mobilizing virtually all the steppe peoples supports this view. But what of the Mongols' far more numerous sedentary subjects? How did their message play out in the agricultural zones of the empire? For guidance on this matter, we can look briefly at the situation in the eastern Islamic lands.

Muslim writers of the period could hardly ignore the shock of the Mongolian conquest and approached the task of explaining this cataclysm to their co-religionists in several ways. Most commonly, they treated the onslaught as Divine punishment for religious laxity. Or, if they wished to place a more positive gloss on the event, they focused attention on the Mongols' destruction of the heterodox and feared Ismāʿīlīs or on the rapid advance of the Faith into new territory in Inner and East Asia.[15] And beyond these mainly religious arguments, Muslims who sought to justify Mongolian rule could also invoke, with some hope of success, select elements of the Mongols' ideological message.

Juvaynī, a mid level official in the Mongolian administration of Iran, made repeated use of this option in his famous history, completed in 1260. The very title of this work, *The History of the World Conqueror*, embodies one key part of their message — universal dominion. This claim, however,

[14] On this institution, see Allsen 1986, 500-521.

[15] For a survey of views, see De Weese 2006, 23-60; Biran 2007, 108ff.

plays a secondary role in the body of the work. His account of the rise and expansion of their empire begins by pointedly contrasting the extreme poverty of the Mongols prior to Chinggis Qan with their great prosperity afterwards; he then attributes this miraculous transformation to their leader's "good fortune [*dawlat*]." Indeed, to drive his point home, Juvaynī makes the Mongolian case the supreme example of the phenomenon, one that provides incontrovertible evidence for the very existence of royal glory.[16] Moreover, such was the potency of Chinggis Qan's "powerful good fortune [*dawlat bā quvvat*]" that it lived on, according to Juvaynī, after his death, disrupting the plans and dashing the hopes of the Mongols' enemies.[17] The latter assertion, of course, was entirely consistent with Mongolian belief that the founding father's spirit, properly venerated, continued to serve the Mongolian cause in various and powerful ways.

In Juvaynī's narrative, Chinggis Qan's successors, starting with Ögödei, possessed similar good fortune.[18] Not surprisingly, Möngke, whom Juvaynī served, is depicted as enjoying this commodity in great abundance. He sat upon a "throne of good fortune [*bakht*]," a fortune that brought about good weather, foiled rivals and defeated enemies. And since his luck was manifest before his enthronement, it is cited as a sure sign of his coming power and majesty.[19]

While all descendents of Chinggis Qan, Hülegü for instance, possessed a measure of good fortune, it was by no means evenly distributed.[20] Qaghans had more than princes of the blood and Chinggis Qan had more than other qaghans. Consequently, in life as in death, a qaghan's vast reserves had to be disseminated for the commonweal. This need was widely understood and reported in the Persian sources. Rashīd al-Dīn, another noted historian in Chinggisid service, relates that on the eve of military action, a subordinate of the Yuan Emperor, Temür (1294-1307), calls upon his sovereign's "good fortune [*dawlat*]" to ensure victory.[21] Today we may view such invocations in psychological terms, as a means of building moral and instilling confidence, but the Mongols and their Persian servitors understood these flows of fortune quite differently. Juvaynī offers a particularly helpful passage on these transfers. He tells us

[16] Juvaynī/Q I, 14-16; Juvaynī/B I, 19-22.

[17] Juvaynī/Q II, 183; Juvaynī/B II, 453.

[18] Juvaynī/Q I, 158; Juvaynī/B I, 201.

[19] Juvaynī/Q III, 34, 39, 82; Juvaynī/B II, 571, 574, 602. Cf. also Rashīd/K I, 475, 584-585, 589; Rashīd/A 131; Rashīd/B 58, 205, 211.

[20] Juvaynī/Q III, 132; Juvaynī/B II, 633.

[21] Rashīd/K I, 677; Rashīd/B 328.

that after his enthronement Ögödei remained in Mongolia, while "the commanders of the court and the bondsmen of [his] good fortune [*bandagān-i dawlat*] led armies and troops of horsemen to the East and West."[22] Clearly, the qaghan both delegates authority to members of his guard/household establishment and bestows upon them the good fortune that underwrites their success. It tells us further something about Juvaynī's understanding of these matters that his Persian construction, *bandagān-i dawlat*, so nicely conveys the dual meaning of the Mongolian, *kešikten*, "guardsmen" and "fortunate ones."

The qaghan's obligation to redistribute his luck, however, was by no means limited to military commissions; he had a far more general responsibility. This duty is noted by Rashīd al-Dīn, who records that at Ögödei's enthronement all the Chinggisids and notables present knelt and exclaimed "may the realm be made fortunate [*mubārak bāl*] by his qanship [*khāniyat*]."[23] The expectation here is that his limitless fund of good fortune will circulate throughout the land to the benefit of all his subjects. Again it is worthwhile to look more closely at the terminology used here: in the fourteenth century Yemeni *Hexaglot*, the Arabo-Persian *mubārak* is equated with the Turkic *qutlugh* and the Mongolian *qutuqtu*, both of which mean "lucky" or "fortunate."[24] Rashīd al-Dīn, like Juvaynī, chose his words well.

This brings us to the question of Persian political vocabulary and political culture and the extent of their compatibility with steppe terms and traditions. For this purpose we can profitably turn to another passage in Juvaynī in which he asserts "the splendor [*farr*] of the daily increasing good fortune [*dawlat*] of Chinggis Qan and his descendents," phrasing he later repeats with specific reference to Möngke.[25] In this instance, the key term is *farr*, the New Persian form of Middle Persian *khvarənah* "royal glory." Thus we have a Persian Muslim literatus, employed by the Mongols and thoroughly conversant with their political institutions, equating the special good fortune of the Chinggisids with that of the storied Iranian rulers of yore. This, however, is not too surprising since pre-Islamic Iran was the primary political model for the ʿAbbāsids, who took over the notion of royal good fortune as part of their inheritance from the Sasanians.

---

[22] Juvaynī/Q I, 159; Juvaynī/B I, 202.

[23] Rashīd/K I, 453; Rashīd/A, 52; Rashīd/B, 31.

[24] *Hexaglot* 207 (203C7).

[25] Juvaynī/Q I, 16; III, 51; Juvanyī/B I, 23; II, 583.

Just how deeply embedded this idea was in Perso-Islamic political culture can be seen in the history of the word *dawlat*. It derives from the Arabic verb *dāla*, "to change, turn, or rotate," and as a noun means, in both Arabic and Persian, "rotation, change of time, turn of fate, good fortune, state, dynasty, and "empire." Its range of meanings can be compared to the Mongolian *kešik* which comes from the Turkic *kezik*, "order, sequence, or turn."[26] And, as already discussed, in the Chinggisid age, *kešik* comes to mean "guard, good fortune," and as an institution functioned, in the early empire at least, as the central government of the realm.

Although the semantic development of these two terms is not exact, they are similar and reveal, in my view, basic elements of the political cultures of the steppe and the eastern Islamic world that were compatible and recognizable, most specifically the close identification of governmental authority with special good fortune. This is not to argue that because of such similarities Persians enthusiastically flocked to the Chinggisid standard, but rather that they had a way of fitting the Mongols into a well established historical framework and into indigenous ideas of political legitimacy. The situation was not unlike that faced by the Chinese subjects of the Mongols. While there was much ambivalence in Chinese attitudes toward their Chinggisid masters, the doctrine of the mandate of heaven was for them immediately recognizable and provided justification for individuals, if they desired, to embrace or accept Yuan authority.[27] The same, I think, can be said of Mongolian ideas about good fortune in Iran: it gave those who wanted to work for the empire an acceptable rationale for doing so and, at the same time, encouraged passive acceptance of their rule on the part of the majority who did not.

To sum up, the Mongols communicated their ideology in a compact formula, individual elements of which were familiar to their subjects, both nomadic and sedentary. As befits a vast and diverse empire, their political message had something for everyone.

Bibliography and Abbreviations

Allsen, T. T. 1986. 'Guard and Government in the Reign of the Grand Qan Möngke, 1251-59'. *Harvard Journal of Asiatic Studies* 46/2, 495-521.

[26] Doerfer 1963, 467-470.

[27] Such ambivalence is found, for instance, in the views of the Ming founder, a one time subject of the Yuan. See Dardess 1978, 6-7.

Allsen, T. T. 1996. 'Spiritual Geography and Political Legitimacy in the Eastern Steppe'. In: H. J. M. Claessen and J. G. Oosten (eds), *Ideology and the Formation of Early States*. Leiden, 116-135.

Dardess, J. 1978. 'Ming T'ai-tsu on the Yüan: An Autocrat's Assessmant of the Mongol Dynasty'. *Bulletin of Sung and Yüan Studies* 14, 6-11.

Biran, M. 2007. *Chinggis Khan*. Oxford.

de Rachewiltz, I. 1973. 'Some Remarks on the Ideological Foundations of Chinggis Khan's Empire'. *Papers on Far Eastern History* 7, 21-36.

De Weese, D. 2006. '«Stuck in the Throat of Chingiz Khan:» Envisioning the Mongol Conquests in Some Sufi Accounts from the 14th to the 17th Centuries'. In: J. Pfeiffer & S. A. Quinn (eds), *Historiography of Post Mongol Central Asia and the Middle East: Studies in Honor of John E. Woods*. Wiesbaden, 23-60.

Doerfer, G. 1963. *Türkische und Mongolische Elemente im Neupersischen*, vol. I: *Mongolische Elemente im Neupersischen*. Wiesbaden.

Gnoli, G. 1996. 'On the Persian *Farnah*'. *Acta Iranica*, 3rd Series 30, 83-92.

Golden, P. 1982. 'Imperial Ideology and the Sources of Political Unity amongst the Pre-Činggisid Nomads of Western Eurasia'. *Archivum Eurasiae Medii Aevi* 2, 37-76.

Gurevich, A. 1992. *Historical Anthropology of the Middle Ages*. Chicago.

Helms, M. W. 1993. *Craft and the Kingly Ideal: Art, Trade, and Power*. Austin.

Hexaglot: Golden, P. B. (ed.) 2000. *The King's Dictionary: The Rasūlid Hexaglot, Fourteenth Century Vocabularies in Arabic, Persian, Turkic, Greek, Armenian and Mongol*. Leiden.

ISH: de Rachewiltz, I. (ed.) 1972. *Index to the Secret History of the Mongols*. (Indiana University Uralic and Altaic Series 121.) Bloomington.

Juvaynī/B: Juvaynī, 'Atā-Malik. *The History of the World Conqueror*. (Trans.) John A. Boyle. Cambridge, Mass. 1958. 2 vols.

Juvaynī/Q: Juvaynī, 'Atā-Malik. *Ta'rikh-i Jahāngushā*. (Ed.) Mirza Muhammad Qazvīnī. (E. J. Gibb Memorial Series 26.) London 1912-37. 3 vols.

Litvinskii, B. A. 1972. 'Das K'ang-chü — Sarmatische Farnah'. *Central Asiatic Journal* 16/4, 241-289.

Pakhomov, E. A. 1970. *Monety Gruzii*. Tbilisi.

Rashīd/A: Rashīd al Dīn. *Jami' al-tavārīkh*. (Ed.) A. A. Alizade. Moscow 1980. Vol. II, pt. 1.

Rashīd/B: Rashīd al Dīn. *The Successors of Genghis Khan*. (Trans.) John A. Boyle. New York 1971.

Rashīd/K: Rashīd al Dīn. *Jami' al-tavārīkh*. (Ed.) B. Karīmī. Tehran 1959. 2 vols.

SH: de Rachewiltz, I. (trans.) 2004. *The Secret History of the Mongols: A Mongolian Epic Chronicle of the Thirteenth Century*. Leiden. 2 vols.

Skrynnikova, T. D. 1997. *Kharizma i vlast v epokhy Chingis-Khana*. Moscow.

Weber, M. 1978. *Economy and Society*. G. Roth & C. Wittich (eds). Berkeley. 2 vols.

YWL: Su Tianjue (ed.) 1967. *Yuan Wenlei*. Taibei.

DIALECTAL TRACES IN BEILU YIYU

Ákos Bertalan Apatóczky

The Sino-Mongol glossary *Beilu yiyu* (北虜譯語)[1] contains a significant body of Middle Mongol lexicon providing us with many interesting linguistic and philological problems. Its taxonomy classes it as an (Eastern) Middle Mongol source along with many other Sino-Mongolian works left to us in Chinese script such as the Secret History of Mongols and the bilingual glossaries of the *Yuan* and *Ming* dynasties. Although there seems to exist a generally accepted view in academic circles concerning the essentially homogenous dialectal nature of Middle Mongol[2] with marked and sometimes controversial differences between its Western and Eastern characteristics, however, in particular cases one finds extraordinary occurrences of forms or even regularities uncommon in other sources, or divergent from Middle Mongol «proper».

Problems start right with the reconstruction of the original Middle Mongol data encrypted in Chinese script. It is a difficult task to distinguish dialectal or substandard forms from those improperly transcribed or not following the well established transcription practice of the more consistent and precise Sino-Mongol sources[3]. Yet, after ruling out the possible transcription errors and inconsistencies, a large number of unusual forms still remain, in which cases one might come to a conclusion that a certain source is most likely differing from what we are used to, simply because it represents a different dialectal entity. This seems to be the situation with the BLYY as well. In this paper I will review the linguistic position of the BLYY compared to other sources of Middle Mongol and to some modern peripheral Mongolic languages that show analogous developments.

---

[1] Also known as *Yiyu* (譯語), Menggu yiyu (蒙古譯語) etc. Abbreviated as BLYY. The earliest version of this glossary that is still extant is from the *Dengtan Bijiu* 登壇必究 encyclopedia (1599). The data incorporated in BLYY however are likely to be dated earlier. See more about the history, titles and versions of the BLYY and other Sino-Middle Mongol sources in: Lewicki 1949, 5-15; de Rachewiltz& Schönbaum (eds), Mostaert 1977, vii-xix; de Rachewiltz 2006; Rybatzki 2003, 57-61; Franke 1968, 204; Apatóczky 2008, Chapter 1; Apatóczky 2005, 13.1-13.2.

[2] Rybatzki 2003, 62.

[3] On the usage of diacritical Chinese characters see Lewicki 1949, 49-50; Haenisch 1952, 31-32; de Rachewiltz 1977, xxi-xxii; Manduqu 1998, 37-38; Apatóczky 2008, 2.3-2.5.

Preservation and change of initial h-. Describing Middle Mongol phonology, one of the first and most remarkable phenomena which scholarly works usually start with is the initial *h-* that was still extant in Middle Mongol, and which has — with the prominent exception of some peripheral modern Mongolic languages — gradually disappeared. As it was to be expected, in most cases the initial *h-* is attested in *Beilu yiyu* (e.g. *harban* 'ten', *hodun* 'star', *heki* 'head' etc.). The more interesting parts are where it is not, or where it has already undergone a change:

617 *ildü* (*yi-er-du*[4] 亦兒度 Chin. *yao-dao* 腰刀) 'sword' SH *üldü*, Hy *üldü*, Zyyy *üldü*, VdI *hüldü*.

Here the BLYY item, similarly to other Eastern Middle Mongol sources, has no initial *h-*, while the Western Middle Mongol material of the *Vocabulary of Istanbul* has it.

The most exceptional occurrences in the entire material of BLYY are the entries in which the initial *h-* in front of a labial vowel has turned into *f* (*hU-* > *fU-*):

502 *fula'an* (*fu-la-an* 伏剌案 Chin. *hong* 紅) 'red' SH *hula'an*, Hy *hula'an*, Zyyy *hulā*, RY *fulian*, Mgr. *fulān/xulaŋ*, Baoan *fulaŋ*, Santa *fulaŋ/xulaŋ* (cf. also 389 *fula'ana*).

369 *füni* (*fu-ni* 伏你 Chin. *yan* 煙) 'smoke' SH *hüni*, MA *huni(n)* 'smoke', Dag. *xoŋ*, Mgr. *fune*, Baoan *fənɛ*, Santa *funi*.

284 *fünege* (*fu-nie-ge* 伏捏革 Chin. *ling-gou* 狑狗) 'fox' SH *Hünegen (daba'a)* (toponym), KdG *hünken/hüngen*, Hy *hünege*, MA *hünegen*, RH *hüngen*, Mgr. *funəgə/funəgɜ*, Santa *funiəγə*.

In these entries BLYY material shows similarity with the contemporary (seventeenth century) Jurchen and with present-day Monguor, Baoan and Santa data, on the other hand in none of the other Middle Mongol sources can this phenomenon be observed.

Palatal prebreaking, that is the assimilation of the sound *i* to the vowel of the subsequent syllable just like actual palatal breaking (*i* > *yV*) is universally not attested in Middle Mongol[5]. The dialect represented in the BLYY — in accord with other Middle Mongol sources — does not show this assimilation in general. There are, however, some exceptions: *qumusu* 'finger nail', *ǰürken* 'heart', *šoroqai* 'soil, earth', *nudur[γ]a* 'fist', *ǰē* (< **ǰege* < **ǰige*) 'son-in-law'. Out of these, only *ǰürken* and *nudur[γ]a* have

---

[4] Note that the pinyin transcription given for Chinese characters is in no way representative in terms of its quondam pronunciation and is only given here to make the identification of the characters more convenient.

[5] Rybatzki 2003, 61.

their prebroken counterparts in other Middle Mongol works, moreover, even some present-day peripheral Mongolic languages have maintained these words in unbroken forms.

44 *šoroqai* (*shuo-luo-hai* 勺羅害 Chin. *tu* 土) 'earth, soil' SH *širo'ai*, Hy *šira'u*, Zyyy *širuwai*, MA *šira'ū, široi, širū*, AT *sirui*, Dag. *ʃirō* 'pebbles, coarse sand', Yogor *šɔrū*/*šorū*, Mgr. *ɕirū*, Baoan *ɕiru*, Santa *ʂəura*, Mong. *siruγai*, *siroi*.

216 *ǰē köwü*/*köwǖ* (*zhe kou-wu* 折扣兀 Chin. *wai-sheng* 外甥) 'sister's son; son-in-law' AT *ǰige*, Dag. *dʒə̄*, Yogor *dʒī*, Mgr. *dʑē*, Santa *dʐə*, Mong. *ǰige*.

562 *qumusu* (*qu-mu-su* 取目速 Chin. *zhi-jia* 脂甲) 'finger nail' AL *kimusun*, MA *kimusu(n)*, RH *qimsūn*, Dag. *kimtʃ*, Yogor *χəməsən*, Mgr. *tɕimusə*, Baoan *ɢəmsəŋ*, Santa *ɢɯmusun*, Mong. *kimusu(n)*.

563 *nudur[γ]a* (*nu-du-er-a* 奴堵兒阿 Chin. *quan-tou* 拳頭) 'fist' SH *nudurqa*, Hy *nudurqa*, Zyyy *nudurwan*, MA *nudurqa*, AT *nudurаγ*, Dag. *ŋodruγ*[w], Yogor *nudurɢa*, Mgr. *nudurɢa*, Baoan *nədɢa*, Santa *nudərax*, Mong. *nidurγa*.

576 *ǰürken* (*zhu-er-ken* 主兒揹 Chin. *xin* 心) 'heart' SH *ǰürüge(n)*, AL *ǰürke*, *ǰirüge(n)*, Zyyy *ǰirkōn*, Hy *ǰürüken*, AT *Jürken*, *Jürüken* (prop.), AL/Poppe, Introd., p. 146, RH *jirüke*, Dag. *dʒury*[w], Yogor *dʒyrgen*, Mgr. *dʑirgɜ*, Baoan *dʑirge*, Santa *dʐuγə*, Mong. *ǰirüken*.

The word *ǰürken* along with words like *emgen* 'old woman' *qulγuna* 'mouse, rat' *turqa* 'thin' also represent another key change, the reduction of a short vowel in an open position of a non-initial syllable that is so typical in many modern Mongolic languages. In this respect the BLYY is close to the Western Middle Mongol MA data (*qulγuna*, *turqan*/*turγan*) and the Jurchen RY has similar items too, e.g. *turha*.

Transformation of diphthong sequences. Middle Mongol by and large preserved the diphthong sequences that formed mostly following the loss of a medial[6]. In BLYY words like *büdü'ün*, *daba'a*, *deliü*, *kira'u*, *šibau*, *šiliüsü*, *taulai* etc. are representative examples, but then again many of the words have already had their diphthongs replaced by long vowels. Without striving for completeness, I give a short list of this kind of entries with their Middle Mongol and present-day Mongolic counterparts:

23, 29, 124 *dolō* (*duo-luo*) 'seven' SH *dolo'an*, Hy *dolo'an*, Zyyy *dolōn*, VdI *dolān*, MA *dolān*, AT *doloγan*, RH *dolān*, Dag. *dolō* (vs.

[6] On the loss and preservation of medial see Rybatzki 2003, 61-62; Apatóczky 2008, 2.4.

dolōn 'seventh'), Yogor *dolōn*, Mgr. *dolōn*, Baoan *dələŋ*, Santa *dolon*, Mong. *doloγa(n)*.

216 *ǰē köwü/köwǖ* (*zhe kou-wu* 折扣兀 Chin. *wai-sheng* 外甥) 'sister's son; son-in-law' AT *ǰige*, Dag. *dʒə̄*, Yogor *dʒī*. Mgr. *dẓē*, Santa *dẓə*, Mong. *ǰige*.

219 *bȫ* (*bei* Chin. *duan-gong*) 'shaman' SH *bö'e*, Hy *bö'e*, Zyyy *bȫ*, Mgr. *bō*, Mong. *böge*.

262 *al<a> sǖl* (*su-lu*) 'tail' SH *se'ül*, Hy *se'ül*, MA *se'ǖl/sǖl/sü'ǖl*, AT *segül*, RH *seül*, Dag. *səuļ*, Yogor *sȳl*, Mgr. *sūl*, Mong. *segül*.

402. *tǖküi noγō* (*tu-kui*) 'raw' MA *tǖküi*, Dag. *tuiγun*, Mgr. *tūgu*, Baoan *tugu*, Mong. *tügükei*.

412 *budā* (*bu-da* Chin. *fan*) 'rice' SH *buda'an* 'porridge', AL *budaan* 'noodle', Hy *buda'an* 'porridge', MA *budān* 'rice, porridge, noodle, food', RY *buda*, RH *budān* 'food, meal', Dag. *budā*, Yogor *budān*, Mgr. *budā* 'thick gruel, dense porridge', Santa *budan*, Mong. *budaγa*.

419 *darasu ū-* (*ou*) 'to drink' SH *u'u-*, AL *au-*, MA *u'ū-/ū-*, AT *uu-*, Dag. *ō-*, Yogor *ū-*, Mgr. *ū-*, Baoan *ū-*, Mong. *uuγu-/uγu-/aγu-*.

467 *qunāsu* (*hu-na-su* Chin. *zhe-er*) 'lined coat' Dag. *xonēs*, Mgr. *xʊnādzə*, Mong. *quniyasu*.

516 *tōdu[γ]* (*tuo-du* Chin. *jiu* 'pigeon') 'bustard' MA *toγdai*, Mong. *toγodaγ*.

580 *bǖr* (*bu-er* Chin. *yao-zi*) 'kidneys' SH *bö'ere/bökörey*, AL *bȫre*, Hy *bö'ere*, Zyyy *bǖr*, AT *bögere*, RH *böire*, Yogor *pȳre/bȳre*, Mgr. *bōro*, Baoan *bə̄rə*, Santa *boro*, Mong. *bögere*.

591 *dürē* (*du-le* Chin. *deng*) 'stirrup' Hy *dörö'e*, Zyyy *dür<r>ē*, VdI *dörie*, MA *dörē*, AT *döröge*, RH *dörē*, Dag. *durə̄ng̦*, Yogor *durē*, Mong. *döröge*.

610 *mǖr* (*mu-er* Chin. *wang-zi*) 'the outer rim of a cart wheel' SH *mö'eren*, Hy *mö'er*, Dag. *m*^{w}*ə̄r*, Mong. *möger*.

In some cases both the diphthongoid and the long vowel variants of a word remained extant:

212 *köbe'ün* (*ke-bo/bai-wen* 可伯文 Chin. *hai-er* 孩兒) and 208 *köwü/köwǖ* (*kou-wu* 扣兀 Chin. *er-zi* 兒子) 'son, child' SH *kö'ün* and *kö'üt* (plur.), Hy *kö'ün* and *kö'üt*, Zyyy *keü*, VdI *keün*, MA *kü'ǖn/kǖn* and *kü'ǖt* (plur.), AT *köbegün* and *köbegüd* (plur.), RH *köün*, *keüket* (plur.), Dag. *kək*^{w}, Yogor *kȳn/kȳken*, Mgr. *kəū/kō*, Baoan *kuŋ*, Santa *kəwaŋ* (plur. *kəwas*), Mong. *köbegün*, *keü-* (in *keüken*, *keüked*).

334 *bowurul morin* (*bao-wu-lun mo-lin* 保兀倫莫林 Chin. *hong-sha ma* 紅沙馬 'red roan') 'grey, grey haired horse' and 319 *būrul morin* (*bei/bo-luo-er mo-lin* 孛羅兒莫林 Chin. *qing ma* 青馬 'grey horse') 'partly grey, roan, greyish (horse)' SH (*ǰosoto*) *boro*, MA *būrul*, AT *buγurul*, RH *būrul (saqaltu)* 'a grey bearded man', Dag. *bōrul*, Yogor *būral*, Mgr. *bōrol*, Mong. *boγurul*.

ö > ü merger. In terms of the amalgamation of *ö* into *ü* that is considered to be a distinctive feature of a postulatory Eastern Middle Mongol dialect versus the *ö > e* change in Western Middle Mongol, BLYY data show typical Eastern characteristics (Written Mongol equivalents are given in parentheses)[7]: *bürbügü/bümbügü* 'round' (bömbüger, bömbür), *ǰ̄ülgen* 'soft, weak' (ǰögelen), *kümüldü[r]ge* 'breast strap of the harness' (kömüldürge), *küngen* 'light (not heavy)' (könggen), *künǰile* 'coverlet, quilt, scarf' (könǰile), *mündür* 'hail, hailstone' (möndür), *münggü* 'silver' (mönggü(n)), *mür* 'way, road' (mör), *mǖr* 'the outer rim of a cart wheel' (möger), *bǖr* 'kidney' (bögere), *mürün* 'river' (mören), *meis(ü)/müsü* 'ice' (mö(l)sü(n)), *hüčiken[ü]dür* 'yesterday' (öčige(l)dür, öčökedür), *üčüken* 'small' (öčügüken/üčügüken, öčüken/üčüken), *ülüs-* 'to starve' (ölüs-), *ürbi* 'stork, heron' (örüb/örbi), *süsü* 'gall' (sösün, čösün), *dürē* 'stirrup' (*döröge*).

Some of the words, however, preserve *ö*, e.g. *bödene/bödöne* 'quail, lark' (bödöne), *örmü[g]* 'coarse, of fabric made from camel hair or sheep's wool' (örmüge(n), ermüge(n)), *ötüge* 'bear' (ötege, ötöge), *ötügü* (ötegü).

Labial harmony. Another important phonologic attribute, the lack of labial harmony in words with *o-a* arrangement is frequent in (mostly Western) Middle Mongol, giving the impression of a middle position in BLYY[8]. Other words are lacking (e.g. *olan* 'many, much', *olam/olang* 'girth', *ǰo'a[s]* 'coin', *oraitu* 'to get late', *dürē* 'stirrup') and some displaying labial harmony (e.g. *qōlo[i]* 'throat', *qolo* 'far', *qoyor* 'two', *torqo* 'badger').

Vocabulary. One of the most apparent attribute of a dialect is its differing lexicon from other dialects. BLYY is rich in lexical items unknown or uncommon in modern Mongolic or in other Middle Mongol sources. There are archaic words in BLYY that have completely disappeared in modern

---

[7] Rybatzki 2003, 62.

[8] Rybatzki 2003, 62.

Mongolic languages, e.g. 166 *or[γ]an* (*wo-er-wan* 我兒完 Chin. *min* 民) 'people' SH *orqa*, Hy *orqon*; and 312 *taunan* (*tao-nan* 討難 Chin. *wu-sui* 五歲) 'five years old stallion'[9]. Larger is the number of items that later became obsolete in modern Mongolic languages but in some form or other have equivalents either in some of the modern peripheral Mongolic languages or in Middle Mongol. Many of them are loanwords:

63 *bač̌ar* (*ba-zha-er* 把扎兒 Chin. *jie-shi* 街市) 'market' Hy *baʒar* 'city', Uighur of Ming *bazar*, Chag. *bāzār*, Dag. *badʒir*, Mgr. *badzar* < Uighur, Mog./Weiers *bɔz'ɔr*, Baoan *badzar*; (< Pers. *bāzār*).

68 *dem* (*de-mu* 得目 Chin. *bao* 堡) 'walled village, a settlement', Uighur of Ming *tam* 'wall', Baoan *dam* 'wall', Dag. *ɖam* (店, 旅店) (or read *dam* cf. Mong. *dam* 'barrier, hindrance') (< Chin. *dian* 店).

95 *dangna<u>su* (*dang-nao-su* 黨惱速 Chin. *tu-dui-zi* 土堆子) 'dust-heap, mound of earth' SH *danglasun* 'fistful of soil', RH *tanglasun* 'brick'.

115 *nač̌ir* (*na-zhi-er* 納只兒 Chin. *xia* 夏) 'summer' Dag. *nadʑir*, Bur. *nažar*.

158 *dudu* (*du-du* 堵督 Chin. *du-du* 都督) 'governor of capital, viceroy, military governor' Turk *totoq*, Tib. *todog* (cf. Ecsedy 1993, 69-75.), Mong. *düdü* (< Chin. *du-du* 都督).

160 *čerbin* (*che-li-bin* 扯力賓 Chin. *ba-zong* 把總) 'sergeant, Darkhan in charge, military commander, chancellor' SH *čerbi*, AT *čerbi*, Zyyy *čerbi*, TMEN № 176.

170 *ötügü* (*wo-tu-gu* 我土故 Chin. *lao-le* 老了 'old, grown old') 'old' AL *ötegü*, Hy *ötögü (gü'ün)*, MA *ötegü*, Mong. *ötegü*.

174 *šanšeng/šanšing* (*shang-sheng* 賞生 Chin. *dao-shi* 道士) '(Taoist) priest' Dag. *ʃenʃing* 'physician' (< Chin. *xian-sheng* 先生).

180 *tesman* (*te-si-man* 忒四蠻 Chin. *man-la* 滿剌) 'Muslim priest' cf. ЗОГРАФ 1984, 39. *dašman* 'Muslim clergyman', Poppe 1955, 39 *dašmad* 'Muhammadan clergy' (< Turk < Pers. *danišmand*).

194 *ebin* (*a/e-bin* 阿賓 Chin. *da-ye* 大爺 'uncle') 'uncle' SH *ebin*, Hy *ebin*.

[9] See the analogous words in written Mongol: *γunan* 'three years old stallion', *dönen* 'four years old stallion'.

217 *otuči* (*wo-du-chi* 我堵赤 Chin. *tai-yi* 太醫) ‘doctor, physician’ Zyyy *otoči*, Hy *otoči*, MA *otači*, Dag. *otuʃ* ‘female shaman’, Bur. *otošo* (rare), Mong. *otači*.

239 *vayiduri* (*fa-yi-du-li* 法一堵力 Chin. *liu-li* 琉璃 ‘opaque’) ‘beryl’ Khal. *vinder’yaa*, Mong. *binderiya/vaiduri/viduri*, Uighur *vaiduri*; (< Tib. < Sanskrit *vaidurya* ‘beryl’).

256 *saiǰa*[10] (*sai-zha* 賽扎 Chin. *zan-zi* 簪子) ‘hairpin’ Khal. *cais*, Mong. *čaisa/čayisa* (< Chin. *chai-zi* 釵子).

345 *haul-* (*hao-la* 好剌 Chin. *pao* 跑) ‘to run, to overrun’ SH *ha’ul-*, Dag. *xaul*, Mgr. *xaulə-*, Baoan *xɵl-*.

352 *dörgene* (*duo-er-han-nie* 朵兒汗捏 Chin. *sang* 桑) ‘mulberry’ SH *Döregene* (prop.).

383 *ǰaγaq* (*yi-ha-ha* 義哈哈 read *cha* 叉 instead of *yi* 義 (乂) Chin. *he-tao* 核 椡 character variant for *tao* normally written as 桃) ‘walnuts’ Hy *ǰi’aq*, RH *jaġaq*, Baoan *dʐanɢax*

391 *čom güilesü* (*shuo-mu gui-le-su* 勺木鬼勒速 Chin. *zhen-ren* 榛棯, read *ren* 仁 instead of *ren* 棯) ‘hazelnut’ Ramstedt/KalmWb *tsöm* ‘cornel’, Karachai-Balkar *čum*, Hung. *som* ‘cornel’ TESz, Ligeti 1986, 292-293, Manduqu *šomur güilesü* = *šid* ‘hazelnut’ (incorrect).

405 *qabaq* (*ha-ba-ha* 哈把哈 Chin. *hu-lu* 葫蘆 ‘bottle-gourd’) ‘gourd’ Hy *qabaq*, TMEN № 1419 (< Turk).

410 *ütmü[g]* (*wu-tu-mu* 五禿木 Chin. *mo-mo* 饝饝 ‘steamed loaf’) ‘dumpling, steamed loaf’ Zyyy *üdmek*, Hy *ütmek*, VdI *ötüme* ‘bread’, RH *ötmek*, Uighur of Ming *ötmäk*, Dag. *utum* ‘snack, biscuit’, Mgr. *ʂdəma*.

424 *širke* (*shi-er-ke* 失兒克 Chin. *cu* 醋) ‘vinegar’ ‘Phags-pa *širge*, Hy *širke*, Uighur of Ming *sirkä*, Poppe 1955, 41 *širge*, TMEN № 1237, precl. Mong. *sirkü* (< Turk).

449 *künǰi[r]* (*kun-zhi* 困直 Chin. *zhi-ma* 芝麻 ‘sesame’) ‘hemp, Cannabis sativa’ MA *künǰid*, Witsen *kentschir*, Uighur of Ming *kändir* ‘hemp’ and *künčit* ‘sesame’, TMEN № 1647, Yogor *kendʒer*, Baoan *kəntɕir*, Santa *kəntʂɯ*, Mong. *kendir*.

---

[10] Although this loanword has a corresponding modern Mongol pair of equivalents, the Chinese dialect it was borrowed from had a different phonologic setup to the one that Khalkha was borrowing from.

473 *čaru[q]* (*yi-lu* 義魯 read *cha* 叉 instead of *yi* 義 (乂) Chin. *xie* 鞋) 'shoes, slippers' Zyyy *čaru[q]*, Hy *čaruq*, RH *čaruq*, Mgr. *tɕarɔɢ*, Mog./Weiers *tʃɔr'ɔ*, TMEN № 1044 (< Turk).

519 *čibčiġ(ai)* (*chi-bu-chi-ge* 赤補赤革 Chin. *shan-he* 山鶴) 'sparrow, lark' AL *čipčiqai* 'sparrow' (< Turk), Chag. *ćimćik*, Manduqu *čibčig* = *qatan-u boljomor* 'lark'.

523 *bildu'ur*[11] (*bin-du-er* 賓堵兒 Chin. *jiao-tian-er* 叫天兒 'a small bird [that cries to the sky]') 'a small bird like a sparrow or a lark' SH *bilǰi'ur*, cf. de Rachewiltz 2006, 365-366, RH *bildür/bildūr* 'nightingale'.

In some instances Jurchen influence can also be assumed, e.g.

425 *ǰüši'ün* (*zhu-shi-wen* 主失文 Chin. *suan* 酸) 'sour' RY *ǰusu* (cf. Kara 1991, 156. "read *ǰušu*"), Dag. *dʒusū* 'vinegar', Manchu *jušuhun*.

404 *qalgi noγō* (*ha-er-ji nu-wu* 哈兒吉奴惡 Chin. *jie-cai* 芥菜 'mustard') 'nettle' RY *harhi*, Dag. *xalān kur*, Manchu *hargi*, Mong. *qalaγai*.

Additionally there are a couple of Jurchen loanwords:

394 *haši* (*ha-shi* 哈失 Chin. *qie-zi* 茄子) 'egg-plant' RY *haši*, Manchu *hasi*, (Mong. *čêse, čêǰe* < Chin. *qie-zi*) (< Jurchen/Manchu).

45 *ula* (*wu-la* 五剌 Chin. 江 *jiang*) 'river' SH *Ula* 'the Ula river', RY *ula*, (Mong. *mören*) Manchu *ula* (< Jurchen/Manchu).

The conspicuous case of *meis(ü)/müsü* 'ice' has more equally acceptable explanations: either the transcribers did a good job so the word reads *meisü* (somewhat as in modern Dagur), or they made an error and the item reads *müsü*:

51 *meis(ü)/müsü* (*mei-su* 每速 read 母 *mu* instead of 每 *mei* or read *meis* cf. Dag., Chin. *bing* 冰) 'ice' SH *mölsün*, Hy *mölsün*, Zyyy *mölsü*, VdI *mölsün*, MA *mölsün*, RH *mölsün*, Uighur of Ming *muz*, Dag. *məis*, Yogor *mösən*, Mgr. *molsə/moɟə*, Baoan *melsəŋ*, Santa *məsuŋ/maŋsuŋ/mənsun*, Barin *mɵs*, Bur. *mülhen*, Mong. *mö(l)sü(n)*.

Conclusion. We have seen that the lexical data of the BLYY consists on the whole of both phonologically and lexically typical Middle Mongol items. Nevertheless there are numerous cases of atypical occurrences as well that might be attested in other Middle Mongol sources separately, but no other Middle Mongol source has them all. The most uncommon of

[11] Along with many other suggestions on difficult cases in BLYY, it was Prof. Igor de Rachewiltz who offered this reconstructed form in our personal correspondence.

these phenomena is the initial *hU- > fU-* change unprecedented in any other Middle Mongol source. The mere existence of the infrequent forms listed in this paper leads us to reflect upon the situation. The language that served as a source for the BLYY most likely might have been a relatively late version of Middle Mongol, in which linguistic changes leading to the formation of a dialect (initial *hU- > fU-* change, palatal prebreaking, long vowels replacing diphthong sequences etc.) had already taken place in some instances. The other possiblity is that BLYY is much older (from about early *Ming*) than its oldest extant edition (1599), and even by the time of the recording of other, better dated *Yuan* and *Ming* sources, the dialect of BLYY was so different to them that in terms of the mentioned changes it seemed to be a vanguard of some modern Mongolic languages. For some trends even foreign influence could be considered to be responsible (e.g. in the case of initial *hU- > fU-* and for some lexical changes the possibility of Jurchen influence cannot be precluded). All these opinions can be accounted for and the acceptance of any of them suggests that the lexicon of BLYY may serve as a starting point for further studies of Middle Mongol dialects.

Bibliography and Abbreviations

AL (Leiden Manuscript): Houtsma 1894, Poppe 1927-28, Saitō 2006.

Apatóczky, Á. B. 2005. 'Yiyu (Beilu yiyu) 16 shijide Hua Meng cidian zhi fenxi' '譯語(北虜譯語)16世紀的 華蒙詞典之分析' [A linguistic analysis of the Yiyu (Beilu yiyu), a Sino-Mongol glossary of the sixteenth century]. In: *4th International Junior Scholars' Conference on Sinology*, National Dong Hwa University-Harward University. Hualian, 13.1-13.22.

— forthcoming. '*YIYU. An Indexed Critical Edition of a Sixteenth Century Sino-Mongolian Glossary*'. London 2008.

AT (Altan tobči): Ligeti 1974, Vietze & Lubsang 1992.

Bao, Zhaolu 保朝鲁 2002. *Mukadimate Mengguyu cidian* 穆卡迪玛特蒙古语词典 [The Mongol dictionary of Mukaddimat]. Kökeqota.

Baoan (dialect): Chen 1985, Sun *et al.* 1990.

Benkő, L. (ed.) 1967-76. *A magyar nyelv történeti-etimológiai szótára.* [A historical-etymological dictionary of the Hungarian language]. Budapest. 3 vols.

BLYY (Beilu yiyu): Apatóczky 2005, 2008.

Bur. (Buryat language): Черемисов 1973, Sun *et al.* 1990.

Черемисов, К. М. 1973. *Бурятско Русский словарь.* Moscow.

Цэвэл, Я. 1966. *Монгол хэлний товч тайлбар толь* [A concise explanatory dictionary of the Mongolian language]. Ulaanbaatar.

Chag. (Chagatai language): Eckmann 1966, Vámbéry 1867.

Chen, Naixiong 陈乃雄 *et al.* (eds) 1985. *Boo-an kelen-ü üges* [Vocabulary of the Baoan language]. Kökeqota.

Chin. (Chinese): Mathews 1943.

Dag. (Dagur/Dahur dialect): Engkebatu *et al.* 1984, Sun *et al.* 1990.

de Rachewiltz, I. 1972. *Index to the Secret History of the Mongols*. (Indiana University, Uralic and Altaic Series 121.) Bloomington.

— 2006. *The Secret History of the Mongols. A Mongolian Epic Chronicle of the Thirteenth Century*. Leiden · Boston.

— 2006. 'Some Remarks on the Chih-Yüan I-Yü 至元譯語 alias Meng-Ku I-Yü 蒙古譯語, the first known Sino-Mongol Glossary'. *Acta Orientalia Hungarica* 59/1, 11-28.

— & Anthony Schönbaum (eds) 1977. Mostaert, Antoine, *Le matériel mongol du Houa I I Iu* 華夷譯語 *de Houng-ou (1389)*. (Mélanges chinois et bouddhiques XVIII.) Bruxelles.

Doerfer, G. 1963-75. *Türkische und mongolische Elemente im Neupersischen* 1-4. Wiesbaden.

Eckmann, J. 1966. *Chagatay Manual*. (Indiana University, Uralic and Altaic Series 60.) Bloomington.

Ecsedy, I. 1993. 'Kínai méltóságnevek a türk birodalom területén' [Titles of Chinese origin in the territory of the Turk empire]. *Keletkutatás*, 69-75.

Engkebatu *et al.* 1984. *Daγur kelen-ü üges* [Vocabulary of the Dagur (Dagur) language]. Kökeqota.

Franke, W. 1968. *An Introduction to the Sources of Ming history*. Kuala-Lumpur-Singapore.

Golden, P. B. 2000. *The King's Dictionary. The Rasûlid Hexaglot: Fourteenth Century Vocabularies in Arabic, Persian, Turkic, Greek, Armenian and Mongol*. Leiden.

Haenisch, E. 1952. *Sino-Mongolische Dokumente vom Ende des 14. Jahrhunderts*. Berlin.

Hajmal, L. 1994. 'Witsen's "Dagur" Material'. *Acta Orientalia Hungarica* 47, 279-326.

Houtsma, M. T. 1894. *Ein türkisch-arabisches Glossar. Nach der Leidener Handschrift*. Leiden.

Hugejiletu & Sarula (ed.) 2004. 呼格吉勒图-萨如拉: *Basibazi Menggu yu wenxian huibian*. 八思巴字蒙古语文献汇编 [A collection of Mongol literature in 'Phags-pa script]. Huhehaote.

Hung. (Hungarian): Benkő 1967-76.

Hy (Huayi yiyu): Lewicki 1949, Haenisch 1952, Kuribayashi 2003.

Kane, D. 1989. *The Sino-Jurchen Vocabulary of the Bureau of Interpreters*. (Indiana University, Uralic and Altaic Series 153.) Bloomington.

Kara, G. 1990. 'Zhiyuan Yiyu. Index alphabétique des mots mongols'. *Acta Orientalia Hungarica* 44, 279-344.

— 1991. 'Jurchin notes'. *Acta Orientalia Hungarica* 45, 149-158.

— 1998. *Mongol-magyar szótár* [Mongolian- Hungarian dictionary]. Budapest.

Karachai-Balkar: Суюнчев 1965.

KdG (Kirakos of Gandzak): Ligeti 1965.

Khal. (Khalkha dialect): Цэвэл 1966, Kara 1998.

Kuribayashi, H. 2003. *Word- and Suffix-Index to Hua-yi Yi-yü Based on the Romanized Transcription of Lajos Ligeti*. (CNEAS Monograph series No. 10.) Sendai.

Lessing, F. D. *et. al.* 1960. *Mongolian-English Dictionary*. Berkeley · Los Angeles.

Lewicki, M. 1949. *La langue mongole des transcriptions chinoises du XIV*[e] *siècle. Le Houa-yi yi-yu de 1389.* (Travaux de la Société des Sciences et des lettres de Wroclaw, Seria A, Nr. 29.) Wroclaw.

Ligeti, L. 1956. 'Le Po kia sing en écriture 'phags-pa'. *Acta Orientalia Hungarica* 6, 1-52.

— 1962. 'Un vocabulaire mongol d'Istanboul'. *Acta Orientalia Hungarica* 14, 3-99.

— 1965. 'Le lexique mongol de Kirakos de Gandzak'. *Acta Orientalia Hungarica* 18, 241-297.

— 1966. 'Un vocabulaire sino-ouigour des Ming. Le *Kao-Tch'ang-Kouan yi-chou* du bureau des traducteurs'. *Acta Orientalia Hungarica* 19, 117-199, 257-316.

— 1974. *Histoire secrète des Mongols. Texte en écriture ouigoure incorporé dans la chronique Altan tobči de Blo-bzań bstan-'jin.* (Monumenta Linguae Mongolicae Collecta 6.) Budapest.

— 1986. *A magyar nyelv török kapcsolatai a honfoglalás előtt és az Árpád-korban* [The Turkish connections of the Hungarian language before the Hungarian conquest and in the Árpád epoch]. Budapest.

MA (Mukaddimat al-Adab): Bao 2002, Poppe 1938.

Manduqu: Manduqu 1995.

Manduqu, Ö. 1995. *Mongγol yi yu toli bičig* (*Menggu yiyu cidian* 蒙古译语词典) [Mongol yiyu dictionary]. Kökcqota.

— 1998. *Quva yi yi yu* (*Hua Yi yiyu* 华夷译语) [Hua Yi yiyu]. Hailar.

Mathews, R. H. 1943. *Chinese English Dictionary*. Harvard.

Mgr. (Mongour dialect): Qasbaγatur *et al.* 1985, Sun *et al.* 1990.

Mog./Weiers (Moghol/Weiers): Weiers 1971.

Mong. (Written Mongolian): Lessing *et al.* 1960.

'hPags-pa (script): Hugejiletu & Sarula 2004, Ligeti 1956, Poppe 1957.

Poppe, N. N. 1927-28. 'Das mongolische Sprachmaterial einer Leidener Handschrift'. *Известия Академии Наук СССР* 1927, 1009-1040, 1251-1274; 1928, 55-80.

— 1938. *Монгольский словарь Мукаддимат ал-Адаб*. Moscow.

— 1955. 'Turkic Loan Words in Middle Mongolian'. *Central Asiatic Journal* I/1, 36-42.

— 1957. *The Mongolian Documents in ḥP'ags-pa Script*. (Ed.) John R. Krueger. Wiesbaden

Qasbaγatur *et al.* (eds) 1985. *Mongγor kelen-ü üges* [Vocabulary of the Monguor language]. Kökeqota.

Ramstedt/KalmWb: Ramstedt 1935.

Ramstedt, G. J. 1935. *Kalmükisches Wörterbuch*. Helsinki.

RH (Rasûlid Hexaglot): Golden 2000.

RY (Ruzhi guan yiyu): Kane 1989.

Rybatzki, V. 2003. 'Middle Mongol'. In: J. Janhunen (ed.), *The Mongolic Languages*. London, 57-82.

Saitō, Yoshio 2006. *The Mongolian words in* Kitâb Majmû' Tarjumân Turkî wa-'ajamî wa-Muğalî. *Text and index*. Kyōto.

Santa (dialect): Sun *et al.* 1990.

SH (Secret History of the Mongols): de Rachewiltz 1972, 2006; Ligeti 1974.

Суюнчев, Х. И. 1965. *Русско-карачаево-балкарский словарь.* Moscow.

Sun Zhu 孫竹 *et al.* (eds) 1990. *Menggu yuzu yuyan cidian* 蒙古语族语言 词典 [Dictionary of the group of Mongol languages]. Xining.

TMEN: (Türkische und mongolische Elemente im Neupersischen): Doerfer 1963-76.

Uighur of Ming: Ligeti 1966.

Vámbéry, H. 1867. *Ćagataische Sprachstudien.* Leipzig.

VdI (Vocabulary of Istanbul): Ligeti 1962.

Vietze, H.-P. & Gendeng Lubsang 1992. *Altan Tobči. Eine mongolische Chronik des XVII. Jahrhunderts von Blo bzaṅ bstan 'jin. Text und Index.* Tokyo.

Weiers, M. 1971. *Die Sprache der Moghol der Provinz Herat in Afghanistan.* (Abhandlungen der Rheinisch-Westfälischen Akademie der Wissenschaften 49.) Göttingen.

Witsen (Wisten's "Dagur" material): Hajnal 1994.

Yogur (dialect): Sun *et al.* 1990.

Зограф, И. Т. 1984. *Монгольско-Китайская Интерференция.* Moscow.

Zyyy (Zhiyuan yiyu): Kara 1990.

INDOCHINA, VIETNAMESE NATIONALISM AND THE MONGOLS

Paul D. Buell

Looking back from the limited perspective of the early 13th century steppe, when the Mongol Empire first emerged, an extended confrontation with a minor power in the jungles of northern Indochina, with the state that became Vietnam, appeared unlikely in the extreme. But, in fact, such a confrontation did take place, with two major consequences. One was a serious weakening of the most dynamic of the Mongol successor states, Qubilai-qan's China. Like the United States in the 20th century, it found Vietnam a quagmire consuming human and non-human resources at a prodigious rate. The second consequence, even more significant over the long term, was the emergence of a renewed and self-conscious Vietnam. It was soon well along the road to uniting the entire east coast of the Indochinese peninsula as well as interior areas. This was a new Vietnam that never forgot the shock of Mongol invasion and has based so much of its national identify on heroic resistance to it.

In the mid-13th century, when the Mongols first came into contact with Indochina, there was, strictly speaking, no Vietnam. Certainly there was no state even remotely similar to the Vietnam of today. Vietnamese speakers did dominate in what is today north Vietnam. There they ruled a highly Sinified state usually known by its Chinese name, Annam 安南, "pacifying the south."[1] Although Vietnamese, this state was weak with little sense of national identity and disunited. Powerful clans were more interested in fighting each other than mobilizing against any potential enemy.[2]

Further south, central Vietnam, the area around modern Huế, was dominated by the kingdom of Champa, by then largely Muslim although once subject to substantial Indian cultural influence. In spite of their geographical position, in what is now Vietnamese heartland, the Cham

---

[1] Since the 11th century this same area was known locally as Đại Việt 大越, "Great Việt," in the manner of a Chinese dynasty.

[2] See K. W. Taylor 'The Early Kingdoms' (Tarling 1992, 137-182). Dominating at the time of the Mongol invasions was the Trần 鎮 clan, positioned in Thăng-long, 昇龍, the modern Hà nội 河内.

people were not Vietnamese but spoke a Malayo-Polynesian language.[3] This contrasts to Vietnamese, a Mon-khmer language heavily influenced by the Thai tonal system and which has been subject to centuries of Chinese influence. This has left an enormous residue in the Vietnamese literary language.

The center of the kingdom was the large and prosperous city called Zhancheng 占城, by the Chinese, Champāpura by the locals, near modern Da Nang. Its greatest asset was its ideal positioning both for international trade and river traffic, quite unlike the inland capital of Annam, upland and in an area with fewer waterways. Champāpura's location was also ideal defensively, as the Mongols were to find out.

South of Champa were hill tribes and Cambodians. The latter spoke a language related to Vietnamese but lacking tones. Like the Vietnamese, the Cambodians were Buddhist, but Theravada Buddhists, not Mahayana like the Vietnamese, whose religious orientation was strongly influenced by China.

The Mongols first came into contact with the first of these cultures, that of Annam in the mid-13th century as they advanced into what is now Yunnan 雲南, then ruled by the Thai state of Dali 大理. They seem to have been interested in the Yunnan plateau in its own terms, as a possible center for their own tribal presence, and because of its position on the flank of the Southern Song 宋 Empire (1125-1279), their main enemy in China. Once positioned in Yunnan, other areas became accessible to the Mongols, including Burma, invaded in 1277, and Vietnam.

Leading the Mongol advance south was Möngke Qan (r. 1251-59) himself, seconded by his younger brother, prince Qubilai (ruled in China 1260-1294). The entire episode, which focused on Sichuan 四川, with the advance farther south through the mountains of the Sino-Tibetan borderlands in many ways an afterthought, is well known and relatively well documented.[4] There is, for example, abundant biographical material available on some of its participants, including the imperial *jarquci* Saiyid Ajall (1211-1279), later a principal figure in Mongol efforts to organize their conquests.[5] Thanks to Sayyid Ajall and others like him, Yunnan became truly a part of China for the first time in its history.

---

[3] On the history of Champa see Taylor (Tarling 1992). Also see C. Wheeler 'One Region, Two Histories, Cham Precedents in the History of the Hội An Region' (Tran & Reid 2006, 163-193).

[4] On the reign of Möngke and his campaigns in China see Buell 2003.

[5] See P. D. Buell 'Saiyid Ajall' (de Rachewiltz *et al.* 1993, 466-479).

Less well known is the exploratory advance towards the sea taking place after the conquest of Yunnan. It was led by figures such as Uriangqadai (1201-1272), the son of the great Mongol general Sübe'etei-ba'atur (1176-1248).[6] The claimed purpose was to was to subdue "various barbarians, who had still not submitted"[7] in the general vicinity of Yunnan, which became a domain of Mongol princes as well as eventual province of Mongol China.

Among these "barbarians" were the peoples of Jiaozhi 交趾, using an old name for Annam. Given the weakness of the Annamese kingdom at the time, the Mongols had no problem penetrating it and their cavalry performed rather well in the relatively flat areas in the uplands and along the Red River, the center of Annamese life. This was in 1257-58. Once positioned near the Annamese capital, the Mongols sent envoys to the king, Trần Thái-Tông 陳太宗 or Trần Cảnh 陳煚, (r. 1225-1258) and invited him to submit. He refused and began almost 40 years of Vietnamese outright resistance or prevarication. After being defeated on the rivers and on land, knowing that he could not face the Mongols if they attempted to take his capital, Thái-Tông took refuge in an island in the sea and thus placed himself out of Mongol reach. Uriangqadai and his subordinates then advanced to and took Thăng-long where they discovered that one of their envoys had been killed, a serious breach of diplomatic protocol to the Mongols. True to tradition, they massacred the city but were forced to retreat again to the safety and coolness of the Yunnan Plateau after only nine days, due to the damp and hot north Vietnam climate (summer 1258).[8]

Once Mongol armies were safely away, Thái-Tông returned to his ruined capital, send back the two Mongol envoys that he still held captive,

---

[6] There is substantial material on Uriangqadai, including a *Yuanshi* biography 2978-2982.

[7] *Yuanshi* 4633. In addition to the lengthy section on Annam in the *Yuanshi*, which provides the fullest account, the other principal Chinese source for the Mongol advance into Indochina are two texts in the *Yuan wenlei*, 'Annam' (41, 25a-26a), and 'Zhancheng' (41, 33a-35b). These texts are supplemented by biographies on the principal participants. Vietnamese sources, which will be discussed in more detail in a later article, include the *Đại Việt sử ký* 大越史記, 'Historical Record of Vietnam,' of Lê Văn Hưu (1230-1322), completed in 1272 and containing considerable information about the first Mongol invasions of Vietnam and local reactions to them, and the later *Đại Việt sử ký toàn thư* 大越史記全書, 'Completed Historical Record of Vietnam,' of Ngô Sĩ Liên (fl. 15th century). On these works see Yu Insun 'Lê Văn Hưu and Ngô Sĩ Liên: A Comparison of Their Perception of Vietnamese History' (Tran & Reid 2006, 45-71).

[8] *Yuanshi* 4633-4634.

and abdicated in favor of his son, Trần Thánh-Tông 陳聖宗, or Trần Hoàng 陳晃, (r. 1258-1278), whose two decades of prevarication allowed the Annamese to build up their strength and avoid collision with their powerful adversaries. They did not give up their claim to be the arbiters of the Vietnamese world. To placate them, Thánh-Tông sent ambassadors, hostages and tribute, that is, local Vietnamese products such as spices and aromatics, and talented individuals of interest to the Mongols, including shaman and doctors, although he never appeared himself, despite repeated requests.[9]

Two patterns thus became apparent from the time of the first encounters between the Mongols and the Vietnamese. One was a refusal to surrender, and willingness to hide out until the danger was past, marshalling resources, for a counterattack, when and if this became possible. The other was the tendency to tell the Mongols what they wanted to hear, as long as nothing substantial was given up. Thus, while tribute was sent, Thánh-Tông had no intention whatever of leaving Vietnam and personally accept Mongol rule, although his court was forced to accept the presence of a Mongolian *daruqaci*, "imperial representative."[10]

During much of the 20 year reign of Thánh-Tông, the Mongols were preoccupied with internal disputes, as the unified empire split up, and Qubilai, who inherited Mongol China, faced external and internal competitors.[11] Annam was far from his mind. This changed as the Mongols finally began in the late 1260s a serious effort to conquer Southern Song and unify China for the first time in centuries.

As the Mongols advanced deeper and deeper into the Chinese south, their pressures increased on Annam. In 1276, the Song capital fell to Mongol armies and in 1279 the last major Song forces were crushed in a great land and sea battle off what is modern Macau, at Yaishan 厓山. The Mongols had learned how to best the south Chinese on their own element, the sea.[12] Annam and Mongol China were now neighbours on two sides, north as well as west, and pressures on Annam to submit in more than theory now intensified.

After Thánh-Tông's death, his son Trần Nhán-Tông 陳仁宗, or Trần Khâm 陳昑, (r. 1278-1293), succeeded to the throne but did so, according to the Mongols, illegally. They should have asked Qubilai first. This fact,

---

[9] *Yuanshi* 4634.

[10] *Yuanshi* 4635.

[11] See the relevant sections in Buell 2003.

[12] For full details, see Buell 1985-86.

and the refusal of any Annamese ruler to come of court and personally present tribute, resulted in a lengthy diplomatic correspondence. It is summarized in detail by the *Yuanshi* 元史 from various sources. Qubilai's ministers tried in every kind of diplomatic doublespeak to assert the inferiority of the king of Annam and his position as a subordinate of Qubilai and his new Yuan 元 Dynasty (1260-1368). The Annamese did what they needed to do to keep the Mongols off their neck but never gave in on substance, arguing precedent with the Mongols in the best Chinese fashion with abundant quotation of early sources on the proper position of subordinate rulers vis-à-vis a "Chinese" emperor.[13]

The Annamese managed to keep the Mongols talking for some time and continued to do so without much disadvantage until 1281 when Qubilai lost patience and ordered an invasion of Champa. Annam was ordered to participate by supporting Mongol armies. Since it was situated along the direct Mongol line of advance, the position of Annam now became more difficult.

Qubilai had become interested in Champa for two primary reasons. One was the size of Champa's trade with the South Seas, trade that the Mongols wished to control if not take over.[14] Another reason seems to have been the possible presence of Song refugees in Champa, plotting a restoration.[15] Thus, immediately after the battle of Yaishan, which took place on March 19, 1279, the Mongols stepped up their efforts, begun some years before, to secure the submission of King Indravarman (r. 1266-?). In Champa Mongol efforts were led by the general Sögetü (died 1285), Minister of the Right and a hero in the final wars against Song.[16]

At first, the Champa king cooperated, but as the physical presence of the Mongols in Champa grew, so did resistance. One bone of contention became Champa interference with Mongol envoys to other points, as far afield as India. In the end, the Mongols made preparations for war as the Champa king mobilized his armies. The pattern once seen in Annam repeated itself in Champa. The king had no intention of submitting. The Mongols finally had no choice but to attack or abandon attempts to expand their influence south.[17]

The war against Champa that followed and went on for nearly four years was well financed, well supported and well led with ample troops

[13] *Yuanshi* 4638-4640.

[14] Rossabi 1988, 213-214.

[15] Rossabi 1988, 94.

[16] See his biography in the *Yuanshi* 3150-3153.

[17] *Yuanshi* 4660-4661.

but Champa proved a most trying adversary. Part of the problem was the physical location of the well defended Champa capital in a land of jungle crisscrossed with rivers and small streams. A concerted attack by land and sea from multiple directions was required to take the city. Once taken, it and other Champa cities proved as difficult to defend as they were to capture since the Mongols were never able to control the interior. As the United States Army and Marines found out in their time, terrain strongly favored an enemy that blended in with the surroundings and made good use of hit and run tactics, the case in the 13th century as in the 20th. A second problem for the Mongols was the difficulty of coordinating many different forces and supplying them, from points as far away as Canton and Fujian 福建, the true base of Yuan sea power.[18]

It was this coordination and supply issue that ultimately brought down the whole enterprise. The main Mongol supply lines stretched down the Vietnamese coast and here the weakness lay as the Vietnamese moved from being uncooperative, to sullen hostility, to cooperation with Champa and outright resistance, as they refused to permit the passage of a new Mongol army bound for Champa under prince Toqan.[19]

During these years the dominant personality in Annam was not the king, but his clansman Trần Quốc Tuấn 陳國峻 (1228-1300) who, with a little help from other princes supporting him, became the Vietnamese national hero in the fight against the Mongols. It was he who led the battle against renewed Mongol invasion, this time by Toqan's horsemen.

The key to a successful defense was preventing any juncture between Toqan's army and Mongol forces, under Sögetü, situated near Champa. This the Vietnamese did. Toqan was able to penetrate Vietnam, and even take the capital of Thăng-long, but the Vietnamese pursued a scorched earth policy to deny valuable supplies and sought to engage Mongol troops using the rivers and streams rather for ambush rather than fighting them in the open. There Toqan's advantage in cavalry would have proven overwhelming. The Vietnamese also let the Mongols wear themselves down in a climate they were both unused and unsuited to. In the end, Toqan was forced to retreat, leaving Sögetü, who found only an empty

---

[18] See Buell 1985-86, Deng 1999. Deng speaks of a huge Mongol fleet for offensive operations (pp. 188-189). On the campaign and the siege of the city of Champa in particular see details in the *Yuan Wenlei* 元文類 41:33b-35b, *Yuanshi* 4661-4664, Rossabi 1988, 215-217.

[19] *Yuanshi* 4641-4643. By this time, to insult Qubilai even more, the Annamese king had even declared himself an emperor, theoretically equal to Qubilai.

camp rather than the army he was supposed to rendezvous with, in the lurch. The latter was defeated and died in battle.[20] This was in 1285.

The Mongols came back two years later, in even larger numbers, again under prince Toqan, but Trần Quốc Tuấn used some of the same tactics to defeat this new invasion. In this case they destroyed Toqan's supply base, forcing him to retreat. Toqan's armies were not destroyed, but the Mongol fleet was, at the Battle of Bạch Đằng白藤 River (1288). Even the Mongol admiral, Omar, died.[21]

Although the Mongols soon abandoned Champa as untenable, the war in Annam went on until the end of Qubilai's reign. His successor, Temür Öljeitü (r. 1294-1307), finally gave it all up, even plans for a renewed assault on Japan.[22] In the end, a Vietnamese quagmire had entrapped the Mongols just as it was later to entrap Americans and others. Vietnam lost most of the battles but won the war.

One of the most impressive elements of Yuan China's Indochinese expeditions was the sizes of the armies employed. Contrary to conventional wisdom on the subject, not mere expeditionary forces, but quite large Yuan armies were sent and reinforced, accompanied by a considerable naval armament, fleets as large as those mobilized to attack Japan or for the final subjugation of Song. This was not a minor effort and thus, the Yuan defeat was not a minor one. Judging by the magnitude of the forces involved, Yuan's Vietnamese quagmire must have been far more costly in material and human resources and in prestige than much smaller, if more famous expeditions against Japan and Java. In fact, only to subjugate Song during the final push were greater forces mobilized for a single operation.[23]

Given this fact, one may speculate whether or not the Indochinese defeat of Yuan was not one cause of the decline of that dynasty which became more and more noticeable as the 14th century progressed, particularly in terms of Yuan inability to control its south. South China too became a quagmire and was quasi-independent long before the Mongols in Beijing had to flee liberating Ming 明 armies.

---

[20] *Yuanshi* 3152 3153; *Yuan Wenlei* 41:25b-26a; Taylor 1992, 149; Insun 2006, 63 (Tran & Reid 2006); Rossabi 1988, 217-218.

[21] *Yuanshi* 4645-4648.

[22] *Yuanshi* 4650

[23] While we may reject the Vietnamese nationalist claims of truly huge armies, as many as 500,000 under Prince Toqan, if we take the figures of the *Yuanshi* at face value, the Mongols may have had armies of up to 200,000 all told, possibly more, operating in Indochina at any one time. These are just the land forces. Thousands of ships, both warships and supply vessels, were also employed. See Deng 1999, 188-189.

For the Vietnamese, the decline of Yuan influence in Indochina meant the rise of their own. The "king" of Annam had declared himself an emperor and set up a true imperial court to rival that of Qanbaliq. He had problems asserting himself in this role, but the Vietnamese never forgot their claimed equality with China, even if it came to irritate the Ming as much as it did the Mongols of Yuan. Nonetheless, in the end it was the Vietnamese who conquered Champa, in the 15th century, not the Mongols and certainly not the Ming, in spite of the obvious power of the fleets led by the eunuch Cheng Ho 鄭和.[24] And from Champa the Vietnamese kept on going south, the area around what is now Saigon becoming Vietnamese no later than the end of the 18th century.[25]

The Vietnamese thus emerged strengthened from their conflict with the Mongols and maintained powerful armies. And even when these were defeated, there was always the jungle, as the Ming found out too. They even, briefly, thanks to a fortuitous discovery of a better way to seal off gunpowder explosions in canon and increase canon range, became technologically a leading military power by world standards.[26] Fortunately, the Portuguese, who preferred to trade rather than fight, never had to fight against the Vietnamese. They might have lost badly. The technology of canon, of course, they seem to have borrowed initially from the Ming or possibly the Mongols, and then improving on it.

Not only did Vietnam emerge more militarily powerful after its Mongol encounters, but it emerged more unified as well. Just as in Japan the myth of the Kamikaze that saved Japan from invasions became a major symbol of Japanese nationhood, so resistance to the Mongols became a symbol of what it was to be Vietnamese. The whole episode is taught in the schools of Vietnam to this day and the heroes of Vietnamese resistance such as Trần Quốc Tuấn are celebrated. In some ways, there never was a truly unified Vietnam before the Mongols and a truly disunited Vietnam, even when it was divided into competing halves, after them. The French, who ultimately made a physical national unity permanent even when they wished to divide Vietnam in support of their own political interests, only helped advance a process that had begun in the 13th century as small

[24] On later Vietnamese relationships with Champa see Wheeler 2006 (Tran & Reid 2006); Taylor 1992, 166-156.

[25] On Vietnam's Mekong, see Li Tana 'The Eighteenth-Century Mekong Delta and Its World of Water Frontier' (Tran & Reid 2006, 147-162).

[26] See Sun Laichen 'Chinese Gunpowder Technology and Đại Việt' (Tran & Reid 2006, 72-120).

groups of Vietnamese ambushed Mongols and waded into the streams to take pot shots at them with their bows.

Bibliography

Buell, P. D. 2003. *Historical Dictionary of the Mongol World Empire*. (Historical Dictionaries of Ancient Civilizations and Historical Eras 8.) Lanham, Md. · Oxford.

— 1985-86. 'The Sung Resistance Movement, 1276-1279: The End of an Era'. *Annals of the Chinese Historical Society of the Pacific Northwest* III, 138-186.

Deng, G. 1999. *Maritime Sector, Institutions, and Sea Power of Premodern China*. (Contributions in Economics and Economic History 212.) Westport · Connecticut · London.

de Rachewiltz, I. *et al.* (eds) 1993. *In the Service of the Khan, Eminent Personalities of the Early Mongol-Yuan Period (1200-1300)*. (Asiatische Forschungen 121.) Wiesbaden.

Rossabi, M. 1988. *Khubilai Khan, His Life and Times*. Berkeley · Los Angeles.

Su Tianjue 蘇天爵 1962. *Yuan Wenlei* 元文類. Taibei 台北.

Song Lian 宋濂 *et al.* 1976. *Yuanshi* 元史, 15 volumes. Beijing 北京.

Tarling, N. 1992. *The Cambridge History of Southeast Asia*, four volumes. Cambridge.

Tran, Nhung Tuyet & A. Reid 2006. *Việt Nam, Borderless Histories*. Madison, Wisconsin.

NAQAČU THE GRAND MARSHALL, A MONGOL WARLORD IN MANCHURIA DURING THE YUAN-MING TRANSITION

Hok-lam Chan

In the waning days of Mongol rule in China under the last Yuan emperor Toqon Temür 妥懽貼睦爾 (Shundi 順帝, r. 1333-70) whose reign was ripped by corruption and factionalism, few Mongol military leaders rose to the challenge of confronting the dynasty's external enemies to leave their name in history. In earlier times, both Chaghan Temür 察罕帖木兒 (?-July 1362) and Bolod Temür 孛羅帖木兒 (?-August 1365) scored many victories against the anti-Yuan Chinese regional warlords but they descended to feuding among themselves to protect their own interests at the expense of Mongol solidity.[1] After their passing, Chaghan's adopted son Kökö Temür 擴廓帖木兒 (?-September 1375), who was given charge of defending the Mongol position in the western front, appeared to be the last strongman the Yuan court could count on for survival. But Kökö, who was Chinese and known as Wang Baobao 王保保, was less interested in prolonging the Mongol cause than establishing himself as an independent warlord in northwest China even though he did fight and defeat the forces of Zhu Yuanzhang 朱元璋 (1328-98), founder of the Ming dynasty before he ended his life in Qara Noqai, Mongolia.[2]

Naqaču, known in Chinese as Nahachu 納哈出, was unique in the Mongol military leadership. He was a commander who maintained a strong influence in the Northern Yuan regime after Toqon Temür's exit from the capital Daidu 大都 (modern Beijing); and he independently pressed forward Mongol interests in the northeastern region during the reign of his feeble successors Ayushiridara 愛猷識理達臘 (r. 1371-78) and Toqus Temür 脫古思帖木兒 (r. 1379-88). He was a distant descendant of

---

[1] For a general historical background, see Dardess 1973, Epilogue; Han Rulin 1986, vol. 2, chaps. 6, 7; *The Cambridge History of China* 6, chap. 7. See also H. Franke 'Toγon Temür' (*Dictionary of Ming Biography,* 1290-1293 [hereafter DMB]); Qiu Shusen 1991, chap. 8.

[2] For the biographies of Chaghan Temür and Bolod Temür, see *Yuan shi* 141:3384-3393, 207:4601-4605. On their rivalries, see Dardess 1975, 142-150. On Kökö Temür, see Qian Qianyi 1982, *juan* 11; *Ming shi* 124:3709-3710. See also J. Dardess 'Kökö Temür' (*DMB* I, 724-728).

the prominent Mongol general Muqali 木華黎 (1170-1223), the close comrade of Činggis Qan (r. 1206-27) in the conquest of North China and western regions. Naqaču was well respected by his clansmen who thrived in many parts of Manchuria but were concentrated in the Sungari River 松花江 valley and the Daning 大寧 and Liaoyang 遼陽 circuits in Liaodong 遼東 peninsula.[3] His career took the same path as that of his ancestors. Naqaču became the last chief councillor (*chengxiang* 丞相) of the Branch Central Secretariat at Liaoyang and other areas in Manchuria at the fall of the Yuan court at Daidu. The Branch Secretariat governed seven circuits (*lu* 路): Liaoyang, Guangning 廣寧, Daning, Dongning 東寧, Shenyang 瀋陽, Kaiyuan 開元, Helanfu-Shui Dada 合蘭府水達達, and one superior prefecture (*fu* 府): Xianpingfu 咸平府, split from the Kaiyuan circuit. These circuits comprised the whole of Manchuria, and covered the regions of modern Liaoning, Jilin and Heilongjiang, southern Russia, the Sakhalin island (then known as Guwei 骨嵬), and portions of North Korea. A great part of the Liaoyang and Dongning circuits were former territories of the Koryŏ kingdom lost to the Mongol invasion in 1247-59. The Branch Secretariat was first founded in the Liaoyang area in 1287 under Qubilai Qaghan (r. 1260-72); it was changed to its present name in the following year with the administrative seat established at Liaoyang circuit and became increasingly important.[4]

With this extensive military and administrative experience, Naqaču was able to consolidate his position as a warlord in the northeastern front of the crumbling Mongolian empire and expanded his influence in the Liaodong peninsula by making forays into Chinese and Korean territories. Thus he placed himself in a delicate triangular relationship between the Mongol-Yuan state, Koryŏ — which was a subjugated Mongol vassal but now faced the new ruler of China, and the Chinese Ming dynasty. He alternated his relations with the rulers of Koryŏ who had attempted to throw off the Mongol yoke and yet sought his assistance to counteract Chinese encroachment, but he remained a staunch foe of the Ming dynasty, often

---

[3] For the biography of Muqali and some of his descendants, see de Rachewiltz *et al.* 1993, 3-12. For his genealogical tree, see Hambis 1954, tableau 5, facing p. 40. On Muqali's military exploits, see briefly *The Cambridge History of China* 6, 259-261, 357-360. For Ming sources on Naγaču 's origin, see n. 5 below.

[4] See *Yuan shi* 59:1395-1400. Cf. Farquhar 1990, 391-393. On the administrative geography of the Yuan empire, see Yanai 1913/II, 268-432, and map facing p. 432. Okada Hidehiro remarked in his 1985 study that "actually, in Yuan times there was enough reason to regard the Liao-yang teng ch'u Hsing Chung-shu Sheng that governed Manchuria as a province of the Koreans." (Okada 1985, 181).

using the Koreans to offset its pressure and fought many battles against the Chinese armies to secure his own interests. As a result, Naqaču appears frequently in the Korean history *Koryŏ sa* 高麗史 (1451) as well as in the *veritable records* of the founder of the Ming dynasty, *Ming Taizu shilu* 明太祖實錄 (1417), which provide rich information for a reconstruction of his biography and assessment of his place in Mongol history. There are no Mongolian biographical sources.[5]

Naqaču's origins are rather obscure and his date of birth is unknown. Chinese sources first mentioned Naqaču when he was captured in May 1355 by Zhu Yuanzhang, the future Ming emperor Taizu (r. 1368-98), when Zhu launched his forces attacking the city of Taiping 太平 (Anhui) to clear the Mongol occupation. When the city fell, a number of Mongol commanders and Yuan officials were captured. Naqaču was identified as an offspring of Muqali's lineage and was listed as a myriarch commander.[6] Although Zhu treated Naqaču well considering his prominent Mongol pedigree, he was despondent during captivity. When Zhu sent a former Yuan captive Huang Chou 黃儔, a Chinese myriarch commander, to make an inquiry, Naqaču expressed gratitude to the hospitality but confided that as a Mongol, his heart always remained in the northern grassland. Impressed by his candid loyalty, Zhu released him over the objection of his subordinates, notably General Xu Da 徐達 (1332-85). Xu, who later led an expeditionary force against Toqon Temür's stronghold in Daidu and expelled the Mongols further north, favored his execution to eliminate an adversary. Zhu apparently hoped that his generous treatment of Naqaču might mollify the Mongols' enmity and induce their troops to defect.[7]

In January 1356, Naqaču headed home unscathed, returning to Daidu and then rejoined the Mongol forces. He was assigned to a military commandary in Liaodong, and by 1362 according to the *Koryŏ sa* held the rank of vice councilor of the Branch Secretariat of Liaoyang, occupying

---

[5] For Korean sources, see Chŏng 1908-1909, *juan* 40-44, 46-50, 133-137 [hereafter: *KRS*]. For Chinese sources, see *Ming Taizu shilu*, *juan* 3, 52-203 [hereafter: *MTZSL*]. See also Qian Qianyi 1982, *juan* 12; and Gu Yingtai 1936, *juan* 15. For Naqaču's biography, see *Ming shi*, 129:3799 [hereafter: *MS*]; and Hok-lam Chan 'Naγaču' (DMB II, 1083-1085). For other Ming sources, see Hambis 1969, 13:19. See also Serruys 1959b, 75:92, 324.

[6] *MTZSL* 3:31-32; *MS* 129:3799.

[7] *MTZSL* 3:38-39. On Xu Da, see *MS* 125:3723-3730; E. L. Farmer 'Hsu Ta' (DMB I, 602-608).

the Shenyang area.[8] It happened that in November 1361, a splinter group of the anti-Yuan Red Turbans of the Song 宋 state of Han Liner 韓林兒 (?-January 1367) headed by Pan Cheng 潘誠, Sha Liu 沙劉, Guan Duo 關鐸, and others crossed the Yalu River 鴨綠江 with a following of over one hundred thousand men and raided Sakchu 朔州 inside Koryŏ. They overran several cities, trounced the Korean defense, and took the capital Kaegyŏng 開京 (modern Kaesŏng 開城) to the south in late 1361. Shortly thereafter King Wang Chŏn 王顓 (r. 1352-74) fled with his retinue. (Wang Chŏn was known to the Mongols as Bayan Temür 伯顏帖木兒, and in Koryŏ chronicles by the Chinese canonized name Kongmin 恭愍, conferred by the Ming court in 1385.) The king then summoned General Yi Sŏnggye 李成桂 (1355-1408), later T'aejo 太祖 (r. 1392-98) of Chŏsen 朝鮮's Yi dynasty, and his comrades to the rescue, and they successfully recaptured the capital in February 1362 after a fierce battle, killing Sha, Guan, and a large number of enemy soldiers. The decimated Red Turbans hastily retreated across the Yalu and the chaos in Koryŏ ended.[9] About this time, Naqaču took advantage of the Korean turmoil, and guided by a native Korean named Cho Sosaeng 趙小生, led troops across the Yalu to raid the northern cities of Samch'ŏl 三撒 (Pukch'ŏng 北青) and Holmyŏn 忽面 (Hongwŏn 洪原) along the coast. The Koreans suffered several setbacks, but in August, under the command of Yi Sŏnggye, they routed Naqaču's forces after a face to face confrontation between the two senior commanders in the battlefield, in the plain of Hamju 咸州 (modern Hamhŭng 咸興). Naqaču then sued for peace, presenting horses to both King Wang Chŏn and Yi Sŏnggye, and ceased military hostilities.[10] *Koryŏ sa* carries no further reports on him until the inauguration of the Ming dynasty.

Naqaču appears in the historical record next from a Chinese contemporary account on the plight of Toqon Temür. It was reported in Liu Ji 劉佶's *Beixun siji* 北巡私記 (Private account on the Northern Journey) that on his flight from Daidu to Shangdu 上都, the summer capital Kaiping 開平 in Inner Mongolia in September 1368, Toqon Temür promoted *Yäsü Buqa 也速不花, then chief councillor of the Branch

8 *KRS* 40:2a.

9 *KRS* 39:25b-26, 29b-30b, 31a-33b, 39a-43b; 40:1a-1b. See also *Yijo sillok* vol.1, 1:7a-7b. For a more recent review of the Red Turbans' invasion of Koryŏ on bilateral relations, see Qu Wenjun 2000, 34-37.

10 *KRS* 40:2a, 2b, 5a-10a. See also *Taejo sillok* 1:7b-9a.

Secretariat at Liaoyang to head the Central Secretariat, and appointed Naqaču as his replacement with the title of Grand Marshall (*taiwei* 太尉). At that time Toqon Temür's Korean empress née Ki 奇, was angry with King Wang Chŏn for executing her brother Ki Ch'ŏl 轍, a powerful court official, and his associates in July 1359 on charges of sedition. She sought to coax her husband to direct Naqaču to invade Koryŏ to avenge their deaths, but her scheme failed. Toqon Temür and his followers fled to Yingchang 應昌 in Inner Mongolia (on the Dalai Nūr, 230 miles north of Peking) and founded the Northern Yuan court.[11] Naqaču set up his headquarters in Jinshan 金山, northwest of Kaiyuan 開原, Liaoning (about 70 miles north of Shenyang) on the northern bank of Eastern Liao River 東遼河, with more than one hundred thousand followers. His military forays reached as far as Long'an 龍安 (Nong'an 農安), Yitong 伊通 River and up the Sungari valley, a center of the Jurchen settlement, and down the Liaodong peninsula to Koryŏ's border. Naqaču thus emerged as one of the strongest of the independent military leaders of the Northern Yuan deployed in various regions of Mongolia and Manchuria. Apart from the senior Mongol military commanders at the exile capital Yingchang, they included *Yäsü Buqa at Daning 大寧, *Äsän Buqa 也先不花 at Kaiyuan, Hong Baobao 洪保保 at Shenyang, Liu Yi 劉益 at Deliying 得利贏 city, Gaizhou 蓋州, Gao Jianu 高家奴 at Mt. Pingding 平頂山, Liaoyang, and others, each with a strength ranging from several tens of thousands to several thousand soldiers.[12]

In January 1368, Zhu Yuanzhang inaugurated the Ming dynasty and the reign of Hongwu 洪武 (1368-98), which replaced the Yuan as the suzerain state of East Asia, ushering in a new era of Northern Yuan-Korea-China triangular relations. In an effort to contain the Chinese thrust, Naqaču sent a delegation in January 1369 to negotiate with the Korean king for a joint defense agreement against the Ming ruler. Meantime, to offset possible alliance between the two, Zhu Yuanzhang dispatched an envoy in June to invest King Wang Chŏn as "King of Korea", and to confer formal recognition of Koryŏ as a vassal state. The king, who had received the same title from Toqon Temür, was now eager to free himself from the Mongol yoke, and readily accepted the emperor's demand to use the Ming

[11] See Liu Ji, *Beixun siji*, in Luo Zhenyu (comp.), Yunchuang congke (ed.) 1914, 2a, 3b. On the conspiracy of Empress Ki's brothers to overthrow the Korean king and subsequent execution, see Ikeuchi Hiroshi 1917, 117-136.

[12] See *MTZSL* 66:1241-1243; Bi Gong *et al.* 2002, 8:4a-4b. On these developments, see Wada Sei 1955, 270-275; Chen Wenshi 1967, 240-244.

calendar and comply with the ritual formalities, but he still received embassies from Northern Yuan and from Naqaču in particular.[13] Then in January 1370, Wang Chŏn launched a series of incursions into Liaodong under the command of Yi Songgye with the aim of recovering their territories from Northern Yuan and crushing the forces of the Ki family faction. Naqaču was not targeted, but to promote cordial relations, he immediately sent envoys to the Korean court presenting local products as well as requesting an official title. The king was pleased and awarded Naqaču the honorary rank *Samjung taegwang sado* 三重大匡司徒 (Third Ranked Great Assistance Minister of Learning). Thereafter, the Koreans marched north to destroy Dongningfu 東寧府 (south of present Pyongyang 平壤), in the southernmost edge of Liaoyang circuit under Mongol rule, then penetrated deeper into the territories of the enemy, ravaging cities and towns on the way. By end of the year they captured Liaoyang, the administrative seat of Shenyang circuit, and the king demanded that Yäsän Temur and Naqaču submit. But the Koreans, led by Yi Songgye, had to retreat owning to cold weather and a shortage of provisions. To avoid a complete rupture in relations, Naqaču continued to send tribute products to Koryŏ through the end of King Wang Chŏn's reign.[14]

Naqaču's power and influence in Liaoyang and his flirtation with Koryŏ worried the Ming court. In June 1370, in view of the attacks launched by Mongol generals of Northern Yuan against Tongzhou 通州 and Datong 大同 in the previous year, Zhu Yuanzhang was particularly concerned that Naqaču might join forces with the Northern Yuan. To forestall this, Zhu sent an envoy carrying a letter to both the Yuan ruler and Naqaču, attempting to persuade each to submit in order to avoid open warfare. But the diplomatic sally drew no response. (It was not known then that Toqon Temür had already died a month earlier.) The Ming emperor then took a more direct approach. In March 1371, he secured the surrender of Liu Yi, a senior official from the Liaoyang Branch Secretariat, and appointed him commander of a newly created regional military

---

[13] *KYS* 41:21b; *MTZSL* 44:866-867. The Ming record, however, dated this event in September 1369. For a succinct account of such triangular relationship in East Asia during this time, see Ikeuchi Hiroshi 1918, 56-90, 161-179; Suematsu Yasukaza 1965, 234-256. See also Ye Quanhon 1991, chaps. 1, 2; briefly, D. N. Clark 'Sino-Korean tributary relations under the Ming' (*The Cambridge History of China*, vol. 8 · *The Ming Dynasty 1368-1644*, part 2. D. Twitchett & F. W. Mote (eds). Cambridge 1998, 272-284).

[14] *KYS* 44:255, 45:678; *Taejo sillok* 1:11b-12a. On the seizure of Dongningfu, see Ikeuchi Hiroshi 1918, 206-248.

commission of Liaodong (*Liaodongwei zhihuishisi* 遼東衛指揮使司). But three months later Liu was killed by his rival Hong Baobao who fled to Naqaču's camp.[15] In July, concerned with Naqaču's hostility, the emperor dispatched Huang Chou to Jinshan to deliver to him a strongly worded communication calling for him to lay down arms. This time Naqaču was outraged; he detained the envoy, and later reportedly had him executed. The emperor then installed the *Ding Liao* (Pacifying Liaodong) *duwei* 定遼都衛, a superior military commission in Liaodong under the charge of Ma Yun 馬雲 and Ye Wang 葉旺 to maintain a permanent defensive base against external foes, which would also facilitate military excursions into the heartland. This permanent Ming military presence heightened the apprehension of Naqaču and Koryŏ and forever changed the political and military landscape of the region.[16]

In February 1372, alarmed by news that Toqon Temür had recruited Kökö Temür with an army of 100,000 strong for a major offensive, Zhu Yuanzhang assembled a huge force under the command of three eminent generals in response. Xu Da, who commanded a 150,000 cavalry force, was to exit via Yanmen Pass 雁門關 in Shansi and march across the Gobi Desert to Qara Qorum 和林. Feng Sheng 馮勝 (1330?-95) and Li Wenzhong 李文忠 (1339-84) each commanded smaller armies. Feng was to conquer the western prefectures of the Gansu corridor, and Li to march from Yingchang to subdue pockets of the Mongols in Inner Mongolia and Manchuria. Another general, Wu Zhen 吳禎 (1328-79), assumed charge of the shipment of rations and provisions to Liaodong in support of the expeditionary forces, and to take initiatives to strike at Mongol positions to coordinate the military movement. It turned out that though Xu's subordinate young general Lan Yu 藍玉 (?-March 1393) defeated part of the Mongol army by the Tula River in April, he himself suffered a disastrous defeat when the two main armies met for a decisive battle inside Mongolia in the following month. Li Wenzhong's expedition also suffered considerable losses from a Mongol surprise attack, but he managed to bring the army back to China. In Gansu Feng Sheng marched as far as Dunhuang 敦煌 (Gansu), winning several victories and capturing much livestock, thus putting the region under permanent Ming rule. These victories, however, could not compensate for defeats on many other fronts.

[15] *MTZSL* 41:816; 44:859; 52:1030; 61:1191-93; 65:1230.

[16] *MTZSL* 66:1241-1243, 1249-1251, 1358-1359.

In sum, these Ming expeditions had the reverse effect Zhu Yuanzhang had hoped for and provided Naqaču and Koryŏ new incentives for defiance.[17]

At the start of the Chinese Mongolian campaign, *Koryŏ sa* recorded an intriguing incident. It claimed that on March 1, 1372, *Yüsän Buqa 於山不花, Naqaču, Gao Jianu and others from Liaodong attacked the Korean cities of Nisong 泥城, Kanggye 江界 and others south of the Yalu River. This is rather odd because Naqaču had been on good terms with Koryŏ; how could he join force with the rival Mongols in Liaodong attacking its ally's territories? It is probable that remnants of the Mongols from Dongningfu concealed their identity to seek revenge, and that the Koreans exaggerated their threat in order to impress the Ming of their precarious situation. In reality, the presence of the Ming military commission in Liaodong made the Koreans quite apprehensive of the Chinese motive, and they stealthily maintained friendly relations with Northern Yuan and Naqaču as a counter balance.[18] Meanwhile, despite Xu Da's setback in the north, his subordinate Wu Zhen scored some successes in Liaodong against the Mongol positions at Tieling 鐵嶺 and Kaiyuan. In October he sent back to the Ming capital a number of high ranking captives, mostly Chinese and Korean officials serving the Mongols as senior administrators. His military actions infuriated Naqaču, who launched a counterattack late in the year. His forces overran a Chinese grain depot at Niujiazhuang 牛家莊 (near Haicheng 海城, south of Liao River) in Liaoyang, burning over 100,000 bushels of grain, and killing over 5,000 soldiers, dealing a severe blow to the Chinese supply line in the northeastern region. As a result, Wu Zhen was demoted to the position of commander of the Ding Liao Guard, and the emperor appointed the veteran naval commander Liao Yongzhong 廖永忠 (1323-75) to take charge of the supply line to Liaodong.[19]

While pursuing hostilities against the Ming to protect his interest in the Liaodong peninsula, Naqaču sought cordial relationship with Koryŏ as it was in their mutual interest. He continued to dispatch envoys to present tribute products of horses and camels to King Wang Chŏn to strengthen the anti-Chinese alliance to the ire of the Ming court. The latter had

---

[17] *MTZSL* 71:1321-23; 72:1332; 73:1338, 1349; 74:1358-59. For a general description of these campaigns, see Chen Wenshi 1967, 244-247; E. L. Dreyer 'Military Origins of Ming China' (*The Cambridge History of China*, vol.7 · *The Ming Dynasty 1368-1644,* part 1. F. W. Mote & D. Twitchett (eds). Cambridge 1998, 100-103.

[18] *KRS* 43:11a. For the general background, see Suematsu Yasukaza 1965/I, 234-256. For comment on the *KRS* account, see Li Xinfeng 1998, 306-312, esp. 307.

[19] *MTZSL* 74:1360, 75:1395-96, 76:1407.

already been quite displeased with Koryŏ over its flirtation with Northern Yuan, disruption in submission of tribute products and creating incidents that harmed Ming envoys. In March 1373 Naqaču sent a certain Wen *Qara Buqa 文哈喇不花 as envoy to Koryŏ; he was a Korean and was awarded an honorary official position at the Korean court.[20] But in late 1374, Wang Chŏn was murdered by a eunuch in his inner chamber and prince Sin U 辛禑 (child name Monino 牟尼奴) ascended the throne as usurper (r. 1374-87), unleashing a political storm that engulfed Northern Yuan, the Ming court, and Naqaču. Sin U immediately sent a delegation to the Ming capital announcing the king's death and requesting that the emperor bestow a canonized name on the late king and recognize his succession. His request was rebuffed and the insult motivated him to turn to Northern Yuan. Naqaču, on the other hand, again sent *Qara Buqa to present to the new king two camels and four horses as a token gesture of congratulation. This time *Koryŏ sa* noted that Naγaču sent his "son" along, evidently this person had become his adopted son, which was not an unusual custom among the Mongols in their treatment of the Koreans.[21]

In the meantime, apparently with Koryŏ's backing, Naqaču continued his hostilities against the Ming positions in Liaodong. In December 1374 he made a surprise attack on Liaoyang, but was repelled by the defenders. Then two years later, perhaps delayed while courting the support of the new Korean king, in January 1376, he launched a large-scale offensive against Liaodong. After being repulsed at Gaizhou, he turned to Jinzhou 金州, but again encountered stiff resistance. He lost this battle, during which his able lieutenant Nayira'u 乃剌兀 was wounded and captured by the Chinese, while his forces suffered heavy casualties. Naqaču then abandoned his adventure and turned north, narrowly surviving an ambush set by pursuers on his return journey. After this debacle Naqaču waged few offensives; he was presumably busily regrouping his forces to strike at the Ding Liao Guard with Korean assistance, while the Ming remained vigilant and was able to prevent any major actions.[22] Naqacu continued to dispatch Wen *Qara Buqa with gifts for Sin U, in 1377, 1379, and again in 1380 and 1383, while the king also reciprocated by returning envoys with gifts for Naqaču. In March 1377, the Northern Yuan court, addressing Sin U in his child name, invested him with the title "Chief Councillor of

---

[20] *KRS* 43:15a, 44:2b, 3a.

[21] On King Wang Chŏn's murder and Sin U's enthronement, see *KRS* 44:34a, 131:29a-29b, 133:2b-4a. On Sin U's pursuit relations with Ming and Naqaču's response, see *KRS* 133:5a, 9b; 44:2b, 3a. For details, see Ikeuchi Hiroshi 1918, 161-179.

[22] *MTZSL* 94:1636, 102:1727-29; *Liaodong zhi* 5:67b-68a, 70a-70b (pp. 605, 606).

[Yuan's] Conquered Eastern Province and King of Koryŏ" (征東省左丞相高麗國王) as delegated ruler of a vassal state. Sin heartily accepted, hence he adopted Northern Yuan's era-name Xuanguang 宣光 (1370-78) and ceased using Ming's Hongwu era-name, but he revived the latter usage a year later, and continued to send tribute products to the Chinese ruler to gain recognition and avoid open rupture of relations. Amid these volatile developments, Zhu Yuanzhang sent another message in September 1378 to Naqaču to persuade him to surrender, but his Mongol adversary remained adamant and relations deteriorated.[23]

Naqaču apparently laid low during the next few years, and while *Koryŏ sa* continued to note his close contacts with Sin U on plans to strike at Ming positions in Liaodong, Ming sources do not record any major military confrontations until late 1387. The delayed actions need some explanation. On the one hand, Naqaču was still attempting to regroup after his earlier defeats but was less successful as more Mongol commanders from 1378 to 1385 had been defecting to the Ming with their following, thus he was considerably weakened and posed no serious threat to the Chinese.[24] On the other hand, the Ming ruler was preoccupied with several major military campaigns from 1377 to 1385 in Tibet, Guangdong, Guangsi, Guizhou and Yunnan against recalcitrant local rebels and ethnic minorities, and lacked resources for additional adventure.[25] Nevertheless, Zhu Yuanzhang also took steps preparing for the eventual showdown in Liaodong. He had commanded Ma Yun to lead an attack on Daning in July 1379, regaining the city in December, then in 1381 gave orders to install the Fuzhou Guard 復州衛. In August and September 1386 three more guards, the Dongning Guard and the Shenyang Central Guard 中衛 and Left Guard 左衛 were established, and there was a defense force of more than one hundred and ten thousand strong in Liaodong.[26]

Zhu Yuanzhang made preparations against Naqaču in early 1385, after more Mongol commanders and leaders surrendered from the Jurchen settlement, indicating that he was increasingly isolated. In January 1387

---

[23] *KYS* 133:20a, 20b, 23b, 31a, 33a;134:6b, 7a, 13b, 18b; 135:1a,18b; *MTZSL* 119:1942-1944. For details, see Ikeuchi Hiroshi 1918, 252-270.

[24] See, for example, *MTZSL* 118:1930; 119:1936; 132:2098; 137:2164; 138:2173; 140:2203; 142:2235; 143:2248; 144:2268; 146:2289; 147:2324; 150:2359, 2368; 153:2400; 156:2428; 159:2459; 161:2506; 175:2661. See also Wada Sei 1955, 292-296; Chen Wenshi 1967, 248-251.

[25] See, for example, *MTZSL* 111:1851,1902; 121:1959,1960; 122:1972,1974; 130:2061; 134:2136;138:2179, 2180;141:2225, 2227; 158:2446; 162:2514;171:2620; 172:2634.

[26] *MTZSL* 94:1636, 102:1727-1729, 125:1999, 139:2189, 178:2699,179:2706.

Zhu appointed General Feng Sheng as commander-in-chief, with Fu Youde 傅友德 (?-December 1394) and Lan Yu as deputies, to lead an army of 200,000 against Naqaču in Jinshan. Toward the end of March, Feng Sheng led his troops to the north of the border walls, fortified Daning and other outposts in the region. A garrison of 50,000 troops was left at Daning while the main force continued northeast. In July 1386 Feng camped to the west of Jinshan. As a strategic ploy he returned to Naqaču his former lieutenant Nayira'u, who had been captured by the Ming forces in 1376 and had been in Ming's custody. Feng sent him to Naqaču with a letter urging him to surrender to the Ming forces and to accept the suzerainty of the new regime in China. Nayira'u's diplomacy led Naqaču to cease his fighting and to surrender to General Lan Yu in October.[27]

However, the surrender was jeopardized by an incident at Lan's camp when Naqaču arrived. An altercation broke out between Naqaču and Chang Mou 常茂 (?-October 1391), the duke of Zhengguo 鄭國公, a general in the expeditionary force. Chang slapped Naqacu's upper arm with his sword causing Naqaču to storm out of their meeting. When Naqaču's spouse and followers at the Sungari valley heard about the incident, they became angry and dispersed; some vowing reprisal. Informed of the situation, Feng Sheng sent Guantong 觀童, a former subordinate of Naqaču who had surrendered to the Ming, to soothe the dissidents. Finally on July 14, having realized that the Ming forces were well positioned from the north and east for a joint assault, and seeing no hope of resistance, Naqaču made his formal surrender to Lan Yu. A few days later Lan Yu arrived in Jinshan to receive his submission. It was reported that over two hundred thousand of his men went to the Chinese side; and they, together with countless sheep, horses, camels, and supplies formed a hundred *li*. The rest of Naqaču's forces in the Sungari valley, shocked by the surrender of their chieftain, disbanded, heralding a stunting victory for the Ming court.[28] In September, to tighten surveillance of the followers of Naqaču who had dispersed over the Liaodong peninsula, a new military guard, called Daningwei, was created. A month later, it was changed into a regional military commission (*du zhihuishi si* 都指揮司), with Daning as the administrative seat[29].

---

[27] *MTZSL* 180:2721-1722; 181:2731-2732; 182:2746, 2748-49. See also Wada Sei 1955, 299-303; Chen Wenshi 1967, 250-252.

[28] *MTZSL* 182:2748-2752, 183:2757-2758. See also Wada Sei 1955, 304-310, Chen Wenshi 1967, 252-255.

[29] *MTZSL* 182:2753-2754; 184:2765-2766, 2769.

On October 12 1387, Feng Sheng presented to the capital some 3,300 members of Naqaču's subordinate Mongol and Chinese military personnel, 290 horses, 100 pieces of gold, silver and copper seals, insignia, hundreds of senior officials from his own administration, a total of 189 myriarch and chiliarch commanders and some 1,400 members of miscellaneous junior administrative positions. A congratulatory memorial enumerating Naqaču's crimes and lauding the emperor's ingenious stratagem was submitted to court in advance. Upon Naqaču's arrival at court on the following day, Zhu Yuanzhang personally embraced him and gave orders to send lavish gifts to Naqaču and his followers. Delighted over his submission, the emperor awarded him a first-grade costume and the rank of marquis of Haixi 海西侯 (West of the Sea) in deference to his former jurisdiction over the Jurchen settlement, with an annual stipend of 2,000 bushels of rice, and additional gifts. His followers also received titles and rewards. In return Naqaču presented to the emperor 308 horses. All the lavish imperial favors were apparently intended to keep him contented, but Naqaču had now lost all power, and he remained in residence in Nanjing. Although his Mongol civilian followers were allowed to stay in their own settlements, his troops were subsequently incorporated into the Chinese army and scattered to assignments in garrisons in Inner Mongolia, the Beiping area, Shandong, Nanjing, and also in regions far to the south.[30]

Despondent over his new status, Naqaču was given to excessive use of liquor, and his health declined. Nevertheless, in July 1388, he received a summons to join General Fu Youde in his expedition against the rebellious tribesmen in Yunnan. By this time he had become very sick and was under the care of a court physician, but he felt obligated to comply with the imperial command. As the expeditionary force included many of his former troops, Naqaču's presence in the campaign was deemed useful to guarantee their loyalty. According to the *Ming veritable record*, while the expedition was on its way to Yunnan, Naqaču died on Hongwu 21/7/29(August 31, 1388) on a ship near Wuchang 武昌, probably around sixty years of age. His remains were brought back and buried outside one of the southern gates of Nanjing.[31] There was no further mention of this once-powerful Mongol warlord in Chinese official accounts, but the *Chosŏn* (*Yijo*) *sillok* 朝鮮 (李朝) 實錄 of Emperor T'aejo records an interesting incident. It says that late in 1388 a Korean Hanlin scholar-

[30] *MTZSL* 184:2763-2767, 2772-2774, 185:2775-2776, 2778, 2781-1783; 186:2788. On Naqaču's ennobled title, see also Serruys 1959a, 211-212.

[31] *MTZSL* 192:2891.

official Yi Saek 李穡 (1328-96) was sent by King Sin Ch'ang 辛昌 (r. 1388), the usurper Sin U's son who reigned only one year, as envoy to the Ming court. Yi tried to address the Celestial Ruler at a court audience in Chinese. Zhu Yuanzhang, however, was unable to understand the speech, and jokingly remarked that Yi spoke Chinese like Naqaču! Apparently Naqaču did acquire a smattering of Chinese, but his skills did not pass muster.[32]

We know little about Naqaču's progeny, but according to Chinese records, he was survived by a son named Čaqan 察罕 who inherited his father's marquisate. However, on September 12, 1388, the title was changed from Haixi to Shenyang. This was probably because the title held by Naqaču referred to the land of the Jurchen tribes, which seems to be anachronistic, and Shenyang, a city in Liaodong, reflected contemporary reality. In May 1390, the Ming emperor sent Čaqan and three meritorious Chinese commanders to Dongchang 東昌 prefecture, Shandong, to drill the troops there. Two months later, like many other ennobled generals, he was assigned a company of 120 soldiers as his retinue, and in August he was rewarded a string of 400 cash for his work. In March 1392, he was summoned to return to Nanjing.[33] A year later, however, Čaqan was implicated in the conspiracy of Lan Yu, the powerful Ming general who was charged with plotting a rebellion. The nature of Čaqan's alleged involvement was revealed in two confessions he made in the record of the trial's proceedings. This was known as *Nichen lu* 逆臣錄 (Record of the Nefarious Officials), written by officials commissioned by the emperor in the aftermath of the trial.[34]

In his confession Čaqan revealed that on Hongwu 26/1/14 (February 25 1393) he attended a drinking party at the home of *Nayir Buqa 乃兒不花, a former Mongol military officer who had surrendered to the Ming. There he learned that the Duke of the Liang State 涼國公 (Lan Yu) was plotting a major uprising and was soliciting the assistance of the Mongol officers with promises of rich rewards and the opportunity to return to their northern home. The next day (February 26) was the *shangyuan* 上元 festival and Čaqan held a party at his own home where several of his

---

[32] *Yijo sillok* vol.1, *Taejo sillok* 1:25a.

[33] *MTZSL* 193:2894-2895, 201:3009, 202:3030, 203:3040, 216:3178; see also Serruys 1959a, 213.

[34] For Lan Yu's biography, see *MS* 132:3863-3866; see also E. L. Dreyer & Hok-lam Chan 'Lan Yü' (DMB I, 788-791). The *Nichen lu* was reprinted by the Peking University Press in 1991. On Lan's rebellion, see T. P. Massey 1992.

guests, both Chinese and Mongol military officers, confided to him the same seditious intention related by a messenger from the Duke. He and his companions then met Lan Yu in person, learned of the scheme, and later frequented the Duke's home for further deliberations before the plot was exposed and the culprits and conspirators arrested. As a result, Lan Yu was executed in March 1393, implicating over fifteen thousand civil and military officials who met the same fate. Čaqan was put to death on May 18 for high treason, becoming one of the most senior Mongol commanders who fell victim to the alleged political conspiracy. The veracity of his involvement with Lan Yu could not be collaborated, but his ignominious death was a sad end to Naqaču's immediate family.[35]

All in all, Naqaču must be recognized as a great Mongol military leader true to his ancestral heritage in the waning years of the Mongolian empire in China. He did not unswervingly commit to Toqon Temür's successors of Northern Yuan; instead, he became a powerful, independent warlord in the Liaoyang province and provided strong leadership to his clansmen and other Mongol tribesmen who flourished in the regions he controlled against the encroachment of the Korean and Chinese adversaries. A shrewd Mongol in the shadow of Muqali, Naqaču was condemned as wicked and malevolent by the Chinese but hailed as brave and resourceful by the Koreans. He was both feared and hated, but also respected by his enemies.[36] At the vortex of a complex triangular relationship between Northern Yuan, Koryŏ, and Ming China, he was able to pursue artful diplomatic and military strategies to exploit the common and contradictory interests among the Mongols, the Koreans and Chinese. He fought courageously and refused to surrender to the Ming ruler like his compatriots. As a result, he was able to prolong and expand the Mongol presence and influence in the Liaodong peninsula some twenty years after the fall of Daidu and left a strong, though mixed legacy to the Chinese and Koreans in Manchuria. In short, Naqaču was an ambitious and resourceful Mongol loyalist who occupied a prominent position in the fluid relations between Northern Yuan, Koryŏ, and Ming China during the late 14th c.

Bibliography

Bi Gong 畢恭 *et al.* (eds.) 2002. (*Jiajing*) *Liaodong zhi* (嘉靖) 遼東志. (*Xuxiu Sikuquanshu* 續修四庫全書 646.) Shanghai.

---

[35] See *Nichen lu* 1:23-24; on a related confession by a fellow Mongol officer, see also *ibid.* 4:197-198; *MTZSL* 225:3296-3297; 227:3312.

[36] See for example, the remarks in *MTZSL* 184:2773; *KRS* 40:7b, 10a.

Chen Wenshi 陳文石 1967. 'Mingdai qianqi Liaodong de bianfang 明代前期遼東的邊防'. *Bulletin of the Institute of History and Philology, Academia Sinica* 中央研究院歷史語言研究所集刊 37.1, 237-270.

Chŏng In-ji 鄭麟趾 1908-09. *Koryŏ sa* 高麗史 (1451). Tokyo.

Dardess, J. W. 1973. *Conquerors and Confucians: Aspects of Political Change in Late Yüan China*. New York.

de Rachewiltz, I. *et al.* (eds) 1993. *In the Service of the Khan: Eminent Personalities of the Mongol-Yuan Period (1200-1300)*. Wiesbaden.

Dictionary of Ming Biography, 1368-1644. (Eds) L. C. Goodrich & Chaoying Fang. New York 1976.

Farquhar, D. M. 1990. *The Government of China under Mongolian Rule: A Reference Guide*. Stuttgart.

Gu Yingtai 谷應泰 1936. *Ming shi jishi benmo* 明史紀事本末. Shanghai.

Hambis, L. 1954. *Le Chapitre CVIII du Yuan Che*. Leiden.

— 1969. *Documents sur l'histoire des Mongols a l'époque des Ming*. (Bibliothèque de L'Institut des Hautes Études Chinoises XXI.) Paris.

Han Rulin 韓儒林 (ed.) 1986. *Yuanchao shi* 元朝史. Beijing.

Ikeuchi Hiroshi 池内弘 1917. 'Kōrai Kominō no Gen nitai suru hankō no undō 高麗恭愍王の元に對する反抗の運動'. *Tōyō Gakuhō* 東洋學報 7.1, 117-136.

— 1918. 'Kōrai Komin ōchō no Tōneifu seibatsu ni tsuite no kō 高麗恭愍王朝の東寧府征伐に就きての考'. *Tōyō Gakuhō* 東洋學報 8.2, 206-248.

— 1918. 'Kōrai-matsu ni okeru Ming oyobi Kita-Gen tono kankei 高麗末に於する明及び北元との関係'. *Shigaku zasshi* 史學雜誌 29:1-4, 56-90, 161-179, 251-271, 372-389.

Li Xinfeng 李新峰 1998. 'Gongminwang houqi Ming Gaoli guanxi yu Ming Meng zhanju 恭愍王後期明高麗關係與明蒙戰局'. *Hanguoxue lunwenji* 韓國學論文集 7, 306-312.

Liu Ji 劉佶 1933. *Beixun siji* 北巡私記 · *Guoxue wenku* 國學文庫. Beiping.

Massey, T. P. 1992. *Chu Yüan-chang and the Hu-Lan Cases of the Early Ming Dynasty*. (PhD diss., University of Michigan 1983.) Ann Arbor.

Ming shi 明史. (Eds) Zhang Tingyu 張廷玉 *et al.* Beijing 1974.

Ming Taizu. *Nichen lu* 逆臣錄. (Collated) Wang Tianyou 王天有 & Zhang Heqing 張何清. Beijing 1991.

Ming Taizu shilu 明太祖實錄. (Eds) Yao Guangxiao 姚廣孝 *et al.* Taibei 1962.

Okada Hidehiro 岡田英弘 1985. 'The Koreans in Manchuria in the Yüan Times'. *Hanguo xuebao* 韓國學報 (Korean Studies) 5, 181-199.

Qian Qianyi 錢謙益 1982. *Guochu qunxiong shilue* 國初群雄事略. Beijing.

Qiu Shusen 邱樹森 1991. *Tuohuantiemuer zhuan* 妥懽貼睦爾傳. Changchun.

Qu Wenjun 屈文軍 2000. 'Hongjinjun huodong dui Gaoli zhengju he Yuan-Li guanxi de yingxiang 紅巾軍活動對高麗政局和元麗関係的 影響'. *Zhejiang shida xuebao* 浙江師大學報 (*shehui kexueban*) 25.5, 34-37.

Serruys, H. 1959a. 'Mongols ennobled during the early Ming'. *Harvard Journal of Asiatic Studies* 22, 209-260.

Serruys, H. 1959b. *The Mongols in China during the Hung-wu period (1368-1398).* (Mélanges Chinois et bouddhiques 11). Bruxelles.

Suematsu Yasukaza 末松保和 1965. 'Rai-matsu Sen-sho ni tsuite tai Min kankei 麗末鮮初に於ける對明關係'. *Seikyū shisō* 青丘史草 1, 234-256.

The Cambridge History of China, vol. 6. *Alien Regimes and Border States, 907-1368.* (Eds) H. Franke & D. Twitchett. Cambridge 1994.

Wada Sei 和田清 1955. 'Minsho no Manshū keiryaku 明初の滿洲經略', part 1; rpt. in *Tōashi kenkyū* 東亞史研究 : *Manshū hen* 滿洲篇. Tokyo, 260-336.

Yanai Watari 箭内亙 1913. 'Mansen ni okeru Gen no kyōiki 滿洲に於ける元の疆域'. *Mansen rekishi chiri* 滿洲歷史地理 2, 268-362.

Ye Quanhong 葉泉宏 1991. *Mingdai qianqi Zhong Han guojiao yanjiu* 明代前期中韓國交研究. Taibei.

Yijo sillok 李朝實錄, vol.1, *Taejo sillok* 太祖實錄. Tokyo 1953.

Yuan shi 元史. (Eds) Song Lian 宋濂 *et al.* Beijing 1978.

Comparative Analysis of Original Texts on One Verse Composition in the Secret History of the Mongols

Sharav Choimaa

According to the *Secret History of the Mongols* (SHM), Temüjin made an alliance with Wang-khan and Jamuqa, in order to overpower the three Merkids and free his wife Börte Üjin. After living together for a year and a half, Temüjin and Jamuqa separated from each other. Their separation, as seen in the *SHM*, was the result of Jamuqa's veiled words. In reality it was caused by the incompatibility of their characters and forethoughts, and it is commonly understood that it would have been impossible for them to have a common outlook and keep together in the future.

After Temüjin had parted from Jamuqa, notable and powerful people in the state of "All the Mongols" came to join him. Among them were Jelme's younger brothers Ča'urqan and Sübe'edei Ba'atur, together with their men. By this time, Altan Qučar and Sača Beki, along with their men, having deliberated, conferred upon Temüjin the title of Čingis Qan for the first time (in the year 1189). Immediately after his recognition as a khan, Temüjin granted important positions to his followers and the men close to him. Then Sübe'edei Ba'atur (1176-1248), from the clan of the Jarchigudai Uriankhai pledged allegiance to Temüjin as Jelme, his elder brother, had done before. These words appear in paragraph §124 of the *SHM*. Let us compare how they occur in the *SHM* and in the chronicle the *Golden Button* (GBL) by Blo-bzaṅ bstan-'jin (the first lines in italics refer to the *SHM* §124, the second ones to the *GBL* folio 33b-34a):

sübe'etei-ba'adur ügülerün
sübegedei baγatur ügülerün

quluqana bolju quriya[l]dusu
quluγan-a bolju quriyaldusu :
qara keri'e bolju qada'un bügün-i qarmaldusu
qara keriy-e bolju γaduγun bükün-i qurimaldasu :
nembe'e isgei bolju nemürleldün sorisu
nemüry-e šejegei[1] metü nemüreleldün qoyisuγai[2]

[1] (*šajaγai*).

isgei bolju ger jük gerisgeleldün sorisu
kerisge[3] šejegei[4] bolju : ger jüg kerisleldün[5] quriyasu

ke'eba[6]
kemebe[7]

In particular this passage of both sources has been translated in various ways by scholars. Some words have been given unlikely interpretations. As far as the *SHM* is concerned, the translators have relied on the parallel Chinese translation.

The *Golden Button* by Blo-bzaṅ bstan-'jin has been published in modern Mongolian; appearing in the Cyrillic script three times in Ulaanbaatar, in the years 1957, 1990 and 1998. Let us check the verses compared above, as translated in the 1990 and 1998 Cyrillic editions:

"*Сүбээдэй баатар өгүүлсэн нь:*
Хулгана болж хураалдсу.
Хар хэрээ болж
Хатуу бүхнийг хурималдсу.
Амраг шаазгай мэт
Амраглан хураасугай.
Хэрээ шаазгай болж
Гэр зүг
Гэрслэлдэн хураасу хэмээв"

["Sübe'edei Ba'atur said: | I'll become a mouse and will gather precious things. | I'll become a black raven | And I'll gather everything difficult (to find). | As a loving magpie | Let me collect lovingly. | I'll become a raven and a magpie | And towards the tent | I'll hoard up and protect as a fence."]

This translation contains severe errors. However, this is just an example of how necessary textological research is, collating any source text with other sources, when rendering a text in the Mongolian language.

---

[2] [*qorisuyai*]. — Due to the fact that the stroke for *r* was not as big in Pre-Classical Uighur-Mongolian script as it is today, it was very similar to the stroke for the vowel *i*. Also the letters *y i w* were very unclear and undistinguishable from each other when written in a medial position, since there was no other way to write them than with a "shin" stroke.

[3] (*keriy-e*).

[4] (*šajayai*).

[5] (*gerlen*).

[6] de Rachewiltz 1972, 52-53.

[7] *GBL,* folio 33b-34a.

We propose below how this passage could look in the Uighur-Mongolian original of the *SHM*, by collating the originals of the *SHM* and the *Golden Button* by Blo-bzaṅ bstan-'jin, and considering any other available Pre-Classical (Middle) Mongolian sources as well as available data in Altaic languages:

sübegedei baγatur ügülerün quluγana bolju quriyaldusu : qara keriy-e bolju γadaγun (~ *γaduγun*) *bükün-i qarmaldusu*[8] *: nemürge sisegei bolju nemürleldün qorisu : kerisge*[9] *sisegei bolju ger jüg kerisgeleldün*[10] *qorisu kemebe* 'Sübe'edei Ba'atur said: «I'll become a mouse and will gather. I'll become a black raven and I'll gather everything that is outside. I'll become a felt cloak and protect by covering. I'll become a felt like a railing and protect by encircling the goods and chattels»'.

To justify our reconstruction, let us briefly explain several capital matters, relying for some words on the studies and translations of previous scholars, and on the peculiarities of earlier classical writings.

1. Since both the translators and transcribers of the *SHM* in Chinese and the *güüsi* Blo-bzaṅ bstan-'jin had to use a very old and worn out text in Pre-Classical Uighur-Mongolian script, none of them could avoid making mistakes. As a matter of fact, since the initials *s* and *q* in Pre-Classical Uighur-Mongolian script had a very similar shape when written with a bamboo pen, the transcribers of the *SHM* took the word *qorisu* for *sorisu,* which led to erroneous translation. Such mistakes appear not infrequently in the Chinese transcription of the *SHM*, and in fact we can find *so'or čölö-tüi* in the paragraph §172 of the *SHM*, *tere so'or-tur* in §162, *tere so'or-tur* in §177, and *naiman-i busangqui so'or-tui* in §208. All of these instances are merely *qoγur* 'between', where the letter *q* has been incorrectly read as *s*, causing the faulty transcription. As we intend to write another article about the faulty rendering of these two letters, let us leave this point for now.

2. While the faulty reading of *sorisu* appears in the Chinese transcription of the *SHM*, Blo-bzaṅ bstan-'jin reads the initials *s* and *q* correctly. He fails, however, to understand the whole word as *qorisu* or

[8] In the Mongolian *Twenty-one's Dictionary* (1717) the word *qarmaqu* is explained as 'to collect, to fill in one place'.

[9] Ibid., *keresge* (*хэрсэг*) is defined as a manufacture of wooden balusters put in balconies, or a series of stones put horizontally on the terraces of a palace (as to prevent people from falling)'.

[10] Ibid., *keresgekü* (*хэрсэглэх*) is defined as 'to protect by putting something perpendicularly as a fence'.

qorisuγai. This may have happened because the graphemes were very unclear in the Uighur-Mongolian original. The *güüsi* Blo-bzaṅ bstan-'jin understood the verses in the whole, but since initial *s* had long been dropped in the 17th century, *šejegei* would have mislead him in several instances as an unknown word. This word is our *эсгий,* which in Pre-Classical and Middle Mongolian had the form *sisgei* or *sisegei.* The absolutely incomprehensible form this word had for contemporaries clearly illustrates why the bird name *šajaγai* appears instead in the parallel gloss.

Here another question arises. If the form *sisegei* was used in Middle Mongolian written and spoken language, why then does it appear written *isgei* precisely in this line of verse? The reason is supplied by the language of the *SHM* itself. Let us quote two passages from the *SHM*. While we find the transcription *sisgei tu'urqatu* 'that one living inside felt walls' in paragraph §202, *isgei tu'urqatan* 'those living inside felt walls' appears in the following one, §203. This confirms that by the end of the 14th century the initial *s* was beginning to be dropped. But in Blo-bzaṅ bstan-'jin this same word is written in the old way.

3. Scholars are still finding numerous instances of words beginning with a vowel in Modern Mongolian, which have dropped the initial consonant. This is the case of our present word. Besides having in the *SHM* evidence that the Modern Mongolian *isegei* (Khalkh. *эсгий*) was written and pronounced *sisegei* in the Middle Mongolian language, we can also find a confirmation for this in the dictionary of *Muqaddimat al-Adab* (*sisegei* 'felt', *sisegei da'urya* 'felted cloth', *sisegeiči* 'felt maker', *sisügei čadur* 'felt tent')[11], in the *Hua-yi yi-yu* glossary (華夷譯語) where *sisige* occurs, as well as in dialects such as Dagur or Moghol where the Pre-Classical Mongolian form has been preserved.

4. Since the word lettered as *sisegei* was completely incomprehensible for the 17th century's historian Blo-bzaṅ bstan-'jin and his scribes, when they copied *kerisge, šejegei* according to the original of the *SHM* in their hands, the later copyists added the erroneous gloss of *keriy-e šajaγai* 'raven and magpie'. This is the reason why the authors of the modern version of the *Golden Button* in Mongolian have erred so frequently. It is probable that the same Blo-bzaṅ bstan-'jin, not having well understood the main word *isgei,* copied some other words with a "corrected" shape instead. It is necessary to keep in mind that in Pre-Classical Uighur-

---

[11] Poppe 1938, 323.

Mongolian documents the shape of the consonants *s j č* were very similar inside a word.

5. The word *nemürge* 'mantle', to which we have referred particularly in these verses, appears as *nembe'e* in the Chinese transcription, the *güüsi* Blo-bzaṅ bstan-'jin wrote it instead as *nemüry-e.* This can be clearly explained only through the peculiarities of the Pre-Classical Uighur-Mongolian way of writing, and about this word Professor Bürenbat, from the Inner Mongolian University, has already provided convincing explanations.

6. In the short composition in verse quoted here from the *SHM*, *qorisu* appears written as *sorisu.* Besides being an evident spelling error, this word does not have anything to do with *sori-* (Khalkh. *сорих* 'to try out, to test') in point of meaning. Sübe'edei Ba'atur's words should mean that he would protect the Khan's properties as a fence, as felt, as a mantle, and also defend him from his enemies. To clarify this matter, the meaning of *qoriqu* in Pre-Classical and Middle Mongolian is 'to protect, to defend'. This is confirmed by data from other Altaic languages, especially, by the Old Turkic language. In Old Turkic we have *qorï-* 'to guard against, protect from', *otïγ qorïdï* 'he protected the pastures', according to Mahmud al-Kashgari's dictionary[12]. The Finnish scholar Martti Räsänen has observed the existence of the verb *qorï- ~ kory-* 'to protect, to defend; to watch, to guard' in many Turkic languages, and pointed out its etymological relation with Mongolian *qori-*[13]. Drawing a conclusion from what is stated above, it is clear that Sübe'edei Ba'atur meant to protect his Khan's properties as a felt mantle and as a fence.

7. In the Chinese original of the *SHM* the compound *ger jüg* is translated as 'dwelling, home' in the parallel gloss, but dismissed in the abridged translation at the end of the paragraph. The majority of scholars have taken the second element to be the Mongolian word *jüg* (Khalkh. *зүг*) 'direction; towards', but in the given context this meaning does not fit. In ancient and modern Turkic languages we can find several variants of this word: *yük ~ yok ~ jük ~ čük* 'a tent, its furnishings and the cattle; everything that belongs to a tent and its inhabitants'[14]. We can further see a connection between *jüg* in the *SHM* and *jüγ,* an ancient word indicating 'dwelling-place', which scholars have traced and studied in the Tungus-

---

[12] DTS 458.

[13] Räsänen 1969, 282.

[14] DTS 285.

Manchurian languages. In any case, the word *jüg* in this passage of the SHM does not have the meaning 'direction; towards'.

By way of conclusion, we would like to stress the importance of considering closely the fact that the original, transcribed in Chinese characters, was taken from a text in Uighur-Mongolian script, and the need to compare that original with other, later Mongolian sources, in order to deepen our knowledge of the *SHM.*

Bibliography and Abbreviations

DTS: *Drevnetjurkskij slovar'*. Leningrad 1969.

GBL: (The Golden Button) *Altan tobči*. Ulaanbaatar 1990.

de Rachewiltz, I. 1972. *Index to The Secret History of the Mongols*. (Uralic and Altaic Series 121.) Bloomington.

Poppe, N. N. 1938. *Mongol'skij slovar' Mukaddimat al-Adab*. Moskva · Leningrad.

Räsänen, M. 1969. *Versuch eines etymologischen Wörterbuchs der Türksprachen*. (Lexica Societatis Fenno-Ugricae XVII:1.) Helsinki.

SHM: (The Secret History of the Mongols). De Rachewiltz, I. 2004. *The Secret History of the Mongols · A Mongolian epic chronicle of the thirteenth century*. (Brill's Inner Asian Library 7/1-2.) Leiden.

PARADIGMS OF THE IMAGE OF THE MONGOLS IN MEDIEVAL RUSSIA

Charles J. Halperin

In an original, stimulating essay, Donald Ostrowski has surveyed models of the influence of the Tatars (Mongols)[1] on Russian history structured in the form of eight paradigms. The first three of theses paradigms apply to medieval and early modern Rus' and will be discussed here.[2] The remaining five encapsulate modern historiography.[3]

According to Ostrowski, Paradigm 1, "Punishment for Sins and the Wrath of God," describes the Tatars with graphic epithets and attributes the Mongol conquest of Rus' to God's punishment of Rus' for its sins. This paradigm ended in northeastern Rus' "within fifteen years" (1237-1252). Paradigm 2, "Realpolitik of Rus' princes and Church leaders," reflects the *modus vivendi* of Rus' ecclesiastical and political leaders with their new Mongol overlords. After 1252 in areas of the Rus' church subordinated to the Byzantine Patriarch, "pejorative" terminology disappeared and descriptions of Tatar depredations were "neutralized." Ostrowski credits John Fennell[4] as the first scholar to identify this attitude of the Rus' sources. The Byzantine-Jochid ulus alliance lasted, with exceptions, until 1453. The closest the sources came to explaining the many trips of Rus' princes to the Horde is contained in the Galician-Volynian Chronicle *sub anno* 1287, noting that the Rus' had been "conquered" (*pokoreny*) by the Tatars, "by God's wrath." The role of Jochid Khans in settling land disputes in Rostov is treated in a matter-of-fact manner in the fourteenth-century "Tale about Tsarevich Peter."[5] Paradigm 2 lasted in Church sources until 1448, but continued thereafter in state documents. In Paradigm 3, "Anti-Tatar Attitude of the Russian

---

[1] The medieval East Slavic sources, written in Slavonic, called the entire Mongol army, including its non-Mongol elements, "Tatars," and later applied the term to the entire population of the Jochid ulus, including assimilated Kipchaks.

[2] In the thirteenth century the East Slavic states included Kiev and Galicia-Volynia, now part of Ukraine, so calling them collectively "Russia" would be incorrect. The contemporary term "Rus'" is used instead.

[3] Ostrowski, forthcoming. I wish to express my most sincere appreciation to Dr. Ostrowski for an advance copy of his article.

[4] Fennell 1970, 105-111.

[5] Ostrowski cites Halperin 1975, 323-335.

Orthodox Church," the Church developed an extremely anti-Tatar, but essentially anti-Islamic, ideology, epitomized in the "Legend of the Battle against Mamai" (*Skazanie o Mamaevom poboishche*), "Discourse upon the Ruin of the Rus' Land" (*Slovo o pogibeli russkoi zemli*), and "Tale of the Destruction of Riazan' by Batu" (*Povest' o razorenii Riazani Batyem*), all dated to the second half of the fifteenth century.[6] While the *Zadonshchina* "admitted that Batu conquered the Rus' land, that is to say 'it was God who punished Rus' for its sins,' nevertheless after Kulikovo the situation of Rus'-Tatar relations was no longer as it had been 'in early times'." This Church attitude is summed up by the term "Tatar Yoke," based upon the "yoke of slavery" in the sixteenth-century "Life of Merkurii of Smolensk," which can be attested first in Latin in Daniel Printz's account of his embassy to Moscow in 1575. The "Tatar Yoke" became dominant in mainstream Russian historiography via Shcherbatov.[7]

Ostrowski's informed, if highly compressed and selective, depiction of the evolution of Rus' attitudes toward the Tatars adumbrates ideas previously expressed in his monograph.[8]

On the whole Ostrowski implicitly accepts my interpretation of the gingerly use by Rus' sources of the vocabulary of political sovereignty in depicting Rus'-Tatar relations.[9] I had previously missed the invocation of Tatar sovereignty in the passage in the Galician-Volynian Chronicle *sub anno* 1287. However, the reference in the *Zadonshchina* to "old times" does not pertain to sovereignty; it merely contrasts Batu's successful campaign against Rus' with Mamai's failure.[10]

The chronology of Paradigm 1 is problematic. Ostrowski's conception of the "neutral" attitude of the Rus' sources toward the Tatars during Paradigm 2 was much influenced by John Fennell's article, but Fennell saw no distinction between the Rus' sources before and after 1252. Ostrowski correctly rejects, albeit without comment, Fennell's minimization of the negative depiction of the Tatar "conquest" itself, but still retains his paradigm for the period from 1252 until 1448. However, Ostrowski cites some evidence that the attitudes of Paradigm 1 did not disappear in 1252 — the reference to "God's wrath" in the Galician-

---

[6] For the purposes of this article I accept Ostrowski's textual datings.

[7] Ostrowski cites Halperin 1984, 26-30.

[8] Ostrowski 1998, 144-148, 156-160, reviewed by Halperin 1999, 517-518. In his monograph Ostrowski makes greater use of my publications than space permitted in the article discussed here.

[9] Halperin 1985; Halperin 1986; Halperin 1998-1999, 98-117.

[10] Including the epic *Zadonshchina* among works by the Church is highly dubious.

Volynian Chronicle *sub anno* 1287 from Paradigm 2 and the allusion to God's punishment of Rus' for its sins by Batu in the *Zadonshchina* from Paradigm 3. There are additional invocations of the divine punishment of the Orthodox for their sins in the *Skazanie o Mamaevom poboishche*,[11] in Bishop Vassian's "Epistle to the Ugra River" from 1480,[12] and in sixteenth-century redactions of the vita of Aleksandr Nevskii.[13] Nor did anti-Tatar epithets disappear after 1252. The Novgorodian Chronicle described the 1259 Tatar census-takers as "accursed Tatars, eaters of unclean flesh",[14] and Bishop Serapion, of Vladimir, in sermons written probably after 1252, described the Tatars[15] as a "merciless people," "merciless heathen" and "pagans." Serapion probably influenced the allusion to the Tatars in the canons of the Rus' Church Council of 1274 as "godless and unclean infidels'."[16] Therefore, Paradigm 1 *never* disappeared.

How Ostrowski would reconcile Paradigm 2 with some sources from 1252-1448 which he does not, perhaps for reasons of space, discuss, cannot be anticipated, but their content does not seem "neutral" in attitude toward the Tatars. Grand Prince Mikhail of Chernigov was executed in the Horde in 1246, and his full Vita cannot be attested until the fourteenth century. In a Pauline manner it derives the khan's authority from God. Nevertheless the Tatars try to coerce Mikhail to apostacize, and for his refusal, martyr him, hardly a neutral image.[17] The portrait of the devastation of Rus' by the Tatars in Serapion's sermons can hardly be called neutral.[18] The nefarious activities of *baskak* Akhmat took place during the 1280s and are recorded in unedifying detail in the northeastern chronicles.[19] Ostrowski has argued elsewhere that the concept of "Tatar oppression" (*nasilie tatarskoe*) invoked to explain Metropolitan Maksim's departure from Kiev to Vladimir in 1299 was a specific allusion to Horde divisions at that time and is better translated as "Tatar violence," but

---

[11] *Povesti o Kulikovskoi bitvy* 1959, 44, 48.

[12] Halperin 1986, 154-159, especially 155.

[13] Isoaho 2006, 312, 352; the 1554 Vasilii-Varlaam edition of the vita of Aleksandr Nevskii for the Tsar's Great Menology and the Iona Dumin redaction under Patriarch Iov.

[14] Halperin 1986, 67.

[15] Serapion does not name the Tatars in his sermons and neither do the 1274 Church canons, but in context both clearly refer to them.

[16] Halperin 1986, 71-75, 75.

[17] *Ibid.*, 48-53.

[18] *Ibid.*, 70-75. Serapion's praise of the Tatars as "noble savages" in his last sermon, a literary cliché, does not alter the import of his sermons as a whole.

[19] Halperin 1986, 75-80.

unless that violence touched Kiev, Maksim would not need to leave, so it could not have meant only intra-Tatar violence. I believe the concept of "Tatar oppression" was more general here, and in either case the term can hardly be called "neutral."[20] This incomplete list of additional sources is sufficient to make the point that there was no uniform "neutral" paradigm toward the Tatars in Rus' during 1252-1448.

Ostrowski follows Fennell in dating the end of the "neutral" attitude toward the Tatars, at least on the part of the Russian Orthodox Church, to 1448. This dating is tentative and uncertain. 1448 was, in the view of the A. A. Shakhmatov, and then Ia. S. Lur'e, the date of the hypothetical compilation which was the common source of the Novgorod Fourth and Sofia First Chronicles, which in turn contain the most extensive and "anti-Tatar" narrative texts about the battle of Kulikovo Field in 1380 and the sack of Moscow by Khan Tokhtamysh in 1382. Fennell and now Ostrowski consistently date all embellished narratives about events in Rus'-Tatar relations during the fourteenth century, including the Tver' uprising of 1327, to a time after 1448. The problem, discussed in Ostrowski's monograph but not in this article, is that neither Shakhmatov, nor Lur'e, nor M. A. Salmina, the leading authority on the chronicle tales, stuck to this dating. Lur'e antedated the hypothetical compilation of 1448 to 1425 at the latest. Such a dating seriously impugns Ostrowski's imputed attribution of the sea-change in Russian Church attitudes toward the Tatars to the removal of the "constraints" imposed upon the Russian Church by Byzantine foreign-policy interests, which could not have taken place earlier than 1438, with Metropolitan Isidor's expulsion from Moscow for proclaiming the Union of Florence. Salmina dated the "chronicle tales" about the battle of Kulikovo and Tokhtamysh's sack of Moscow to the sixteenth century,[21] leaving a half-century gap in which the Russian Church did not shift its views despite the removal of Byzantine control. Ironically, Ostrowski rejects the 1448 dating of the common source of the Novgorod Fourth and Sofia First Chronicles, though retaining the 1448 ideological divide, arguing that even the Short Redaction of the "Chronicle Tale" of 1380 was composed between 1449 and 1462. Ostrowski's 1448 chronology is therefore both argumentative and artificial.

Concerning 1380 Ostrowski asserts that Grand Prince Dmitrii Donskoi of Moscow was aiding Khan Tokhtamysh by defeating Tokhtamysh's enemy, Emir Mamai. "Objectively" this was true, but there is no evidence of any communication between Donskoi and Tokhtamysh before

[20] Halperin 1984, 31-39; Halperin 1986, 64; Ostrowski 1993, 83-101.

[21] Halperin 2001, 248-263.

Kulikovo. Ostrowski's interpretation is, in fact, foisted by the Rus' chronicles onto Tokhtamysh himself, who supposedly informed Donskoi that Tokhtamysh had subsequently defeated their mutual enemy Mamai, a convenient political spin which should not be construed as expressing Russian motivations for riding into the steppe against Mamai.[22]

Ostrowski does not repeat in this article his assertion that in 1380 Donskoi led a mixed Rus' and Tatar army against a mixed Rus' and Tatar army under Mamai.[23] Mamai might have had Riazan' troops in his forces. However, there is no evidence of Tatars in Donskoi's army, unless, as Ostrowski argues later,[24] he was thinking of descendants of Tatar immigrants already in Muscovite service. However, such an assertion would perforce rely on legendary genealogies, such as that of the Godunov clan which claim the Tatar emir Chet-Murza as their ancestor, or on the case of Andrei Serkizov, killed at Kulikovo, supposedly the son of the Tatar émigré Serkiz, which is first recorded only in the Short Chronicle Tale of 1380, dated by Ostrowski to at least three quarters of a century after the battle, and then attested in genealogies which probably derive from the chronicle narrative.

Ostrowski does not date the end of Paradigm 3; since Paradigm 4 begins with the eighteenth century, the seventeenth century escapes discussion. For Paradigm 3 Ostrowski agrees with Keenan's unconvincing notion of a major cultural divide between Church and Court in Muscovy during the second half of the fifteenth and the sixteenth centuries.[25] Keenan's schema is suspect even on linguistic grounds.[26] It is true that the Muscovite diplomatic papers do not voice the same kinds of virulent anti-Tatar rhetoric as contemporary Church sources, but the language of diplomacy is not infrequently disingenuous. Keenan and Ostrowski take Court assertions of Muscovite tolerance of Islam at face value, but not Court declarations extolling the Russian conquest of Kazan' in religious terms: in Kazan' Ivan IV had converted mosques into churches, in Kazan' God had raised Christianity over Islam.[27] In his foreign policy Ivan often played the "fellow Christian" card. In negotiations with Poland-Lithuania

---

[22] Halperin 1976, 41.

[23] Ostrowski 1998, 155. This assertion is accepted by Sheiko 2004, 196.

[24] Ostrowski 2002, 37.

[25] Notably Keenan 1967b, 548-558; Keenan 1971, especially 53-58; Halperin 1974, 173-178. Keenan and Ostrowski do not date the ultimate fusion of Church and state attitudes toward the Tatars.

[26] Halperin 2007, 1-24.

[27] *SRIO* 1887, 372, 426.

Ivan bemoaned the sufferings of Christians at Muslim hands while Russia and Poland-Lithuania engaged in war; the Muslims here are clearly the Ottomans and their Crimean Tatar vassals, very likely a reflection of Ostrowski's anti-Tatar, anti-Muslim Paradigm 2.[28] The context of Habsburg-Russian negotiations over succession to the Polish-Lithuanian throne was expressed in religious terms: election of Bathory, an Ottoman client, would help Islam, but election of Ivan or his son Fedor, or the Holy Roman Emperor Maximilian or his son Ernst, would cement an anti-Ottoman alliance of all parties.[29] Finally, the sub-text of Ivan's appeal to the Pope to mediate the Livonian War, which led to the Possevino mission, was that in gratitude for Papal mediation of a truce, Ivan would endorse Church Union, which would, once again, facilitate an anti-Ottoman crusade.[30] Of course, Ivan was totally insincere in both cases about going to war with the Ottoman empire, and in the latter about a church union, but the rhetoric of Ivan's foreign policy echoes earlier Rus' descriptions of the Juchid ulus Tatars via the Crimean Tatars.

Even absent a complete history of the concept of the Tatar Yoke, Ostrowski's "find" in Printz is of major importance. However, a Latin invocation of the concept cannot be assumed to originate in the Church and only in the Church, and the absence of Russian allusions to the phrase until the importation of the *Synopsis'* from Kiev in the seventeenth century makes any assertions that it represented Church opinion in the sixteenth century highly speculative. Were Ostrowski to argue that Church texts which do not mention the "Tatar Yoke" per se contain a "Tatar Yoke mentality," such logic would stand in sharp contrast to Ostrowski's positivistic interpretation of the evolution of the concept of Third Rome, which makes no allowance for a "Third Rome mentality."[31]

Ostrowski's premise that Rus' attitudes toward the Tatars might have changed has great merit in positing that all expressions of opinion on the subject were not identical.[32] I would argue, however, that there was a single overriding paradigm for the entirety of the thirteenth to seventeenth centuries. Instead of alternating or sequential paradigms, however, I see simultaneous variations, contradictions and exceptions. In a manuscript

---

[28] *SRIO* 1887, 279 (1549), 557 (1558); *SRIO* 1892, 128 (1563), 663 (1570); *Posol'skaia kniga po sviazam Rossii s Pol'shei (1575-1576 gg.)* 2004, 45-46, 48-59, 65, 66, 96 (1575-1576).

[29] *PDSDR* 1851, 590.

[30] *Ibid.*, 768.

[31] Ostrowski 1998, 219-243, and more recently, Ostrowski 2006, 170-179.

[32] See Seleznev 2004, 34-48.

culture it would have been extremely difficult, if not impossible, to impose hegemonic homogeneity upon written culture. Changes occurred, but in degree more than in kind. The following, in outline form, constitutes an alternative interpretation of the image of the Tatars in Rus' sources.[33]

The first Mongol incursion into the Western steppe in 1223 was perceived by some as eschatological, as evidenced by a passage quoted by Ostrowski. According to the Novgorodian chronicler, some thought the Tatars were the peoples mentioned by Methodius of Patara, clearly an allusion to the peoples of Gog and Magog who would be unleashed at the end of time. This apocalyptic hysteria, which the chronicler did not share, soon passed, since the world did not come to an end.

From 1237-1238 through almost the middle of the sixteenth century, the Rus' dealt with the Tatars as infidels, hostile instruments of God's wrath against Rus' sins. This prejudice did not preclude cooperation with the Tatars when circumstances required it. The Tatars did not care what Rus' sources wrote about them, so there were no political consequences for depicting Tatar misdeeds on parchment. This overall paradigm could be balanced by other themes, for example, the chivalric treatment of Evpatyi by Khan Batu in the "Tale of the Destruction of Riazan' by Batu," dated variously anywhere from the fourteenth to the seventeenth centuries.[34] This same theme occurs in the chivalric depiction of the fleeing Tatars in the *Zadonshchina*.[35]

Moreover, Rus' attitudes toward the Tatar Khans, descendants of Chinggis Khan, were far more complicated, since the khans were, even when they acted evilly, accorded an exceptional degree of respect as "tsars," that is, legitimate rulers like the Byzantine Emperors also called "tsars," no matter what their misdeeds. This deference to Chingissids persisted long after the overthrow of the Jochid ulus.

---

[33] DeWeese 2006, 24 summarizes Muslim reaction to the Mongol conquests: "The repertoire of religious explanations of the Mongol conquests ranges from the initial expressions of sheer horror at the destructiveness of the Mongol advance, interpreted in terms of apocalyptic expectations, through conspiracy theories suspecting collusion between the Mongols and particular rulers with the Muslim world, through the penitential responses recognizing the Mongols as the instrument of divine punishment of a sinful world, through occasional idealizations of the simple virtue of the Mongols employed in critiques of Muslim society, through the historical and genealogical interpretations that found a place for the Mongols within the framework of the Muslim vision of Adam's descendants, and finally to the providential explanations that found in the Mongol invasion a key, ultimately, to the expansion of the *Dar-al-Islam*."

[34] Halperin 1986, 39-43, especially 40-41.

[35] Halperin 1976, 9-22.

By the second half of the fifteenth century, changing political realities, namely the fragmentation of the Horde, permitted a more imaginative attitude toward the Tatars, a fictionalizing tendency which subjected Batu, the bell-weather of Rus' attitudes toward the Tatars, to comic disdain. This occurs in the vita of Merkurii of Smolensk and the "Tale of the Death of Batu,"[36] in the "*Yarlik* of Akhmad," which Keenan dates to the seventeenth century[37] but could have been written a century earlier,[38] in the interpolated narratives of Olgerd's envoy to Mamai Bartiash and Dmitrii Donskoi's envoy to Mamari Vasilii Tiutchev in the *Skazanie o Mamaevom poboische*, which might date as early as the late fifteenth century or as late as the seventeenth century, even if Mamai was not a Chingissid,[39] and in chivalric elements in the *Kazanskaia istoriia* (Kazan' History), which Keenan interprets as reflecting a seventeenth-century mentality.[40]

Bishop Vassian of Rostov in 1480 denied the legitimacy of the Chingissid clan. This assertion constitutes a major exception to all Rus' paradigms on the Tatars. Although his "Epistle to the Ugra River" was recopied, no original sixteenth-century author ever quoted or developed Vassian's ideas on the Golden Kin, not even in descriptions of the conquest of Kazan'. Therefore, one may conclude that Vassian went too far even for the most rabidly anti-Tatar ideologues of the mid sixteenth century.[41]

The mixture of attitudes toward the Tatars found in seventeenth-century Muscovy, when they might have been influenced by European literature, remains unstudied.

In conclusion, as it stimulates fresh thinking, Ostrowski's ambitious attempt to elucidate the paradigms of Rus' attitudes toward Tatar influence constitutes a positive contribution to understanding Rus'-Tatar relations and the impact of the Mongols on Russian and world history.

Bibliography and Abbreviations

DeWeese, D. 2006. '«Stuck in the Throat of Chingiz Khan»: Envisioning the Mongol Conquests in Some Sufi Accounts from the 14th to 17th Centuries'. In: J. Pfeiffer & Q. Sholeh (eds), in collaboration with E. Tucker, *History and Historiography of*

---

[36] Halperin 1983, 50-65.
[37] Keenan 1967c, 33-47.
[38] Halperin 1986, 165-166.
[39] *Ibid.*, 107-115 on the *Skazanie*, 112-113 on Bartiash and Tiutchev.
[40] Keenan 1967a, 143-183. Halperin 1986, 161-165.
[41] Halperin 1986, 154-159.

Post-Mongol Central Asia and the Middle East. Studies in Honour of John E. Woods. Wiesbaden, 23-60.

Fennell, J. 1970. 'The Ideological Role of the Russian Church in the First Half of the Fourteenth Century'. In: *Gorski Vijenac: A Garland of Essays Presented to Professor Elizabeth Hill.* Cambridge, 105-111.

Halperin, C. J. 1974. 'A Heretical View of Sixteenth-Century Muscovy: Edward L. Keenan, *The Kurbskii-Groznyi Apocrypha*'. *Jahrbücher für Geschichte Osteuropas* 22, 161-186.

— 1975. 'A Chingissid Saint of the Russian Orthodox Church: «The Life of Peter, *tsarevich* of the Horde»'. *Canadian-American Slavic Studies* 9, 323-335.

— 1976. 'The Russian Land and the Russian Tsar: The Emergence of Muscovite Ideology, 1380-1408'. *Forschungen zur osteuropäischen Geschichte* 23, 7-103.

— 1983. 'The Defeat and Death of Batu'. *Russian History* 10, 50-65.

— 1984. 'The Tatar Yoke and Tatar Oppression'. *Russia Mediaevalis* 5, 20-39.

— 1985. *Russia and the Golden Horde: The Mongol Impact on Medieval Russian History.* Bloomington, IN.

— 1986. *The Tatar Yoke.* Columbus, OH.

— 1998-99. 'The East Slavic Response to the Mongol Conquest'. *Archivum Eurasiae Medii Aevi* 10, 98-117.

— 1999. Review of Donald Ostrowski, *Muscovy and the Mongols.* In: *The Sixteenth Century Journal* 30, 517-518.

— 2001. 'Text and Textology: Salmina's Dating of the «Chronicle Tales» about Dmitry Donskoy'. *Slavonic and East European Review* 79, 248-263.

— 2007. 'The «Russian» and «Slavonic» Languages in Sixteenth-Century Muscovy'. *Slavonic and East European Review* 85, 1-24.

Isoaho, M. 2006. *The Image of Aleksandr Nevskiy in Medieval Russia. Warrior and Saint.* Leiden · Boston.

Keenan, E. L. 1967a. 'Comings to Grips with the *Kazanskaya istoriya*: Some Observations on Old Answers and New Questions'. *Annals of the Ukrainian Academy of Arts and Sciences in the United States* 31-32, 143-183.

— 1967b. 'Muscovy and Kazan: Some Introductory Remarks on the Patterns of Steppe Diplomacy'. *Slavic Review* 34, 548-558.

— 1967c. 'The *Yarlik* of Axmed-Khan to Ivan III: A new Reading — A Study in Literal Diplomatics and Literary Turcica'. *International Journal of Slavic Linguistics and Poetics* 11, 33-47.

— 1971. *The Kurbskii-Groznyi Apocrypha. The Seventeenth-Century Origin of the "Correspondence" Attributed to Prince A.M. Kurbskii and Tsar Ivan IV.* With an appendix by D. C. Waugh. Cambridge, MA.

Ostrowski, D. 1993. 'Why Did the Metropolitan Move from Kiev to Vladimir in the Thirteenth Century?'. *California Slavic Studies* 16, 83-101.

— 1998. *Muscovy and the Mongols: Cross-Cultural Influences on the Steppe Frontier 1304-1547.* Cambridge, England.

— 2002. 'Troop Mobilization by the Muscovite Grand Princes (1313-1533)'. In: E. Lohr & M. Poe (eds), *The Military and Society in Russia 1450-1917.* Leiden, 19-40.

Ostrowski, D. 2006. 'Moscow the Third Rome as Historical Ghost'. In: S. Brooks (ed.), *Byzantium: Faith and Power (1261-1557): Perspectives on Late Byzantine Art and Culture*. New York, 170-179.

— forthcoming. 'The Mongols and Rus': Eight Paradigms'. In: A. Gleason (ed.), *A Companion to Russian History*. Oxford, England.

PDSDR 1851: *Pamiatniki diplomaticheskikh snoshenii drevnei Rossii s derzhavami inostrannymi*. Chast' pervaia. *Snosheniia s gosudarstvami evropeiskimi*. [Tom I. St. Petersburg, izdanie. II otdelenie E. I. V. Kantseliarii = *Pamiatniki diplomaticheskikh snoshenii s Imperieiu rimskoiu*. Tom I: *S 1498 po 1594 god*.]

Posol'skaia kniga po sviazam Rossii s Pol'shei (1575-1576 gg.) 2004. L. V. Sobolev (compiler). Moscow-Warsaw. [= Pamiatniki istorii Vostochnoi Evropy. Istochniki XV-XVII vv. Tom VII.]

Povesti o Kulikovskoi bitvy 1959. Moscow.

SRIO 1887: *Sbornik russkogo istoricheskogo obshchestva* tom 59. St. Petersburg. [= G. O. Karpov (ed.), *Pamiatniki diplomaticheskikh snoshenii drevnei Rossii s derzhavami inostrannymi = Pamiatniki diplomaticheskikh snoshenii moskovskogo gosudarstva s Pol'sko-litovskim* Tom II (1533-1560).]

SRIO 1892: *Sbornik russkogo istoricheskogo obshchestva* tom 71. St. Petersburg. [= G. O. Karpov (ed.), *Pamiatniki diplomaticheskikh snoshenii drevnei Rossii s derzhavami inostrannymi = Pamiatniki diplomaticheskikh snoshenii moskovskogo gosudarstva s Pol'sko-litovskim* Tom III (1560-1571).]

Seleznev, Iu. V. 2004. 'Ideino-religioznaia otsenka sovremennikami russko-ordynskikh otnoshenii 1240-1270-kh gg.'. In: A. O. Amel'kin & Seleznev, *Nashestvie Batyia i ustanovlenie ordynskogo iga v obshchestvennom soznanii Rusi XIII-XVII vekov*. Voronezh, 34-48.

Sheiko, K. 2004. *Lomonosov's Bastards: Anatolii Fomenko, pseudo-history and Russia's search for a post-Communist identity*. PhD dissertation, University of Wollongon (Australia).

ON THE ROMANIZATION OF VPHAGS.PA MONGOL

Juha Janhunen

A written language with a non-Roman script can be rendered in Roman letters by two different methods. The first method is that of transliteration, in which the non-Roman script is transferred into Roman letters segment by segment, so that the Romanized sequence of letters has an unambiguous and reconvertible relationship to the original script image. This is not to say that each segment of the original script has to be transliterated by only one Roman letter, for in many cases it is both practical and inevitable to operate with sequences of letters (digraphs or trigraphs). The second method is that of transcription, in which the original script is ignored in favour of the underlying linguistic substance. The linguistic substance, or sequence of sounds, is most adequately Romanized in terms of the phonemes of the underlying language. In this case, too, it is often necessary to use a sequence of letters for a single phoneme, but this does not invalidate the transcription as long as the phonemic distinctions are correctly transmitted and the phonotactic patterns observed.

It is important to realize that transliteration and transcription are, in principle, two alternative methods, only one of which can be applied at a time. This means that as a rule, it is impossible to combine a transliteration and a transcription in a single system of Romanization, unless the orthography of the language to be Romanized is perfectly phonemic, which is rarely the case. Which one of the two approaches, transcription or transliteration, is chosen in each given case, depends on the goals and presuppositions of the Romanization enterprise. In many cases, especially when dead languages with obsolete writing systems and inadequate orthographies are concerned, it is impossible to obtain enough phonological information on the underlying language to attempt a phonemic transcription. In such cases the only option is to approach the language by the method of transliteration. For successful transliteration, only an understanding of the original graphic sequence is required.

Transliteration is also the most suitable approach to scripts that are, or have been, used for several different languages. For reasons connected with the history of scholarship, the principles of phonemic (or even phonetic) transcription as used for different spoken languages are often very different, and it is difficult to conform the values of the Roman letters across the boundaries of well-established learned traditions. However, when several languages are written in the same non-Roman script it is always reasonable to make an effort to Romanize them according to a single unified system. For instance, the many languages using the Arabic script are best Romanized by using always the same Roman letters to denote the same Arabic letters, including non-standard and additional letters not used in Arabic itself. Another example is offered by the Ancient Uighur script, which can conveniently be Romanized according to unified principles irrespective of whether it is applied to Uighur, Mongol, or Manchu (before the script reform).

For practical reasons, it is also convenient, though not always possible, to Romanize a given language according to uniform principles irrespective of what the original writing system is. There are many languages that are, or have been, written in several different writing systems. In such cases, it often happens that all the writing systems concerned are in some respects phonemically inadequate, though their shortcomings are not necessarily identical. We might say that each writing system, together with the orthographical conventions that accompany it, reflects a slightly different picture of the phonological reality of the underlying language. Obviously, systems that reflect different pictures of the phonological reality cannot yield identical results when Romanized. Even so, it is a useful goal not to introduce more variation in the Romanizations than is present between the original non-Roman scripts. Segments that have the same distinctive status in two or more scripts, as used for a single language, should, in principle, be Romanized in a uniform way.

Middle Mongol is a language that is documented in several different scripts. All these scripts have, moreover, been used, to write also other languages. In this situation, one would expect that specialists on Middle Mongol would have paid special attention to the problems of transcription and transliteration. This is not exactly so, however, for Middle Mongol studies is a field that has always been dominated by philologists, for whom, understandably, the contents of the documents are more important than their form. The issue of Romanization, which belongs more intimately to the sphere of linguistics, has therefore been pushed aside as a relatively minor one, to which the best solution is the one dictated by the tradition of scholarship. To some extent, the same situation is true of Mongolic studies, in general. Written Mongol, for instance, is a language whose non-Roman system of writing involves complicated theoretical issues of segmental analysis[1]. Even so, most Mongolists continue to Romanize Written Mongol in terms of an antiquated system that does not fill the requirements of linguistic critique.

Middle Mongol studies is an example of a tradition that has tried to solve the Romanization issue by combining features of transcription and transliteration. This approach[2] has the advantage that all Middle Mongol data will appear in a more or less uniform Romanized shape irrespective of what the original writing system is. On the other hand, the peculiarities of the individual writing systems are not given much attention, and there has been no attempt to coordinate the Middle Mongol Romanization with the Romanizations of other languages written in the same scripts. Moreover, there has been a tendency to ignore the fact that Middle Mongol itself involves a considerable degree of local and chronological variation. Some local forms of language going under the label of Middle Mongol, especially those recorded in the Arabic script, would better be classified as early Western Mongolic, while others, especially the language of Preclassical Written Mongol, are in some respects more ancient than, or dialectally different from, the Proto-Mongolic level of reconstruction.

The problems inherent in the current praxis of Middle Mongol Romanization may be illustrated by the convention that requires the phonemes *k g* in back-vocalic words to be Romanized invariably as <q>, as in <qahan> for †*ka*(*x*)*an* 'emperor' and <qajar> for †*gajar* 'place'. This convention reflects the circumstance that most script systems used to record Middle Mongol do not distinguish the sounds of *k* (unvoiced and/or aspirated) vs. *g* (voiced and/or unaspirated) in back-vocalic words. However, there are also script systems, such as the Uighur script, that do not distinguish these sounds in front-vocalic words, either, but in spite of this they are normally Romanized by separate letters, as in <niken> for †*nike/n* 'one' and <irgen> for †*irgen* 'people'. In fact, any attempt to give a phonemically imperfect orthography a phonemic interpretation can only lead to arbitrary decisions. For instance, it is impossible to tell when the presumably original Proto-Mongolic shape **nike/n* 'one' became **nige/n* and (Common Mongolic) **nege/n* — most of the script systems used for Middle Mongol simply do not tell us such details.

It may be concluded that knowing the phonemic system of a language is one thing and phonemizing individual lexical items of the language, not to mention entire texts, is another. Although we have a fair understanding

---

[1] Balk & Janhunen 1999.

[2] On which cf., e.g., Rybatzki 2003, 55-64.

of the segmental paradigm and phonotactic features of Middle Mongol, there are both sporadic idiosyncracies and positional developments that make it impossible to accurately transcribe the language of the Middle Mongol documents in terms of segmental phonemes. It is considerably safer to approach each writing system used for Middle Mongol as a separate object of transliteration, rather than transcription. This will in the following be illustrated with the case of the vPhags.pa script.

The vPhags.pa script is one of the most phonetically perfected medieval scripts of Asia[3]. Although not adapted for showing tonal distinctions, it has a large selection of consonant and vowel letters, sufficient to express the relevant segmental distinctions, as well as even some non-phonemic details, of the languages recorded in it. Based on the **dbu.can** variety of the Tibetan script, the vPhags.pa script is essentially a verticalized derivative of the latter[4], though some additional letters were designed after other models, including, apparently, the Devanagari script. In any case, the Tibetan origin of the vPhags.pa script is evident from the fact that the vPhags.pa letters are grouped into blocks which structurally correspond to Tibetan-type syllables.

The principle of grouping the letters into syllabic blocks was of particular relevance when the vPhags.pa script was applied to write other languages with an essentially monosyllabic lexical structure, such as Chinese[5], while it was of less significance when languages with predominantly polysyllabic words, such as Middle Mongol, were written. For Middle Mongol, it would have been more important to indicate word boundaries, which is normally not done in the vPhags.pa Mongol documents. Even so, the Middle Mongol documents preserved in the vPhags.pa script[6] reflect the phonological properties of the underlying language considerably more accurately than, for instance, the Uighur script does. This means that a Romanized transliteration of vPhags.pa Mongol will yield a result that is much closer to the actual phonemic structure of the language than a Romanization of the Uighur script can be.

The distinction between transliteration and transcription is not new to vPhags.pa studies, and it has also been recognized by most scholars working on the Middle Mongol documents in the vPhags.pa script. In fact,

---

[3] Cf. e.g. Kara 2005, 51-62.

[4] van der Kuijp 1996, 437-438.

[5] Luo & Cai 2004, Coblin 2007.

[6] Poppe 1957, Ligeti 1972-1973, Junast 1990-1991, Tumurtogoo 2002, Hugjiltu & Saruul 2004, cf. also Michalove 2004.

some scholars offer systematically two parallel Romanizations, involving both a transliteration and a transcription, while others prefer to work mainly with a transliteration. However, irrespective of the method, the actual principles applied in the Romanization of vPhags.pa Mongol so far illustrate a wide range of practical conventions, which differ from one author to the other[7]. It is therefore useful to reconsider the issue in order to create a more generalized approach that could better serve the interests of Middle Mongol studies. In the following, a numbered list of issues (1-11) is presented which, in the author's opinion, should be considered and, if possible, applied in the field. Note that the vPhags.pa letters and syllables are quoted below in a horizontalized order (left to right).

(1) As has already been implied above, transliteration is, indeed, the only adequate method of quoting vPhags.pa material from any language. Although the vPhags.pa script was segmentally capable of expressing the phonemic distinctions of the languages written in it, the orthographical conventions used for the individual languages were not always necessarily phonemic. Moreover, the actual vPhags.pa orthographies did not always reflect chronologically coherent forms of speech. vPhags.pa Chinese, for instance, was to some extent a 'composite' language, which did not correspond to any single variety of spoken Chinese of the time[8]. In a similar way, vPhags.pa Mongol incorporated both orthographical and grammatical features that were probably not in line with the actual spoken language. For some details, it seems that vPhags.pa Mongol was a transcription of the language underlying Written Mongol, which, on the other hand, was not fully coherent with the spoken forms of Middle Mongol as used in the Yuan period.

(2) In all vPhags.pa studies, it is important to remember that, in spite of the Tibetan origin of the script, the principal language to which the vPhags.pa letters were applied was Middle Mongol. This means that it is, indeed, reasonable to assign Romanized values to the vPhags.pa letters under consideration of their role in vPhags.pa Mongol. The transliteration of vPhags.pa Mongol should therefore be taken as the uniform basis for transliterating other languages written in the same script. The validity of this principle has occasionally been questioned by specialists on vPhags.pa Chinese[9], but it is difficult to see how else the often inherently multi-lingual vPhags.pa documents could be Romanized at all. It would be more

[7] Cf. e.g. Damdinsuren 1986, 21-24.

[8] Coblin 2007, 34-36.

[9] Coblin 2007, 58-59 *et passim*.

or less impossible to apply different standards to, for instance, Middle Mongol and Chinese elements occurring in a single text.

(3) When choosing the Romanizational values for the individual vPhags.pa letters, it is practical to start from the systems available for Romanizing the regular Tibetan script. At the same time, an effort should be made to correlate the Romanization with the Romanized image of the Uighur script as used for Written Mongol. In fact, this is what has been done by most scholars working on vPhags.pa Mongol, but the problem is that the Romanizations that have been used for Written Mongol have, in general, not been quite up-to-date. As a result, many of the problems involved in the conventional Romanizations of Written Mongol have been transferred to the Romanization of the vPhags.pa letters.

(4) Although some authors prefer to incorporate detailed allographic information in the Romanization[10], this is best ignored when vPhags.pa Mongol material is transliterated for linguistic purposes. Allographic variants of letters may be of crucial importance for the historical and textological identification and dating of individual documents, but as far as they do not reflect linguistic realities they need not to be considered in the Romanization.

(5) On a practical level, the Romanization of vPhags.pa Mongol should exclude any non-standard letters or symbols that are not compatible with the regrettably very limited alternatives permitted by most modern communication devices. Diacritics should also be avoided, and any expanded letter form should simply be replaced by either a basic letter or a sequence of basic letters (digraph or trigraph), as is also done in the most common (Wylie) Romanization of the regular Tibetan script. Typical non-standard letters used by many authors in vPhags.pa Mongol studies include <č ǰ š ž> as well as <ñ ŋ>[11], which are conveniently, and with no loss of information, replaced by the simple letters ꡄ **c** ꡆ **j** and the digraphs ꡚ **sh** ꡔ **zh** ꡇ **ny** ꡃ **ng**, respectively. Digraphs are also best used for the letters ꡁ **kh** ꡉ **th** ꡍ **ph** ꡅ **ch** (voiceless aspirates) as well as **ts** ꡐ **dz** ꡒ (dental affricates), while a trigraph is needed for **tsh** ꡑ (voiceless aspirated dental affricate). Most other consonant letters can be Romanized by a single letter each: ꡀ **k** ꡈ **t** ꡌ **p** (voiceless unaspirated stops), ꡂ **g** ꡊ **d** ꡎ **b** (voiced or weak unaspirated stops), ꡛ **s** ꡕ **z** (dental sibilants), ꡋ **n** ꡏ **m** (nasals), ꡙ **l** ꡘ **r** (liquids), ꡓ ꡧ **w** ꡗ **y** ꡜ **h** (glides).

[10] Cf. e.g. Hugjiltu & Saruul 2004, 9-10.

[11] Cf. e.g. Poppe 1957, 19.

(6) Two special letters not directly derived from the Tibetan alphabet but used in vPhags.pa Mongol are ꡢ and ꡣ, which denote back velar consonants (basically, back allophones of **k* **g*). Among the Romanizations used for these letters there are the non-standard symbols <ɢ> (small capital G) and <γ> (*gamma*), but it is clearly much more convenient to use the basic Roman letter **q** (back velar stop) and the digraph **qh** (back velar fricative), respectively. It should be noted that in native Mongol words, the letter ꡢ **q** is normally used to denote both a strong (voiceless aspirated) and a weak (voiced and/or unaspirated) back velar obstruent, as in ꡢ ꡘꡞ ꡗ ꡉꡋ **qa ri ya than** for †*kariya-tan* 'subordinates', ꡢ ꡆꡘ **qa jar** for †*gajar* 'place', ꡆꡘ ꡙꡞꡢ **jar liq** for †*jarlig* 'order'. This convention of vPhags.pa Mongol represents a deviation from the general phonemic accuracy of the script and may be due to the influence of the Uighur script, as used in Preclassical Written Mongol.

(7) An important property of the vPhags.pa script, and a difference with regard to the regular Tibetan script, is that the vowel letters ꡠ **e** ꡞ ꡞ **i** ꡟ ꡟ **u** ꡡ ꡡ **o**, which have also the positionally conditioned initial variants ꡦꡞ **i** ꡦꡟ **u** ꡦꡡ ꡦꡡ **o**, occupy a separate segmental slot in the linear graphic sequence. Even so, the alphasyllabic origin of the script[12] is still visible in the convention which leaves one unmarked vowel without a graphic representation after a syllable-initial consonant letter. Some authors incorporate this feature in the transliteration by writing no vowel letter in these cases[13], or by placing the 'missing' vowel in parenthesis[14]. It seems, however, that the principles of the script are better observed if the unmarked vowel is consistently Romanized as a segmentally manifested **a**, as in ꡎ **ba** for †*ba* 'and'. This is also the established praxis in the Romanization of the regular Tibetan script.

(8) The vowels **ö* **ü* (rounded front vowels) are in the vPhags.pa script rendered by the digraphs ꡠꡡ **eo** ꡠꡟ **eu**. These have normally been Romanized by the diacritically marked 'umlaut' letters <ö ü>, but a segment-by-segment transliteration with Roman digraphs appears a much better choice, e.g. ꡛꡠꡟ ꡏꡠ **seu me** for †*süme* 'temple'. This convention not only allows us to avoid using diacritics, but it also corresponds to the actual structure of the vPhags.pa script. It may be added that the vPhags.pa script often ignores the distinction between **ö* **ü* and **o* **u* (the corresponding back vowels), in which case, of course, the Romanization

---

[12] On the term, cf. Bright 1996, 384.

[13] E.g. Hugjiltu & Saruul 2004, 11-13.

[14] Cf. e.g. Junast 1990, 9, Michalove 2004, 17.

also has to ignore it, as in the common **mong kha** for †*möngke* 'eternal', in which the palatal vocalism of the word is nevertheless signalled by the 'palatal' velar letter **kha**[15].

(9) The vPhags.pa letters and , which derive from the regular Tibetan letters **va.chung** ('little *a*') and **xa.chen** ('big *a*'), respectively, are in most Romanizations of the vPhags.pa script, as also in the common Romanization of the regular Tibetan script, represented by apostrophes and/or simply zero. This is, however, contrary to the principles of the Tibetan script, in which these two elements clearly function as consonant letters. In a transliteration it is therefore inevitable to mark them with regular basic letters of the Roman alphabet, and the two most readily available letters are **v** for and **x** for [16]. In actual usage, the letter **x**[17] functions as an 'empty' base for the unmarked vowel **a,** as in **xa li ba** for †*aliba* 'whatever', as well as for the vowel **e** in the combinations **eo** **eu**, as in **xeu lu** for †*ülü* [negation particle]. In this function, **x** is occasionally replaced by **v**, and examples like **veu ge vu** ~ **xeu ge vun** for †*ügeü-n* [caritive particle] show that the two 'empty' initials do not involve any phonemic distinction[18]. The vowels **i** **u** **o**, in their initial variants **i** **u** **o**, do not require a consonantal initial, as in **u sun** for †*usun* 'water', though they can take one, especially in non-Mongolic items, as in **xom** ~ **om** for †*om* [magic syllable].

(10) The letter **v** is also used word-internally to indicate the hiatus ('), that is, the intervocalic zero (Ø) which in Middle Mongol had replaced the original medial *x. In these cases, it is a question of contracted vowel sequences[19], which had not yet developed to the long monophthongs (double vowels) of Modern Mongol. The role of **v** as a hiatus marker reflects directly the use of **va.chung** in the regular Tibetan script as an intra-syllable base for syllable-final vowels[20]. In these cases, the structure of the script requires that a vowel is read both before and after **v**. Depending on the type of the vowel sequence there are different possibilities:

---

[15] On the historical background of the word, cf. Poppe 1957, 70-72.

[16] Balk 2005 *passim*.

[17] Cf. also Coblin 2007, 46.

[18] Junast 1990, 17-18.

[19] Hugjiltu 1999.

[20] For a somewhat different interpretation, cf. Kara 2005, 56.

(a) If no other vowel is indicated, **a** is read on both sides of **v**, as in **qava nu** for †*kaan-u* 'of the emperor', **cha qavan** for †*cagaan* 'white'.

(b) If the first vowel is indicated by a separate vowel letter, the second one has to be read as **a**, as in **ya buva su** for †*yabu-asu* 'if one goes'.

(c) If the second vowel is indicated by a separate vowel letter, the first one has to be read as **a**, but the phonemic implication is that of a sequence of two identical vowels, as in **khave khu** for †*kee-kü* 'to say'.

(d) If both vowels are indicated by separate vowel letters, a syllable boundary is generally assumed to exist before the intervocalic **v**, though it is not always clear whether it really is there in the actual script, as in **beu theu veg sen** for †*bütüe-gsen* 'completed'. The vowels written on the two sides of **v** can also be identical, as in **kheu vun** for †*küün* 'man'. Note that in the regular Tibetan script both the main consonant letter and the syllable-final **va.chung** can take a marked vowel letter. However, in native Tibetan words the syllable-final **va.chung** cannot be followed by any other final segment.

(e) In some cases, especially if contraction would take place in two consecutive syllables, a segmental **h** is written instead of **v**, as in **i haven** ~ **vi haven** ~ **vi he ven** for †*ixeen* 'protection'. This suggests that, under special conditions, intervocalic **x* could still survive in Middle Mongol as a separate segment, though it was subsequently eliminated. There are, of course, also examples in which **x* is preserved and segmentally marked in initial position, as in **ha chi heu re** for †*xaci xüre* 'consequence'.

(11) Probably the most difficult issue of vPhags.pa Romanization involves the extra vowel letter that medially has the allographic variants and initially . It has been traditionally claimed that this letter represents 'a vowel more closed than *e*'[21]. Accordingly, the distinction between vs. has been expressed in the Romanization either as <ä> vs. <e>[22], or as <e> vs. <ė> or <é>[23]. However, it is misleading to claim that Middle Mongol had two different 'vowels' when it actually only had, in the vPhags.pa script, two different vowel letters with related functions. Clearly, it is a question of an orthographical convention, rather than of a phonemic feature of the underlying language. Even so, it goes without

---

[21] Poppe 1957, 25.

[22] Ligeti 1972, 13-15.

[23] By most other scholars, cf. also Michalove 2004, 12.

saying that, in an adequate system of transliteration, the letter has to be Romanized in an unambiguous way. As a preliminary solution, and without making any claim about the corresponding phonemic reality, we will Romanize it by the digraph **ie**. The Romanization need not be the same for all positions, however, and in any case it is necessary to consider the distributional properties of both **ie** and **e**. There are four positions to be considered:

(a) In initial position, only the initial variants of the letter **ie** are attested. For reasons not fully understood, but apparently connected with the paleographical origin of the distinction between **ie** vs. **e**, the letter **e** is completely blocked from this position. In fact, it is the letter **ie**, and not **e**, that represents the vowel letter **e** of the regular Tibetan script, while the origin and intended function of the letter **e** remain disputed[24]. As a possibility, one might think of a connection with the Uighur script, in which the vowel **e* is expressed by the basic unmarked 'tooth'[25], which not only functionally but also physically resembles the vPhags.pa letter **e**, though in the Uighur script the 'tooth' also marks the vowel **a*. However this may be, in view of the distributional situation, there is no obstacle to simplifying the notation **ie** to **e** in initial position, e.g. **ie ne** > **e ne** for †*ene* 'this'.

(b) Another context in which the letter **ie** occurs is after a vowel, in which case it stands for the second component of a diphthongoid vowel sequence. The actual vowel in these sequences was originally **i*, and it must still have been phonemically †*i* in Middle Mongol, as is also evident from Written Mongol. The vPhags.pa convention of writing it with the letter **ie** may or may not imply that it was phonetically developing towards the quality of [e], as has happened in many forms of Modern Mongol. Irrespective of this, there is no contrast between **ie** and **i** in the position after another vowel letter, which means that it is possible to simplify the notation **ie** to **i** in this position, e.g. **xeuie les** > **xeui les** for †*üile-s* 'works', **de le geie** > **de le gei** for †*delekei* 'world'. It should be noted that the diphthongoids can also be written by using the sequence **yi**. The latter is the only possible choice after **a**, as in **da la yi** for †*dalai* 'sea' as well as after an initial **ie** > **e**, as in **e yi mu** for †*eimü* 'like this'.

(c) Elsewhere, the letter **ie** appears only immediately after a word-initial consonant letter, a position in which both **e** and **i** can also

---

[24] Coblin 2007, 53-62.

[25] Romanized as 'glyphic' **v**, cf. Balk & Janhunen 1999, 23.

occur. In practice, however, the letter **ie** is conspicuously rare and limited mainly to a number of fixed items and contexts. In fact, the systematic complementarity of **e** and **ie** is valid in some post-consonantal positions, as well, notably after **y**, where only **ie** is attested. In this position, then, the notation **ie** may be simplified to **e** with no loss of information, as in **yie ke** > **ye ke** for †*yeke* 'big'.

(d) After most other consonant letters, **e** and **ie** can actually contrast, which means that the distinction has to be observed in the Romanization. Even so, the occurrence of **ie** in vPhags.pa Mongol is normally connected with exceptional circumstances. The most common example of the letter is **dieng ri** for †*tenggeri* 'sky', an item that also otherwise involves idiosyncratic orthographical deviations from the phonemic reality[26]. Thus, the fact remains that vPhags.pa Mongol exploits the graphemic opposition between **e** vs. **ie** only very marginally. This allows most occurrences of **ie** to be Romanized as either **e** or **i**, which are also better in line with the actual segmental structure of the language.

There remain several other aspects of the vPhags.pa script which are of relevance to the issue of Romanization, though they are not central features of vPhags.pa Mongol. Since the vPhags.pa script made it possible to write words from several different languages, including not only Middle Mongol but also contemporary forms of Chinese and Tibetan, in a single text and in the same writing system, the users of vPhags.pa Mongol are likely to have been familiar with many of the features present in vPhags.pa Chinese and vPhags.pa Tibetan. On the other hand, the users of vPhags.pa Chinese and vPhags.pa Tibetan may not always have been familiar with the true meaning and background of the conventions of vPhags.pa Mongol, which is why there may be language-specific differences in the application of the principles of the script. These are particularly evident in vPhags.pa Chinese.

Among the most important features of vPhags.pa Chinese is the frequent use of the medial letters **w** **y**, which in the Romanization may be viewed as positional variants of the consonant letters **w** **y**, as in **xwang** (*wang* 王), **hyang** (*xiang* 向)[27]. The letters **w** **y** are also used as finals, as in **gaw** (高 *gao*), **qhway** (*huai* 懷). It may be noted that the letter **w** is likewise attested as a 'final' (postvocalic rounded vowel) in vPhags.pa Mongol, as in **thaw la yi** for

26 On the historical background of the word, cf. Poppe 1957, 68-70.

27 The examples, accompanied by the Pinyinized Standard Mandarin shapes without tones, are quoted from the facsimiles of steles and xylographs in Luo & Cai 2004.

†*taulai* ‘hare’, while the use of the letter **y** as a ‘final’ (postvocalic palatal vowel) is rendered unnecessary by the other conventions available for writing the relevant sequences, that is, **ie** and **yi**, cf. e.g. **na yi man** for †*naiman* ‘eight’. Of these, the letter **ie** is also attested as a final in vPhags.pa Chinese and may in this usage be Romanized as **ie** > **i**, as in **shui** (水 *shui*).

An intricate issue of vPhags.pa Chinese with relevance also to vPhags.pa Mongol is the question concerning the function(s) of the letter **e**. Basically, this letter occurs in vPhags.pa Chinese in contexts very similar to those observed in vPhags.pa Mongol, and there is no reason not use the same Romanization for the two languages. Thus, there are examples of **e** as the main vowel of a syllable without a final, as in **be** (*bie* 别), with a final, as in **sen** (*xian* 先), and in the combinations **eu eo**, as in **xeu** (*yu* 魚), **zheung** (*rong* 戎), **geon** (*juan* 眷). There are also examples of **e** in combination with a medial, as in **gwe** (*jue* 決), as well as in combination with both a medial and a final at the same time, as in **swen** (*xuan* 宣). In many of these positions, though not in all, **e** can potentially contrast with **ie**, cf. e.g. **zie** (*xie* 謝), **thien** (*tian* 天), **zhwie** (*rui* 芮). From the point of view of the Romanization it is irrelevant what the exact phonemic and phonetic distinction between the correlates of the letters **e** vs. **ie** was. In any case, the material suggests that, in the underlying form of Chinese, it was a question of two separate vowel phonemes or phonemic sequences.

The letter **e** can also contrast with the medial letter **y**, as in **ge** (*jie* 結) vs. **gya** (*jia* 家)[28]. A problem is, however, that the two letters **e** **y**, are often graphically confused in the extant sources, and the confusion may even extend to the medial letter **w**. Thus, a word normally written with **y** can appear in the sources also with **e**, e.g. **gyang** ~ **geng** (*jiang* 江). On this basis, and considering also the preserved ‘alphabetical’ lists of the vPhags.pa script, it has been proposed that virtually all occurrences of **y** should actually be read as **e**, which, in turn, should be analyzed not as a regular vowel letter but as a medial letter, implying a sequence of a palatal medial consonant and the main vowel *a*[29]. Unfortunately, this looks rather like an overinterpretation of the situation. The confusion between **e** **y** **w** may be a fact, but when Romanizing the script we only have to consider what is actually written.

---

[28] Coblin 2007 nos. 764, 794.

[29] Coblin 2007, 56-58.

It has to be concluded that vPhags.pa Chinese does not offer any easy explanation of why the vPhags.pa script has the opposition between the vowel letters **e** and **ie**. There is nothing in vPhags.pa Chinese that would require us to assume that **e** was inherently supposed to write a medial, rather than a regular main vowel. Both vPhags.pa Mongol and vPhags.pa Chinese suggest that this letter basically denoted a regular vowel, though it may, of course, have been qualitatively different in the two languages. Even so, it is important to note that the two vowel letters contrast much more systematically and more frequently in vPhags.pa Chinese than they do in vPhags.pa Mongol. This, on the other hand, would seem to suggest that the original design of the script may, in fact, have been based on considerations that extended beyond Middle Mongol and comprised also contemporary Chinese, or at least the Chinese elements that had to be included in Middle Mongol texts.

Most other properties of vPhags.pa Chinese are also compatible with the principles proposed here for the Romanization of vPhags.pa Mongol. For some details, however, modifications may have to be made in order to incorporate the syntagmatic specifics of vPhags.pa Chinese into the Romanization. vPhags.pa Chinese has, for instance, the sequences **ha hi**, as in **jhang** (*zhuang* 莊), **nhing** (*neng* 能), which are generally assumed to denote two specific vowel qualities, distinct from the corresponding 'basic' vowels written as **a i**[30]. Although the sequences **ha hi** as such are unambiguous, the **h** in them may be confused with the **h** of the initial di/trigraphs **kh th ph ch tsh sh zh qh**. In cases of ambiguity, the segmental boundary has to be indicated by an apostrophe ('), or by some other convention, in the Romanization, e.g. **si** (*xi* 西) vs. **shi** (*shi* 施) vs. **s'hi** (*si* 司) vs. **shhi** (*shi* 師). This, like all other idiosyncracies of vPhags.pa Chinese, is a marginal issue, which does not in any way invalidate the prospects of a unified Romanization for all languages written in the vPhags.pa script.

Sample text. In conclusion, a brief extract of Romanized vPhags.pa Mongol is presented below. The text is quoted from an edict of Sechen (Khubilai) Khaghan, issued in the Year of the Ox (1277/1289). (薛禪皇帝牛年聖旨)[31]. For the sake of comparison, a parallel Romanization of the same text in Written Mongol (modern orthography) is presented[32]. Line

[30] Coblin 2007, 49-52.

[31] No. 1 in Hugjiltu & Saruul 2004, 1-4; cf. also the commentaries to similar texts in Poppe 1957, 67-85.

[32] *Ibid.*, on the principles of Romanization, cf. Janhunen 2003.

breaks are shown by the slash (/). Presumablc mistakes or misreadings in the original text are corrected in square brackets.

vPhags.pa Mongol: **mong kha dieng ri yin khu cheu[n] dur / ye ke su ja li yin vi haven dur / qavan jar liq ma nu / che ri vu dun no yad da / che rig ha ra na / ba la qa dun da ru qas da no yad da yor / chi qun ya bu qun el chi ne davul qa qui / jar liq / jing gis qa nu ba qava nu ba jar liq dur do yid er khe vud sien shhi ngu[d] dash mad xa li ba / xal ba qub chi ri xeu lu xeu jen dieng ri yi jal ba ri ju hi ru ver xeo gun xa thu qa yi / - - -**

Written Mongol: **muivggae tvgri jiv guicu[v] dur / yagae suu jali jiv vibagav dur / qaqhav jarliq manu / carig ut uv nuyat da carig varan e / balqhat uv taruqhas da nuyat da yur/ciquv yabuquv vlcin e tuqhulqhaqui / jarliq / civggis qav u bae qaqhav u bae jarliq tur tujit vrgagut siyavshevg ut tashmat valibae / valbae qhubciri vuilu vuizav tvgri ji jalbarizu virugar vuigguv vaduqhai / - - -**

Notes on the notation. In the present paper, the systematic transliterations of all non-Roman scripts are quoted in boldface. Other Romanizations are quoted in pointed brackets (<>), while transcriptions and reconstructions of actual phonemes and phonemic sequences are quoted in Italics. Linguistic reconstructions are indicated by an asterisk (*), while 'readings' of items in non-Roman scripts are preceded by a cross (†). The syllable boundary of the regular Tibetan script is indicated by a period mark (.), while in the Romanization of the vPhags.pa script it is indicated by a space. Word boundaries are indicated only if they are marked in the original script.

Acknowledgement. The author thanks Dr. Michael Balk (Berlin) for comments and Dr. Wu Yingzhe (Huhhot) for supplying the vPhags.pa font used in the present paper. The font was designed at the Academy of Mongolian Studies, Inner Mongolia University.

Bibliography

Balk, M. 2005. 'On letters, words, and syllables: Transliteration and Romanization of the Tibetan script'. Online version: http://ead.staatsbibliothek-berlin.de/2005/bloomington.pdf.

Balk, M. & J. Janhunen 1999. 'A new approach to the Romanization of Written Mongol'. In: J. Janhunen & V. Rybatzki (eds), *Writing in the Altaic World.* (Studia Orientalia 87.) Helsinki, 17-27.

Bright, W. 1996. 'The Devanagari Script'. In: P. T. Daniels & W. Bright (eds), *The World's Writing Systems.* Oxford · New York, 384-390.

Coblin, W. S. 2007. *A Handbook of 'Phags-pa Chinese.* (ABC Dictionary Series.) Honolulu.

Damdinsuren [Damdinsueren], A. 1986. *Mongol doerwoeljin bichig.* Ulaanbaatar.

Hugjiltu 1999. 'On contraction in Mongolian h̲P'ags-pa documents'. In: J. Janhunen & V. Rybatzki (eds), *Writing in the Altaic World.* (Studia Orientalia 87.) Helsinki, 123-131.

Hugjiltu [Hugejiletu] & Saruul [Sarula] 2004. *Basibazi Mengguyu Wenxian Huibian.* (Aertaixue Congshu.) Huhehaote.

Janhunen, J. 2003. 'Written Mongol'. In: J. Janhunen (ed.), *The Mongolic Languages.* (Routledge Language Family Series 5.) London · New York, 30-56.

Junast [Zhaonasitu] 1990-91. *Basibazi he Mengguyu Wenxian.* I. *Yanjiu Wenji.* II. *Wenxue Huiji.* Tokyo.

Kara, G. 2005. *Books of the Mongolian Nomads: More than Eight Centuries of Writing Mongolian.* First English Edition. Translated from the Russian by John R. Krueger. (Indiana University Uralic and Altaic Series 171.) Bloomington.

van der Kuijp, L. W. J. 1996. 'The Tibetan script and derivatives'. In: P. D. Daniels & W. Bright (eds). *The World's Writing Systems.* New York · Oxford, 431-441.

Ligeti, L. 1972-73. *Monuments en écriture 'phags-pa. Pièces de chancellerie en transcription chinoise.* (Monumenta Linguae Mongolicae Collecta, vol. III. Indices Verborum Linguae Mongolicae Monumentis Traditorum, vol. III.) Budapest.

Luo Changpei & Cai Meibiao 2004. *Basibazi yu Yuandai Hanyu.* (Zengdingben.) Beijing.

Michalove, P. 2004. *A Guide to Reading Mongolian Texts in the 'Phags pa Script.* (The Mongolia Society Special Papers. Issue Fifteen.) Bloomington.

Poppe, N. 1957. *The Mongolian Monuments in ḫP'ags-pa Script.* Second Edition, translated and edited by John R. Krueger. (Göttinger Asiatische Forschungen 8.) Wiesbaden.

Rybatzki, V. 2003. 'Middle Mongol'. In: J. Janhunen (ed.), *The Mongolic Languages.* (Routledge Language Family Series 5.) London · New York, 57-82.

Tumurtogoo [Toemoertogoo], D. 2002. *Mongol doerwoeljin uesegiin durasxalyn sudalgaa: Udirdxal, ex bichig, uegsiin xelxee, nomzuei.* (Monuments in Mongolian Language II.) Ulaanbaatar.

Louis Kervyn, Joseph Mullie and the Beginnings of Khitan Studies

Daniel Kane

Everyone with any interest in Khitan knows that the field was initiated with an article by a Belgian priest, Father Louis Kervyn, published in the *Bulletin catholique de Pékin* in 1923. Kervyn's colleague, Joseph Mullie, sent a copy of the article to Pelliot, who published it in *T'oung Pao* in the same year. It was through this article that scholars came to know of the Khitan script, and it marks the beginnings of Khitan studies. Haneda[1] was quick to notice that the script in the Liao imperial tombs at Qingling, attached to Kervyn's article, was the same as the inscription on the stele in front of the tomb of Empress Wu in Xi'an, which was previously thought to be in Jurchen. Equally important was the fact that the inscription in Xi'an, generally known as the Langjun inscription, was clearly a bilingual. This led to many attempts to try to decipher the Liao imperial inscriptions on the basis of the Langjun inscription. This work has proceeded slowly but steadily, but there is still a long way to go. It has taken over eighty years to achieve even a partial translation of the Langjun inscription, and decipherment of the imperial epitaphs is still at its initial stages. Kervyn's article initiated this field. But apart from the fact that he was a Belgian missionary working in Inner Mongolia, practically nothing is known about Kervyn himself.

Louis Kervyn (Chinese name 梅嶺蕊 Mei Lingrui) was born at Hooglede, Belgium on the 3 March 1880. He was educated at the 'minor seminary' (the first four years of high school) at Brugges from 1893-1899. One of his fellow students was Antoine Mostaert, later to achieve fame for his researches into Mongol language and culture. Joseph Mullie was a few years younger. However, as Aubin[2] noted, the CICM congregation at that time prized only missionary achievement, and in no way encouraged intellectual work. It was not expected that Mostaert, Grootaers, Mullie, Henri Serruys, Paul Serruys and other CICM priests would distinguish themselves as scholars.

Kervyn entered the noviatiate of the CICM fathers in 1899. He studied philosophy at Scheut from 1900-05, and theology at the Louvaine Jesuit

[1] Haneda 1925.

[2] Aubin 1999, 31-45.

Seminary from 1902-05. He was ordained on 16 July, 1905 and departed for China on 27 September of the same year. He studied at the Songshuzuizi Language College from 1905-06, was made Deputy Parish Priest at Chaoyang from 1906-08 and Acting Parish priest of Tongjiayingzi from 1908-10.

During this time Kervyn made an enormous effort to compile a huge volume of nearly 900 pages, entitled *Méthode de l'Apostolat moderne en Chine*, which was published in Hong Kong in 1911[3]. The book was granted the *imprimatur* by the Bishop of Eastern Mongolia, Koenraad Abels. It was favourably reviewed (presumably by Mullie) in *Missions Catholiques* in 1912: "*La Méthode de l'apostolat moderne en Chine* est une oeuvre remarquable. Longtemps désirée par tous les missionaires d'Extrême-Orient, elle constitue, pour la première fois, à côté d'une multitude de publications protestantes du même genre, un traité vraiment professional des conditions dans lesquelles s'exerce actuallement la propagation du catholicisime de l'empire chinois ... Grâce à une rare sûreté de méthode et le logique, l'auteur a condensé dans son texte, l'expose substantiel et sans lacune grave de ce qu'il faut savoir... Sur toutes ces questions palpitance d'intérêt de controversées entre missionaires, l'auteur répand de vives lumières avec une surprenante profondeur de coup d'oeil..."[4]. However, as Aubin remarked[5], readers of the late twentieth century feel a sense of discomfort even from reading the table of contents. The mandarinate is a "regime of corruption", a "regime of incompetents", a "regime without honour", "slaves of superstition" and so on. Chapter headings include "pride", "immorality", "egoism", "materialism" and the like, leading to the conclusion that the Chinese are "of an inferior nature". The Chinese clergy also suffer from certain congenital defects: a lack of a sense of administration, ambition for promotion to high office, lack of generosity and so on. Even almost a century after its publication, it is occasionally mentioned as a "negative example". A recent example is Pierre Lefebvre: "A large tome published by Fr. L. Kervyn in Hongkong claimed that «the nature of the Chinese expresses itself in a singular poverty of resources, of virtues and of natural qualities». He asserted that the «indigenous» priests should have «at least the humility or the good spirit to perform the appropriately narrow and minor ministry which is their due, instead of envying the privileges of the immediate superiors and to encroach on their rights and refuse to take

[3] Kervyn 1911.
[4] Quoted in van Hecken 1972, 111-113.
[5] Aubin 2000, 175-176.

directions from them»"[6]. The general aim of Lefebvre's article is to explain that the missionaries saw themselves as part of the *mission civilisatrice*, and the Chinese as "the Other". The way they perceived 'the Other' may appear offensive to people of a later generation, but such was the intellectual and social milieu in which they worked.

It is clear from many contemporary writings that Kervyn was not alone in these attitudes. However, it did not take the sensibility of the late twentieth century to realise the extraordinary offensiveness of this book, even by the standards of the early twentieth century. Van Hecken notes that "there was nevertheless much criticism of this work, and it was declared *taboo* by some people because of the unfavourable description of Chinese customs. The *Missions Catholoqies* gave Kervyn's response to this criticism: "Le R. P. Kervyn … remercie vivement les missionaires qui ont signalé les lacunes et les défauts de son livre, *Méthode* etc. et leur annonce que l'ouvrage sera remanié à leur entière satisfaction". As van Henken noted[7], this never happened. Van Henken goes on to say that this work "has not always been highly appreciated" by modern missionaries, but that the mentality of missionaries has evolved since Kervyn's day.

Despite its value as a collection of documents on the history of the Church in China, including various imperial edicts and with relevant Chinese characters given in the text, it was removed from the libraries of the CICM libraries, and CICM students training for missionary work in China in the 1920s barely heard of it.[8]

It is not known what effect this episode might have had on Kervyn's career, his relations with his fellow missionaries or his reputation in China. He was recalled to Scheut in September 1912 to lecture in philosophy, and to work in the archives. He was posted back to Eastern Mongolia in September 1913, to a number of posts in fairly rapid succession. In 1919 he was appointed *curé* in Haobaotu (號保圖), the most northern and most desolate of the CICM missions in Eastern Mongolia. At one stage an assistant was sent to keep him company, but that arrangement did not last. He stayed there until 1932, living more or less as a hermit. In his obituary we read, "In this rigorous climate, in this solitude, he was like a hermit in the Sahara, a man who prepared for the conversion of the Mongols in the milieu in which they lived. He also attracted to himself poor Chinese families who had come to find in these northern regions a corner of the earth to eke out a bare existence." Whether or not he went there

[6] Lefebvre 2002.

[7] van Henken 1972, 113-114.

[8] Aubin 2000, 161-184.

voluntarily, or was more or less in exile, is not clear from the records. Haobaotu is 140 *li* to the north of Dayingzi, the location of the Qingling tombs, and 150 *li* from the prefecture of Linxi (Balin), the site of the Liao Supreme Capital.

At that time, of course, neither Kervyn nor anyone else knew that. However, another Belgian priest, Joseph Mullie, had been on the track of the location of the Liao Supreme Capital and the Liao tombs for more than a decade. Mullie visited Baitazi in 1911 and 1912, but the local mandarin assured him he had seen no Khitan inscriptions there. The study of the travel notes of Chinese travellers to the Khitans translated by Chavannes[9] led Mullie to a second visit to Balin in 1920. He also visited Baitazi, where he was shown a large subterranean cave full of water, in which the roofs of some buildings could be seen, and around which were the ruins of other buildings. Mullie suspected the Liao imperial tombs might be found under the water, but there was no way to access whatever it was. Mullie noted that "the Christians in Haobaotu" in 1920 knew that there was an underground cavern full of water near Baitazi. The location stood well with the historical texts. Mullie came to the conclusion that Baitazi was not the Supreme Capital of the Liao, but Qingzhou, the location of the imperial tombs. Presumably Kervyn came to know of Mullie's views at this time.

Mullie wrote up the results of his research in a very substantial article, "Les Anciennes Villes de l'Empire des Grands Leao au royaume Mongol de Bārin", published in *T'oung-Pao* in 1922. In the same year, local Chinese decided to try to get at the treasures they presumed to be in the imperial tomb.

At this point in the story one cannot help but recall the Chinese proverb about "the old man at the mountain pass lost his horse: how was he to know this was not his good fortune". It was the hermit of Haobaotu, Louis Kervyn, in exile either self imposed or otherwise, who was on the spot when the local Chinese decided to open the tomb to access whatever treasures might be in it. It is certainly to Kervyn's credit that he hurried to the site of the excavations. His article published in the *Bulletin catholique de Pékin* makes exciting reading. Kervyn thought the tomb belonged to Daozong, thus the title. Mullie later pointed out that the tomb must have been that of Shengzong, the emperor preceding Daozong. Kervyn remarks that the local people suspected there were 'treasures of inestimable value' in the cave. Mullie suggests it was *he* who gave them the idea that the cave might contain a tomb of a Liao emperor. As Kervyn related the series of events, "In the spring of the year 1922 it occurred to the Chinese, who had

---

[9] Chavannes 1897-98.

settled not far from this Mongol territory, to try to get their hands on these treasures … The tomb was a vast subterranean chamber, build into a mountain of granite. It was full of water. The cave was about 5.5-5.6 metres deep, and about 9 metres across. The top of an ornamental gate with an imperial dragon was on the northern side. The grave robbers tried to siphon out the water, but had to resort to using buckets, which took many days. Eventually they found only a lot of debris, which also had to be cleared away. To their distress, it was clear that it had been pillaged before. The coffin of the emperor was found, opened, in the last chamber. His skeleton, deprived of its head, was strewn on the ground. Not having found any treasures, the grave robbers decided to take the wood used for the imperial coffins, which could fetch a high price."

Kervyn followed these excavations from a distance, but he knew from "un confrère familiarisé avec l'étude du *Leao-che*" (presumably Mullie) that some "documents" should be found in the emperor's tomb. Kervyn must have been referring to the epitaphs. But, as Kervyn went on, "How to get ones hands on them? On the one hand, the circumstances of the opening of the tomb were seen in a bad light, but from a linguistic and archaeological point of view the [texts] were invaluable". The grave robbers had been chased away by Mongol soldiers at the beginning of their work, but returned after the danger had disappeared. They quarrelled amongst themselves, government soldiers threatened to stop their work, eventually Chinese soldiers sent by the Magistrate of Linxi (who wanted to exploit the tomb for his own benefit) arrested the ringleaders and detained them in the local *yamen*. Taking advantage of the lull in the grave robbing, Kervyn arranged for three Chinese to copy the inscriptions of the texts engraved on four stelae which were discovered at the bottom of the mud. The three were not strong enough to lift the stelae, which Kervyn estimated to weigh 600-600 kilograms. They were about six metres from ground level, and it was not possible to bring them to the surface where they could be photographed. None of the Chinese copyists knew how to make a rubbing, so they had to copy them by hand, one unfamiliar character at a time. The job had to be done accurately, and lasted five days. After two days, the grave robbers, having been released from jail, returned to the tomb. The three copyists had to take precautions. While one sat perched above the inscription, copying stroke by stroke, his two companions guarded him with drawn daggers.

Two of the stelae were in Chinese, two in Khitan. The Khitan inscriptions were 583 and 856 words in length. The stelae were four feet wide and 8 inches thick. To protect them they were covered with stones of equal size, and the two separated by coins with the reign title *Qingning yuannian* (1055-56) and *Dakang* (1095-85). "The discovery was marvellous. A real treasure had been unearthed in China. Eventually, when everything of any value, including the wood for the coffins, had been removed, the grave robbers left. The stelae were recovered with earth, and water began to seep into the cave again. The water of the mountain regained its rights in this old subterranean empire."

Mullie sent Kervyn's article to Pelliot, who published most of it (without the photographs) in *T'oung-Pao,* thus making the discovery known to the scholarly world at large. A photo of one of the Khitan inscriptions was attached to Kervyn's article in the *Bulletin catholique de Pékin.* Immediately after its publication, Mullie wrote a long article, "Les Sépultures de K'ing des Leao", providing a partial translation of the Chinese inscription with a detailed philological, geographical and historical commentary. He also included photographs of both Khitan inscriptions and the text of four Chinese inscriptions. (The photographs in Kervyn's original article were not reproduced in the *T'oung-Pao* reprint, apparently for technical reasons.) Mullie sent his article to Pelliot in 1924. However, it was apparently lost in Pelliot's library, and not found until 1931. It eventually appeared in *T'oung-Pao* in 1932 with a photo of a rubbing of a third inscription, provided by Tang Zuozong to Mullie in 1931. In 1930 Tang Zuozong, the son of Tang Yulin, the governor of Rehe, removed the four inscriptions from the tomb of Daozong and Xuanyi, and had them transferred to Mukden (Shenyang). Mullie explained that he had been waiting in vain for rubbings of the stelae discovered at Qingling, but water had invaded the tomb and it was not possible to repeat the long and costly work which the Chinese undertook in 1921. He goes on to say that "through the intermediary of Reverend Father L. Kervyn, the curate of Haobaotu to the south of Baitazi (the Qingzhou of the Liao), I received however a copy of the two Khitan steles and three Chinese steles." Mullie went on to mention Kervyn's article in the *Bulletin catholique.* He pointed out that the tomb could not have been that of Daozong, as Kervyn thought, but of Shengzong and his two wives, Rende and Qin'ai. He says Kervyn had been misled by the dates on the coins separating the epitaphs from their covers, from the Qingning and Dakang periods. Mullie notes, "Here there is an obvious mistake. On the coins, of which I have been able to make a hastily traced copy, there are the following characters: *Qingning yuanbao* and *Dakang tongbao:* the words *yuanbao* and *tongbao* indicate clearly that these are coins. They were sold to a goldsmith in Chifeng county; only two were able to escape from the melting pot." Again, there is more to this than meets the eye, as we shall see from some excerpts from Mullie's diary given below.

Mullie went on to say, "Reading Kervyn, one has the impression that the people of that area knew for generations the history of Qingzhou and of Qingling. That is by no means the case. One can ask in vain a local Mongol or Chinese the name of the ruins of Baitazi, but no one can answer. Some individuals learnt of the historical significance of Qingzhou and Qingling since the excavations began at Bārin … The guides who accompanied me in my visit to Qingling in 1919 were naturally intrigued by the numerous vestiges of superb monuments and above all the presence of the room of water in the mountain. This room of water, of which the local Christians had already advised Reverend Father L. Heyns, curate of Dayingzi (Bārin) … was itself the main cause of my excursion in the valley Warīn maňga. To establish that Baitazi was indeed Qingzhou and not Shangjing, it was necessary to find the Qingling tombs, because there was no Qingzhou without Qingling. From the first question on the subject of ancient tombs in the environs of Baitazi, Father Heyns told me about this famous room of water, of which people had told him many beautiful things. This indication gave me the hope to find the Qingling tombs there. I was not deceived. In running through the ruins of Baitazi, and those of Qingling, which excited general curiosity, my guides made all possible suppositions, to laugh about them five minutes later. Evidently they could not help thinking what interest these ruins might have for me, and by way of conversation they asked me questions. I would not say that their intention was to know the objective truth, but I had no reason to hide my opinion about Baitazi and its environs, especially as they showed themselves very devoted, and gave me from their side very useful information on the country, which they had run through in the course of their hunting. *This 'indiscretion' on my part ran its course,* (emphasis added) and two years later, in 1922, when two successive bad harvests introduced hard conditions, even famine at certain families, some remembered Qingling, because they hoped to find there the means to procure some money to buy the food which was lacking in so many hearths."

Mullie's article was sober scholarship, and a reassertion of his sinological acumen, historical research and actual fieldwork. But in Kervyn's article one can still feel the sense of excitement of discovery, and the realisation that this was a find of great value. Yet Kervyn was never to mention the matter again, at least not in any of his books or articles. One can only wonder why. Some clues to this may be found in the diaries of Joseph Mullie preserved in the KADOC archives. The following entries are relevant:

17 July 1922. Oude sapeken gevonden om te identificeren. (Old coins found, to be identified.)

10 December 1922. P. Dewolf ook gepasseered, & L. Kervyn, L. Heyns & Raf Verbois, L. Kervyn had sapeken uit de keizerlijke K'itangraven (Barin) mee. Eischte 27$ voor 27 stuk: anders scheur ik er mijn broek aan. Had ze mij eerst verkocht aan 0.10$ per stuk. Hij verkocht ze te Hata aan een zilversmid en ze werden gesmolten. (Fr. Dewolf also came by, together with L. Kervyn, L. Heyns and Raf Verbois. L. Kervyn had some coins from the royal Khitan tombs (at Barin) with him. He demanded $27 for 27 pieces. Otherwise I would be tearing my trousers. (Cf. I would be ripped off: I would suffer a financial loss). They had first been offered at 10 cents each. He sold them in Hada to a silversmith, and they were melted.)

23 June 1923. P. L Kervyn verkocht mij de K'itanopschriften (een alschaft) en geeft ze dan zelf uit! Vraagt foto's ...? Om uit te geven? Wie betaalt? (Fr. L. Kervyn sold me the Khitan incriptions and then published them himself! He asked about the photos…? So as to publish them? Who is paying?)

10 December 1923. De 2 K'itan pei's laten fotografeeren in de staadt. 't is duur. (I had the two Khitan stelae photographed in the city. It was expensive.)

26 May, 1924. P. Schotte vraagt foto van de K'itan opschiften voor 't museum. (Fr. Schotte asked for a photo of the Khitan inscriptions for the museum.)

There do not seem to be any further diary entries after that. Mullie was called back to Belgium to teach in 1926. From these entries we can derive the following insights:

(1) Kervyn sold Mullie photographs of the Khitan inscriptions, and then published them himself. Mullie was writing for *T'oung-Pao,* Kervyn for the *Bulletin catholique de Pékin*. Mullie was clearly angry that Kervyn had published the photos after having sold them to him. Mullie had been working on the location of the Liao tombs for years. Kervyn 'scooped' him in a local publication.

(2) Kervyn offered to sell Mullie some silver coins from the tombs, at a price ten times what had apparently been agreed to before. Mullie did not buy the coins. So Kervyn sold them to a silversmith and they were melted down for the value of the silver. Mullie does not say what happened to the proceeds of this sale.

In addition to *Méthode,* Kervyn published a number of other books, mainly of a devotional or ethnographical nature, and eighteen articles[10]. His obituary[11] says he also published many articles under pseudonyms, because "Fr. Kervyn wanted above all else to pass his life unnoticed". Only one article was on the Liao tombs; two if one includes the reprint in *T'oung-Pao.* After these, Kervyn seems never to have mentioned this discovery again. Amongst Kervyn's later publications, from the point of view of the present article, the most interesting is *L'Empire chinois et les Barbares,* published in Beijing in 1933 as part of a series *Politique de Pékin*. In this booklet of 74 pages, which covers China's relations with the Xiongnu, Khitans, Jurchens, Mongols and Manchus, four pages are devoted to the Liao. Kervyn notes the early references to them in the Chinese histories, the rise of Abaoji, the establishment and expansion of the Liao state and its relations with the Song, the Koreans and the Tanguts. He notes the rise of the Jurchens and the eventual defeat of the Liao. But there is not a single word in this book about the discovery of the Liao tombs at Qingling, or the Khitan script, or any reference to the significance of that discovery.

Mullie left China in 1926 to become one of the major figures in European sinology. He was eventually awarded the Medal of Commander of the Order of Orange-Nassau by the Queen of the Netherlands (1956); elected to the Royal Flemish Academy (1955) and Grand Officer of the Order of Leopold (1958). He retired from the Academy in 1972 and was appointed Honorary Member of the Academy in the same year.

Kervyn stayed in Haobaotu until 1932, when the mission passed from the hands of the CICM fathers to another order. He was posted to Chaoyang, in Rehe, succeeding his brother, Joseph. Kervyn's health continued to deteriorate, and he was transferred to Xiaomiao'ergou (小廟兒溝). He had few duties, and spent most of his time in the church praying for others. He died there on the 24 January, 1939. A brief obituary[12] appeared in the journal *Missions de Scheut*:

> "In 1905, he embarked for the Diocese of Eastern Mongolia where his brother Joseph was already working. During the 33 years which he passed in this area, most of his time was spent in the ministry of various Christian communities, except during the period from 1908 to 1909, during which he taught theology in the seminary at Songshuzuizi. Even before he had heard of Fr. de Foucauld, Fr.

[10] Grootaers & van Coillie 1939, 57-58.
[11] *In Memoriam* 1939.
[12] *Ibid.*

> Kervyn chose a life of prayer and penance as the main means of conversion. He was deeply convinced of the impotence of the missionary to lead even a single soul to the faith. Trusting in the merciful aid of God, he consecrated many hours to prayer every day, and led a life extraordinary for its poverty and mortification. From 1919 to 1932, he was *curé* at Haobaotu, the most northerly and most distant mission in the Parish of Rehe. In this rigorous climate, in this solitude, he was like a hermit in the Sahara, a man who prepared for the conversion of the Mongols in the milieu in which they lived. He also attracted to himself poor Chinese families who had come to find in these northern regions a corner of the earth to eke out a bare existence. Father Kervyn was spiritually gifted, and wanted to leave his *confrères* the fruits of his meditations and his readings of the Holy Fathers. He edited two works: *Acts of Grace after the Holy Mass* and *The Priestly Blessing*, which give witness to a life of intense spirituality. We are also indebted to him for his work and his erudition on various studies of ethnology, which were published in journals such as *Politique de Pékin, Missions catholiques* and others. Most of the time these works were published under a pseudonym, because Fr. Kervyn wanted above all else to pass his life unnoticed. He continued his life of study, prayer and penance until the end. Only God knows how many souls his virtues gained for the Church. Like Moses praying on the mountain and obtaining victory for the Israelites fighting on the plain, Fr. Kervyn was the unknown aide of many missionaries who were struggling with the numerous difficulties of the practical apostolate. His prayers surely obtained the grace of Heaven for many pagans which led them to the Church of Christ."

In this obituary, there is not a word about *Méthode,* the tome of nearly 900 pages, nor about Kervyn's articles about the Liao tombs, or the Khitan inscriptions, the main reason his name is remembered today.

In a seminar paper entitled "De K'i-Tan inscripties van de graven der Liao-dynastie (907-1125)" given to the Eighth Congress of the Oriental Association of the Netherlands, held in Leiden from 6-8 January, 1936, Mullie discussed the circumstances of the discovery of the inscriptions. Here he revealed that he sent Pelliot a copy of Kervyn's article, who reproduced most of it but without the photograph, and that he had written another article which he sent to Pelliot in 1924. This, however, was mislaid in Pelliot's library, and was not found until 1931, and was eventually published in *T'oung-Pao* in 1933. Mullie summarised his own researches, in particular his having located the location of the Liao tombs, and mentions in passing that Kervyn was able to obtain some rubbings of the Khitan inscriptions from the tombs after they had been opened by grave robbers. Professor Duyvendak "made some observations, and expressed his appreciation of the initiative of Prof. Mullie, who is to be thanked for the discovery of the Liao inscriptions".[13]

It is ironic that *Méthode*, the work which the young Kervyn presumably thought would be his *magnum opus*, was consigned to oblivion except for an occasional negative mention, whereas the article on the Khitan inscriptions for which he is most remembered seems to have been one which he either regarded as of no importance, or which he preferred not to mention. The biographical and bibliographical sketch compiled by the Kervyn family[14] mentions several of Kervyn's books, but not his article on the Liao tombs. Kervyn's article will still be justly remembered for its announcement of the discovery of stelae in the Khitan script, but Kervyn only knew about the location of the Liao tombs due to the exhaustive researches of Mullie. Kervyn was the man on the spot, and arranged for copies of the stelae to be made: this was his great contribution. But Mullie's research paved the way. It is equally ironic that Kervyn's article, which Mullie probably regarded as a footnote to his own two scholarly articles, is now mentioned in almost every study of Khitan, while Mullie's works on this discovery are mentioned rarely.

We can conclude that the discovery of the location of the tombs can be attributed to Mullie, the excavations done by grave robbers, and the initiative in arranging for copies to be made of the Khitan inscriptions to Kervyn. Merit for the discovery and publication of the first Khitan inscriptions belongs to all.

Bibliography

Aubin, F. 1999. 'The young Father Mostaert's Forerunners'. In: K. Sagaster (ed.), *Louvain Chinese Studies IV, Antoine Mostaert (1881-1971), C.I.C.M. Missionary and Scholar* · Volume One: Papers. Leuven, 31-45.

— 2000. 'Quelques échoes des prêtres chinois dans les missions de Scheut (Mongolie-Interiéure et Chine occidentale, Dix-neuvième-vingtième siècles)'. In: K. De Ridder (ed.), *Footsteps in Deserted Valleys - Missionary Cases, Strategies and Practice in Qing China*. (Louvain Chinese Studies VIII.) Leuven, 175-176.

Chavannes, E. 1897-98. 'Voyageurs Chinois chez les Khitan et les Jouchen'. *Journal Asiatique,* Ser. 9/9, 377-422; Ser. 9/11, 361-439.

[13] Concluding comments to Mullie 1936, 59.

[14] Kervyn de Meerendré 1978.

Grootaers, W. A. & D. van Coillie 1939. *Proeve eener Bibliographie van de Missionarissen van Scheut*. Brussels, 57-58.

Haneda Toru 1925. 'Kittan moji no shin shiryō' [New materials for the study of the Khitan script]. *Shirin* X/1. [Reproduced in *Haneda Hakushi shigaku rombusho* (Collected articles on history by Doctor Haneda), Vol. II. Kyoto 1957, 420-434.]

'In Memoriam R.P. Louis Kervyn'. *Missions de Scheut* No. 2, February 1939, 60.

Kervyn, L. 1911. *Méthode de l'Apostolat Moderne en Chine*. Hongkong.

— 1923. 'Le tombeau de l'empereur Tao-tsong (1101), une découverte intéressante'. *Bulletin catholique de Pékin* X/118, 236-243, 2 photos.

— 1923. 'Le tombeau de l'empereur Tao-tsong des Leao et les premières inscriptions connues en écriture K'i-tan'. *T'oung-Pao* XXII, 292-301.

— 1933. *L'Empire chinois et les Barbares*. Pékin.

Kervyn de Meerendré, H. *Des Kervyn dans l'Eglise. Fragments biographiques rassemblés pour l'Association Kervyn*. [Privately printed, June 1978.]

Lefebvre, P. 2002. 'L'Autre dans la tradition missionaire récente'. *Expérience et recherches missionaires* 168/September. [Reproduced SEDOS Bulletin (www.sedos.org).]

Mullie, J. 1922. 'Les Anciennes Villes de l'Empire des Grands Leao 大遼 au Royaume Mongol de Bārin'. *T'oung-Pao* XXI, 105-231.

— 1933. 'Les Sépultures de K'ing des Leao'. *T'oung-Pao* XXX, 1-25.

— (no date). 'De K'i-Tan inscripties van de graven de Liao-dynastie (907-1125)'. Oostersch genootschap in Nederland, *Verslag van het Achtste Congres*. Leiden, 6-8 January 1936, 57-59.

van Hecken, J. 1972. *Documentatie betreffende de Missiegeschiednis van Oost-Mongolia, Je-Ho-Erh*, Deel VII. Leuven, 111-113.

SUR QUELQUES VERS DU BODHICARYĀVATĀRA MONGOL

György Kara

La version mongole du *Bodhicaryāvatāra* (ou *Bodhisattva-caryāvatāra-saṃskāra*) de Śāntideva, poème qui comprime 913 quatrains, est un des plus importants monuments bouddhiques du moyen mongol. Traduit du tibétain par Chos-kyi 'od-zer au début du XIVe siècle, xylographié plusieurs fois sous les Yuan, il fut remanié par l'érudit Biligtü güši des Urat au XVIIIe siècle (qui changea surtout l'orthographe ancienne), puis incorporé dans le Tanjur mongol imprimé durant le même siècle. M. Igor de Rachewiltz a publié ce texte, le *Bodhi-saduva-nar-un yabudal-dur oroqui neretü šastir,* en transcription avec une introduction, l'index des mots et le fac-similé en 1996. Ce qui suit ici est une petite contribution à l'étude du *Bodhicaryāvatāra* mongol, où j'offre des corrections et l'interprétation de quelques passages du texte du Tanjur mongol imprimé, en les comparant avec leur source, la traduction tibétaine *Byang chub sems dpa'i spyod pa la 'jug pa* (selon l'édition de F. Weller et Mdo 'grel, vol. XXVI, La, de l'édition mandchoue du Tanjur tibétain).

Voici la liste des mots et expressions que je vais examiner:

ülügü = *ülü'ü,* négatif préverbal des formes imparfaites et futures avec la particule interrogatif dans les strophes IV 2, 45; VI 60; IX 49, au lieu de *ülükü,* le même négatif avec la particule emphatique *kü*.

esegü = *ese'ü,* négatif préverbal des formes parfaites avec la particule interrogatif dans les strophes VII 4, 5; IX 130, au lieu de *esekü,* forme emphatique (mais voir *ese kü* dans IV 13d).

ögkü, forme du future de *ög-* 'donner', dans II 59, au lieu de *ükükü* < *ükü-* 'mourir'.

eregüd-ün küčün-iyer 'par la force de (mes) fautes' au lieu de *erkes-ün küčün-iyer* 'par la force de (mes) droits' dans IV 13.

buyuly-a 'joug' (cf. khalkha *buulga*) dans IV 20.

an 'étant', adverbe modal de *a-* 'être', dans VI 61a *amidu an bögetele,* au lieu de *ene* 'ceci'.

amidu-bar, instrumental, dans VI 61d *amidu-bar aǰu yayun kereg,* au lieu de *amidu ber* etc.

budungγui 'obscur' (cf. khalkha *budangui* 'obscur; obscurité' et mong. *budang* 'brouillard') et *bolila-* 'cesser' (itératif < *boli-*) dans la strophe VIII 185, au lieu de *bodongγui* (cf. mong. *bodo-* 'penser') et *bulila-*'forcer, employer la force'.

edüged-ün dans les strophes II 54, 57: tib. *tha mal* 'ordinaire, habituel' (mais voir *edüged-tür* dans IX 46ab[1]).

tegetele yaγun 'pourquoi transférer?' dans VI 45.

yasutan 'ceux qui ont des os ...' au lieu de *ǰasutan*[2] dans X 10

kölgen tanu au lieu de *kölgeten-ü* dans X 49.

II 54, selon le manuscrit de Delhi, f. 7b, ll. 26-30

edüged-ün ebečin-eče ayubasu (ber) **:** ota=čiyin ügeber yabuqu kereg bolbasu el-e **:** tačiyangγui terigüten ǰaγun gem-ün ebečin-e kürtegsen-i d̲aki ügüle=d̲ele yaγun **::**

Même si l'on craint une maladie ordinaire, il faut suivre la parole du médecin. Alors qu'est-ce que l'on peut dire de celui qui a la maladie de cent vices, tout d'abord *la maladie de* l'attachement passionné?

Mdo 'grel |tha mal nad kyis 'jigs na yang| |sman pa'i ngag bzhin bya dgos na| |'dod changs la sogs nyes brgya yi| |nad kyis rtag btab smos ci dgos|

II 57

üčüken edüged-ün ergi nuras-ača ber **:** uqaǰu sereǰü aγdaqu bögetele **:** mingγan nur-a-dur [= ber-e-dür] kürtele unaǰu odqu **:** öni ergi nur-a-yi taki yaγun ügületele **::**[3]

Si l'on doit faire attention avec précaution *au bord* des petites précipices ordinaires, qu'est-ce que l'on peut dire de la précipice qui dure et dans laquelle on peut tomber jusqu'à mille lieues?

---

[1] Tanjur: *edüged-tür yabuγči kümün tačiyangγui* **:** *maγad teden-e ügei kemebesü* **:** *'Si celui qui va dit qu'il est sûr que ceux (susmentionnés) n'ont pas d'attachement exagéré ...', mais voir le manuscript de Delhi, f. 46b, ll. 2-5: *edüged-d̲ür abuγči tačiyangγui* **:** *maγad teden-e ügei kemebesü* **:** 'Si l'on dit qu'il est sûr que ceux-là n'ont pas d'attachement exagéré qui occupe proprement ...', traduction des vers tibétains *re zhig nyer len sred pa ni| |med ces nges pa nyid ce na|* où *nyer len* 'action de prendre proprement' (aussi 'la cause des causes', etc., mong. *čiqula abulγ-a*) semble être, selon l'interprétation mongole, l'attribut de *sred pa* (mong. *tačiyangγui*) 'attachement exagéré'.

[2] Ou *ǰisüten* 'ceux qui ont un certain teint, visage, etc.'.

[3] Manuscrit de Delhi, 8a ll. 7-11: *üčügüken edüged-ün ergi nura-a ber* **:** *uqaǰu sereǰü aγdaqu bögetele* **:** *mingγan bere-dür kürtele unaǰu odqui* **:** *öni ergi nurasi d̲aki yaγun ügületele* **::**

Mdo 'grel |g.yang sa tha mal chung ngu la'ang| |bag yod gnas par bya dgos na| |dpag tshad stong du lhung ba yi| yun ring g.yang sar smos ci dgos|

II 58

ene edür böged ülü ükükü kemen : nuta saγuqu yosutu busu bui : minu nögčiküi ükükü tere čaγ : saγar ügei maγad böged iren bui ::

En disant qu'aujourd'hui je ne mourrai pas, il n'est pas convenable que je sois en repos. Mon temps de décéder, de mourir, arrivera certainement, sans tarder.

Mdo 'grel |de ring kho na mi 'chi zhes| |bde bar 'dug pa rigs ma yin| |bdag ni med par 'gyur pa'i dus| |de ni gdon mi za bar 'byung|[4]

II 59

nada ken ber ögkü [*xyl.*: 'wkwkwy][5] ayul ügey-yi : egün-eče kerkiǰü maγad tonilqu bi : saγar ügei ükün bögetele : kerkin nuta saγumui bi ::[6]

Qui me donnera l'intrépidité (*ou* la sécurité)? Comment pourrai-je m'échapper d'ici avec sûreté? Alors que je mourrai sans doute, comment *pourrai* je rester calme?

Mdo 'grel |bdag la mi 'jigs su yis sbyin| |'di las ji ltar nges thar zhes| |gdon mi za bar med 'gyur na| |ci phyir bdag yid bde bar 'dug|

II 60

urida bolǰu bütüǰü nögčigsen-eče : ülekü inu edüge nadur yaγun bui kemen : bi teden-dür quričan tačiyaǰu bür-ün : baγši-yin ǰarliγ-luγ-a qarsilabai ::[7]

Si je dis: «De ce qui est achevé auparavant, *mais* qui est passé, qu'est-ce qui me reste maintenant?» - et si je suis passionnément attaché à telles choses, j'ai violé le précepte du Maître.

Mdo 'grel |sngon chad myong ste zhig pa las| |bdag la lhag pa ci yod na| |bdag ni de la sngon zhen nas| |bla ma'i bka' dang 'gal bar byas|

---

[4] Finot II 59: «La mort ne viendra pas aujourd'hui!» Fausse sécurité! Elle vient inexorablement, l'heure où je ne serai plus.

[5] Ligeti: *ükükü* [= *ögkü*]. Le manuscrit de Delhi a une autre forme erronée.

[6] Ms. de Delhi, f. 8a, ll.16-19: *nada ken ber ögkü* [ms: 'wykb'kw] *ayul ügey-yi* : *egün-eče kerkiǰü maγad tonilqu bi* : *saγar ügei ükün bögetele* : *kerkin nuta saγumu bi* ::

[7] Delhi MS f. 8a, ll. 19-23: *urida bolǰu bütüǰü nögčigsen-eče : ülekü inu edüge nadur yaγun bui kemen : bi teden-ṯür quričaǰu tačiyaǰu bürün : baγši=yin ǰarliγ-i* [*ms.*: y'r'yq-y] *köndebei* ::

II 61

enegeken qalaγun amin kiged tegünčilen : öri sadud nököd-iyen tebčiǰü bür-ün : qaγus-iyar γaγčaγar odqu ele bolbasu : amaralduqun ülüldükün-ü kereg inu γaγun ::

Si l'on *doit* quitter cette même vie précieuse, les parents et les amis, et *doit* aller, tout seul, dans incertitude, à quoi bon faire des amis et des ennemis?

Mdo 'grel |gson tshe 'di dang de bzhin du| |gnyen dang bshes pa rnams spangs nas| |gcig pu ga shed 'gro dgos na| |mdza' dang mi mdza' kun ci rung|

IV 2-3

ečüs-iyer tuγurbin ǰasaγsan üile be : taki ken ber sayitur ülü qadan : aman aldan baribasu [= barabasu] ele : üiledkü-gü ülü-gü kemen qadaγdaqu bögetele :: yeke bilig-ten burqad kiged : bodhi-saduva-nar onoǰu qadaǰu bür-ün : öber-iyer ber basa basa onoγsan : tegün-i taki talbitala yaγun ::[8]

Même si l'on a promis d'accomplir une action commencée en hâte (*lit.* de la fin), sans mûre réflexion, on doit réfléchir s'il faut la faire ou ne pas *faire*. Néanmoins on ne doit pas abandonner ce qui est examiné et réfléchi par les très sages Bouddhas et par les Bodhisattvas, et que l'on a examiné à plusieurs reprises.

Mdo 'grel |bab col brtsams pa gang yin pa'am| |gang zhig legs par ma brtags pa| |de ni dam bcas byas gyur kyang| |bya 'am gtang zhes brtag pa'i rigs| |sangs rgyas rnams dang de'i sras| |shes rab chen pos gang brtags shing| |bdag nyid kyis kyang brtag brtags pa| |de la bshol du ci zhig yod|

IV 13

qamuγ amitan-a tusa kürgegčin[9] : toγ-a tomsi ügei burqad[10] nögčibesü ber : bi öber-ün eregüs-ün[11] küčün-iyer : teden-e emčilegdekü ber ese bolba ::

---

[8] Manuscrit de Delhi, f. 10b, ll. 23-27: *ečüs-iyer tuγurbin ǰasaγsan üile be : d̲aki ken ber sayitur ülü qadan : aman aldan barabasu el-e : üiled=kügü ülü-gü kemen qadaγdaqu bögetel-e :: yeke bilig-d̲en burqad kiged bodisung*[= *bodistv*]*-nar : onoǰu qadaǰu bürün : öber-iyen basa basa onoγsan : tegün-i d̲aki talbi=d̲al-a yaγun ::*

[9] Tanjur: *kürgegčid,* pluriel plus récent que *kürgegčin.*

[10] Tanjur: *burqan.*

[11] Tanjur: *erkes-ün* au lieu de *eregüd,* plur. de *eregü* 'faute, défaut, vice; crime' = tib. *nyes pa.*

Bien que d'innombrables Bouddhas, ceux qui rendent service à tous les êtres vivants, aient passés, je n'ai pas pu, par la force de mes fautes, être guéri par eux.

Mdo 'grel |sems can thams cad phan mdzad pa'i| |sangs rgyas grangs med 'das gyur kyang| |bdag ni rang gi nyes pas de'i| |gso ba'i spyod yul ma gyur to|

IV 20

tegün-ü tulada ilaǰu tegüs nögčigsen : yeke dalai-daki keyisügči buγulγ-a[12] modun-u : nüken-dür yasutu menekey-yin küǰügün učiraqui-dur adali : kümün-ü bey-e masi olquy-a berke kemen nomlaǰuγui ::

C'est pourquoi le Bhagavat a prêché qu'il est très difficile à obtenir une existence (*lit.* corps) humaine, de même *qu'il est difficile* que le cou d'une tortue se trouve par hasard dans l'orifice d'un joug de bois qui flotte sur le Grand Océan.

Mdo 'grel |de nyid phyir na bcom ldan gyis| |rgya mtsho chen g.yengs gnya shing gi| |bu gar rus sbal mgrin chud ltar| |mi nyid shin tu thob dkar gsungs|

IV 42

öber-ün čaγ-iyan ülü meden : aman aldan ügülekün γalǰaγu ülügü bui [:] tegüber nisvanis-i daruquy-ača : nasu aburida ülü ičuγdaqui ::

Ne sont-ils pas fous ceux qui font des promesses sans savoir *la mesure de* leur propre temps? C'est pourquoi on ne doit jamais renoncer à vaincre les passions.

Mdo 'grel |bdag gi tshod kyang mi shes par| |smra ba ji ltar smyon pa min|[13] |de ltas nyon mongs gzhom pa la| |rtag tu phyir mi ldog par bya|

Si je parle sans savoir même ma mesure, comment peux-j'être autre qu'un fou? Ainsi je ne me détournerai jamais d'élimination des passions.

V 109

eden-ı bey-e-ber böged üiledteküi : ama-bar ügülegsen-iyer yaγun-i bütügeküi : otači-yin šastir-i uribasu : ebedčiten-e tusa bolqu yaγun ::[14]

[12] Ligeti: *boγolγ-a*.

[13] Tib. *min* pour *min nam*.

On doit faire ces choses par le corps. Qu'est ce que l'on peut achever par *la simple* récitation *des textes*? A quoi sert aux malades si l'on prononce *les mots du* traité d'un médecin?

Mdo 'grel |lus kyi 'di dag spyad par bya| |tshig tsam brjod pas ci zhig 'grub| |sman dpyad bklags pa tsam gyis ni| |nad pa dag la phan 'gyur ram|

VI 15

qoor-a-tu[15] moγai singsiγul kiged ölösküi : umdaγasqui terigüten ǰobalang-luγ-a : qabangγu[16] terigüten ǰobalang-ud-i: öd̲ ügei[17] daγusqun-i ese-gü üǰebe či ::

Est-ce que tu n'as pas vu les fins prématurées de *ceux qui avaient* douleurs comme celles *causées par* serpents venimeux, moucherons, faim *ou* soif, *ou* douleurs comme celles *causées par une* tumeur?

Mdo 'grel |sbrul dang sha sbrang dag dang ni| |bkres skom la sogs tshor ba dang| |g.yan pa la sogs bcas pa yi| |don med sdug bsngal cis ma mthong|

VI 16

qalaγun küiten kei qur-a kiged : ebedküi ükükü aškiqui[18] terigüten-dür : nada ülü emgenikü buyu : emgenikü bögesü ǰobalang-ud munda nemeyü [*xyl.:* amuyu] ::[19]

Je ne doit pas me plaindre *des douleurs causées par* chaleur, froid, vent, pluie, maladie, mort[20] claques et caetera. Si je m'y plains, la souffrance croîtra intensément.

Mdo 'grel |tsha grangs char dang rlung sogs dang| |nad dang 'ching dang rlog sogs la| |bdag gis gze re mi byas te| |de ltar byas na gnod pa 'phel|

---

[14] Manuscrit de Delhi, f. 39a, l. 32, f. 39b, ll. 1-3: *eden-i bey-e-ber üiledteküi* : *amabar ügülegsen-iyer yaγun-i bütügeküi* : *otači-yin šastir-i uribasu* : *ebečiten-e tusa bolquγu yaγun* ::

[15] Manuscrit de Delhi, f. 21a, l. 27: *qorotu,* forme préclassique.

[16] Manuscrit de Delhi, f. 21a, l. 27: *qabangγui.*

[17] Cf. turc ancien *ödsüz.*

[18] Lessing 57: *aski-* 'асгих'; Cewel id., lire ашгих; cf. MNT *ašgi-*.

[19] Manuscrit de Delhi, f. 21b, l. 1-2: *ede* [= *nada*] *ülü yarar*<'>*qaγdaqu buyu* : *yararqa=basu ǰobalang-ud munda nemeyü* ::. Le verbe *yararqa-* est dérivé de *yara* 'blessure', cf. *niγur* + *(u)rqa-* > *niγurqa-*; *sečen* + *rke-* > *sečerke-*; *tala* + *rqa->* *talarqa-*, etc.

[20] La traduction tibétaine de *'ching* 'lier; captivité', normalement rendu en mongol par *külikü* < *küli-* 'lier, attacher'.

VI 45

köbegüked ǰobalang ülü kereglen bögetele : ǰobalang-un siltaγan-dur sinuqayiraǰu : öber-ün kü üiledügsen gem-iyer ǰobaγuldabasu : busud-ta tegetele yaγun ǰ-e bui ::

Les enfants ne souhaitent pas la souffrance, toutefois ils convoitent la cause de la souffrance. Si l'on souffre du mal commis par soi-même, pourquoi s'irriter contre autrui (*lit.* transférer à autrui)?

Mdo 'grel |byis pa sdug bsngal mi 'dod cing| |sdug bsngal rgyu la brkam pas na| |rang gi nyes pas gnod gyur pas| |gzhan la bkon du ci zhig yod|[21]

VI 47

minu kü nigül kilinčas-a qadquγdaǰu : nadur qoor üiledügčid : tegüber tedeger tamu-dur odbasu : bi teden-i ese-gü qokiraγulbai ::

Si ceux qui sont irrités par mes péchés et vices et me font du mal et c'est pourquoi ils iront à l'enfer, c'est moi qui les ais ruiné, n'est-ce pas?

Mdo 'grel |bdag gi las kyis bskul byas nas| |bdag la gnod byed rnams 'byung ste| |de yis sems can dmyal dong na| |bdag gis de dag ma brlag gam|

VI 60-61

ker ber oluγsan ed̲-iyer amiban teǰigeǰü : buyan üiledüged nigül-iyen arilγasuγai kemebesü : olǰa-yin tulada urin töröbesü : buyan-iyan baraǰu nigül ülü-gü boluγuǰai :: buyan-u tulada amidu an bögetele : ker ber tere buyan baraγdaǰu bür-ün : imaγta nigül kilinča kü üiledün : amidu-bar aǰu yaγun kereg ::

Si l'on dit: «Je veux me nourrir (*lit.* je veux nourrir ma vie) des biens achevés, pratiquer le mérite et détruire mon péché», cependant si l'on irrite dans le désir des biens, n'ira pas on détruire son mérite et ne deviendra pas cela un péché? On doit vivre pour *pratiquer* le mérite, mais si ce mérite-là est détruit, et si l'on commet toujours des péchés, pourquoi doit-on vivre?

Mdo 'grel |gal te rnyed pas gson gyur na| |sdig zad bsod nams bya zhe na| |rnyed pa'i don du khros gyur na| |bsod nams zad sdig mi

[21] Finot VI 45: Je n'aime pas ma douleur, mais j'aime la cause de ma douleur, fou que je suis! C'est de mon péché qu'elle est née: pourquoi en vouloir à une autre?

'gyur ram| |gang gi don du bdag gson pa| |de nyid gal te nyams gyur na| |sdig pa 'ba' zhig byed pa yi| |gson pa des ko ci zhig bya|[22]

VII 4cd-5ab

ükül-ün eǰen-ü aman-dur oroγsan-iyan : eǰiy-e-de ese-gü medebe či :: öber-ün nököd-iyen ǰerge-ber alaquy-yi ber : čimada ese-gü üǰegdebe [:]

Est-ce que tu n'as pas entendu, en ce moment même, que tu es entré dans la bouche du Seigneur du Mort? Est-ce que tu n'as pas vu que tes compagnons étaient tués l'un après l'autre?

Mdo 'grel |'chi bdag khar ni song gyur b/pa| |ci ste da dung mi shes sam| |rang sde rim gyis gsod pa yang| |khyod kyis mthong par ma gyur tam/ram|

VIII 185

tegün-ü tulada köbegüked-ün aburi bolilan : edüge merged-i daγuriyaǰu : seregdeküi üges-i duraduγad : noyir kiged budungγui sedkil-i qariγulsuγai ::[23]

C'est pourquoi, en quittant les manières puériles, maintenant je veux imiter les sages et, en me rappellant les paroles de prudence, je veux refuser le sommeil et l'esprit brouillon.

Mdo 'grel |de bas byis pa'i spyod pa chog| |bdag gis mkhas pa'i rjes bsnyags te| |bag yod gtam ni dran byas nas| |gnyid dang rmugs pa bzlog par bya|

IX 49

ali ayalγu sudur-tur orolduγči : tegün-i burqan-u ǰarliγ kemekü bögesü : olangki yeke kölgen tan-u[24] sudur-luγ-a : adali kemen ülü-gü taγalamui yaγun ::

---

[22] Cf. de la Vallée Poussin VI 60-61: Mais, dirais-tu, les biens prolongent la vie, et je pourrai longtemps détruire mon péché, accroître le mérite? Mais ne t'irrites pas dans le désir des biens, car tu détruirais le mérite et accroîtrais le péché! [Prolonger la vie, dites-vous?] Maudite soit la vie, si je manque le but unique de ma vie, si ma vie se passe entière dans la péché!
Les mêmes vers chez Finot: «Mais, dis-tu, grâce à mes profits, je vis, et en vivant j'use mes péchés et je gagne du mérite.» Quand on se fâche pour une question de lucre, c'est le mérite qu'on use et le péché qu'on gagne. Si le but de ma vie disparaît, à quoi bon cette vie elle-même qui ne produit que du mal?

[23] Ligeti, de Rachewiltz: *bulilan, bodongγui*.

[24] Voir dans le manuscrit de Delhi, f. 46b, ll. 12-15: *ali ayalγu sudur-tur orolduγ=či : tegün-i burqan-u ǰarliγ kemekü bögesü : olangki yeke kölgen tan-u : sudur-luγ-a adali kemen ülü-gü taγalamu yaγun* ::; où mong. *tan-u* rend tib. *khyed cag gi*.

Si vous considérez que chaque mot qui se trouve dans vos sūtras représente la parole du Bouddha, pourquoi ne pas accepter que la plupart du Grand Véhicule sont similaires aux sūtras?

Mdo 'grel |ngag dang mdo sde la 'jug ste| |gal te sangs rgyas gsung 'dod na| |theg chen phal cher khyed cag gi| |mdo dang mtshungs 'dod min nam ci|

IX 130ab

egüdügsen siltaγan inu buyu kemebesü : egüdügsed-i onon esegü baraluγai [:]

Si *vous* dites: «Ce qui est créé a sa cause», *je vous réponds:* «Est-ce que nous n'avons pas finir la discussion des *choses* créées?»

Mdo 'grel |dngos rnams de rgyu'am rang bzhin na| |dngos po rnam dpyad zin min nam|

X 10

olom ügegü γal metü müren-ü dotor-a baγtaγdaǰu : oγtačiqui[25] miqan inu kunda čičig-ün[26] öngge-tü yasutan : minu buyan-u küčün-dür tngri-ner-ün bey-e olǰu bür-ün : tngri-ner-ün ökid-lüge nigen-e Mandakid-tan[27] naγur-tur aqu boltuγai ::

Que *les êtres* serrés dans la rivière (Vaitaraṇī) sans gué et pareille au feu, *ceux* dont les chairs *sont* hachées et dont les os ont la couleur de la fleur *kunda,* obtiennent, par la force de mon mérite, des corps du dieux et séjournent avec les filles des dieux au lac (= fleuve) Mandākinī!

Mdo 'grel |chu bo rab med me dang 'dra nang bying ba dag| |sha kun zhig gyur rus gong me tog kun da'i mdog| |bdag gi dge ba'i stobs kyis lha yi lus thog nas| |lha mo rnams dang lhan cig dal gyis 'bab gnas shog|[28]

:: *naγan nasutu Iγor baγši ǰaγun namur-un amur-i üǰekü boltuγai* ::

---

[25] Manuscrit de Delhi, f. 53a, l. 20: *oγtalaqui*.

[26] Manuscrit de Delhi, f. 53a, l. 21: *künda čečeg önggetü*. Dans les langues mongoles vivantes, les consonnes sourdes mais non-aspirées des mots d'origine indo tibétaine sont substituées par des consonnes démi-sonores, par exemple, *gunda* au lieu de *kunda*, Les voyelles du mot *čičig* montrent l'influence d'un dialecte du Sud, cf., par exemple, baarin *čičig*.

[27] Manuscrit de Delhi, f. 53a, l. 25: *Mandaki-nista naγur*[-*tur*] *aqun boltuγai* ::

[28] Cf. Finot, X 10: Que les êtres plongés dans la Vaitaraṇî aux ondes brûlantes comme le feu, avec leurs chairs en lambeaux, leurs corps et leurs os pâles comme le jasmin, obtiennent, par la force de mes mérites, une nature céleste et se jouent dans la Mandâkinî avec les Apsaras!

Bibliografie

Cewel, Ya. 1966. *Mongol xelnii towč tailbar toli*. Ulaanbaatar.

de la Vallée Poussin, L. 1905-06. *Introduction à la pratique des futurs Bouddhas*. Poème de Çāntideva. Traduit du sanscrit et annoté par L. de la Vallée Poussin. (Extrait de la *Revue d'histoire et de littérature religieuses* X-XII/1905-07; *Muséon* 11/1892, 87-115; *Muséon* 15/1896, 306-318.)

de Rachewiltz, I. 1996. *The Mongolian Tanǰur Version of the Bodhicaryāvatāra*. Edited and transcribed, with a word-index and a photo-reproduction of the original text (1748). Wiesbaden.

Finot, L. 1920. *La marche à la lumière: Bodhicaryavatara*. Poème sanscrit de Çantideva. Traduit avec introduction par L. Finot. (Les classiques de l'Orient II.) Paris.

Lessing, F. *et al.* 1995. *Mongolian English Dictionary*. Bloomington, IN.

Ligeti, L. 1966. *Śāntideva: A megvilágosodás útja. Bodhicaryāvatāra. Čhos-kyi'od-zer fordítása*. Budapest.

Lokesh Chandra (ed.), *Bodhicaryāvatāra*. 1. *Pre-Canonical Mongolian Text*. 2. *Tibetan Commentary by Blo-bzaṅ dpal-ldan*. With a foreword by Walther Heissig. (Śatapiṭaka Series 230). New Delhi 1976.

Matics, M. L. 1970. *Entering the Path of Enlightenment; the Bodhicaryāvatāra of the Buddhist Poet Śāntideva*. London.

Padmakara Translation Group 2006. *The Way of the Bodhisattva* [by] Shantideva. Revised translation and new preface by Padmakara Translation Group. Foreword by the Dalai Lama. Boston.

Tumurtogoo, D. & G. Cecegdari 2006. *Mongolian Monuments in Uighur-Mongolian Script (XIII-XVI Centuries)*. Introduction, transcription and bibliography. Taipei, Taiwan.

Wallace, V. A. & B. A. Wallace 1997. *A Guide to the Bodhisattva Way of Life* by Śāntideva. Translated from the Sanskrit and Tibetan. Ithaca, New York.

Weller, F. 1950. *Über den Quellenbezug eines mongolischen Tanjur-textes*. (Abhandlungen der Sächsischen Akademie der Wissenschaften zu Leipzig. Philologisch-historische Klasse. Band 45, Heft 2.) Berlin.

A STUDY OF NAI-XIAN (1309-68)

Yuan-Chu Ruby Lam

In a research on Turks in China under Mongol rule, published in 1983, Igor de Rachewiltz ranked Nai-xian (Nai-hsien) as one of the ten men who "distinguished themselves for their literary accomplishments in Chinese, their calligraphic skill, and their active support of Confucianism" during the Yuan era. The other nominees mentioned in the article were the two senior scholar-officials Nao-nao (1295-1345) and Ma Tsu-ch'ang (1279-1338).[1] By placing these three names side by side we are able to make a remark on Nai-xian's name. Nao-nao's name was rendered by two identical characters, transcribing the pronunciation of a foreign name, having no meaning in Chinese. As for Ma Tsu-ch'ang, he chose to use a Chinese first-name, and also his surname Ma shows Chinese influence. In comparison with these two names, Nai-xian's name was a hybrid one, using elements of both names.

Nai-xian was born in 1309 to a Qarluq family that had settled first in Nan-yang 南陽 of Henan province and later moved southeastward to a port city commonly known as Ningbo in Zhejiang province. Like the name of his elder brother Ta-hai, a *jinshi* in the 1318 palace examination, also Nai-xian's name sounded alien in the ears of the Chinese. But when it was written down on paper, the two characters 迺賢 not only designated Nai-xian's family origin but also carried a meaning: The first character *nai* has a major component meaning west, and was written with a radical indicating movement, thus indicating the meaning of coming from the west. As for the second character *xian* 'virtue', it was usually chosen to name a son born in a well-educated family. Therefore, the name Nai-xian, carrying the meaning 'a sage coming from the west' was most appropriate for a Chinese-educated Qarluq, identified by his ethnicity. However, none of his friends nor Nai-xian himself are known to have made remarks on neither this name nor his other, chosen or given Chinese style (*zi*) name which he used alternatively for signature.

Nai-xian's *zi* was Yi-zhi 易之, sometimes used together with He-lu, indicating the ethnic origin of his family (合魯易之); other variants of his

[1] de Rachewiltz 1983, 291-292.

zi were Nanyang Nai-xian Yi-zhi, or just Nai-xian Yu-zhi. When he called himself just Nai-xian, the attached identity would switch to Nanyang (Nanyang Nai-xian 南陽迺賢). Such a practice is attested by two seals which he affixed on a painting in 1347.[2] It is no question that Nai-xian was very meticulous about the arrangement of his name, and he never added the place name Yin-xian (Ningbo) to his name. Nevertheless, other Yuan contemporaries were not so attentive, and made up several other combinations for him. Later in his life, he was often addressed Ma Yi-zhi, but he never used this surname to sign his work.[3] Down to the Qing dynasty, various other homophonic words were used as his name, but none of those fabrications was as meaningful as the original.

I. *A Chinese-Qarluq poet*. Nai-xian was a third generation Qarluq living in Southern China. It is reasonable to assume that Chinese was the only language he spoke, and that Confucian education was the only education he had received. However, it is noticeable that admirers of his poetry invariably mention his ethnic background in their praise for him, as if thus more merits could be given to him. In Da-du, Nai-xian's poetry was circulated and read by the most famous and influential senior official-scholars. Ten of them wrote the preface, loaded with praises, for his poetic work, the *Jin-tai ji* 金臺集. Nai-xian started composing it during his first trip to Da-du in his early twenties, the last poem in this work, however, is dated 1351, at this point he was already forty-two years old. The work was printed in 1355[4] by a close friend who is twice mentioned in Nai-xian's poems. His name was Xu Zhongyu, printed in small size on the edge near the end of the volume. Because of Xu's special efforts in reproducing the calligraphy, written by the authors of the original preface, this work became a rare book and an item of collection in the Ming dynasty.[5]

Being a young Qarluq scholar coming from the south, Nai-xian was capable in securing good relationships with many well-established intellectuals in the state capital Da-du. Upon arrival, he most likely enrolled in the Imperial College or was involved in the newly founded Academy of Scholars in the Kui-zhang Pavilion.[6] This would explain why

---

[2] See his poem on the *Jia dan you-ji tu* of Zhao Yong (1290-1360s?). In this poem Nai-xian used the assumed name Zi-yun shan-ren 紫雲山人.

[3] Another of his assumed names was He-shuo wai-shi 河朔外史, indicating his interests in history. He started to use this name after a study tour in north China.

[4] The dating is fixed by the date of the last preface.

[5] Cf. Ye Shi, *Shui-dong riji*, *juan* 8, 92.

[6] Cf. the *Jin-tai ji* preface written by Jie Xisi (1274-1344) who served at this academy.

several high-ranking scholar-officials serving in those two places became acquainted with him and recognized his poetical talent. In his late twenties, Nai-xian established himself as a fine Qarluq poet. His friend Wei Su (1303-1372) asked him to edit his poems, published in 1337.[7] They stayed in touch with each other ever since. Nai-xian, however, was not as fortunate as his friend, who was initially recommended in 1342 to serve in the court as a literary retainer. In 1364, after several promotions over two decades, he was appointed a first-class bachelor in the Hanlin Academy (2b in rank).[8] As for Nai-xian, he got a much lower appointment in the Hanlin and Historiography Academy in 1362, probably through Wei Su's recommendation.

It is noteworthy that Nai-xian's reputation as a poet was met with indifference in the South. During his time, there were two literary characters, Dai Liang (1317-1383) and Yang Weizhen (1296-1370), who were known to be the leaders among poets in South China. Nai-xian was mysteriously shunned by both of them.[9] This exclusion was not due to the fact that they had never heard about Nai-xian, common friends of poetry were found among their respective followings, but there is no testimony indicating that Nai-xian ever attended their literary gatherings. The reason why Nai-xian was popular in Da-du, but not an active member in the poetic circle in the South outside his home district deserved attention.[10]

It was primarily through Chen Yuan and the English translation of his work the *Western and Central Asians in China Under the Mongols*, that Nai-xian was reintroduced and has since become a popular subject for research. From among 132 Yuan western region intellectuals, Nai-xian was chosen by Chen Yuan for an extensive study.[11] According to Chen Yuan, ten percent of the poems collected in Nai-xian's *Jin-tin ji* were composed for his Taoist friends. Therefore, he placed him in the group of Buddhist and Taoist of men letters from the Western Regions. Chen made a further notion about Nai-xian by saying "Nai Hsien could not give up the idea of being of some use in the world; so he strove to prolong his life by practicing asceticism."[12] However, except in his poetry, we can not find any other evidence to prove that Nai-xian was indeed devoted to Taoism.

---

[7] Nai-Xian's name is given in the *Wei Tai-pu Yun-lin ji* as that of the editor.

[8] For Wei Su's biography see Goodrich & Fang 1976/II, 1464-1467.

[9] For a note on the omission by Dai Liang, see Chen Yuan's translated work (2000, 124-125). Cf. also the *Hui-hui jiu shi lei ji* (Wu Jianwei 2002, 449-450).

[10] For a study of Nai-xian's activities, see Hsiao Ch'i-ch'ing 1994, 227-230.

[11] See Chen Yuan's translated work (2000, 85-94).

[12] *Ibid.*, 92.

In recent decades, several Chinese scholars have been writing about Nai-xian. They came to the conclusion that Nai-xian was an outstanding poet but a loser in seeking appointments, and thus living in financial difficulties. Their assessment is largely based on the reading of Nai-xian's own poetry. These writings led to the interpretation that he was occasionally frustrated and longing for home while staying in Da-du awaiting an appointment through recommendation. However, based on accounts made by those who had known Nai-xian personally, also a different portrait can be drawn. Thus, Nai-xian has been publicized on Internet by a Chinese Islamic newsletter that considered him to be a Muslim.[13] This identification is based on a single poem in the *Jin-tai ji*, entitled *The Crescent Moon*. This poem begins telling about a child from southern China that never knew the feeling of sorrow. When the child sees the new moon, he calls it a silver hook. The poet's family members are so excited about the matter that they invite the poet to go upstairs with them to take a better look at the new moon. This poem was written during Nai-xian's second trip to the capital, around 1350. In fact, in addition to his longing for home which was arisen by the new moon, we can see that, at the same time, he was accompanied by his family. Although he mentions in this poem that he stays at home poor and miserablely, he was able to stay and actively participate in various activities in Da-du for another three, four years.

He was once regarded by a friend to be so short of material goods that he was not able to make a living. But when he, prior to his departure for his appointment in Da-du, temporarily headed a local academy, it is reported in the same account that he had donated his stipend to fix the local Confucian temple and to hire an instructor for the academy.[14] Another one of his local friends said that Nai-xian refused to receive a bride by asking a favor from a dignity, but he was willing to accept financial aid from the same dignity who was his friend.[15] The conflicting informations concerning Nai-xian's standard of life are either insufficient or rather intriguing, which helps to raise the question about the livelihood of Central Asian households in Yuan China.

---

[13] See *Mu-si-lin tongxun* at: muslimtx@sina.com.cn. Moreover, because of the feasibility of the Internet, more of Nai-xian's missing poems have been retrieved from local gazetteers and have become available on the Web.

[14] Cf. Zhu You 1983, *juan* 5.7a-10a.

[15] Cf. Wu Sidao 1983, *juan* 8.4b-5b.

II. *Nai-xian's quest for recognition.* When the civil service examinations were finally restored in 1313, there were educated Central Asians who were qualified to take the examinations and to share the same special treatment as given to Mongolian candidates. Nai-xian's brother attended the second triennial examination, and passed the 1318 palace examination. According to the rules, he must have been twenty-five years of age or older at the time of the examination. This means that Nai-xian was only nine years old when his brother earned the *jinshi* degree. Having passed the examination, his brother was assigned to various regional offices, but he never received an appointment near the capital; Nai-xian, on the contrary, was living in Da-du for quite a number of years during his two stays. The fact of not being able to choose one's own service location might have discouraged Nai-xian from seeking an office through the civil-service examinations.

The interruption of the examinations might be another reason why Nai-xian was not interested in taking a degree. When Nai-xian was qualified to take the provincial examination in 1335, the institution of examinations was suddenly abolished after the provincial examinations had been held that year. The next six years, a period critical for Nai-xian if he wanted to follow his brother's footsteps, were wasted. Whether Nai-xian took the provincial examination in 1335 is unclear; it is mentioned nowhere in the available sources concerning him. However, the single undated preface of the *Jin-tai ji*, written by Yu Ji (1271-1348), who complains about his own poor health and the deterioration of his eyesight, helps to place the date of this preface into the early 1330s. Yu Ji, an influential senior scholar-official uses here the term *xiao-lian* to address Nai-xian, and calls him a friend although the latter was almost forty years younger than himself. The term *xiao-lian* used to be given to a candidate who had passed the provincial examination. Moreover, at the end of this preface, Yu Ji encourages Nai-xian to seek for an official appointment. But, the term *xiao-lian* can also be interpreted as a polite form used by Yu Ji to address a young scholar coming from the southern provinces. Therefore, we can not rely solely upon Yu Ji's one-time address of Nai-xian to determine whether he actually took the civil service examination.

More than half of the scholar-officials who wrote a preface for his *Jin-tai ji* bring up the issue of seeking for an office. All of them express the single opinion that Nai-xian should receive an appointment so that he can put his literary talent to use. Other composers of a preface indicate that Nai-xian was pursuing a path different from civil examinations. According to Huang Jin (1277-1357), a palace examination *jinshi* from 1315, for instance, Nai-xian was a man with high morality, who did not care about writing examination essays in order to earn a position in the government. He also states that Nai-xian had been living in Da-du for many years, so he was familiar with various court and institutional regulations and rituals.[16] Huang's observation about Nai-xian imply that he was qualified for recommendation, one of the way to select officials. Moreover, what concerns the rules of the civil-service examinations, the requirements were focused on the Confucian classics. Nai-xian's devotion to poetry indicates that in his early twenties, he had decided to follow a different path to enter officialdom, namely recommendation. In 1362, at the age of fifty-three, Nai-xian finally got his first literary appointment at the Hanlin and Historiography Academy to serve in the office of compilers (8a in rank). After passing the palace examination, this office was sometimes granted to a successful *jinshi* candidate.

Nai-xian died of misdiagnosed sickness on 25 April 1368 at the age of fifty-nine. At that time, he was between two literary appointments and was temporarily assigned to conduct secretarial tasks in a military headquarters near Da-du.[17] Although he lived his entire life under the Yuan, he was not given a biography in the official *Yuan History*. As for his biography in the *Xin Yuan-shi*, it fails to dig deeper into the accounts given by his contemporaries. However, even we could patch together all the available sources about him, there would still remain holes that can not be filled. For instance, we do not know enough about his family, how he could afford to make trips to Da-du in the 1330s and 1340s and how he could stay there for a number of years. We are vaguely informed that he had high-ranking relatives on his maternal lineage. But, unlike other meritorious families who had close ties with the Mongolian ruling authorities, Nai-xian's were not influential or powerful enough to get him a position through recommendation when he was young.[18] In the end, although his official career was brief and remained on an initial level, Nai-xian was able to serve in a position matching his scholarly aptitude. In his decade-long search for recognition and recommendation, he unexpectedly succeeded, we do not know how, to smooth his way and enter the hall of intellectual excellence.

---

[16] Nai-xian 1916-22.

[17] Chen Gaohua 2005, 256. Chen was the first who quoted this important source material to relate about the date and condition of Nai-xian at the end of his life.

[18] For a vague note on his family background, cf. for instance, Nai-xian's preface to his poem *Yi Qing tang* (Nai-xian 1916-22, *juan* 1.3b-4a).

In addition to being a poet, Nai-xian won in modern times also the recognition of an accomplished traveler, mainly due to his *He-shuo fang gu ji* 河朔訪古記 (*Touring the Antiquities in North China*), a work in the style of both prose and poetry.[19] Nai-xian recounts here a study tour he had made from Ningbo to Da-du in 1345. His trip included also Nanyang regarded by his family as their hometown as stated in his itinerary. Although this work was a travelogue by structure, it actually presented of author's research and knowledge of Chinese history. The complete *He-shuo fang gu ji* is long lost. The current version of three chapters on regions of the modern Henan and Hebei provinces was created by withdrawing materials from the *Yong-le da-tien*. Like the *Jin-tai ji*, which was prefaced by an unusually large group of famous scholars, Nai-xian had asked also here at least six scholarly friends to write prefaces for this work. These prefaces were written between the late 1340s and 1363. Unfortunately, only two of them, an earlier one by Wang Wei (1323-1374) and a latest one by Liu Renben, survived and they are kept separately in the author's collective works. Reading the two extant prefaces, we notice that Nai-xian's effort in producing a geo-historical work gave again rise to the idea of his appointment through recommendation based on the work in question, just as it had happened earlier in connection with the *Jin-tai ji*. That is to say, while his friends gave high praise to his scholarship, their attention was drawn to official appointment, asking at the same time whether it could award Nai-xian with a position in an adequate office. In Liu's preface, written in 1363 after Nai-xian's appointment, the clear message that the work justified the appointment is expressed. Two of the poems written for this work were included in the *Ji-tai ji*; Chen Yuan selected one of them to make special comments, because it vividly describes the suffering that a commoner faced in the late Yuan period.[20] It is noticeable that by this time, Nai-xian was writing more about what he had seen at the end of the dynasty in everyday life than about his literary interests.

In retrospect, the issue of what motivated Nai-xian to strive for recognition remains unclear. He left an ambiguous picture of a man who was either eager to sell his talents in order to serve or of a scholar who was interested in pursuing a career of his own choice. Nevertheless, important

---

[19] Additionally was his calligraphy recognized as a national treasure. His copy of the *Nan cheng yong gu shi tie* was purchased from Henan province in 1999 by the Palace Museum in Beijing. See the homepage of *Dian cang*, Art & Collection; see also Wang Naidong 1989, 84-86.

[20] Chen Yuan 2000, 121-123.

is that he produced two major works of his time. They were written from the viewpoint of a third generation Qarluq living in Yuan China. Although he was getting high marks from scholar-officials at court, for unknown reasons, he had to overcome more obstacles than was customary, before receiving his first low-ranking appointment. Also Nai-xian's ethnic family background did not facilitate his seeking for an office, as would have been expected. But, just because he was not confined to an office, he could continue to think and write independently and mature in his scholarship. After his first devotion to poetry, he started a different project, visiting and writing about historically significant ancient places. Additionally, he also began to write about the poor people he had seen in the country. These writings in poetic style were also incorporated in his above-mentioned work *Touring the Antiquities in North China*. In a different paper, I shall continue to write about Nai-xian's special interest in Chinese history and the geo-historical work which he produced at a time when the Mongolian regime was collapsing before his eyes. Being a Chinese-educated Qarluq, Nai-xian had the privilege to spend his whole life in pursuit of his own intellectual interests. Even if his writings had been aimed at impressing his patrons in order to earn him a literary appointment, the final and eternal goal which he achieved was beyond the poet's imagination.

Bibliography

Chen Gaohua 陳高華 1988. 'Yuandai de Ha-la-lu ren 元代的哈剌魯人'. *Xi bei minzu yanjiu* 西北民族研究 1, 145-154.

— 2005. 'Yuandai shiren Nai-xian shengping shiji kao 元代詩人迺賢生 平事蹟考'. In: *Chen Gaohua wenji* 陳高華文集. Shanghia, 227-251.

Chen Yuan 陳垣 2000. *Xiyu ren Hua hua kao* 元西域人華化考. Shanghai.

Ch'ien Hsing-hai 錢星海 (translated and annotated by L. C. Goodrich) 1966. *Western and Central Asians in China Under the Mongol*: *Their transformation into Chinese*. (Monumenta Serica at the University of California.) Los Angeles.

de Rachewiltz, I. 1983. 'Turks in China Under the Mongols: A Preliminary Investigation of Turco-Mongol Relations in the 13th and 14th Centuries'. In: M. Rossabi (ed.), *China Among Equals. The Middle Kingdom and its Neighbors, 10th-14th Centuries*. Berkeley · Los Angeles · London, 281-310.

Goodrich, L. C. & Chaoying Fang 1976. *Dictionary of Ming Biography 1368-1644*, 2 volumes. New York · London.

Hsiao Ch'i-ch'ing 蕭啓慶 1994. 'Yuanchao duo zu shiren quan de xingcheng chutan 元朝多族士人圈的形成初探'. In: *MengYuanshi xinyan* 蒙元史新研 (New Studies in Mongol-Yüan History). Taibei, 227-230.

Ke Shaomin 柯劭忞 1988. *Xin Yuanshi* 新元史. Beijing.

Liu Renben 劉仁本 1966. *Yu-ting ji* 羽庭集. (Qian-kun zhengqi ji 08.) Taibei.

Nai-xian 迺賢 1916-22. *Jin-tai ji* 金臺集. [China, no placename].

— 1994. *He-shuo fang gu ji* 河朔訪古記. (Yuandai biji xiaoshuo.) Shijiazhuang.

Qi Chongtian 齊冲天 1980. 'Lun Yuandai minzu shiren Nai-xian 論元代民族詩人迺賢'. *Nei Menggu shehui kexue* 3, 107-111.

Shan Yiwei 單義委 2004. 'Nai-xian yu Yuandai you-shi 迺賢與元代遊士 (Naixian and Traveling Scholars of the Yuan Dynasty)'. *Yuan-shi ji minzu-shi yanjiu ji-kan* 17, 261-266.

Wang Naidong 王乃棟 1989. 'Xiyu shaoshu minzu shufa jia yi-cunzuopin kao 西域少數民族書法家遺存作品考'. *Gu-gong bo-wu-yuan yuan-kan* 1, 80-88.

Wang Wei 王禕 1991. *Wang Zhongwen ji* 王忠文集. Shanghai.

Wei Su 危素 1985. *Wei Taipu ji* 危太樸集. Taibei.

Wu Jianwei 吳建偉 (ed.) 2002. *Hui-hui jiu shi lei ji* 回回舊事類記. Yinchuan.

Wu Sidao 烏斯道 1983. *Chun-cao zhai ji* 春草齋集. (Jing yin Wen-yuan-ge Si-ku-quan-shu 171.) Taibei.

Yang Lian 楊鐮 2003. *Yuan shi shi* 元詩史. Beijing.

Zhang Danfei 張丹飛 1997. 'Nai-xian he tade Jin-tai ji 迺賢和他的金臺集 (Some Remarks on Poet Nai xian and His *Jin-tai ji*)'. *Minzu wenxue yanjiu* 1, 24-27.

Zhang Jing 張晶 1997. 'Lun shaoshu minzu shiren zai Yuandai zhong hou qi shi feng pi bian zhong de zuoyong 論少數民族詩人在元代中後期詩 風丕變中的作用 (The Role of Ethnic Minority Poets in Changing of Poetic Style in the Late Yuan Dynasty)'. *Minzu wenxue yanjiu* 1, 9-12.

Zheng Zhen 鄭真 1983. *Ying-yang waishi ji* 滎陽外史集. (Jing yin Wen-yuan-ge Si-ku-quan-shu 173.) Taibei.

Zhongguo Lidai huihua 中國歷代繪畫. (Gugong bowu-yuan cang-hua ji 故宮博物院藏畫集 IV.) Beijing, 1983.

Zhu You 朱右 1983. *Bai-yun gao* 白雲稿. (Jing yin Wen-yuan-ge Si-ku-quan-shu 167.) Taibei.

Dumdadu Mongγol Ulus 'THE MIDDLE MONGOLIAN EMPIRE'

Dai Matsui

Introduction. There is a small fragment among the Mongolian texts brought back from East Turkestan by the German Turfan expeditions. It is housed now at the Berlin-Brandenburg Academy of Sciences (Department Turfanforschung), under a signature U 5981[1]. In the present paper, I consider this fragment, particularly the unclear phrase reconstructed as *Dumdadu Mongγol Ulus* 'The Middle Mongolian Empire' and the related historical problems.

U 5981: Revised edition. L. Ligeti was the first scholar to provide an edition of the fragment[2]. He included the edition again in his corpus of the Pre-classical Mongolian monuments, without any further remarks[3]. In 1993, D. Cerensodnom and M. Taube published the philological edition of the Mongolian texts of the German Turfan collection with photographic reproductions and included also our fragment[4], basically following Ligeti's edition. So did Tumurtogoo in his recent corpus of the Uigur-Mongolian monuments[5]. Apart from these editions, no other scholar in the field of Mongolian philology or Mongolian history has paid attention to the fragment.

In 1997, I had the chance to examine the original fragment: it is 6.7 x 13.7 cm, a mediocre paper with rough *vergeé* (4 / cm) and colored beige clair. I present here a revised edition as the result of my examinations, even though it does not offer many new findings in addition to those of precedings scholars.

---

[1] It is now available in the "Digital Turfan Archiv" of the Berlin-Brandenburg Academy (http://www.bbaw.de/forschung/turfanforschung/dta/u/images/u5981seite1.jpg). Most of the Pre-classical Mongolian monuments of the German Turfan collection are now housed at the Berlin State Library Haus II (Potsdamer Straße), while our fragment is housed at the Academy (Jägerstraße) because it had been misunderstood as an Old Uigur manuscript as shown by the signature U(igur).

[2] Ligeti 1971, 150-153.

[3] Ligeti 1972, 251.

[4] BTT XVI, Nr. 79.

[5] Tumurtogoo 2006, 171.

[MISSING]

(1)	[	]
(2)	[	kü](č)ü (av)γ-a buu
(3)	[kürgetügei	](.) edüge bas-a
(4)	[	](e)düge a̱n-e
(5)	[	]DWN yaγu ke
(6)	[	eyin] ke'gülüged bu̱rün
(7)	[	](.) kürged (q)arabas olm-a
(8)	[	](.) ba taṉluγ-a
(9)	[	dum]dadu mongγo[l] u(l)us-un
(10)	[	temeče]ǰü buu qaltuγai ken-ü
(11)	[	](.) keleletügei a̱yin
(12)	[	](..)TWN ČWB'T kibesü
(13)	[	ke]men nišaṯu bičig
(14)	[ögbei	-W]N [e](ki) sar-a-in
(15)	[	büküi-d](ü)r bičibei

English translation. (1)........... (2-3)...... [They shall not use] violence. .... (3)...... Even now (4).............. Now, this (5)................ anything (6)............... After (We) let announce [thus], (7)............... slave and jar (8)............... We together with you (9)............... of the Middle Mongolian Empire (10).............. [They shall] neither argue nor make demands. Whose (11)............... [they] shall tell. Thus (12)............... (???) If [they/you] torment(?), (13)............ (13-14)(Thus) saying, [We gave] (this) document with the stamp sealed. (14-15)[On the XXth day] of the first month of the [spring/autumn/winter of the year of XX], (15)when [We were at XX, We] wrote (this document).

Notes. (3) The beginning of the line may be restored as *kürgetügei* (< v. *kürge-* 'to cause to arrive; to send, deliver'). Cf. Cleaves and BTT XVI, Nrn. 68-70[6], for *küčü avγa kürge-* 'to bring might and strength; to use violence, behave violently'.

(6) We should follow Ligeti and restore *eyin* 'thus' before *ke'egülged* (~ *kemegülged* < v. *kemegül-*) 'let tell'[7]. Thus far *ke'egülged* has been read here as *kemegülged*, though the hook of -M- is not written. If it is not a simple error, it may reflect the contemporary colloquial pronunciation

[6] Cleaves 1953, 47; BTT XVI, Nrn. 68(11,13), 69(8-9), 70(14).

[7] Ligeti 1971, 152-153; BTT XVI, 185.

kēülü'ed as seen in the 'Phags-pa Mongolian inscriptions or the *Secret History*[8].

(7) Here the context is not clear. I suggest *kürged* (conv. < v. *kür-* 'to reach, arrive at') as another alternative to the reading *künesün* 'provision' as was done by earlier scholars. The next two words have not been studied enough so far. We may tentatively read the first one *(Q)'R'B'Z* = *(q)arabas* < Uig. *qarabaš* 'slave'. The next, which has been deciphered until now as *WLS-'*, might be *'WLM-'* = *olm-a* < Uig. *olma* 'jar, pitcher'[9].

(9) The expression *[dum]dadu mongyo[l] u(l)us* 'the Middle Mongolian Empire' and the problems related with it, will be analyzed below.

(10) For the sentence *temečeǰü buu qaltuyai* '[they] shall neither argue nor make demands', see Ligeti[10].

(12-13) The context of these lines seems to belong to the *Poenformel* section. Here we may expect a phrase such as *yosu ügei üiles üiledübesü ülü ayuqun ta/müd* 'If (you/they) commit unlawful behavior, don't you/they fear (the punishment)? [= you/they shall be punished]'[11]. For this reason *ČWB'T kibesü,* lit. 'if (you/they) make/do «*ČWB'T*»', should also bc a kind of unlawful behavior, and in the beginning of line 13 we may restore *ülü ayuqun ta/müd.* Although the letters *ČWB'T* are rather clear, no word of this form is attested so far and earlier scholars did not explain it. Here I tentatively assume *ČWB'T* = **ǰobad*, plural of **ǰoban*, a deverbal noun from v. *ǰoba-* 'to torment' with the converb *-n*,[12] and translate **ǰobad ki-* as 'to indulge in tormenting; to torment'. Yet the orthographical problem still remains as in the Classical Mongolian orthography, the initial *ǰ-* of the v. *ǰoba-* is always written with *Y-*. From the context it seems inappropriate to relate *ČWB'T* to *čuba* 'raincoat, short fur vest', *ǰoba* ~ *ǰobaya* 'dangerous mountain trail, a narrow valley'[13] or Uig. *čupan* 'minor official; shepherd'[14].

(14) See Ligeti for the restoration of *ögbei* '[We] gave (the document)'[15]. This word should be followed by the designation of the date

---

[8] Junast 1991, 114, 120, 144; Matsukawa 1995, 43; *SH* 10:06:10, 06:37:04.

[9] ED 146.

[10] Ligeti 1971, 153.

[11] BTT XVI, 167; cf. Matsukawa 1995, 43-44.

[12] E.g., Cleaves 1954, 125: *nayadun čenggen-iyer* 'by playing and rejoicing' < v. *nayad-* 'to play; to enjoy oneself' and v. *čengge-* 'to exult, be happy or merry'; Poppe 1991, 49: *šinggen* 'fluid' < v. *šingge-* 'to be absorbed'.

[13] Lessing, 203, 1077; MKT 1283, 1361.

[14] ED 397-398

[15] Ligeti 1971, 153.

of issue, and in fact we can restore some more letters before *sar-a* 'month'. The word just before *sar-a*, on which a black stamp is sealed, might be *eki* 'first', since I could slightly identify the strokes *[ ]KY* while examining the original. In the damaged part preceding **eki*, we can see a stroke of a final *-N*, which apparently belongs to the genitive *-[u]n/-[ü]n*. This speaks for the fact that the name of the month was either *qabur* 'spring', *namur* 'autumn' or *übül* 'winter' all of them taking this genitive suffix, but not *ǰun* 'summer' which requires the genitive in *-u*.

Analysis. Although the fragment does not provide any dating information, we may safely regard it as issued under the domination of the Chaghatai Khanate during the fourteenth century, judging from the black round stamp (ø 2.6 cm), which is rarely seen on Yuan documents.

My analysis shall concentrate on the phrase *[dum]dadu mongγo[l] u(l)us* 'the Middle Mongolian Empire' in line 9 of the text. While the last two words *mongγo[l] u(l)us* can be read undoubtedly, the anterior half of the first word is severely damaged, and *[dum]dadu* is only a hypothetical restoration proposed by Ligeti; however, in his later edition he did not mention it again[16]. Cerensodnom and Taube also followed his later reading, and refered to his proposal of *[dum]dadu* only in a footnote to the text[17]; Tumurtogoo did not make any remark concerning the expression[18]. However, I would raise again Ligeti's proposal, because some Western sources attest appellations such as 'the Middle Empire' for the Chaghatai Khanate, corresponding to *Dumdadu Mongγol Ulus* in our fragment.

First to be noted are appellations *Imperium Medium* 'the Middle Empire' and the like in Latin sources. They were first collected by H. Yule and later remarked on by P. Pelliot as follows: Guillaume Adam describes the empire of «Doa or Caydo», i.e., Du'a or Qaidu, with the appellation *Medium Imperium* 'the Middle Empire' between 1314 and 1328. By this period Qaidu, the Ögödeid leader of the anti-Yuan Mongols in Central Asia, had already passed away (d. 1301), consequently this 'Middle Empire' clearly stands for the Chaghatai Khanate in Central Asia ruled by the descendents of Du'a[19]; *Imperium Medium* 'the Middle Empire' as seen in a letter from Pope Benedict XII of 1338 and in the report by the Franciscan friar John of Marignolli, who brought the Pope's letter to the

[16] Ligeti 1971, 151-152; 1972, 251.
[17] BTT XVI, 184.
[18] Tumurtogoo 2006, 171.
[19] Pelliot 1959, 129.

Yuan[20]; *Imp. de Medio* 'the Empire in the Middle' as seen in Andrea Bianco's atlas of 1436[21].

Besides these, we also have Latin appellations for the Chaghatai Khanate such as *Imperium Medie* 'the Empire of Media' by the Franciscan friar Pascal of Vittoria or on the Catalan Map, as well as *Imperium Medorum* 'the Empire of Medes' in the *Portulano Mediceo* in the Laurentian Library. They are apparently misnomers of *Imperium Medium* or *Imperium de Medio* mentioned above[22].

Concerning these Latin attestations, noteworthy is also the narrative of the famous Muslim traveler Ibn Baṭṭūṭa. In his *Riḥlat*, he introduces the Chaghatai Khanate under the reign of Ṭarmāšīrīn (< Mong. Darmaširi(n) < Skt. Dharmaśrī, r. 1326-34) as follows: *bilāduhu mutawassiṭatun baina 'arba'atin min al-dunyā al-kibāri wa hum maliku al-ṣīni wa maliku al-hindi wa mailk al-'irāqi wa al-maliku ūzbaku* 'His (= Ṭarmāšīrīn's) [ruling] country [is in] the middle between the four of the powerful kings on the earth, i.e., King of China, King of India, King of Iraq and King Özbeg'[23]. Here *bilāduhu mutawassiṭatun* 'his country [is in] the middle' is not completely parallel with the phrase *Dumdadu Mongγol Ulus* or *Imperium Medium*, yet it seems not an accident that he uses the word *mutawassiṭ* 'middle' for the Chagahtai Khanate[24].

Yule explained the reason of the use of *Imperium Medium* and the like for the Chaghatai Khanate with the fact that it lies "between Cathay and Persia"[25]. However, I would suppose that the Latin appellations should be originated from the Mongolian expression *Dumdadu Mongγol Ulus* to be reconstructed in our fragment, which must have been adopted by the Chaghatai Khanate as their official state name.

The appanage in Central Asia given by Činggis-qan to his second son Čaγatai was the origin of the Chaghatai Khanate. However, it was not

---

[20] Yule 1916, 212; Pelliot 1959, 55.

[21] Yule 1916, 85.

[22] Yule 1916, 85, 87, 88; Pelliot 1959, 55.

[23] Defrémery & Sanguinetti (Baṭṭūṭa/DS 31) and Gibb (Baṭṭūṭa/G 556) did not directly translate the original Arabic *mutawassiṭ* as 'middle', while Hikoichi Yajima did so, translating correctly into Japanese as 'mannaka' (Baṭṭuṭa/Y:IV, 172). I would express my sincere gratitude to Dr. Masaki Mukai (Osaka University) and Dr. Yōichi Yajima (Kyoto University) for their kind help in reading the Arabic text.

[24] Baṭṭūṭa/DS is the only Arabic text of *Riḥlat* available to me. As far as H. Yajima confirmed, there exists 29 manuscripts of *Riḥlat* (Baṭṭūṭa/Y:I, 390-398), among which we may also expect an attestation of **bilād al-mutawassiṭat* 'the Middle country' or the like for the Chaghatai Khanate.

[25] Yule 1916, 85.

directly and smoothly inherited by Čaγatai's descendents as they were severely suppressed by the fourth Emperor Möngke, and after the temporary prosperity under Alγu (r. 1260-65/66) and Baraq (r. 1266-71) they were headed by Du'a under the supremacy of the Ögödeid prince Qaidu for nearly thirty years. Only after Qaidu's death (1301), Du'a could re-establish the Chaghatai Khanate in alliance with the Yuan Dynasty to sweep away the Ögödeids in Central Asia[26].

In order to settle his new regime in the Central Asia, Du'a must have had to show off the independence from the Qaidu-Ögödeid domination in various ways. The *Chaghatai-Zeichen*, a double-leaves-like emblem (♈) used frequently in the official stamps sealed on the Mongol and Uigur documents as well as in the coins and mints issued under the Chaghatai Khanate, might be one of the expression: it is never used on the materials before Du'a's reign[27]. Still more, some Chinese sources call the Chaghataid rulers Esen-Buqa (r. 1310-18) and Elǰigidei (r. 1327-30) not by their own names, but 諸王察阿臺 *zhu-wang Cha-a-tai* 'Prince Čaγatai'[28]. This may point to the fact that after Du'a the Yuan dynasty recognized the khanate in Central Asia as specifically "Chaghataid"[29].

Although it is true that no appellation kindred with 'the Middle Mongolian Empire' has been attested in the Persian and Chinese historical sources, it seems probable that Du'a or his descendants took the brand-new official state name *Dumdadu Mongγol Ulus* 'the Middle Mongolian Empire' in order to affirm that their polity was renewed, as did the emperor Qubilai, who in 1271 adopted the official state name *Dai Ön Yeke Mongγol Ulus* 'the Dai-Ön Great Mongolian Empire' [30], adding *Da-yuan* 大元 (> Mong. *Dai-Ön*) to the former state name *Yeke Mongγol Ulus* (>

---

[26] Barthold 1927, 813; Barthold 1956, 128-131; Kato 1977; Sugiyama 1987 = Sugiyama 2004, 356-359; Jackson 1992, 345; Biran 1997, 69-77

[27] Oliver 1891, 8-9; Franke 1962, 406-407; Matsui 1998, 8-11.

[28] *YS*, chap. 31:694, 695, 696; Liu 2006, 398-399.

[29] Du'a himself and the Yuan emperor Temür had the similar concept that Turkestan was to belong to the Chaghataids (TU/H 33; TU/P 40-41).

[30] For *Dai Ön Yeke Mongγol Ulus* as attested in the Sino-Mongolian bilingual inscriptions, see Cleaves 1949, 62; Cleaves 1951, 53. Also noteworthy is that the official state name *Dai-Ön* was widespread among the Mongols, as indicated by the Mongolian edict of 1389 from the first Ming Emperor Hongwu to Aǰaširi, in which the former Yuan emperor (Chin. 元君 *Yuan-jun*) is designated as *Dai-Ön Mongγol qaγan* (Haenisch 1952, 1 & pl. II; Mostaert & Rachewiltz 1977, 1-2; HYYY, 2:03a4; Miya 2006, 15-16).

Chin. 大蒙古國 *Da Meng-gu guo*)[31] to cap a series of his "new deals" after his victory against his youngest brother Ariγ-Böke, such as changing the era name into 至元 *Zhi-yuan* (1264), constructing the new capital *Da-du* 大都 > Mong. *Daidu* ~ Pers. *Dāydū* (1267), campaigning against the Southern Song dynasty (1268), and inventing the 'Phags-pa script (1269). The designation *dumdadu* 'middle' could have been chosen because the Chaghatai Khanate was situated "in the middle" between Yuan, India, the Ilkhanid and the Golden Horde, as explained by Ibn Baṭṭūṭa.

From the mid-fourteenth century onwards, the Chaghatai Khanate was divided into Eastern and Western parts. The latter, which had been undergoing Islamization and Turkicization, became the dominion of the Timurid dynasty, while the Eastern part became the so-called Moghul Khanate, with the self-designation *Moġūl ulus* or *ulus-i Moġūl.* Their dominion — covering the northern steppe and southern oases of the Tianshan mountains with Bišbalïq and Ili valley as their main bases — was called *Moġūlistān*[32]. The name *Moġūl* (< Pers. *Muġūl* 'Mongol') attached to them acknowleged their attachment to the nomadic tradition[33]. They even considered themselves as the legitimate rulers of the whole territories formerly under the control of the Chaghatai Khanate and the Timurids as usurpers[34]. Here we may suppose that the designation *Moġūl ulus* was directly derived from *Dumdadu Mongγol Ulus* 'the Middle Mongolian Empire' which had been first adopted by their ancestors in the Chaghatai Khanate.

Bibliography and Abbreviations

Barthold, W. W. 1927. 'Čaghatāi-Khān'. *The Encyclopaedia of Islam* II, 811-815.

— 1956-58. *Four Studies on the History of Central Asia*, I-II. Tr. by V. & T. Minorsky. Leiden.

Biran, M. 1997. *Qaidu and the Rise of the Independent Mongol State in Central Asia.* Richmond.

Baṭṭūṭa/DS: Defrémery, C. & B. R. Sanguinetti (eds & trs) 1877. *Voyages d'Ibn Batoutah*, Vol. III. Paris.

Baṭṭūṭa/G: Gibb, H. A. R. (tr.) 1993. *The Travels of Ibn Baṭṭūṭa A.D. 1325-1354*, Vol. III. Rep. New Delhi.

[31] *Yeke Mongγol Ulus* is attested in the inscription of the stamp sealed on the Persian letter of 1246 from Güyüg to Pope Innocent IV (Rachewiltz 1983, 274 & pl. I). Its Chinese translation *Da Meng-gu guo* is frequently attested: e.g., the notorious diplomatic correspondence of 1266 from Qubilai to Japan (*YS*, chap. 208, 4625).

[32] Barthold 1956, 137-139; Barthold 1958, 10-11; Mano 2001, 264-274 291-313.

[33] Kim 1999, 316-318.

[34] *MTS*, chap. 66, 929; Kim 1999, 314.

Baṭṭūṭa/Y: Yajima, H. (tr.) 1996-2002. *Dairyokouki*. Japanese Translation of the *Riḥlat ibn Baṭṭūṭa* I-VIII. Tokyo.

BTT XVI: Cerensodnom, D. & M. Taube 1993. *Die Mongolica der Berliner Turfansammlung*. Berlin.

Cleaves, F. W. 1949. 'The Sino-Mongolian Inscription of 1362 in Memory of Prince Hindu'. *Harvard Journal of Asiatic Studies* 12, 1-133 + 27 pls.

— 1951: 'The Sino-Mongolian Inscription of 1338 in Memory of J̌igüntei'. *Harvard Journal of Asiatic Studies* 14, 1-104 + 32 pls.

— 1952. 'The Sino-Mongolian Inscription of 1346'. *Harvard Journal of Asiatic Studies* 15, 1-123 + pls I-XII.

— 1953. 'The Mongolian Documents in the Musée de Téhéran'. *Harvard Journal of Asiatic Studies* 16, 1-107.

— 1954. 'The *Bodistw-a Čari-a Awatar-un Tayilbur* of 1312 by Čosgi Odsir'. *Harvard Journal of Asiatic Studies* 17, 1-129 + pls I-XXIV.

de Rachewiltz, I. 1983. '*Qan, qa'an* and the Seal of Güyüg'. In: K. Sagaster & M. Weiers (eds), *Documenta Barbarorum*. Wiesbaden, 272-281 + 3 pls.

Franke, H. 1962. 'Zur Datierung der mongolischen Schreiben aus Turfan'. *Oriens* 15, 399-410.

Haenisch, E. 1952. *Sinomongolische Documente vom Ende des 14. Jahrhundert*. Berlin.

HYYY: Kuribayashi, H. (ed.) 2003. *Word- and Suffix-Index to Hua-yi Yi-yü*. Sendai.

Jackson, P. 1992. 'Chaghatayid Dynasty'. *Encyclopaedia Iranica* V, 343-347.

Junast 1991. *The 'Phags-pa Script and Mongolian Texts* II: Collected Materials. Tokyo.

Kato, K. 1978. 'The Establishment of the Chaghatay Khanate'. In: The Society for Near Eastern Studies in Japan (ed.), *Oriental and Indological Studies Dedicated to Dr. Atsuuji Ashikaga on His Seventy-seventh Birthday*. Tokyo, 143-160.

Kim, H. 1999. 'The Early History of the Moghul Nomads. The Legacy of the Chaghatai Khanate'. In: R. Amitai-Preiss & D. Morgan (eds.), *The Mongol Empire and Its Legacy*. Leiden · Boston · Köln, 290-318.

Lessing, F. D. 1960. *Mongolian-English Dictionary*. Berkeley · Los Angels.

Ligeti, L. 1971. 'Fragments mongols de Berlin'. *Acta Orientalia Hungarica* 24, 139-164.

— 1972. *Monuments préclassiques* 1, XIII-XIV siècles. Budapest.

Mano, E. 2001. *Bābur and His Times*. Kyoto.

Matsui, D. 1998. 'Uigur Administrative Orders Bearing «Qutluγ-seals»'. *Studies on the Inner Asian Languages* 13, 1-62 + 15 pls.

Matsukawa, T. 1995. 'On the Daiyuan-Ulus Style in the Mongolian Edicts of the 13th and 14th Centuries'. *Machikaneyama Ronsō* 30, 25-52.

Miya, N. 2006: *The Culture of Publication in the Mongol Period*. Nagoya.

MKT: 蒙漢詞典 *Meng-han ci-dian* [Mongγol Kitad toli]. Kökeqota 1999.

Mostaert, A. & I. de Rachewiltz 1977. *Le matériel mongol du Houa-i-i-iu 華夷譯語 de Houng-ou (1389)* I. Bruxelles.

MTS: 明太宗實録 *Ming Taizong shilu* (Institute of History and Philology of Academia Sinica ed.). Taipei (no date).

Oliver, B. 1891. 'The Coins of Chaghatai Mughals'. *Journal of the Asiatic Society of Bengal* 60, 8-16 + m. pls.

Pelliot, P. 1959. *Notes on Marco Polo*, Vol. I. Paris.

Poppe, N. 1991. *Grammer of Written Mongolian*. 4th ed. Wiesbaden.

SH: Kuribayashi, H. & Choijinjab (eds.) 2001. *Word- and Suffix-Index to the Secret History of the Mongols*. Sendai.

Sugiyama, M. 1987. 'Where Were the Western Borderlands of the Dai-Ön Ulus around 1314 AD?'. *Bulletin of the Society for Western and Southern Asiatic Studies* 27. *Kyoto*, 24-56.

— 2004: *The Mongol Empire and Dai-Ön Ulus*. Kyoto.

TU/H: Abū al-Qasim 'Abd Allāh b. Muḥammad al-Qāšānī, *Tārīḫ-i Ūlğāytū*. Ed. by M. Hambalī. Tehrān 1969.

TU/P: Parvisi-Berger, M. (ed. & tr.) 1968. *Die Chronik des Qāšānī über den Ilchan Ölğāytü (1304-1316)*. Göttingen.

Tumurtogoo, D. 2006. *Mongolian Monuments in Uighur-Mongolian Script (XIII-XVI Centuries)*. Taipei.

YS: 元史 *Yuanshi*. Zhonghua shuju (ed.). Beijing 1976.

Yule, H. 1916: *Cathay and the Way Thither*, Vol. III. New ed. by H. Cordier. London. (Rep. New Delhi 1998)

NOTES ON CAUTERIZATION

Ruth I. Meserve

In the *Secret History of the Mongols*, passages §173 and §214 concern the wounding of Öködei (~ Ögödei, 1186-1241), Chinggis' third son and successor (r. 1229-1241). Shot in the neck by an arrow during a battle against the Kereyit at Qalaqaljit Sands in 1203,[1] a companion, Boroqul, sucked the blood from the wound and watched over him during the night. When Ögödei was unable to ride the next morning, Boroqul mounted behind him, held him and again sucked the blood from the wound as they rode back to camp. Although the treatment of such battle wounds has received some attention,[2] the final part of the treatment given to Ögödei has been neglected. Chinggis "... speedily ordered a fire to be prepared, had the wound cauterized, and drink sought for Öködei and given to him."[3] Cauterization was not performed by Boroqul on the evening of their escape, perhaps because it was too dangerous, but such a procedure may have been performed only under certain conditions or required a specialist.

Was cauterization of an arrow wound a standard treatment by the Mongols of the 13th century? During the same time period, various battle wounds from arrows or ballista to the shoulder or chest received a completely different treatment. In one case, Chinggis personally ordered the arrows pulled out, but then instead of cauterizing the wounds, had an ox or water buffalo slaughtered and the injured man placed in the belly of the animal to soak in its hot blood.[4] Can the location of Ögödei's arrow wound, his neck, be the reason for cauterization? When Chinggis himself was wounded in the neck by an arrow (*SH* §145), blood was sucked from the wound, but cauterization was not mentioned. Was it simply omitted or did cauterization require specific symptoms that were not met? Did blood

[1] See de Rachewiltz 2004, 147, 624, 805.

[2] See Kaszuba 1996, 63-64 on the modern reason of air embolism, plus removing any poison; de Rachewiltz 2004, 528-529, too, on sucking the blood to remove the deadly effects of a possible poisoned arrow. Balms were also used on battle wounds and "medicine dissolved in wine"; see, for example, Thackston 1998-99/III, 614.

[3] See de Rachewiltz 2004, 93-94.

[4] Cleaves 1954, 432-33, 435-36, 438, 440.

flow determine its use? In Ögödei's case, he was still bleeding the next day, suggesting the severity of the wound. Although speculative in nature, such questions need to be asked.

Standard medical definitions of cauterization (from Greek: *kauterion*, 'branding iron') give two major types.[5] (1) "Actual" or fire cauterization utilizes a heated implement or burning material applied directly to the body and results in tissue destruction. Throughout their history, the Mongols used wood, stone, bone, metal (iron, brass, copper, silver) including branding irons and stirrups, grasses and lichen, felt, fire needles, etc. (2) "Potential" cauterization uses a caustic substance on the body that also results in tissue destruction. Because cauterization seems so commonplace, its study has been neglected in the region, where the wide reach of the Mongolian empire fostered, developed, and transmitted medical concepts, through its encounters with China, India, Tibet, and the Near East which itself had preserved and greatly advanced ancient Greek medical traditions. In examining this surgical practice during the Mongol Empire, the appropriate generalized term is *cauterization*, which encompasses many different methods. The descriptive terminology used for the cauterization of a wound in the *Secret History* (§173; it is not repeated in §214) was first to kindle a fire "*qal ötör tüle'ülü'et*" and then to cauterize "*qala'un da'a'ulu'at*" the wound.[6] This passage permits a further discussion of cauterization in central Eurasia demonstrating both possible influence and indigenous traditions in the Mongol empire. Only selected examples from various traditions are given with preference for historical incidents relevant to medieval Mongolian medical practices.

Modern Mongolian scholars[7] trace their medical history on cauterization to two main sources found in early Chinese texts. First is an intriguing passage in the medical compilation, *Huang Di nei jing su wen* (ca 2nd-1st century BCE), which presented a geographic orientation (*Su wen* 12) for treatment methods. Cauterization with burning plant matter (*jiu ruo*) as tinder came from the North.[8] Lu and Needham considered the

---

[5] *Dorland's Illustrated Medical Dictionary* 1994, 281; Haubrich 2003, 43.

[6] Ligeti 1971, 128; Haenisch 1962, 30, 154. — In modern Khalkha versions of the *Secret History*, the term *da'a'ulqu-* 'ausbrennen' is sometimes replaced by a more standard term for the procedure: *xairch* from *qayiri-*, *qayira-*, *qaγari-* 'to cauterize,' also used sometimes in the sense of 'to singe'and *qaγarilγ-a* 'cauterization, with a hot iron or other heated substance.'

[7] See, for example, Šagdarsüren 1989, 272.

[8] *Huang Di nei jing. Su wen* 12; Unschuld 2003, 290, 314-315; Lu & Needham 1980, 1, 2. — On the continuing importance of geographic division in imperial Chinese medical discourse see Hanson 2006, 137-142, 163.

North to be "... the northern quasi-Tungusic nomadic element,"[9] but neither ethnic nor language affiliations can be assumed. However, the second source, the 3rd century C.E. *San guo zhi*, concerns the Wuhuan people living on the Mongolian steppe and in Manchuria from the 2nd century B.C.E. They cauterized in a number of ways: by moxa (*ai jui*), by ironing with a heated or burning hot stone (*shao shi dou yu*), and by lying down on heated earth (*shao di wo shang*).[10]

At about the same time, the Mawangdui medical texts (ca 2nd century B.C.E.) suggest that cauterization (Chinese: *jiu*) pre-dated moxibustion (*ai jiu* or *ai rong jiu*), because artemisia (*ai*) used as tinder in moxa was not attested. Cauterization was one of five heat therapies in these texts, along with roasting (*zhi*), hot-pressing (*yun*), fumigation (*xun*) and balneotherapy (immersing part of the body in hot medicinal baths).[11] All of these heat therapies are also a part medical traditions on the Mongolian steppe. Clearly this was a time of development for cauterization techniques. Another tantalizing text was known as the "Frog" or "Toad" Classic of Huang Di (*Huang Di hamajing*, from Dunhuang dating, perhaps, as early as the Han period or to the Sui).[12] Basically an almanac for treatment methods, it included instructions regarding when cauterization should not be performed (compare with Uighur materials below).

Islamic medical traditions regarding cauterization followed two, almost opposite yet interconnected, paths. One, known as "the medicine of the Prophet" (*tibb al-Nabī*), followed a traditionalist view, which cited Muhammad as saying: "There is health in three things: drinking of honey, incision made by the cupper's knife and cautery with fire; I forbid my people to cauterize."[13] Conflicting opinions on the contradictory nature of this saying led to the notion that cauterization was a method of last resort. Even Juvaini (ca 1226-1283), historian of the early Mongol Empire, cited a proverb: "The final remedy is cautery."[14] This gives credence to the idea that it was a well-known and widespread concept. The other path led to the necessary debate in the Islamic world, causing medical scholars to embrace cauterization by fire (Arabic: *kayy*) as a part of wound treatment.

---

[9] Lu & Needham 1980, 2.

[10] Chen Shou 1957, 30:4a-b; Chen Shou 1960, §30, 832, both under Wuwan. — A few other editions have *ai zhi* for moxa.

[11] Harper 1998, 5, 92-97, (texts:) 192-202, 203-212.

[12] Harper 2005, 136-137.

[13] Perho 1995, 11, 53, 109-110; Elgood 1962, 144-146.

[14] Juvaini/Boyle 1958/II, 577. — In his ornate style, the proverb is not applied to a medical event.

Near Eastern medical practices spread into Central Eurasia along with Jewish and Nestorian Christian traditions.

Early Central Asian Turkic examples of cauterization (*tögnä- ~ tügnä-* 'to cauterize') appeared in Kašγari's 11th century compendium as a treatment for both man and animal: "He cauterized his wound" and as a veterinary treatment for a horse ailment (*čildäg*), in which "[a] sore ... appears on the upper chest of a horse[,] ... flows with pus and must be cauterized."[15] This term can be compared to *tö'ēne* in the 15th century manuscript of the *Muqaddimat al-Adab*, reflecting Middle Mongol of the 13th-14th centuries.[16] More important, a Tibetan medical text (Pelliot tibétain 127, line 182) spoke of cauterization and gave very clear indication that different types were practiced by a neighboring non-Tibetan people, where "... 'the Dru-gu [identified as Türk/Uighur] method of iron cautery (*sur-phug?*) is also suitable'."[17] Unfortunately no specifics were given beyond the use of an iron implement. Besides this, lists of foreign medical doctors, who visited the imperial Tibetan court in the 7th and 8th centuries, recorded their traditions or specialties. Cauterization was noted as coming from northern tribes of Tibet, the early Western Türk, the Qarluq, and the medieval Uighurs.[18] Rachmati's work on Turfan medical texts revealed that one minor text (TT VII, 21) marked the days of the month when cauterization was counter-indicated: "(Am 25. Tage ist der Geist in ... Wenn man an diesem Tage diese Stelle) ausbrennt oder eine Wunde macht, so wird man sterben" or "Wenn man an diesem Tage zur Ader läßt, ausbrennt und eine Wunde macht, so wird man sterben."[19] The Tarim Basin city-states such as Turfan and Dunhuang received many traditions, indicative not only of wide transmission, but also of indigenous knowledge of medical procedures due recognition, especially as Uighur influence would impact the Mongol empire.

Not only would Uighur medical knowledge influence impact the Mongol empire, so too would Khitan and Song Chinese expertise. The royal family of the Khitan had an acknowledged bibliophile in Yelu Bei (d. 937), the eldest son of Abaoji (872-926; first emperor of the Liao dynasty, r. 907-926). More interested in learning than the throne, Yelu Bei "... was

---

15 Kašγari/Dankoff 1982-1984(1985)/II, 304; I, 356 respectively.

16 Poppe 1938/1971, 352; for classical and modern Mongolian forms *tögene-e* and *töönö* see Sagaster 1980, 85-88.

17 See Uray 1979, 303-304. In addition, see Finckh 1992 for Tibetan recognition of Mongolian cauterization separate from both Tibetan and Chinese.

18 For example see Rechung 1973, 202; for a recent study of such lists, see Garrett 2007.

19 Rachmati 1972, 320, 406; see also Müller 1923/1965.

skilled in medicine, acupuncture, and cauterization ..." as well as other achievements.[20] Artistic examples of cauterization (or moxibustion and acupuncture) came to the attention of both the Jurchen and the Mongols. Bronze human statues (*tong ren*) showing the loci for cauterization and acupuncture were demanded from Song China by the Jurchen as a condition in a peace treaty when they defeated the Chinese in 1126 at Kaifeng.[21] In 1233, Ögödei sent the envoy Wang Ji to the Song court to negotiate a two-pronged Mongol-Chinese attack on the Jurchen Jin. Wang was given numerous gifts to take back to Ögödei, including one of these bronze figures. Then some thirty years later, Qubilai showed a Nepalese master craftsman, Anige (1244/45-1306), a badly damaged "Bronze Microcosmic Statue for Acupuncture and Moxibustion Demonstration," which revealed "all the joints, arteries and veins."[22] Qubilai told Anige that this was the statue given to the envoy Wang Ji. Qubilai then commissioned Anige to repair or make a new statue which he completed in 1265. The biography of Anige in *Yuanshi* 203 and his official epigraph,[23] by Cheng Jufu (1249-1318) in 1316 at the order of Buyantu (r. 1311-1320), remarked on his exceptional skill.

Care must be taken in assuming that a given treatment belongs to an outside medical tradition. Transmission does not necessarily mean adoption, but usually adaptation, making it local. In the case of cauterization, this meant by substance, by tool, by point of application, by time or season, and by ailment. If anything, the Mongol Empire absorbed much: ideas, craftsmen, and professionals, constantly "up-grading" skills, making innovations and discarding things that did not work. The Ilkhanid ruler Ghazan (r. 1295-1304) had acquired some knowledge not only of Mongolian, but also of Chinese, Indian, Kashmiri, and Tajik medicine. He himself experimented with medicines and contributed to pharmaceutical knowledge.[24] Rashīd ad-Dīn (ca 1248-1318), minister to Ghazan, historian of the Mongols, and physician, aided in the transmission of Chinese medicine to the Ilkhanate, but his greatness as a historian has long overshadowed his medical contribution, found in the *Tansūqnāma* (ca 1313). Comprised of four books, only the first is extant, containing his preface to the work and the translation of a Chinese "Pulse Poem" (*Mai*

[20] Wittfogel & Feng 1946/1949, 497; 254 on Yelu Bei ceding the throne to his younger brother.

[21] Lu & Needham 1980, 133.

[22] Jing 1994, 79; Lu & Needham 1980, 131, 154-155.

[23] Jing 1994.

[24] Thackston 1998-1999/III, 668.

jue) by Gao Yangsheng (fl. 12th C.E.) as well as anatomical drawings (dated to 1113) from Yang Jie.[25] Rashīd ad-Dīn "reshaped" the work to fit "the Spirit of Islam."[26] It is his preface, however, that should be examined more carefully, for "[a] great part … is dedicated to cauterization and its mechanism for the purpose of elaborating how blood circulation repairs the body."[27] Perhaps detailed in the missing books,[28] his interest in cauterization was, no doubt, stimulated by Ghazan's experience with a recurring eye disease. The ailment first appeared in 1299, when "… the people burned wild rue …" (most likely as a fumigant) and prayed to avert the "evil eye."[29] When the ophthalmia struck again in early September of 1303, his physicians failed to cure him with medicines. Ghazan then changed methods (on 19 October 1303): "… in accordance with the treatment of the Cathaian physicians, his regal body was cauterized in two places …," later identified as on the stomach.[30] Most likely, this was real Chinese moxibustion, as the site of burning was not at or near the eyes, but at loci thought to transmit healing via vessels to his eyes. Two weeks later pain from the burning and weakness still left Ghazan unable to ride when camp was broken to move to winter quarters; he traveled first on a platform mounted on an elephant and then by litter.

This then brings us back to the passage in the *Secret History of the Mongols* and the use of cauterization in the Mongol Empire. The seriousness of the arrow wound cannot be denied, as Ögödei could neither sit on his horse nor ride. Blood continued to trickle from the wound. Ögödei's condition was critical. Was cauterization used as a last resort? Certainly it was a possibility. Evidence suggests that cauterization was not automatically called for nor an over-used surgical method. There were choices to treat battle wounds. Well-known in the Mongol Empire, cauterization had a definite place in surgical procedures, utilized under specific conditions and in many different forms. Over the coming centuries, cauterization would continue to be a major type of treatment for man and animal in the medicine of the Mongols.

Bibliography

Chen Shou 1957. *San guo zhi ji jie*. Beijing.

[25] Klein-Franke & Zhu 1996; Miyasita 1967.
[26] Klein-Franke & Zhu 1996, 398-399.
[27] Klein-Franke & Zhu 1996, 400.
[28] Jahn 1970, 135.
[29] Thackston 1998-99/III, 644.
[30] Thackston 1998-99/III, 658.

Chen Shou 1960. *San guo zhi*. Shanghai.

Cleaves, F. W. 1954. 'A Medical Practice of the Mongols in the Thirteenth Century'. *Harvard Journal of Asiatic Studies* 17, 428-444.

de Rachewiltz, I. 2004. *The Secret History of the Mongols*. A Mongolian Epic Chronicle of the Thirteenth Century. Translated with a historical and philological commentary. (Brill's Inner Asian Library, Volume 7/1-2.) Leiden.

Dorland's Illustrated Medical Dictionary, 28th edition. Philadelphia 1994.

Elgood, C. 1962. 'Tibb-ul-Nabbi or Medicine of the Prophet'. *Osiris* 14, 33-192.

Finckh, E. 1992. 'Practice of Tibetan Medicine: Notes on Moxibustion'. In: Ihara Shōren and Yamaguchi Zuihō (eds), *Tibetan Studies, Proceedings of the 5th Seminar of the International Association for Tibetan Studies, NARITA 1989*, I-II. Narita II/443-450.

Garrett, F. 2007. 'Critical Methods in Tibetan Medical Histories'. *Journal of Asian Studies* 66.2, 363-387.

Haenisch, E. 1962. *Wörterbuch zu Manghol un niuca tobca'an (Yüan-ch'ao pi-shi). Geheime Geschichte der Mongolen*. Wiesbaden.

Hanson, M. E. 2006. 'Northern Purgatives, Southern Restoratives: Ming Medical Regionalism'. *Asian Medicine: Tradition and Modernity* 2.2, 115-170.

Harper, D. 2005. 'Dunhuang Iatromantic Manuscripts: P.2856 R° and P.2875 V°'. In: V. Lo & C. Cullen, *Medieval Chinese Medicine: The Dunhuang Medical Manuscripts*. London, 134-164.

Harper, D. J. 1998. *Early Chinese Medical Literature: The Mawangdui Medical Manuscripts*. London.

Haubrich, W. S. 2003. *Medical Meanings: A Glossary of Word Origins*, 2nd edition. Philadelphia.

Huang Di nei jing. Su wen. (Wang Bing zhu; jiao zheng zhe Li Yi deng; Guo xue ji ben cong shu si bai zhong: 142.) Taipei 1968.

Jahn, K. 1970. 'Rashīd ad-Dīn and Chinese Culture'. *Central Asiatic Journal* 14.1-3, 134-147.

Jing, Anning 1994. 'The Portraits of Khubilai Khan and Chabi by Anige (1245-1306), A Nepali Artist at the Yuan Court'. *Artibus Asiae* 54.1-2, 40-86.

[Juvaini] 1958. *The History of the World-Conqueror by 'Ala-ad-Din 'Ata-Malik Juvaini* I-II, translated by John Andrew Boyle. Manchester.

[al-Kašγari, Mahmud] 1982-1984[1985]. *Compendium of the Turkic Dialects (Diwan Lughat at-Turk)* I-III, edited and translated with introduction and indices by Robert Dankoff in collaboration with James Kelly. (Sources of Oriental Languages and Literatures & Turkish Sources VII.) Cambridge.

Kaszuba, S. C. 1996. 'Wounds in Medieval Mongol Warfare: Their Nature and Treatment in the *Secret History*, with Some Notes on Mongolian Military Medicine and Hygiene'. *Mongolian Studies. Journal of the Mongolia Society* 19, 59-67.

Ligeti, L. 1971. *Histoire secrète des Mongols*. (Monumenta Linguae Mongolicae Collecta 1.) Budapest.

Klein-Franke, F. & Zhu Ming 1996. 'Rashīd ad-Dīn as a Transmitter of Chinese Medicine to the West'. *Le Muséon* 109.2, 395-404.

Lu, Gwei-djen & J. Needham 1980. *Celestial Lancets: A History and Rationale of Acupuncture and Moxa*. Cambridge.

Miyasita, S. 1967. 'A Link in the Westward Transmission of Chinese Anatomy in the Later Middle Ages'. *Isis* 58.4, 486-490.

Müller, R. 1923/1965. 'Ein Beitrag zur ärztlichen Graphik aus Zentralasien (Turfan)'. *Archiv für Geschichte der Medizin* XV. (Rpt. *id.* 14, 21-26.)

Perho, I. 1995. *The Prophet's Medicine: A Creation of the Muslim Traditionalist Scholars*. (Studia Orientalia 74.) Helsinki.

Poppe, N. N. 1938. *Mongol'skii slovar' Mukaddimat al-Adab*. (Rpt. ed. Westmead 1971.)

Rachmati, G. R. with sinological remarks by W. Eberhard 1972. *Türkische Turfan-Texte* VII. (Sprachwissenschaftliche Ergenisse der deutschen Turfan-Forschung, Albert Le Coq *et al.*, Opuscule III, Bd. 2.) Leipzig, 190-411.

Rechung, Rinpoche Jampal Kunzang 1973. *Tibetan Medicine Illustrated in Original Texts*. Berkeley.

Sagaster, K. 1980. 'M. M. Haltods Notizen über die mongolische Volksmedizin'. In: H. Franke & W. Heissig (eds), *Heilen und Schenken. Festschrift für Günther Klinge zum 70. Geburtstag*. (Asiatische Forschungen 71.) Wiesbaden, 77-96.

Šagdarsüren, C. 1989. 'Die traditionelle mongolische Medizin'. In: W. Heissig & C. C. Müller (eds), *Die Mongolen*. Innsbruck, 272-273.

Thackston, W. M. 1998-99. *Rashiduddin Fazlullah's Jami'u't-tawarikh: Compendium of Chronicles. A History of the Mongols*, Part Three. (Sources of Oriental Languages and Literatures 45, Central Asian Sources IV/1-3.) Cambridge.

Unschuld, P. U. 2003. *Huang Di nei jing su wen: Nature, Knowledge, Imagery in an Ancient Chinese Medical Text*. Berkeley.

Uray, G. 1979. 'The Old Tibetan Sources of the History of Central Asia up to 751 A.D.: A Survey'. In: J. Harmatta (ed.), *Prolegomena to the Sources on the History of Pre-Islamic Central Asia*. Budapest, 275-304.

Wittfogel, K. A. & Feng Chia-sheng 1949. *History of Chinese Society: Liao (907-1125)*. Philadelphia.

HOW MONGOLIAN WAS HAMGYŎNG-DO?

Johannes Reckel

In the second half of the 14th century, the land on both sides of the Tumen and the Yalu, including the modern Korean provinces of Hamgyŏng and P'yŏng'an was a political and administrative No Man's Land that had slipped out of the control of the Chinese Ming dynasty and had not yet become an integral part of Korea proper.

This area had originally been part of the territory of Korguryŏ and then Parhae. Parhae had a mixed population of Tungusic Malgal and Korguryŏ people[1]. By the time Wang Kŏn founded the Koryŏ dynasty in 918, Parhae was at the point of collapse under the Khitan onslaught and Pongyang, the old capital of Koguryŏ till 668, had become the hunting ground of groups from the Malgal/Mo-ho tribes, renamed Jurchen soon after[2].

By 926 the Khitan of the Liao dynasty had completed the occupation of Parhae. The Khitan were of Mongolian stock, nomads of the eastern Mongolian steppe who never felt at home in the forests and swamps of Manchuria and the wooded mountains on the border of Koryŏ, populated by various Tungusic tribes, mainly hunters and fishers, partly living in villages along the river.

The remnants of the old Koguryŏ-Parhae people had lost their identity amongst the Jurchen, or moved south into Koryŏ and Liao-tung.

Only the Northwest of modern Korea was held by the Khitan by military force, as strategically important roads for military and trade purposes were running parallel to the West Coast between the Koryŏ capital Kaesŏng and China via Liao-tung. In 1010 the Khitan raided the Korean capital Kaesŏng near the West Coast but withdrew very soon afterwards. Koryŏ managed to secure the Northwest nevertheless and between 1030 and 1044 built a Great Wall as border defence between the lower Yalu and the bay of Wŏnsan right across the Korean peninsula. This wall marked the northern frontier of Koryŏ until the old boundaries fell under the Mongol rule in the 13th century.

After 1115 the tribes of the Wild Jurchen all came under the rule of the Wanyen Jurchen of the newly founded Chin dynasty and the frontier

---

[1] Reckel 1995.

[2] *Koryŏ-sa* 1,8: 9th month 918.

became calmer than it had been for centuries. This calm lasted until the first Mongol invasion in 1231 followed by further invasions in 1232, 1235, and 1254. Korea became de facto a protectorate of the Mongols. The Northwest and the Northeast of the Korean territory were formerly made a part of Mongolian-ruled Yüan-China. In 1270 Pyongyang became Tung-ning Fu for 20 years and Hwaju (Yŏnghŭng) at the eastern end of the Great Wall became Shuang-ch'eng for 99 years (1258-1356).

Focusing on the population of the area of Tung-ning and Shuang-ch'eng, we will find the situation in these two territories quite different. Pyongyang, now Tung-ning, had been part of the Koryŏ state for over 200 years before it fell under Mongol rule and the Parhae-Jurchen population in this northwestern area had either left or become completely naturalized by 1270. There have been reports of Khitan monks or more generally of large numbers of Khitan refugees coming to Koryŏ in the early 12th century, going back on ch.19 of the *Kao-li t'u-ching* by Hsü Ching, though this can not be verified by any entries in the *Koryŏ-sa* or other primary sources[3]. There were probably no Mongolian-speaking Khitan colonies in the Northwest around 1270 to justify a Mongol occupation of Pyongyang. When Tung-ning was given up by the Mongols in 1290, a good number of Koreans fled from Pyongyang into Liao-tung beyond the Yalu, where Tung-ning Fu was re-established, for these Koreans feared to be treated as traitors by the returning Koryŏ authorities[4].

A completely different situation existed in the Northeast: Yŏnghŭng, just south of the eastern end of the Great Wall of Koryŏ, had by the middle of the 14th century been just under the Mongol rule for a hundred years as the seat of the Shuang-ch'eng Prefecture. It had always been a border town. Now it was on the other side of the border. The area north of the wall had originally been mainly controlled by different Jurchen tribes, though Koryŏ tried to bind their chiefs into the Korean administrative system by granting them titles and nominal positions. Their tribal areas were made "Kimiju" 羈縻州 similar to the Chinese garrison system ("wei" 衛) among the barbarians. In 1107 the Korean general Yun Kwan built 9 new fortified towns in the Jurchen territory north of Yŏnghŭng. These were but short-lived and the Korean influence north of the wall was finally ended by the founding of the Chin dynasty by the Wanyen Jurchen in 1115.

---

[3] Reckel 2002, 100-101.

[4] Kawachi Yoshihiro 1986, Pang Tong-in 1984.

The situation along the border remained calm and stable for over a hundred years until the arrival of the Mongols. Mongol rule in Yŏnghŭng and further north eroded the old boundaries and by the early 15th century the Tumen and Yalu had become the new Korean border.

Until the arrival of the Mongols in Korea, the area north of the Great Wall of Koryŏ was almost exclusively settled by Jurchen, and the territory of Yŏnghŭng by Koreans. In 1258 the Northeast came under direct Mongol rule. At first this might not have shown in any large scale ethnic shifts, but the first movement of Korean settlers into the old Jurchen area is recorded for the year 1254. On the other hand, Yŏnghŭng remained probably very much Korean. The prefects of Shuang-ch'eng came from the local Korean family of Cho for a hundred years[5]. At the same time the firmly-guarded border along the Great Wall became irrelevant. It did not mark any border any longer. The Jurchen tribes to the North were not any longer under the control of a central Jurchen government. Koreans, who had become Mongol subjects in Shuang-ch'eng or who wished to avoid the Korean authorities for other reasons gradually moved into the fertile plains along the northeast coast of the Korean peninsula.

Among them were the ancestors of the founder of the Chosŏn dynasty (1392-1910), Yi Sŏng-gye, who around the year 1254, just after the arrival of the Mongols in Korea, moved towards modern Kyŏnghŭng on the lower Tumen river. After 35 years these Korean settlers were driven out by the native Jurchen and settled much further south at or around Hamju north of Yŏnghŭng but still in an area mainly populated by Jurchen. Those ancestors of Yi Sŏng-gye all held official posts given by the Mongols, had Mongolian titles and Mongolian names. Yi Sŏng-gye grew up as a Korean among Jurchen, with a father who had been a Mongol officer. Some of his cousins married among the native Jurchen and later rebelled with the help of the Jurchen against Yi Sŏng-gye. On the other hand Yi Sŏng-gye had many friends amongst the Jurchen, too. One of his best friends from the days of his youth was the Jurchen chieftain Turan Temür 豆蘭帖木兒 from Pukchŏng, later known as Yi Chi-ran 李之蘭.

Yi Sŏng-gye's upbringing among the Jurchen of the Northeast made it possible for him to incorporate into the Korean state the vast territory between Yŏnghŭng and the Tumen relatively peacefully.

The blending of Korean and Jurchen elements in Korea's northern border provinces has been fairly well documented[6]. Much more obscure is

---

[5] Reckel 2006, 123.
[6] Reckel 2001, 2002, 2006, 2007.

the presence of the Mongolian element in an area which had been part of the Mongol empire for about a century. The Mongolian influence there must have been historically strong enough to leave traces.

It is widely known that some of the Koryŏ kings had Mongolian names in addition to their Korean ones. The court also adopted Mongol elements of language, dress or rites[7]. There were political reasons for this rather than the physical presence of many Mongols in Kaesŏng at that time. The background in the Northeast was different. The Mongolian names occurred among the common people or low ranking officials in an area outside the borders of Koryŏ.

Yi Sŏng-gye's grandfather (?-1342) was named Yi Ch'un 李春 in Korean and Po-yen T'ie-mu-erh/P'ae-an Ch'ŏp-mok-a 孛顏帖木兒, i.e. Bayan Temür in Mongolian; his father Yi Cha-ch'un 李子春 (1315-61) bore the Mongolian name of Wu-lu-ssû Pu-hua/O-ro-sa Pur-hoa 吾魯思不花, i.e. Ulus Buxa (Mongolian *bayan* 'rich', *temür* 'iron', *ulus* 'people', *buxa* 'bull)[8].

Yi Ch'un had two sons from his first wife, the elder called Cha-hŭng 子興 in Korean and T'a-ssû Pu-hua/T'ap-sa Pur-hoa 塔思不花 in Mongolian (Mong. *tas* 'condor'), the younger was Yi Cha-ch'un, whose Mongolian name has been given earlier. The sons of Yi Ch'un's second wife were called Wan-che Pu-hua/Wan-cha Pur-hoa 完者不花 and Na-hai/Na-hai 那海. The exact Mongolian meanings are not clear except for *pu-hua* 'bull'. But the name Wan-che pu-hua appears also as the name of a Mongolian prince in the *Yüan-shih* ch.108, written in the same Chinese characters. Hambis[9] reads Öljä-buqa. Another name, 完澤 Wan-tse is read Öljäi by Hambis[10]. Both names might go back to Mongolian *öljei* 'luck, fortune'. In the Secret History of the Mongols paragraph 55 we find 完勒只 Wan-le-chih, read Öljei by Ligeti[11]. The second Chinese character has been printed smaller in the original and represents an *-l*, which otherwise does not exist in Chinese closing a syllable. This system of inserting smaller, "diacritical" characters has not been used in the *Koryŏ-sa* or the *Sillok*.

For these two younger sons no Korean names are recorded, an indication that the Mongolian names at that time even among ethnic

---

[7] Lee Ki-moon 1964, Shiratori Kurakichi 1929.
[8] Cf. *T'aejo Sillok* ch.1.
[9] Hambis 1954, 38.
[10] *Ibid.* 34.
[11] Ligeti 1971.

Koreans had preference over the Korean names. Nahai is also a common name often found in the *Yüan-shih*[12].

Sometime before 1364 a daughter of Yi Ch'un married Kim Pang-gwae 金方卦, the *darugači* (Mong. title) of Sam-Haeyang near modern Kilju, at that time deep into the Jurchen territory. They had two sons named Sam-sŏn 三善 and Sam-gae 三介. Their names might be Korean or not. Interestingly enough the *Koryŏ-sa* ch. 40 under the first month of 1364 calls them "the Jurchen Sam-sŏn and Sam-gae". They are described as rebellious bandits who finally disappeared among the local Jurchen. The fact that they are called Jurchen suggests that their father, despite his Korean name, probably not his original name, was himself in fact a Jurchen. Many Jurchen received Korean names from the Korean, or Chinese names from the Chinese authorities. The official Korean or Chinese sources would in that case use only the more recent or newest names. So there might have been an older name of Kim Pang-gwae, as there has been in the well-documented case of Yi Chi-ran[13].

As we have shown, there were ethnic Koreans bearing Mongolian names in the Northeast, and there were likewise many Jurchen in the same area bearing Mongolian names. Some of these Mongolian Jurchen names were in fact by-names, like the frequent Temür. The Mongolian names of the ethnic Koreans often show the same elements. The Mongolian elements amongst the Jurchen names emerged under the direct contact and influence of the Mongols of the 13th and 14th century. It might have started amongst the southwestern Jurchen as the ones who first faced the Mongolian onslaught, as a fashion that rapidly moved east. As for the Mongolian names amongst the ethnic Koreans of the Northeast, there are two possible explanations: They might have emerged under Jurchen influence, as the population of that area was mainly Jurchen, and Mongolian names among the Jurchen were common. But there might also have been a direct Mongolian influence, as the now-Korean provinces of Hamgyŏng-do and part of P'yŏngan-do were integral parts of the Mongol empire.

It should also be mentioned that there were two different transcription systems for foreign names in Korea; the one using the Chinese sound value of the Chinesese characters used to write the names of Mongols, Jurchen and others, the other using the Korean sound value. E.g. the Korean system used the character 乙, the Chinese system the character 兒

[12] Song Ki-jong 1988.

[13] Biography in *Koryŏ-sa* ch. 116; obituary in *T'aejong Sillok* ch.3, fol. 20v°.

to represent the sound *r*[14]. For the Mongolian names recorded in the Korean sources for Jurchen or Koreans only the Chinese system has been used, which makes it very likely that these Mongolian elements were first recorded further west by Chinese or at least non-Korean scribes.

Unfortunately the official annals of the Yüan dynasty, the *Yüan-shih*, contain but little information on Shuang-ch'eng. Shuang-ch'eng was not included in the geography section (*ti-li chih*) of the *Yüan-shih*. Even the annals (*pen-chi*) of the *Yüan-shih* ch. 3 remain silent as to the occupation of Shuang-ch'eng by Mongol forces in 1258. The very few times in the *Yüan-shih* when Shuang-ch'eng is mentioned at all, it always appears in connection with Koryŏ.

In the year 1287[15] the Mongolian prince Nayan, who had received "Manchuria" as his inheritance, rose in rebellion against Kubilai. The rebellion involved several of the princes' and even Korean officials from the border region[16]. Most of the Jurchen and Water Tatars stood behind Nayan[17]. After the death of Nayan in 1288, the rebellion collapsed. Many of Nayan's supporters disappeared amongst the Jurchen[18].

The biography of Lai-a-pa-ch'ih[19] contains the following remarks about his son Chi-seng, who hold an official post among the Water Tatars of the lower Tumen and Ussuri river: "Nayan rose in a rebellion and Chi-seng fought at Shuang-ch'eng of Koryŏ (*kao-li shuang-ch'eng*)". On the one hand we have a Mongolian official fighting in or near Shuang-ch'eng in connection with a Mongolian uprising and at the same time this Shuang-ch'eng is called Korean. There is a slight possibility that the annalist and writer of this part of the *Yüan-shih* did not count Shuang-ch'eng as Mongolian since it did belong to the Mongolian Yüan empire only for a limited time. Anyway, the fighting in 1287-89 in connection with the rebellion must have affected Shuang-ch'eng badly, because in the 8th month 1292 the *Yüan-shih*[20] has the following entry: "Shuang-ch'eng on the border between Koryŏ and the Jurchen reports a famine. The king of Koryŏ has been ordered to send corn over the sea for help".

During all these Mongolian years, Shuang-ch'eng was in reality ruled by two local Korean families, the Cho and the T'ak. The Cho always filled

---

[14] Reckel 2006, 152-169.

[15] *Yüan-shih* ch. 14, 298ff.

[16] *Koryŏ-sa* ch. 14, 59: 5th month 1287.

[17] *Ibid.* ch. 133, 3224: Biography of T'a-ch'u.

[18] *Ibid.* ch. 16, 353: 12th month 1289.

[19] *Ibid.* ch.124, 3143.

[20] *Ibid.* ch. 17, 366.

the office of prefect[21]. A certain Cho Hui had surrendered Shuang-ch'eng to the Mongols in 1258 and in 1356 a cousin, named Cho Ton, of the ruling prefect Cho So-saeng, lead the Korean troops as a traitor into Shuang-ch'eng. Yi Sŏng-gye's father had been a Ch'ien-hu, a "leader of one thousand" in Shuang-ch'eng at that time. And he too changed sides easily. Although the Korean authorities had no say in Shuang-ch'eng for 99 years, it should probably be best regarded as a separate fief of the Cho family under Mongol protection.

The exact line of the northern border of the Shuang-ch'eng prefecture at that time is not known. Somewhere north of the old Great Wall of Koryŏ lay the semi independent Jurchen state of Tung-chen that established itself after the collapse of the Chin dynasty. Shuang-ch'eng and Tung-chen must have had a common border. Officially Tung-chen must have belonged to the Yüan province of He-lan.

In 1211 Chinghis Khan attacked the Chin Empire and in 1212 Liao-yang, the administrative centre of Manchuria was taken by the Mongols. In 1215 Peking fell into Mongol hands and the Chin rule in northern China came to an end as did the central rule of the Wanyen Jurchen over all Jurchen tribes. The Jurchen nation disintegrated again. In the 10th month of 1215, the Jurchen P'u-hsien Wan-nu declared himself king of the state of Ta-chen, being shortly after renamed Tung Hsia, meaning "The Eastern Hsia". The Korean sources tend to call it " Tongjin" (Chin. Tung-chen), meaning "The Eastern (Jur-)chen". The power base of P'u-hsien Wan-nu moved from the Yalu river towards the middle Tumen river. For a while he cooperated with the Mongols. But when the Mongols turned their attention away and towards China and Hsi-Hsia in the West in 1219, he became largely independent until 1233, when Ögedei Khan turned Mongolian attention again eastward. In the 10th month 1233 P'u-hsien Wan-nu was taken prisoner by the Mongols and his state came to an end. And still the Korean sources continued to call the area Tongjinguk, i.e. "The land of Tongjin". As late as 1286[22] Koryŏ was sending an official into Tongjin to fetch back Korean nationals that had fled there. Hence it can be assumed that Tongjin was a close neighbour of Koryŏ.

In 1356 Koryŏ regained souverainity over Shuang-ch'eng. On this occasion the Koryŏ-sa[23] presents a list of several towns that were regained by Koryŏ including far off places like Pukch'ŏng, Hongwŏn and Hamju, which originally were part of the Chin empire and not part of Koryŏ.

---

[21] Biography of Cho Ton in: *Koryŏ-sa* ch. 111.
[22] *Koryŏ-sa* ch. 30, 58: In the 8th month.
[23] Ch. 111, 181; *T'aejo Sillok* ch. 1, fol. 5r°.

Unfortunately the information for that area after the fall of Chin and before the secession of Shuang-ch'eng in 1258 is very meagre. But since this was the time of P'u-hsien Wan-nu, it seems very unlikely that Koryŏ had gained any ground north of the Great Wall during his reign over Tung-chen.

It seems likely that the area of Shuang-ch'eng had grown together with the southern part of the old Chin and Yüan province of Ho-lan during those 99 years, 1258 to 1356, forming a new territorial entity. The Geography (*ti-li-chih*) of the *Yüan-shih*[24] contains only a very short description of Ho-lan Fu in connection and without distinction from the territory, likewise called a *lu* 'province', of the Water Tatars (*shui ta-ta*) and Jurchen. Here a River Ho-lan is mentioned, that empties into the sea. Neither the administrative seat of Ho-lan nor Koryŏ are mentioned. "It is scarcely populated… The population consists of Jurchen and Water Tatars". Tung-chin and the province of Ho-lan must have covered roughly the same area. But Tung-chin was never recognized by the Yüan as an independent state or autonomous region. It seems extremely unlikely that the seat of Ho-lan-fu was anywhere near modern Hamju during the Yüan dynasty[25] despite the *Yongbi och'ŏnga*[26] placing the seat of Ha-ran/Ha-lan 5 Li south of Hamhŭng near modern Hamju.

Apparently Korean settlers had seeped into the area north of the Great Wall following the arrival of the Mongols around 1231 as can be shown by the example of Yi Sŏng-gye's ancestors and by the mission of the Korean official to Tongjin in 1286 to take back fugitive Korean nationals. Somehow many Koreans must have remained north of the Great Wall, so that Koryŏ could claim "back" territory as far north as Pukch'ŏng in 1356.

During the first half of the Koryŏ dynasty nearly all trade routes and general lines of communication with China and the Liao empire ran along the Korean west coast as did the invasion routes of the Khitan. After the downfall of the Khitan in the early 12th century the northern border region became very stable, with the Chin Jurchen showing no territorial interest towards Koryŏ and at the same time keeping a tight control over the various Jurchen tribes along the border. The situation changed under the Mongols with many invasion forces coming down along the east coast. In the 13th century the area between the Tumen River and the Great Wall of Koryŏ became open for Koreans and Mongols alike, and the Mongol

---

[24] Ch. 59, 1400.

[25] Reckel 2006, 40, 255 (34).

[26] Ch. 4, fol. 21v°.

authorities maintained order and peace to a certain degree. Rebellious Mongols like Nayan broke that order occasionally and Japanese pirates broke the peace as well. But real chaos only broke out after the collapse of central Mongolian rule.

In 1359 the rebellion of Red Turbans that had been defeated by the Mongols in Liao-yang extended to Koryŏ and shortly occupied the Korean capital Kaesŏng in 1361. Yi Sŏng-gye successfully drove back the Red Turbans. But since 1362 the notorious bandit Nahachu 納哈出 had established himself in the area between modern Mukden and modern Hamgyŏng province[27]. One of his lieutenants was Hu Pa-tu/Ho Par-tu 胡拔都 (Chin. *hu* 'barbarian'; Mong. *bator* 'hero'[28]). Hu Pa-tu was a Jurchen despite his Mongol name. Nahachu, who had originally served as a general under the Mongols, might himself have been Jurchen for his name reminds us of the Jurchen chieftain Ahachu 阿哈出, whom the Manchu imperial dynasty would later claim as its ancestor. Furthermore, the former prefect of Shuang-ch'eng, Cho So-saeng, joined the ranks of Nahachu in the 2nd month of 1362[29]. In the 7th month of the same year[30] Nahachu and his men clashed with Yi Sŏng-gye's troops at the "Tatar-village" 韃靼洞 (*ta-tan tung/tar-tan tong*) near Hongwŏn. As a vanguard, Nahachu sent Ha-la/Hap-ra 哈剌, Na-yen T'ie-mu-erh/Na-yŏn Chŏp-mok-a 那衍帖木兒 and Pai-yen P'u-hsia/Paek-an Po-ha 伯顏甫下. These three men all bear Mongolian names (*temür* 'iron', *buxa* 'bull', *bayan* 'rich', *qara* 'black'), although they might have been Jurchen. Until 1387 Nahachu and his men remained active in Manchuria and northeastern Korea until they were finally defeated by the Chinese.

Also a fourth ethnic element, Japanese, was active in northeastern Korea. Yi Sŏng-gye fought against a Japanese pirate (*waegu*) called A-ki Pa-t'or 阿其拔都[31] which would be Agi Bator. The *Yongbi och'ŏnga* explains the first element as "dialectal expression for small child" and the second as "hero in Mongolian". Agi sounds very Korean, although a connection with Jurchen-Manchu *age* or Mongolian *aya* 'elder brother' can't be ruled out. This pirate might have actually been a Korean. At that time any pirate was classified as Japanese by the Chinese and Koreans, whereas in the 11th century Jurchen pirates raided the coasts between Korea and Japan. The Chin dynasty kept any independent activity by the

---

27 Cf. Yun Ŭn-suk 2007.

28 According to *Yongbi och'ŏnga* ch. 7, fol. 39r°f.

29 *Koryŏ-sa* ch. 39, 42.

30 *Ibid.* ch. 40, 44.

31 *Yongbi och'ŏnga* ch. 7, fol. 10r°.

various groups and tribes of the Jurchen under tight control. But in the late 14th century there might have been Jurchen, Japanese or even Korean pirates active, as the Korean authority in the Northeast was not yet very well established and the Mongols had retreated into Mongolia.

In this short article I used personal names from the northeastern border region of Koryŏ to show the strong Mongolian influence amongst the various ethnic groups of that area. Only examples were given[32].

Bibliography and Abbreviations

Chosŏn Wangjo Sillok 朝鮮王朝實錄 (incl. *T'aejo Sillok* and *T'aejong Sillok* 太祖實錄, 太宗實錄) 1972. Seoul. (Reprint)

Hambis, L. 1954. *Le chapitre CVIII du Yuan Che* I. (Monographie du T'oung Pao 3.) Leiden.

Kawachi Yoshihiro 1986. 'Ryōyō no Tōnei-I ni tsuite'. *Toyōshi kenkyū* 44:4 89-127. (河内良弘 : 遼陽の東寧衛に就いて).

Koryŏ-sa 高丽史, Bilingual edition Chin.-Korean. Seoul 1965.

Lee, Ki-moon 1964. 'Mongolian Loanwords in Middle Korea'. *Ural-Altaische Jahrbücher* 35, 188-197. (= *Alt'ai Hakpo* 3/1991, 6-12.)

Ligeti, L. 1971. *Histoire Secrète des Mongols*. (Monumenta Linguae Mongolicae Collecta I.) Budapest.

Pang, Tong-in 1984. 'Tongnyŏngbu ch'ip'e so ko'. *Kwandong sahak* 2, 71-83. (方東仁 : 東寧府置廢小考)

Reckel, J. 2001. 'The Ya-in on Korea's Northern Border until the 12th century'. *Göttinger Beiträge zur Asienforschung* 1, 41-85.

— 2002. 'Chaegasŭng – Die letzten Mandschuren Koreas'. In: *Proceedings of the First International Conference on Manchu-Tungus Studies* 1. (Tunguso-Sibirica 8.) Wiesbaden, 95-165.

— 2006. *Nordostasien am Ende der Mongolenherrschaft · Die Jurcen in den Grenzmarken Koreas bis zum Ende des 14. Jahrhunderts*. Göttingen.

— 2007. 'Zur Onomastik der koreanischen Jurcen · Tierbezeichnungen und andere Anspielungen auf das Reich der Natur unter den Geschlechternamen der Jurcen'. *Central Asiatic Journal* 51:2, 208-222.

Shiratori Kurakichi 1929. 'Kōraishi-ni mierutaru Mōkogo-no kaishaku'. *Tōyo gakuhō* 18:2. (白鳥庫吉 : 高丽史に)

Song, Ki-jung 1988. 'T'aejo Sillog-e tŭngjang hanŭn Monggoŏmyŏng-gwa Yŏjinŏmyŏng'. *Chintan Hakpo* 66, 133-149. (宋基中 > 太祖實錄에 登場하는 蒙古語名과 女眞語名; 震檀學報 六十六號)

Yüan-shih 元史, edition Chung-hua shu-chü. Peking 1987.

---

[32] A more complete list of names can be found in Reckel 2006 and Song Ki-jung 1988.

NEW BUDDHIST MONGOLICA FROM DUNHUANG

Volker Rybatzki

During the last decade of the 20th century Chinese archeologists conducted extensive investigations in the northern grottoes of Mogao near Dunhuang[1]. Besides objects of everyday life of the monks who once lived there, also a great amount of literary documents were found during these excavations. The findings included not only documents written in Chinese, Tibetan and Tangut, by far the largest groups, but also documents written in Brāhmī, Uighur and Middle Mongol, the last one both in the Uig.-Mong. and hPags-pa scripts. All these documents were published between 2000 and 2004 by Peng & Wang[2]. The publications, including very good reproductions of every item found, can be called exemplary: the quality of the pictures is very good and the texts thus readable with ease, but also the way of arranging the findings deserves to be mentioned. The authors decided to publish all the findings of a certain grotto together. In this way it is possible to see, for example, which kind of texts were read by a certain monk, and this varies from grottoes where only texts in one language were found, to grottoes with texts in several different languages. Middle Mongol texts were found in 12 grottoes, and with regard to other languages used in the respective grottoes, the findings can be analysed as follows (the first column indicates the grotto in question, the abbreviations in brackets are mine, and refer to second table of this article; the second column refers to the facsimiles of the whole finding of a certain grotto as found in Peng & Wang; the third column indicates the different languages attested in a given grotto):

Grotto	Peng & Wang	Languages
B 119 (Du2)	II/X', XLVI-LII	MMoU, Chin.
B 121 (Du3)	II/X'-XIII'; LIII-LXII	MMoU, Uig., Chin., Tang.
B 127 (Du4)	II/LXXVI-LXXIX	MMoU, Chin., Tang., Tib.
465 (Du5)	II/XVIII'-XXVII'; CX-CXIII	MMoU, Chin., Tang.
B 147 (Du6)	II/XXXII'; CXXII, CXXIX-CLXII	MMoU, Chin., Tib.
B 157 (Du7)	III/II'; IV-XIII	MMoU, Uig., Uig.-Chin., Chin.
464 (Du8)	III/III'-XII'; XXVII-LXVIII	MMoU, Uig., Uig.-Chin., Chin., Tib., Tang., Br.
B 161 (Du9)	III/LXIX-LXXII	MMoU, Uig.
B 162 (Du10)	III/LXXIII-LXXV	MMoU

[1] Whitfield *et al.* 2000.

[2] Peng & Wang 2000, 2004a, 2004b.

B 163 (Du11, DuP1)	III/XV'-XVII'; LXXVI-LXXXVI	MMoU, P, Chin., Tib.
B 168 (Du12, DuP2)	III/XVIII'-XIX'; XCIX-CIV	MMoU, P, Uig.(?), Chin., Tib.
B 172 (Du13)	III/CVIII-CXI	MMoU, Uig., Chin.

Following the list it is interesting to notice that most of the grottoes where Middle Mongol texts were found, include also texts in Chinese and/or Tibetan and Tangut. The amount of Uighur texts found in connection with Middle Mongol texts is rather small, probably pointing to the fact that among Mongols (or persons who were able to read Mongol) in Dunhuang, Uighur was of rather limited significance. Most of the grottoes containing Middle Mongol texts are rather poor, the only exceptions are grottoes 465 and 464 which were highly decorated; all grottoes with the signature B are undecorated, but in B119, B121, B163, B168 some household utensils and clothes were found in addition to texts.

Until the publications of Peng & Wang, only a small amount of Middle Mongol material had been discovered at Dunhuang, namely a short inscription of three pilgrims (DuIss1) and a poem of two lines (Du1)[3]. The last item, once in the possession of P. Pelliot, is nowadays lost. Due to the discoveries of Chinese archeologists at Mogao, the Middle Mongol corpus of Dunhuang has increased dramatically; unfortunately, most of the texts found are very fragmentary. The following table lists all the Middle Mongol documents found until now in Dunhuang, attempting also to identify the content. However, due to the bad state of most of the new documents, only some of them can be identified with certainty. It seems that besides some Buddhist texts, most of the documents are of administrative content. (In some cases where we have a lot of material in other languages than Middle Mongol, and the Middle Mongol material is only of administrative nature, it may be asked if the respective monks were really able to read Middle Mongol; administrative documents as f.ex. edicts, might have been given by the Mongol authorities to people, who were in fact not able to read and understand them.) The abbreviations used in column one of the following table follow the principle employed in my work on Middle Mongol names and titles[4]; the second column attempts to identify the texts; the third column refers to previous publications (the Roman numbers denote the publications of Peng & Wang).

Text	Content	Previous publications
SrnPDu	Subhāṣitaratnanidhi	III/415-417 (B163:77) [DuP1/1]; Ja02/LII/142; Hu04/§48/499-502

[3] For the abbreviations and further references, cf. the table below.

[4] Rybatzki 2006.xvii-xxxii (here all other abbreviations found in this article and referring to Middle Mongol or Uighur documents can be found).

DuP1	Two words, unclear	III/417 (B163:3) [DuP1/2]
DuP2/1	Some letters, unclear	III/419 (B168:3)
DuP2/2	Some words, edict	III/417-418 (B168:4)
DuP2/3	One word	III/418-419 (B168:5)
Du1	Poem	Li72.35
Du2/1	Unclear, juridical?	II/376-377 (B119:7); Tu06/Dun. II/263-64
Du2/2	Civil document	II/377 (B119:8)
Du2/3	Civil document?	II/378 (B119:9)
Du2/4	Unclear, Buddhist?	II/378-379 (B119:13)
Du3	Unclear, Buddhist?	II/379 (B121:40)
Du4/1	List of pers. names?	II/379-380 (B127:10)
Du4/2	Contract	II/380-381 (B127:11); Borjigin 2005
Du5/1	Two words, unclear	II/381-382 (465:8; 12-13)
Du5/2	Some words, civil?	II/381 (465:12)
Du5/3	Some words, unclear	II/381 (465:13)
Du6/1	Some words, unclear	II/383 (B147:12/1)
Du6/2	One word, unclear	II/383 (B147:12/2)
Du6/3	Some words, unclear	II/383-384 (B147:12/3)
Du6/4	Two words, unclear	II/384 (B147:12/4)
Du6/5	Some words, civil?	II/384-385 (B147:12/5)
Du6/6	Only letters, unclear	II/385 (B147:12/6)
Du6/7	Two words, unclear	II/385-386 (B147:12/7)
Du6/8	Chin. title; civil	II/386 (B147:12/8)
Du6/9	One letter	II/386 (B147:12/9)
Du6/10	Two words, unclear	II/386 (B147:12/42)
Du7/1	Some words, unclear	III/398 (B157:21/1)
Du7/2	Some words, unclear	III/398-399 (B157:21/2)
Du7/3	Some letters	III/399 (B157:21/3)
Du7/4	Some words, civil?	III/399 (B157:52)
Du7/5	Some letters	III/399-400 (B157:53)
Du8/1	Pañcarakṣā?	III/401-405 (464:58); Tu06/Dun. VI/266
Du8/2	Writing exercise?	III/400-401 (464:63)
Du8/3	Edict	III/401 (464:71)
Du8/4	Some words, unclear	III/402-403 (464:72/1)
Du8/5	Some words, unclear	III/403 (464:72/2)
Du8/6	Some words, unclear	III/403 (464:162/1)
Du8/7	Some words, unclear	III/403-404 (464:162/2)
Du8/8	Some Words, civil?	III/404 (464:163)
Du8/9	Two words, unclear	III/403 (464:176)
Du9/1-9	Some words and letters	III/404-406 (B161:12/1-9)
Du10	Some words, edict	III/406 (B162:8)
Du11/1	List of offerings?	III/406-408 (B163:3); Tu06/Dun. III/264-265
Du11/2	Some words, unclear	III/409 (B163:40/1)
Du11/3	Some words, civil?	III/410-411 (B163:40/2)
Du11/4	Edict	III/410-411 (B163:42); Matsui 2008; Tu06/Dun. IV/265
Du11/5	Edict	III/411-412 (B163:46); Tu06/Dun. V/265-266
Du11/6	Some words, unclear	III/408-409 (B163:76)
Du12	Some words, civil	III/412-413 (B168:38)
Du13/1	Some words, unclear	III/413-415 (B172:9)
Du13/2	One word	III/415 (B172:11)
DuIss1	Graffiti	Li72a.33-34
DuIss2-29	Inscriptions	II, 376-386, 397-419; Tu06/Dun.I:01-28/34-38

In the preceding list, two documents (Du2/4, Du3) might have a Buddhist content as Du2/4 contains the Uig. word *čambudivip* (< < Skt.

jambudvīpa 'the [Indian] continent, this earth', until now the word is not attested in MMo. sources; in this fragment also the previous line is in Uig.), and Du3 contains the words *tamu* 'hell' and *tonil-* 'to be saved, rescued; to escape (from sufferings)'; another one (Du11/1) might contain a list of offerings, cf. for the nature of this text the edict of the last Yuan emperor Togon temür from 1368 (TogT6) that is somewhat similar in content; this text mentions *maqagala* (< < Skt. *mahākāla* 'name of a Lamaist deity'). Due to the horrible handwriting employed, it is extremely difficult to read this fragment, anyway, some of the readings found in Peng & Wang and Tu06 do not seem to be correct. Two more texts are surely of Buddhist origin.

The first one of these is quoted as SrnPDu [= DuP1/1] in my second list. This is a blockprint fragment in hPags-pa script of the *Subhāṣitaratnanidhi* "A Treasury of Aphoristic Jewels". Comparing this fragment with similar fragments from Turfan, it seems that the fragments of both discoveries belong to the same blockprint edition. However, whereas the fragments from Turfan comprise verses 5-8 and 52-62 of the work, contains the one from Dunhuang verses 313-316. The readings of these new verses as they appear in Peng & Wang, Ju02 and Hu04 are mostly correct, but the same can not be said of the emendations, as one can judge by comparing the the text in hPags-pa script and the one in Uig.-Mong. script[5]. What follows is the transcription of the fragment from Dunhuang (first line), the transcription of the corresponding parts in Uig.-Mong. script (second line, in *italics*), as well as the translation of every verse and remarks concerning grammar, vocabulary, and phonology.

§313/i [M I S S I N G]
qoor kürgegci dayisun ber :
ii [M I S S I N G]
arγ-a medebesü nökör bolun bui :
iii [M I S S I N G]
qooro bey-e-tür qoor-tu buyu j-e :
iv [joqiyan cida]basu ėm bol[umuė]
joqiyan cidabasu em bolumui ::

"If one knows the means, even a harmful enemy becomes one's retainer. Poison is indeed harmful to the body, (but) if one is able to organize it, it becomes medicine".[6]

---

[5] For the transcriptions in hPags-pa script cf. the second table of this article, for those in Uig.-Mong. script, Ligeti 1948, 1973a, and Bosson 1969.

[6] The translation follows Bosson 1969, 268-269.

§314/i yosu·ar oluqsan [ėd idegen-i abta]quė :
yosuγar oluγsan ed idegen-i abtaqui :

ii joqis ügeė [busud-i ülü] ė[ri]gdekuė :
joqis ügei busud-i ülü erigdeküi :

iii jemis modun[-u oqi]-aca abtayu :
jimis modun-u oqi-aca abtayu :

iv te·ünece h[üle·esü] unan buė .·.
tegünece ülebesü unan bui ::

"One should accept properly acquired goods and food, (but) one should not seek for the other unrightful (things). One should take fruit from the top of the tree, (but) if one exceeds that, one falls".

§315/i merged seren ėse yabu·[asu]
merged seren es-e yabubasu :

ii [tere] ja·ura gem törön buė :
ter-e jaγur-a gem törön bui :

iii uqa·atan sa[yi]tur seren yabu·asu :
uqaγatan sayitur seren yabubasu :

iv gem törökü-yin colö berke buė .·.
gem törökü-yin cöle berke bui ::

"If the wise do not act attentively, in that interval harm arises. When the intelligent acts attentively, the opportunity for harm to arise is difficult".

§316/i keji·e ö[·er-ün k]ücün törötele
kejiy-e öber-ün kücün törötele :

ii [M I S S I N G]
tejiyede dayisun-i kündülegdeküi :

iii [M I S S I N G]
kücün dügürbesü jokis-iyar üiledteküi kemen :

iv [M I S S I N G]
busud šastir-tan ügülen buyu ::

"Until one's own strength is born, for that long one should honor the enemy. When one's power becomes complete, one should act properly, the adherents of other *śāstra*s say".

The morphological and orthographical forms attested in SrnPDu do not offer anything new with regard to what is already known from previously published texts written in hPags-pa script[7]. Noteworthy is only the word

[7] Cf. f.ex. Poppe 1957, 27-42.

hüle- 'to exceed' (§314/4), not attested until here in hPags-pa sources, but occuring with an initial *h-* in agreement with MMo. occurences in Arabic script and Chinese characters[8]. The most interesting part of the fragment is formed by its vocabulary, containing several word not attested until now in other hPags-pa texts. In order of occurrence these are: *ėm* 'medicine', *ėri-* 'to seek, look for, demand' → *ėrigde-* 'to seek for', *jemis* 'fruit', *ab-* 'to take' → *abta-* 'to accept, take', *una-* 'to fall', *sere-* 'to wake up' → *seren yabu-* 'to act attentively', *törö-* 'to arise', *cölö* 'opportunity', and lastly, *berke* 'difficult'. Although attested here for the first time in a hPags-pa source, all of these words, with the exception of one, are well attested in other MMo. sources written in Arabic and Uig.-Mong. scripts, or/and with Chinese characters. The only exception is *cölö* 'opportunity'. Due to its rarity, the word has been read correctly only in Peng & Wang (*cölö*), as all the other editors of the text read *colo* in accordance with the orthography of the word as employed in the manuscript; the slightly later Uig.-Mong. occurences were read by Bosson *cola* and by Ligeti *co̲le*[9]. The word is attested only four times in MMo. sources: three times in the *Secret History of the Mongols* (§§172, 195[2]) *cölö* (Haenisch reads: *colo*) 'pause, intermission; Spalte, Lücke, Fuge, Gelegenheit' [§172 = *Altan tobci* folio 63v21-22 *cöle*; §195 is missing in the *Altan tobci*][10], and once in the *Bodhicaryāvatāra* (156v7) *co̲le* 'Freiheit, günstiger Umstand', here is found also the derivation (161v2) *co̲le-tü* '(ein Mensch), der die (günstige) Gelegenheit hat'[11]. Important is the occurrence in the *Altan tobci* as the word is written here clearly CWYL' (*cöle*), i.e. not in the defective way CWL' (*cola* = *co̲le*) as in the other texts in Uig.-Mong. or hPags-pa scripts. The word corresponds to MoL *cilüge/n* ~ *cöle*, KhalL *čölöö/n*, meaning 'space in general; leisure, freedom from work, rest, relaxation, leave; *fitting time, occasion, opportunity*' (*italics* mine)[12].

The last fragment with a Buddhist content is Du8/1 of my second list. The text was found in the highly decorated cave 464 that contained also texts in Uighur, Uighur-Chinese, Chinese, Tibetan, Sanskrit, and Tangut. The fragment Du8/1 might be a fragment of the *Pañcarakṣā*, "The Five Protecting Spells", as already suspected by Peng & Wang, but this statement still needs verification. It is known that a MMo. translation of the

---

[8] Rybatzki 2006, 111-112.

[9] Bosson 1969, 178; Ligeti 1973b, 82.

[10] Mostaert 1953, 120; Haenisch 1962, 29; de Rachewiltz 1972, 84, 104, 211.

[11] Cerensodnom & Taube 1993, 77, 86, 209.

[12] Cf. for the semantics of *cölö* also Bosson 1969, 332: "translates Tib. *go skabs* «a chance of taking place; interval, leisure, space, opportunity»".

Pañcarakṣā was either prepared by Chos-kyi 'Od-zer based on an Uighur version[13], or by Šes-rab Seṅ-ge using a Tibetan one; there is no agreement on the matter of the translator among scholars[14]. Anyway, manuscripts of a version belonging to the 14th century have not come to light until now, and for that reason it still needs to be confirmed that Du8/1 is actually a fragment belonging to the *Pañcarakṣā*.

The text of the fragment is written in Uig.-Mong. script and stands between the lines of a Chinese blockprint. This way of using old Chinese manuscripts is well-known from Turfan where scribes used empty verso pages of old Chinese scrolls, or wrote between the lines of an old Chinese text (as in the case of Du8/1) when copying Buddhist or civil texts. The question arises however, if a text as long and as important as the *Pañcarakṣā* could have been written down in this way. For the moment this answer can not be answered as the fragment is too short and we don't know if Du8/1 is a fragment of the whole text, or only of an extract of it as the *Pañcarakṣā* is in fact a compilation of five different texts. A point of objection to identify the text as belonging to the *Pañcarakṣā* could further be made because the first line of Du8/1 is completely different from corresponding lines in other versions of the text. Although these other versions are later copies, mostly from the 16th-17th centuries onwards, it has been generally agreed among scholars that at least some of them are based on the 14th century original. In order to shed light on the matter, the Dunhuang fragment is here compared with three later versions, supposed to be texts based on the 14th century original. Line one contains the transcription of the Dunhuang fragment (in *italics*), line two the transcription of a version kept in Stockholm (by P. Aalto), and line three and four the transcription of two versions kept in Budapest (by G. Kara)[15].

(1) *-Un cinadu qijaγar-a kürügsen*
(Aalto) qamuγ burqan bodistv-nar
(KaN°3) qamuγ burqan bodhi-saduva-nar
(KaN°78) qamuγ burqan bodistv-nar

(2) *-e mörgümü bi ::*
(Aalto) -a mörgümü bi ·

[13] Elverskog 1997, 55-56 (Nr. 30); Zieme 2005.

[14] Mönhsaihan 2005.

[15] Aalto 1961, 6; Kara 2000, 3-13 (perhaps early 18th century; text repeating a late 17th century edition of the 14th century Mongolian version) [KaN°3], 107-112 (17th century copy of Ayuši guiši's edition of 1587, based on Śes-rab Seṅ-ge's early 14th century translation) [KaN°78].

(KaN°3) -a mörgümü bi ::
(KaN°78) -a mörgümü bi ::

(3) *eyin kemen sonosuγsan minu*
(Aalto) eyin kemen minu sonosuγsan
(KaN°3) eyin kemen minu sonosuγsan
(KaN°78) eyin kemen minu sonosuγsan

(4) *nigen caγ-tur ilaju [tegüs]*
(Aalto) nigen caγ-tur ilaju tegüs
(KaN°3) nigen caγ-tur : ilaju tegüs
(KaN°78) nigen caγ-tur · ilaju tegüs

(5) *nögcigsen rajagriq /// [balγasu]n-u*
(Aalto) nögcigsen rajagriqa balγasun-u
(KaN°3) nögcigsen burqan rajagriq-a balγasun-u
(KaN°78) nögcigsen burqan qaγan-u oron-tur ele :

It is immediately clear that the four texts are more or less identical for what concerns line two to five of the Dunhuang fragment. The translation of MMoU *rajagriq-a* (< < Skt., SktB *rājagṛha* 'Königspalast, Name der Hauptstadt von Magadha') as *qaγan-u oron* 'palace of the king' in line five of KaN°78 is a typical feature of MoL translations based on, or influenced by, Tib., beginning from the 17th century. As in Tib., also in MoL attempts were made since that time to translate every single word of the original Skt./Tib. text, even personal or place names. Thus, Skt. *rāja-gṛha* (← *rāja* 'king' + *gṛha* 'house; dwelling') = MoL *qaγan-u oron* 'place of the king'. All the other differences in these lines are of only little significance and reflect mainly different attitudes in style than in translation traditions. Line one of Du8/1 differs completely, however, as already stated, from the corresponding line of the other versions. Du8/1 has *-Un cinadu qijaγar-a kürügsen-e* 'to the one/those who has/have reached the other limit/border of', whereas the other ones have *qamuγ burqan bodistv-nar-a* 'to all the Buddha-Bodhisattvas'. Although this is a difference at first sight, it is only an apparent one as *-Un cinadu qijaγar-a kürügsen-e* expresses the same idea as *qamuγ burqan bodistv-nar-a*. Describing the same idea or concept with so different words points to the fact that the Dunhuang manuscript of the *Pañcarakṣā* reflects a very different text tradition than the other three manuscripts, as it is also corroborated by the use of pre-classical *qijaγar*, in later orthography *kijaγar*, or *kürügsen-e* (sg.) vs. *bodistv-nar-a* (pl.).

Although I am inclined to consider the Dunhuang fragment to be a part of the *Pañcarakṣā*, it should be remembered that if the first line of Du8/1 is emendated to *[(qutuγtu) bilig]-ün cinadu qijaγar-a kürügsen*, we have a phrase, corresponding to Skt. *(ārya) prajñāpāramitā*, Tib. *('phags-pa) šes-rab-kyi pha-rol-tu phyin-pa*, very common in Buddhist works belonging to the *prajñāpāramitā* philosophy. A work of this genre was found among the fragments of the Turfan collection, and it is thus not impossible that also the Dunhuang fragment belongs to this category of Buddhist literature[16].

If Du8/1 is a fragment of the *Pañcarakṣā*, the differences of the first line have to be stressed as they indicate that the MMoU version as attested in Dunhuang, differed considerably in phraseology and grammar from later versions of the *Pañcarakṣā*. In this case, later versions of the work can be used only cautiously with regard to MMo. matters, a situation contrary to the state of affairs concerning MMo. and later versions of the *Subhāṣitaratnanidhi*[17].

Bibliography and Abbreviations

Aalto, P. 1961. *Qutuγ-tu pañcarakṣā kemekü tabun sakiyan neretü yeke kölgen sudur.* (Asiatische Forschungen 10.) Wiesbaden 1961.

Borjigin, O. 2005. 'A Contract in the Uyghur-Mongolian Script from Dunhuang's Mogao Caves'. *Mongolian Studies* XXVII, 7 14.

Bosson, J. E. 1969. *A Treasury of Aphoristic Jewels: the Subhāṣitaratnanidhi of Sa-skya paṇḍita in Tibetan and Mongolian.* (Uralic and Altaic Series 92.) Bloomington.

Br.: Brāhmī

Cerensodnom, D. & M. Taube 1993. *Die Mongolica der Berliner Turfansammlung.* (Berliner Turfantexte XVI.) Berlin.

Chin.: Chinese

de Rachewiltz, I. 1972. *Index to the Secret History of the Mongols.* (Uralic & Altaic Series 121.) Bloomington.

Elverskog, J. 1997. *Uyghur Buddhist Literature.* (Silk Road Studies I.) Turnhout.

Haenisch, E. *Wörterbuch zum Mangḫol un niuca tobca'an.* Wiesbaden.

Heissig, W. 1976. 'Zwei mutmaßliche mongolische Yüan-Übersetzungen und ihr Nachdruck von 1431'. *Zentralasiatische Studien* X, 7-116.

Hu04: Hugjiltu & Saruul 2004. *Basibazi Mengguyu Wenxian Huibian.* (Aertaıxue Congshu.) Huhehaote.

Ja02: Janchiv, Yo. 2002. *The Mongolian Monuments in hP'ags-pa Script · Texts, Translations, Glossary and Bibliography.* (Monumenta Mongolica III.) Ulaanbaatar.

Kara, G. 2000. *The Mongol and Manchu Manuscripts and Blockprints in the Library of the Hungarian Academy of Sciences.* (Bibliotheca Orientalis Hungarica XLVII.) Budapest.

---

[16] Ligeti 1942, 184-187; Cerensodnom & Taube 1993, 106-108.

[17] Cf. for this statement also Heissig (1976) who showed that MMo. Buddhist texts could be treated in very different ways in later tradition.

KhalL: Literary Khalkha

Ligeti, L. 1942. *Catalogue du Kanǰur mongol imprimé*. (Bibliotheca Orientalis Hungarica III.) Budapest.

— 1948. *Le subhāṣitaratnanidhi, un document du moyen mongol*. (Bibliotheca Orientalis Hungarica VI.) Budapest.

— 1973a. *Trésor des sentences, subhâṣitaratnanidhi de Sa-skya paṇḍita*. (Monumenta Linguae Mongolicae Collecta III.) Budapest.

— 1973b. *Trésor des sentences, subhâṣitaratnanidhi de Sa-skya paṇḍita*. (Indices Verborum Linguae Mongolicae Monumentis Traditorum IV.) Budapest.

Li72: Ligeti, L. 1972. *Monuments préclassiques* II, XIIIe et XIVe siècles. (Monumenta Linguae Mongolicae Collecta II.) Budapest.

Matsui, D. 2008. 'A Mongolian Degree from the Chaghataid Khanate Discovered at Dunhuang'. In: P. Zieme (ed.), *Aspects of Research into Central Asian Buddhism · In Memoriam Kōgi Kudara*. (Silk Road Studies XVI.) Turnhout, 159-178.

MMo(U/P): Middle Mongol (in Uig.-Mong./hPags-pa script); Middle Mongolian

Möhnsaihan, S. 2005. 'Introduction'. In: *Pañcarakṣā · A Mongolian Translation from 1345*. Budapest, 1-7.

MoL: Classical (Literary) Mongol

Mostaert, A. 1953. *Sur quelques passages de L'Histoire secrète des Mongols*. Cambridge.

Peng Jinzhang & Wang Jianjun 2000. *Northern Grottoes of Mogaoku, Dunhuang* (Vol. 1). Beijing.

— 2004a. *Northern Grottoes of Mogaoku, Dunhuang* (Vol. 2). Beijing.

— 2004b. *Northern Grottoes of Mogaoku, Dunhuang* (Vol. 3). Beijing.

Poppe, N. 1957. *The Mongolian Monuments in ḥP'ags-pa Script*. (Göttinger Asiatische Forschungen 8.) Wiesbaden.

Rybatzki, V. 2006. *Die Personennamen und Titel der mittelmongolischen Dokumente · Eine lexikalische Untersuchung*. (Publications of the Institute for Asian and African Studies 8.) Helsinki. [http://ethesis.helsinki.fi/julkaisut/hum/aasia/vk/rybatzki/]

Skt(B): (Buddhist) Sanskrit

Tan.: Tangut

Tib.: Tibetan

Tu06: Tumurtogoo, D. 2006. *Mongolian Monuments in Uighur-Mongolian Script · (XIII-XVI Centuries) · Introduction, Transcription and Bibliography*. (Language and Linguistic Monograph Series A-11.) Taipei.

Uig.: Uighur

Uig.-Chin.: Bilingual texts in Uighur and Chinese

Uig.-Mong.: Uighur-Mongolian (script)

Whitfield, R., Whitfield, S. & N. Agnew, 2000. *Cave Temples of Mogao. Art and History on the Silk Road*. Los Angeles.

Zieme, P. 2005. 'Uigurische Fragmente aus dem *Pañcarakṣā*'. In: S. Grivelet, R. I. Meserve, Á. Birtalan & G. Stary (eds), *The Black Master · Essays on Central Eurasia in Honor of György Kara on His 70th Birthday*. Wiesbaden, 151-164.

AN ESSAY ON THE PHRASE *garîblar evvi* (CHAGATAY) / *garîbdun ger* (MONGOL) IN THE MUQADDIMAT AL-ADAB

Yoshio Saitô

1. The quadrilingual manuscript of the *Muqaddimat al-Adab*, discovered in Bukhârâ by A. Fitrat in 1926, is of great importance since it is the only document ever known to contain a large Mongolian text in Arabic script. The Mongolian and Chagatay words and phrases in the manuscript were published by N. Poppe in 1938 with a transcription in Roman script and a translation in Russian[1]. Poppe's work is based on photographs taken in Leningrad of a handwritten copy made from the original in Bukhârâ in the 1920s. After many years, the whereabouts of the manuscript and its copy became unknown to Mongolists, and only Poppe's edition remained available to them. But, in February 2004, H. Kanno found that the copy of the manuscript made in Bukhârâ about eighty years ago is now in the possession of the Alisher Navoi State Museum of Literature in Tashkent. According to Z. Islamov, the original manuscript seems to be lost. If this is true, the one in the museum is the only existing copy.

Judging from its amount and kinds of calques and loanwords, the Mongolian language in the manuscript, which is a variety of the West Middle Mongol, is strongly influenced by Turkic (and perhaps also by Persian). But in Mongol as well as in Chagatay, loanwords had their own specific semantic features, even though most speakers of Mongol probably were bi- or multilingual. For example, the Arabic word *kitâb* and its variants, which mean "book," are translated with the following words:

	A	P	C	M[2]
Type 1	kitâb	kitâb	kitâb	daftar
Type 2	kitâb	kitâb	bitig	bičig
Type 3	kitâb	nâma	kitâb	daftar
Type 4	kitâb	nâma	bitig	bičig

[1] A voluminous colour facsimile of the museum manuscript, the English title of which was given by Igor de Rachewiltz, was produced in January 2008 by Z. Islamov, H. Kanno, Kh. Khasanov, H. Kuribayashi and Y. Saitô with a grant from the Japan Society for the Promotion of Science as one of their research reports.

[2] A: Arabic, P: Persian, C: Chagatay, M: Mongol.

The form *kitâb* here represents the word *kitâb* and its variants. The word *daftar*, which originally is Greek, entered Mongol through Persian and Arabic, but it is used differently in Arabic and Mongol in this manuscript of the *Muqaddimat al-Adab*.

Another such example is *jimiš*, the word meaning both 'fruit' and 'grape' in Mongol. In most cases the situation in the original manuscript is as follows:

	P	C	M
'fruit'	mîve	yemiš	jimiš
'grape'	angûr	üzüm	jimiš

As it is fervently claimed by A. K. Borovkov[3], to interpret correctly the Mongolian and Chagatay words and phrases, especially those in Arabic, the base language of the dictionary should not be ignored.

In this article, the author would like to present a case where an interpretation is difficult without the knowledge of the Islamic society at the time Zamakhsharî lived, even if its original Arabic word is taken into consideration.

2. In his edition of the *Muqaddimat al-Adab* Poppe has the following entry[4]:

C	M
‹ğryb lârnynk âywwy›	‹ğry bdwn kyr›
gariblarnïng ewi	garibudun ger

His Russian translation of this phrase is 'dom bednyx', i.e. 'house for poor people'.

Let us see what the corresponding Arabic word is and how it is translated into Persian in the original manuscript[5], together with its Chagatay and Mongolian equivalents:

A	P	C	M
‹maṣ°ṭabah›	‹jây ğrybân›	‹ğryb lâr âywwy›[6]	‹ğry#bdn kyr›
maṣṭaba(t)	jâyi ğarîbân	garîblar evvi	garîbdun ger

The Arabic word *maṣṭaba(t)*[7] has the meanings 'large stone bench, platform in front of a house or in a garden; inn for beggars'[8], and 'a long

---

[3] Borovkov 1962, 1964.

[4] Poppe 1938, 178. — A transliterated form is in single French quotation marks (‹ ›). In the author's transliteration, the following symbols are used: # (word-final form of a letter appearing word-medially); ḧ or h (tâ' marbûṭa); ° (sukûn).

[5] f.039b.

[6] In Poppe's edition, a genitive suffix *-nïŋ* (-nïng) is added to *ğarîblar* (gariblar).

[7] The derivation of this word is not clear. Cf. Bosworth 1976, 260.

[8] Steingass 1884, 1012.

and wide bench or stone-platform raised two feet from the ground, on which the people of the East recline; a tavern; a hospice (for strangers), an inn, caravanserai'[9]. To *masṭaba(t)*, a variant of the word, the following meaning 'a long and wide bench, or rather a stone platform, raised two or three feet above the ground, on which the Orientals recline'[10] is given.

The Arabic (-originated) word *ğarîb* has the meanings 'strange, foreign; foreigner, stranger, traveller; odd, extraordinary, unheard-of, rare; forsaken, poor, miserable; raven-black'[11], and 'uncommon, strange, outlandish, foreign; extraordinary; rare; a foreigner, stranger; poor, needy; humble, gentle, docile'[12].

The lexical and grammatical elements of the phrase in the translations in the three languages are:

‹jâ› 'place, room', ‹y› [ezâfe], ‹ğryb›, ‹ân› [pl.] (Persian)
‹ğryb›, ‹lâr› [pl.], ‹âywwy› 'house [poss.]' (Chagatay)
‹ğry#b›, ‹dn› [pl., gen.], ‹kyr› 'house' (Mongol).

The Chagatay and Mongolian equivalents are a word-for-word translation of the Persian phrase.

3. Which meaning does the word *ğarîb* have here? If it means "foreigner, traveller," the meaning of the whole phrase may be an inn for travellers. In our manuscript, however, *xân* and *xânât*, a singular and a plural form of an Arabic word meaning 'inn, caravanserai', are listed on the same page[13]. Therefore, *maṣṭaba(t)*, which originally meant a large stone bench or platform, may signify an inn; somewhat different from *xân* in form or in function if this interpretation is correct[14].

A further possibility is to interpret the word *ğarîb* as 'poor person'. If this is the case, the meaning of *maṣṭaba(t)* is a place where the poor and homeless people stay. The meaning of the Arabic word that Zamakhsharî had in mind is not necessarily a place with a house-type structure, but

---

9 Steingass 1892, 1253.

10 Steingass 1892, 1237.

11 Steingass 1884, 752.

12 Steingass 1892, 886.

13 In the Muqaddimat al-Adab, as in other dictionaries created in the Arabic tradition, nouns are classified according to semantic categories and in the same category such words meaning wall of a city, tower, market, bath house, wine shop, weaver's shop, mosque, school, hospital, church, etc. are listed.

14 If there were many poor people including travellers coming into the city and staying at certain places, the result from the former interpretation would be similar to the one presented below, and a shift of the meaning of *ğarîb* from 'foreigner, traveller' to 'poor person' could be assumed.

could possibly be just a stone platform on which poor people, including beggars, stayed[15]. This is because Zamakhsharî himself chose the word *jâ* 'place, room' for his Persian translation, even though several words for 'house' existed in Persian[16]. The Chagatay translation of this phrase with the word *ev* 'house' may have derived from the interpretation of the phrase by the compiler of the Chagatay part. It may have been the result of the shift of the word's meaning at his time[17]. The Mongolian translation with the word *ger* 'house' is a complete calque of the corresponding Chagatay phrase. If this is correct, we can say that the compiler of the Chagatay part of the manuscript is not Zamakhsharî but someone else[18], and that Poppe's translation 'dom bednyx', i.e. 'house for poor people', may be wrong as a translation of the Persian phrase, but is correct as that of the phrase in Chagatay and Mongol.

4. Shifts of meaning in both *maṣṭaba(t)* and *ğarîb* make the interpretation difficult. At present the author cannot say anything certain about the phrase for he has not yet found any detailed description of *maṣṭaba(t)* in the 11th and 12th century Khwârizm. It is impossible to know what Zamakhsharî meant by the word without the knowledge of the city life in Khwârizm at that time, where he spent most of his life. But, even if we had access to this knowledge, we still would be unable to be completely certain what exactly was meant by the word, since Zamakhsharî stayed in Makka for some time and visited Baghdâd on pilgrimage, and

[15] In the teachings of Islâm, Muslims are encouraged to give alms (*ṣadaqa*; *zakât*) to the poor and beggars. Beggars were allowed to stay overnight under the eaves on the stone platforms at the entrance of the mosques. — Cf. Bosworth 1976, 209: "141. And the one who seeks shelter on the stone benches of the mosques, …".

[16] *xâna*, etc.

[17] Cf. Bosworth 1976, 259-260: "…, and one should note too Zamakhsharî's definition of *maṣṭaba* in his Muqaddimat al-adab, ed. J. G. Wetzstein (Leipzig 1843), …«The place of strangers, of the beggars, and of the destitute and wretched». … The commentary on Abû Dulaf's verse seems to take *maṣṭaba* not so much as a part of the mosque and its outbuildings where beggars congregated, but as a special building, the *dâr al-qaum*, which was their headquarters in a particular town, doubtless a ruin or vacant building in which they squatted". — See also Bosworth 1976, 231: "It is possible … that we should simply explain *al-maṣṭabâniyyûn* as «the destitute people who sleep out on the stone benches and platforms, *maṣṭabas*, of the mosques" …"; "… and *ahl al-maṣâṭib* «those who sleep rough in the mosque precincts» is virtually synonymous with «beggars»'.

[18] Poppe (1938, 6) says that there is a possibility that Zamakhsharî created the Chagatay part.

furthermore, as a great scholar of theology and Arabic philology, he had a profound knowledge of the whole Islamic society.

Bibliography and Abbreviations

The Alisher Navoi State Museum of Literature and The Japan Society for the Promotion of Science 2008. *The Muqaddimat al-Adab: A Facsimile Reproduction of the Quadrilingual Manuscript (Arabic, Persian, Chagatay and Mongol)*. Tôkyô. [Grant-in-Aid for Scientific Research (B), No.17320061, Research Report (1), The Japan Society for the Promotion of Science]

Боровков, А. К. 1962. 'Тюркские глосси в бухарском списке «Мукаддимат ал-Адаб»'. *Acta Orientalia Hungarica* 15, 31-39.

— 1964. 'Монгольские глосси в бухарском списке «Мукаддимат ал-Адаб»'. *Народы азии и африки* 1, 140-145.

Bosworth, C. E. 1976. *The Mediaeval Islamic Underworld: The Banû Sâsân in Arabic Society and Literature*, Part Two: The Arabic Jargon Texts. Leiden.

Поппе, Н. 1938. *Монгольский словарь Мукаддимат ал-адаб* I-III. Москва · Ленинград. (Reprint: Westmead · Farnborough · Hants 1971)

Saitô, Y. 2008. *The Mongolian Words in the Muqaddimat al-Adab: Romanized Text and Word Index (as of January 2008)*. Tôkyô. [Grant-in-Aid for Scientific Research (B), No.17320061, Research Report (2), The Japan Society for the Promotion of Science]

Steingass, F. 1884. *Arabic-English Dictionary*. (Reprint: New Delhi 1985)

— 1892. *A Comprehensive Persian-English Dictionary*. (Reprint: New Delhi 2000)

Inner Organs as Seats of Feelings and Emotions in the Secret History of the Mongols

Alice Sárközi

We love close people from the very bottom of our hearts and seeing them suffer makes our hearts bleed. Our feelings also come from our souls and we can be sorrowful from the very depths of our souls. How is it in the *Secret History of the Mongols*?

The name of the Mongols has always been associated with bloodshed and cruelty. However, their own descriptions about themselves show a different picture representing people with deep and true feelings. They are brave and timid, placid and excited, sorrowful and happy, feel sympathy and suffering, they can have bad characters and family feelings. In this paper we put up the question in which part of the body these feelings reside in the Mongolian cultural sphere. Examining the seats of feelings and emotions of the Mongols we restrict ourselves to examples taken from the *Secret History of the Mongols*, as it is the earliest historical monument written by the Mongols themselves.

Heart is the seat of courage and cowardice. If somebody's heart is weak, it means that he is a coward: when Chinggis qa'an sends Dörbei dokshin to take revenge on the Tümets for murdering Borokul noyan he threatens to flog those that lack courage:

> *to'otu gü'ün jirüge yada'asu nisiquya* (§240) 'if anyone lost heart *and refused to proceed*, they should beat him'.[1]

The great ruler started to wage war upon the Tangut people but he fell off his horse and could not proceed with the campaign. Even then, he refused to think that he and his fellows could ever be suspected of cowardice:

> *Cinggis qahan ügülerün tang'ut irgen bidan-i jürüge yadaju qariba* (§265) 'Chinggis Qa'an said, «The Tang'ut people will say that we turned back because we lost heart»'.

Güchülük Qa'an speaks about his father, Tayang, when he hesitates to attack the Mongols because of the fear that they may be too strong:

---

[1] Transcriptions and translations of the *Secret History of the Mongols* are taken from de Rachewiltz 1972, 2004.

ana'ai-yin eme tayang jirüge yadarun ene üges ügülejü'üi mongqol-un olon qa'aca irejü'üi mongqol-un olongkin jamuqa-lu'a ende bidan-tur bui kündü eme-yin si'eküi qajar-a ese qaruqsan gürdün-ü tuqul-un belji'el-tür ese gürüksen eme tayang jirüge yadarun ese-üü (§194) 'Again *that* woman Tayang! He speaks such words because he has lost courage. Where would this vast number of Mongols come from? Most Mongols, together with Jamuqa, are here with us. *That* woman Tayang, who *dares* not walk further than

A pregnant woman *goes* to urinate;
Who does not *even* venture so far as
A wheel-*tied* calf *reaches* for its feed, has *lost heart*…'.

And, also a high ranking nobleman, Khori-sübechi, abuses Tayang Qa'an with the words:

edö'e ci manaqar erte bö'et yekin jirüge yadamu ci cimayi eyin jirüge yadaqui-yi medeksen bö'esü qadun ber gü'ün bö'esü eke-yi cinu gürbesü-yi abciraju... (§194) 'Now you, how can you lose heart when it is *still so* early in the morning? Had we known that you would have lost courage in this manner, shouldn't we have brought your mother Gürbesü, even though she is *only* a woman…'.

And, about the pursuit of the messenger Itürgen:

qali'udar-un morin qurdun aju'u qali'udar guyiceju bariqu jürüge yadaju (§184) 'Qali'udar's horse being *swifter,* Qali'udar caught up with him, but did not venture to seize him'.

The next passage also expresses loss of courage with the expression "his heart was unable":

ong-qan-aca arqai-qasar qariqui-tur tedüi sügegei-je'ün-ü eme kö'ün tende to'oril-tur aju'u otqu jürüge yadaju (§181) 'Arqai Qasar returned from Ong Qan, but because the wife and children of Sügegei Je'ün were there with To'oril, Sügegei Je'ün did not have the courage to go with Arqai and stayed behind'.

When his herd has been stolen Jochi Darmala was brave enough to pursue the robber alone:

taicar joci-darmala-yin adu'un de'ermetcü abcu otcu'ui joci-darmala adu'u-ban de'ermetcü o[t]taju nököd-iyen jürüge yadaqdaju mün joci-darala nekejü otcu (§128) 'Taichar stole Jochi Darmala's herd of horses and took them away. The same

Jochi Darmala, *thus* robbed of his herd, went *alone* in pursuit, his companions lacking the courage *to go with him*'.

Calm and peacefulness also reside in the heart. When Chinggis qa'an was raised to the throne he remembered those companions who had helped him in difficult times:

tende cinggis-qahan qan bolju bo'orcu jelme qoyar-a ügülerün ta qoyar namayi se'üder-ece busu nökör ügei-tür se'üder bolju setkil minu amu'ulba-je ta setkil-tür aduqai ke'eba se'ül-ece busu cicu'a ügei-tür se'ül bolju jirüge minu amu'ulba-je ta ce'eji dotora minu aduqai ke'eba ta qoyar (§125) 'Thereupon, when Cinggis Qa'an became *qan*, he said to Bo'orcu and Jelme,

«You two,
When I had no friend but my shadow,
Became my shadows; and truly
Brought peace to my mind.
In my mind you shall dwell!»
And he said,
«When I had no whip
But my *horse's tail,* you
Became my *horse's* tail; and truly
Brought peace to my heart.
In my breast you shall dwell»'.

When praising his night-guards he states why they bring peace to his heart:

siljirin büküi boro'on-a
silgütken büküi jü'en-e
citqun büküi qura-da
siltesütei ger minu horcin
jirin(?) *ülü kin buyiju*
jirüge amu'uluqsan
cing setkilten kebte'ül minu
jirqalang oron-tur gürgebe (230 §)
'My true-hearted nightguards
who in the swirling snowstorm
In shivering cold, in pouring rain,
taking no rest,
Stood all around my latticed tent
Bringing peace to my heart,
You have made me gain *this* throne of joy'.

As a counterpart of joy and happiness, sorrow and suffering reside in the heart and also in the lungs. When Chinggis and Jamuka meet after a long and hostile separation, the qa'an recalls the pleasant days of their alliance in the following words:

öljeitü qutuqtu anda minu büle'e
ünen üküldüküi üdür
öre jürüge-ben ebetgü büle'e ci
anggida ber ö'ere yabu'asu
alalduqui üdür
a'usgi jürüge-ben ebetgü büle'e ci (§200)
'You remained my lucky, blessed sworn friend.
On the day one kills and is killed surely,
Your heart was aching *for me*.
Although you separated from me,
And went a different way,
On the day one fights one another,
Your lungs and heart were aching *for me*'.

Chinggis fights against Ong khan who took him as a foster child. Although being enemies Chinggis remembers the generous act of Ong khan to whom he was born in dress, and warns Senggüm, his real son (born naked) not to cause sorrow and suffering to their father:

ci edö'e qan ecige-yin bidan-u jürüge inu ülü jobo'an (§181)
'Now do not pin our father the Qan's heart'.

Sympathy is also connected with the heart. When Chinggis — only Temüjin by then — tries to escape from the Taichiuts, his deadly enemies, he remembers the friendliness of Sorqan shira and his family:

cimbai cilawun qoyar kö'üt inu örö jirüge-ben ebetcü söni namayi üjejü buqa'u minu a[b]cu sulalaju qono'a'ululāi (§84)
'Cimbai and Cila'un felt in their hearts very sorry for me, and seeing me at night they took my cangue, relieved me of it and enabled me to spend the night *resting*'.

The sons of Chinggis quarrel over the heritage and Jochi and Ca'adai grabe each other's collar. Kökö cos stops them warning:

boqda qadun eke'yü'en tosun duran qoru'ulju sün jürüge e'ede'üljü ügülemüi ci
büle'en-ece
bület mün ke'eli-dece ese-'üü törele'ei ta
qala'un-aca
qalat qaqca
qaqunaq-aca ese-'üü

qarula'a ta
jürügen-ece töreksen eke-yü'en
cimatqa'su
cinar inu jekircü
jalira'ulu'asu ülü boli (§254)

'You speak so as to harden the butter of your mother's affection, so as to sour the milk of that august lady's heart.

From the warm *womb, coming forth*
Suddenly, were you *two*
Not born from the same belly?
From the hot *womb, coming forth*
Abruptly, were you *two*
Not issued from a single womb
If you incur blame
From your mother who has borne you
From her heart, her affection
Even if you appease her
It will be of no avail.'

Liver is the seat of family sentiments. The above examples can be familiar to anyone—we also feel happiness, joy, sorrow and symphaty in our hearts. However the following passages speak about the liver and gall in connection with human feelings, that is different from ours.

busu heligetü bulqa irgen-tür morila'uldaju jöb-i tab-i bolqu bolba ke'ejü büküi-tür büri güyük qoyar-a eyin ke'ekde'et eye ügei tarqaqdaba (§275) "So, just at the time when, having been sent to ride against a rebellious people of a different race, we were asking ourselves whether we had been successful, Büri and Güyük spoke to us in this way and we parted in disaccord."

Rebel tribes have different livers: *busu heligetü,* while relatives are of the same liver: *heligen-ü uruq*. When the Merkits raped Temüjin's wife, Börte, he called Jamuka for help:

heligen-ü uru[q] busut-ū bida
haci-yan ker hacilaqun bidu ke'eju
...
...
örö minu ebetba
ebür hemtereba ke'en medejü
helige minu ebetba
ösöl-iyen ösön ... (§105)

'Are we not from one family?
How shall we take our revenge?
My breast is torn apart.
You and I,
Are we not of kindred blood?'.

And, when they succeeded in taking revenge, Temüjin uses the same expressions:

ere hacitu merkit irgen-i
ebür ba anu hoqtorqui bolqaba
helige ba anu hemtelba bida
oro ba anu hoqtorqui bolqaba (§113)
'We emptied the breasts of the Merkit people
Who take their revenge as a man does
And we tore their livers to pieces
We emptied their beds'.

Light-mindedness also resides in the liver. Otcigin, who goes to bed early and gets up late is characterised by Jamuka with the words:

tere hö'elün eke-yin nilqa otcigin heligetü ke'ekdeyü (§195) 'He is the youngest son of Mother Hö'elün. He is called Otcigin the Easy-going'.

Foul character and evil intention. His brothers and the nobles speak about Ong khan when he turns against his adopted son, Temüjin:

ene qan aqa bidan-u üge'ü aburitu
hümegei helige ebüritcü yabuqu
aqa de'ü-yi baraba (§152)
'Our elder brother the Qan
Has a miserable nature; he goes on
Harbouring a rotten liver.
He has destroyed his brothers...'.

And also later:

temüjin kö'ün-tür teyin yabuqsan helige ebüritcü yabumu ker kikün bida ke'eldüba (§152) 'Now, forgetting that he kept himself alive like this thanks to his son Temüjin, he goes on harbouring a rotten liver'.

Characterising the heroic Jürkin people the chronicle says:

irgen-ü'en dotoraca ilqaju helige-tür sölsütü heregei-tür honcitan a'usgi dü'üreng jirügetü aman dü'üreng a'urtan ere tutum erdemütten bökös gücüten-i ilqaju ökeü a'urtan sölsütan omoqtan jörkimes tula jürkin ke'ekdegü yosun teyimü (§139) '... chose *men for him* from among his own people and, having chosen them, gave him strong and mighty *men* who had

Gall in their livers
Thumbs good at shooting,
Lungs filled with courage,
Mouths full of fury,
And, all, men of skill

Because they had fury and gall, and were proud and inflexible, that is the reason why they were called Jürkin'.

Now, courage is housed not only in their hearts, but also in their livers and even in the lungs. Gall is connected with courage at another place, as well. Speaking about the brave mother, Höelün, left alone in the steppe:

üdür söni qo'olai teji'eba
sölsütei töreksen üjin eke
sutan kö'üd-iyen teji'erün (§74)
'Night and day she filled
their hungry gullets.
Born brave, the noble mother,
She fed her high born sons'.

In this short paper I tried to point out where the human feelings of the Mongols where thought to reside in their bodies. Thinking it over we can see the similarities and differences compared with other peoples.

Dear Prof. Rachewiltz, I wish you good luck, good health, success and energy for further valuable publications from the very bottom of my heart.

Bibliography

de Rachewiltz, I. 1972. *Index to the Secret History of the Mongols*. (Indiana University Uralic & Altaic Series 121.) Bloomington, IN.

— 2004. *The Secret History of the Mongols*. A Mongolian Epic Chronicle of the Thirteenth Century 1-2. Translated with a historical and philological commentary by Igor de Rachewiltz. Leiden · Boston 2004.

Ligeti, L. 1971. *Histoire secrète des Mongols*. (Monumenta Linguae Mongolicae Collecta I.) Budapest.

- 1974. *Histoire secrète des mongols. Texte en écriture ouigoure incorporé dans la Chronique Altan tobči de Blo-bzaṅ bstan-'jin*. (Monumenta Linguea Mongolicae Collecta VI.) Budapest.

Sárközi, A. 1978. 'Love and Friendship in the Secret History of the Mongols'. In: L.V. Clark & P. Draghi (eds), *Aspects of Altaic Civilization* II, Proceedings of the XVIII PIAC, Bloomington, June 29-July 5, 1975. (Indiana University Uralic and Altaic Series 134.) Bloomington, IN.

WANG GUOWEI'S COLLATION OF THE SECRET HISTORY OF THE MONGOLS

Borjigijin Ulaan

There are two copies of the *Secret History of the Mongols* (henceforth abbreviated to *SHM*) collated by Wang Guowei, which are kept in the Rare Books' Collection of the Chinese National Library. The original of these two copies is the block-printed edition of Guan Gu Tang (i.e. Ye Dehui's edition, abbreviated here to Ye's edition). The call numbers of their microfilms are 02192 and 02193 respectively.

According to the words of Wang Guowei written in the two copies, they were collated between September 1925 and November 1926. The first one (abbreviated here to Copy A) was first collated in September and October 1925, and the second one (abbreviated to Copy B) was first collated in November of the same year. With regard to Copy A, Wang Guowei wrote a note on the blank page left after Ye Dehui's preface and Ruan Yuan's synopsis, ending with the words "Guan Weng (*the scholarly title of Wang Guowei) wrote this in the eighth month of the Year *Yichou* (*the year of the azure cattle)". There is an additional note above the column of the leaf, ending with the words "the first day of the ninth month, noted again". Here, the year of the azure cattle is 1925, and the first day of the ninth month refers to October 18th of that year in the solar calendar. He also wrote a note reading "Collated by Guan Weng with the edition of Yang of Lingshi in the ninth month of the Year *Yichou*", and "checked with the Mongolian (*the Chinese phonetic transcriptions), added several words" following the original text of Copy A. Concerning Copy B, Wang Guowei wrote a long note on the blank page at the end of the copy. It ended with the words "on the fifth day of the tenth month of the Year *Yichou*, Wang Guowei of Haining (noted)". This fifth day of the tenth month corresponds to November 11th of that year in the solar calendar. The two copies were collated again in November 1926 as Wang Guowei wrote "[I] borrowed Gu Jianpin's manuscript kept in the Han-fen-lou and checked once in the tenth month of the Year *Bingyin* (*the year of the red tiger)" at the end of the note next to the original text of Copy A. Further he wrote "[I] borrowed [Gu Jianpin's manuscript] from the Han-fen-lou and checked it once in the tenth month of the Year *Bingyin*, when correcting several words. Guowei has made this annotation sitting by the oil lamp on the twenty second day". Here the Year *Bingyin* is 1926, and the twenty second day of the tenth month refers to November 26th of that year in the solar calendar. Wang Guowei collated the two copies first with the edition of the Lian-yun-yi Series (i.e. Zhang Mu's edition with the Chinese summarized translation only), and later with the interlinear phonetic transcription of the text, when he "added some words and sentences". One year later, he was able to borrow Gu Guangqi's certified text (abbreviated to Gu's text) kept in the Han-fen-lou Library in Shanghai, so he collated the two copies once again with Gu's text, and "corrected several words". There is a note written by Fu Zengxiang in 1932 (*Year *Renshen*, the year of the black monkey) at the beginning of Gu's text. In this note, Fu Zengxiang mentioned that he "had bargained over the price" when the Han-fen-lou bought the text. He borrowed it later from the Han-fen-lou and passed it to Chen Yuan for his collation. Soon after the Han-fen-lou burned in a fire caused by aerial bombardement.

When collating, Wang Guowei mainly corrected the faulty letterings of Ye's edition following Gu's text (about 59 places corrected in Copy A, and about 40 places corrected in Copy B), except for a few faults in the edition of the Lian-yun-yi Series (about 3 places corrected in Copy A). He also corrected mistakes and filled in lacunae according to context (including the Chinese transcription which Wang Guowei called "the Mongolian"; about 88 places corrected in Copy A, and about 77 places corrected in Copy B). He wrote his corrections and additions outside the columns or by the side of the faulty letterings, and the omissions inside the columns. Wang Guowei mentioned "the corrections which Guan Weng (the title Wang Guowei used for himself) made according to the facsimile copy (i.e. Gu's text), were written with a red brush-pen alongside the lines", in the note following the original text of Copy B.

According to compendia's statistics, the total number of Wang Guowei's corrections is more than 260, of these, about 147 corrections in Copy A and about 117 (except for the repeated corrections of the same error) in Copy B, in which there were about 99 mistakes from Ye's edition and about 165 mistakes from Gu's text that had been corrected. The total number of Wang Guowei's additional corrections is more than 70, of these 19 are in Copy A and about 54 in Copy B (excepting for the repeated additional corrections). The scope of his collation extends to the whole book, including all the three parts, i.e. the Chinese phonetic transcription, the interlinear translation and the summarized translation.[1] He made about 84 corrections, filled in about 8 lacunae in the Chinese phonetic transcription, corrected about 36 cases, and filled in about 11 lacunae in the summarized translation. The rest are mainly corrections and additions to the interlinear translation.

Here are some examples of Wang Guowei's corrections and additions. The examples provided are mainly selected from Wang Guowei's corrections or additions to Gu's text.

I. *Examples for misprints.*

1. In the Chinese phonetic transcription:[2]

qašuiqun → *qamuqun*	(§21, 01:13:06)
üčüyü → *üčügen*	(§35, 01:21:08)
solura → *bolura*	(§74, 02:06:03)
de'üdanr → *de'üner*	(§101, 02:47:01)
nobukin → *noyakin*	(§166, 05:40:02)
ke'elyebei → *ke'eldübei*	(§170, 06:05:10)
yegei qongtaqar → *jegei qongtaqar*	(§180, 06:38:07)
qarbuten → *qarbuyu*	(§195, 07:38:04)
yuruqan → *turuqan*	(§202, 08:25:09)
uduber → *udurar*	(§259, 11:42:10)
sojiqas → *solangqas*	(§274, 12:28:01)
lüiyü'er → *söyü'er*	(§277, 12:34:02)

2. In the interlinear translation:

jiang mu zhe → *jiang lai* (come) *zhe*	(§16, 01:10:01)
sui → *chu* (squab-chick)	(§25, 01:16:03)
ban duo du pi you de → *ban yun* (cyetic) *du pi you de*	(§38, 01:22:08)
da you de → *huo* (fire) *you de*	(§62, 01:43:02)
duan zhe → *qi zhe* (ride on)	(§90, 02:28:01)
die → *song* (send-off)	(§94, 02:37:03)
wen san zhe → *kui san zhe* (sauve qui peut)	(§110, 03:16:05)
zhe → *xing* (understand)	(§118, 03:30:10)
jiao le → *sha le* (killed)	(§128, 04:03:04)
yong → *gan* (liver)	(§139, 04:25:07)
gu you de → *hua* (talk, words) *you de*	(§166, 05:40:06)

[1] Eldengtei and Oyundalai's critical edition of *SHM* (*Meng-gu-mi-shi jiao-kan-ben*, Huhhot, 1980) only collated the part of Chinese phonetic transcription.

[2] The pagination following is that of Kuribayashi & Choijinjab 2001.

ru zhe → *fan zhe* (rebelled) (§177, 06:30:03)
yu zhe → *kan zhe* (chop) (§229, 09:47:10)
dao nian → *yi nian* (will, reminder) (§242, 10:24:03)
gao yan → *gao li* (Korea) (§274, 12:28:01)
qu zhe → *diu zhe* (discard) (§278,12:38:03)

3. In the summarized translation:
lie che ke che er chi hu er hu shan liang jian → *dao che ke che er chi hu er hu shan liang jian* (go to bosom of Mountain Čegčer and Mountain Čiqurqu) (§94, 02:37:08)
su wei shu ri → *su wei shu mu* (number of the nightguards) (§229, 09:49:08)
fang dao → *jing dao*(banner) (§232, 10:06:04)

II. *Examples for inversions.*

1. In the Chinese phonetic transcription:
töre'ünbil → *töre'ülbi* (§§17, 01:10:05; 20, 01:12:07)
obotan boqluba → *oboqtan boluba* (§42, 01:25:02)
jurbu → *jubur* (§115, 03:25:02)

2. In the interlinear translation:
zan xun → *xun zan* (§83, 02:20:07)

III. *Examples for unnecessary additions.*

1. In the Chinese phonetic transcription:
büyü → Ø (§243, 10:25:10)

2. In the interlinear translation:
mo lei shan de → *lei shan de* (of one's waist) (§57, 01:39:05)

IV. *Examples for omissions.*

1. In the Chinese phonetic transcription:
töresen → *töregsen* (§8, 01:05:07)
qunta'u → *qunta'u bolba* (§111, 03:18:05)
üri → *ne'üri* (§118, 03:30:05)
bošoqa-dur činu → *bošoqa-dur činu aju* (§203, 08:28:06)

2. In the interlinear translation:
ceng → *bu ceng* (for *ese*) (§34, 01:21:03)
me → *me dao* (for *ke'en*) (§83, 02:21:02)
you de → *zhou* (axle) *you de* (§124, 03:46:03)
mei → *ri mei* (days) (§136, 04:19:06)
zi de hang → *she* (tongue) *zi de hang* (§169, 05:49:02)

ling zhe → *zhong* (clan) *ling zhe* (§176, 06:19:10)
jiao zi de hang
→ *kou* (mouth) *jiao zi de hang* (§214, 09:16:07)
you de → *shui you de* (with water) (§270, 12:16:01)
jiao a → *jiao ben* (gallop) *a* (§279, 12:49:05)

3. In the summarized translation:
ba a tu → *ba a tu er* (*ba'atur*) (§46, 01:29:01)
wo qin ba er he
→ *wo qin ba er he hei* (*Ökin barqaq*) (§49, 01:31:02)
su bie tai → *su bie e tai* (*Sübe'etei*) (§195, 07:40:07)

V. *Examples for incorrect separations.*

1. In the Chinese phonetic transcription:
Qorčiusun ebügen → *Qorči usun ebügen* (§120, 03:36:02)
šigiqutu qugüčü → *šigiqutuqu güčü* (§202, 08:25:04)
badaiqišiliq → *badai qišiliq* (§219, 09:25:07)

About some corrections and additions, Wang Guowei said that they were made according to "the Mongolian" (i.e. the Chinese phonetic transcription) in particular. For examples, he wrote "*Jungšoi* is namely *Jungso* in Volume Three of the Mongolian" under the column of Vol.8.f.25v.l.2. He also wrote "It is written as *Čangši'ud* in Volume Three of the Mongolian" (*it was misprinted as *Biši'ud* in the Chinese phonetic transcription) under the column of Vol.9.f.10v.l.2. He added a personal name *Taqai* before *Sükegei* in Vol.5.f.12v.l.3, and at the same time wrote "added according to the Mongolian" above the column.

Analyzing all the corrections and additions of Wang Guowei, we can know that many other corrections and additions still referred to the Chinese phonetic transcription even if he had not said whether they were corrected according to "the Mongolian". For examples, there is a sentence reading "the seven sons stood up by the door" in Vol.10.f.42v.l.2 (§245, in the summarized translation). Wang Guowei changed "seven" to "six". It ought to be changed according to the Chinese phonetic transcription, because it appeared as *jirqo'an* (*liu ge* i.e. six, in the interlinear translation) there. The personal name *Alči* added between *Jürčedei* and *Tolun* in Vol.11.f.19v.l.1 (§253, in the summarized translation) also ought to be added according to the Chinese phonetic transcription.

Carefully reading and checking the Chinese phonetic transcription is a precondition for collating and studying the *SHM*. One cannot completely comprehend the textual implications of the *SHM* only by referring to its summarized translation, its interlinear translation or the Latin renderings of its Chinese phonetic transcription. This has got to be commonly recognized by *SHM* scholars. Nevertheless, at Wang Guowei's time the study of the *SHM* had not yet developed so much, there were few Chinese scholars who knew Mongolian language. Wang Guowei dared to check the Chinese transcription of the *SHM* even without knowing Mongolian language. This reflects his attitude toward studies, and shows that his collation is comparatively believable.

It should be pointed out that Wang Guowei had already gradually discovered quite a few problems during the process of collation and study of the *SHM*. Except for trivial problems such as the misprints of Ye's edition and the miswritings of Gu's text, he grasped some of the translation skills of the Ming's translators through the comparison of the Chinese phonetic transcription with the interlinear translation, and discovered deep-seated problems in the grammar of the Mongolian original. I think that most of Wang Guowei's corrections and additions, as well as his notes on them, are still a very important reference for us when collating the *SHM*. His contribution to the collation of the *SHM* deserves our high regard.

Wang Guowei's many corrections concerning the Mongolian grammar are connected with verbs. Examples of this are as follows:

1. For imperative suffixes:

zan xun → *xun zan* (for *eriye*)	(§83, 02:20:07)
xia shao → *xia zan* (for *ba'uya*)	(§142, 04:33:07)
hui qu → *hui qu nin* (for *qaridqun*)	(§148, 05:03:08)
gong ru → *gong ru wo* (for *oroldusu*)	(§164, 05:37:10)
si sha → *si sha wo* (for *qadquldusu*)	(§171, 06:07:09)
xu jing → *xu jing zan* (for *oqjadqaya*)	(§193, 07:23:09)

According to the principles set by the Ming's translators for their interlinear translating, the Chinese words *wo* (I), *zan* (we) and *nin* (you) located immediately after verbs were used as symbol words for the imperative of verbs (corresponding to the Mongolian suffixes). The word *wo* was for the first person singular, *zan* was for its plural form, and *nin* was for the second person.[3]

In a like manner, the word transcribed as *širkulen* (interlinear translation: *zuan ru* [*wo*], §111, 03:18:07) had been changed to *širkusu*. The imperative suffix for the first person singular in ancient Mongolian was *-su/-sü;* it was phonetically transcribed with the Chinese character *su*.

[3] From the editions available, we can get the knowledge that this principle had not been put thoroughly into practice. Many of the imperative suffixes have no correspondence in the interlinear translation. What Wang Guowei added is only a little part of them.

The word *lian* (expressing the Mongolian sound *len*) is a miswriting for *su* due to the resemblance of their corresponding characters.

2. For verb determining suffixes:

The words transcribed as *neyisü irebe* (interlinear translation: *xiang he lai le*, §120, 03:34:09) have been changed to *širkulen*. The coordinating verb determining suffix *-n* (associative) was spelled tighter with *-le-* as one syllable *-len*, and transcribed with one Chinese character: *lian*. The word *su* is a miswriting for *lian* due to the resemblance of their corresponding characters.

The interlinear translations *yu le de you lai* (for *ögtegsen bü'esü*, §6, 01:04:05) and *nu ke* (for *a'urla'asu*, §195, 07:38:02), had been changed to *yu le de you a* and *nu a* respectively. The subordinating verb determining suffix *-'asu/-'esü* (*-basu/besü*) (conditional) was transcribed with the Chinese characters *a su/e su, ba su/bie su*, and interlinearly translated with the Chinese word *a*. The words *lai* in the first case and *ke* in the second one are both miswritings for *a*.

3. For verb tense-bound suffixes:

The Chinese transcription *qarbuten* (interlinear translation: *she you*, §195, 07:38:09) was changed to *qarbuyu*. The suffix *-yu/-yü* used to express the present and future tense of Mongolian verbs, was transcribed with the help of the Chinese character *you*. The word *tian* (expressing the Mongolian sound *ten*) is a miswriting for *you* due to the resemblance of their corresponding characters.

The interlinear translation *xing le you wei* (for *yabuju'ui,* §142, 04:34:08) was changed to *xing le you lai*. The suffix *-ju'ui/-jü'üi* used to express the past tense of Mongolian verbs, was interlinearly translated with the Chinese characters *you lai*. The words *you wei* were not used for this function.

4. For passive voice suffixes:

The interlinear translation *bi wei zhang le* (for *aqalaqdaba,* §277, 12:45:10) was changed to *bei wei zhang le*. The suffix *-qda/-gde* used to express the passive voice of Mongolian verbs, was interlinearly translated with the Chinese character *bei*. The word *bi* is a miswriting for *bei* due to the resemblance of their corresponding characters.

5. For verbal negative suffixes:

The interlinear translation *qi lai hang* (for *bosu'ai-üdü'üi-e,* §245, 10:35:02) was changed to *qi wei hang*. The negative suffix *-üdü'üi-e* was interlinearly translated with the Chinese characters *wei* (not yet). The word *lai* is a miswriting for *wei* due to the resemblance of their corresponding characters.

Some of the corrections concern the case of Mongolian nouns. The following examples can be given:

1. For suffixes of the instrumental case:

The interlinear translation *shan ming* (for *arai-iyar,* §198, 08:02:03) was changed to *shan ming yi zhe*. One of the suffixes of the instrumental case *-iyar/-iyer* was usually transcribed with the Chinese characters *yi ya er/yi ye er,* and the other *-bar/-ber* (*-'ar/-'er*), with *ba er/bie er* (*a er/e er*). There were several Chinese words used for interlinear translation of the instrumental case suffixes such as *jiao*, *yong*, *li*, *hang* and *yi zhe*, etc. The word *yi zhe* appears in the interlinear translations with the slightly changed meaning 'along' or 'down'. Regarding the example of §198, we can find another similar one in §257 (11:36:09), reading *ara-iyar* with interlinear translation *di ming* (place name) *yi zhe* (along). The normal form of both *arai-iyar* and *ara-iyar* should be *arai-'ar*. Here the Chinese transcription of the Ming's translators was close to its spoken pronunciation. *Arai* is the Mountain Arai, and *Arai-'ar* means along the Mountain Arai.

2. For suffixes of the dative-locative case:

The interlinear translation *zi sun hao* (for *uruq-a,* §206, 08:39:10) was changed to *zi sun hang*. One of the suffixes of the dative-locative case *-a/-e* was spelled together with the precedent sound as one syllable, and transcribed in a non-consistent way with different Chinese characters. Its interlinear translation was usually *hang*. The word *hao* is a miswriting for *hang*.

All the above corrections and additions made by Wang Guowei are based on his comprehension of the relationship of the Mongolian grammar and the working principles set by the Ming's translators.

There are many lacunae in the interlinear translations (about more than 90). Except for omissions that occurred during the process of rewriting, many of them appear to be words left without translation by the Ming's translators. Wang Guowei attempted to fill about 24 of the lacunae. For examples:

yun que (lark, for *bilji'ur*)	(§77, 02:09:03)
men you de (with a door, for *qa'atai*)	(§101, 02:47:02)
yi (ant, for *qarča*)	(§103, 02:50:10)
kou zi (button, for önör)	(§105, 03:04:02)
wai mao (appearance, for *qaṭar*)	(§111, 03:18:04)
fu zhuang (clothes, for *qunar*)	(§111, 03:18:10)
ci (stab, for *onglajidqun*)	(§124, 03:46:09)
jian ming (name of arrow, for *qola*)	(§124, 03:47:03)

zuo ji (hurry up, for *öterlen*) (§133, 04:13:01)
lai (come, for *igtünejü*) (§133, 04:13:01)
de (gain, get, for *olon*) (§145, 04:40:01)
gua (blow, for *keyisgen*) (§148, 05:01:05)
qi dao (invocation, for *elbesün jalama*) (§174, 06:16:07)
tu (earth, for *urbang*) (§183, 06:46:02)
qi dao yi (by invocation, for *elbesü'er*) (§189, 07:10:03)
nuo (coward, for *torluq*) (§189, 07:10:04)
mo (silent, for *ni'udqun*) (§190, 07:13:08)
xing niu (contrary, for *mojir(qaqun)*) (§209, 09:02:07)

Among the above examples are some that refer to those in Naka Michiyo's annotated translation of the *SHM* in Japanese "The Veritable Records of Chinggis Qan", such as *yun que* (lark), *yi* (ant), *kou zi* (button), *fu zhuang* (clothes), *tu* (earth), etc. We may say that some of them are obviously wrong, for examples *yi* (ant), *kou zi* (button), *fu zhuang* (clothes), etc.

Besides the faulty additions presented above, there are some other mistakes in Wang Guowei's collation. For examples:

1. In the Chinese phonetic transcription:

qamtudqalduju → *qatudqalduju* (§104, 03:02:02)
qoš → *qoq* (§169, 05:49:10)
yeren tabun → *yesü tabun* (§202, 08:27:01)
nu'ud → *kö'üd* (§267, 12:09:09)

It is indisputable that Wang Guowei would not have made these mistakes if he had known the Mongolian language.

Moreover, Ye's edition used the Chinese character *li* (in, within) with a little character *she* (tongue) on the left shoulder of it to express the Mongol sound *-ri* in the word *qori* in §266 (12:08:05), where Gu's text had used another Chinese character *li* (reason). Wang Guowei corrected the word according to Gu's text. In fact, the *li* in Gu's text was a miswriting for *mai* (cover in) due to the resemblance of their corresponding characters.

2. In the interlinear translation:

The phrase *mo lei shan de* (up to one's waist) was changed to *lei shan de* (of one's waist) (§57, 01:39:05). The original Chinese transcription is *qabirqa-ta*. *-Ta/-te* is one of the suffixes of the dative-locative case, usually expressed by the Chinese character *hang* (in, at, on) in the interlinear translations. The Chinese word *mo* (overflow, go above) is an appropriate one for the suffix here, and should not be deleted. Here the meaning of the sentence is "they danced until there was a ditch up to their waist".

3. In the summarized translation:

The sentence *guan shan ma nei. jiao shou shi tuo kun suo zhe* (*the meaning is not clear) was changed to *guan shan ma nei. jiao shou shi tuo xi suo zhe* (§234, 10:10:05). Its Chinese transcription is *Aqtas-ača asaraju hö'öšin ačiju yabutuqai*. The word *hö'öšin* appeared originally mistakenly as *hö'ögia*, and its interlinear translation is *wang suo* (net). Both *kun suo* (enlacing cord) and *xi suo* (thin string) are mistakes for *wang suo*. Thus, the summarized translation should be *guan shan ma nei jiao shou shi. tuo wang suo zhe* (Let [some of the night-guards] manage some of the geldings and load [hunting] nets on to them!).

As a matter of fact, collating a complex historical document such as the *SHM* demands high knowledge of the ancient Mongolian language and scripts, as well as the ancient Chinese phonology. It is not an easy work for any scholar. Mistakes in the studies are always hard to avoid. I think that the mistakes in Wang Guowei' s collation do not affect his achievements in the studies of the *SHM*.

At present, there appears to be a new upsurge in the study of the *SHM*. Several annotated translations in many languages have been published. Nevertheless, a complete and good critical edition of the original text is still required. We hope that the textual collation of the *SHM* may make greater progress following in the footsteps of Wang Guowei, Eldengtei and Oyundalai.

Finally, I wish to offer my thanks to Ariel Laurencio for helping me to write this article in English.

Bibliography

Ardajab 2005. *Xin-yi-ji-zhu Meng-gu-mi-shi*. Huhhot.

de Rachewiltz, I. 2004. *The Secret History of the Mongols · A Mongolian Epic Chronicle of the Thirteenth Century*. Leiden · Boston.

Cleaves, F. W. 1982. *The Secret History of the Mongols*. Harvard.

Чоймаа, Щ. 2002. *Монголын нууц товчоон Лувсанданзаны Алтан товч эхийн харьцуулсан судалгаа*. Ulaanbaatar.

— 2006. *Монголын нууц товчоо, Монголын нууц товчооны эхийг щинээр хөрвүүлж буулгаж тайлбар хийсэн*. Ulaanbaatar.

Eldengtei & Oyundalai 1980. *Meng-gu-mi-shi jiao-kan-ben*. Huhhot.

Irinchin-ü sergügelte 1987. *Mongγol-un Niγuča Tobčiyan*. Huhhot.

Kuribayashi H. & Choijinjab 2001. *Gencho-hishi-mongorugo-zen-tango-gobi sakuin · Word- and Suffix-Index to the* Secret History of the Mongols. Sendai.

Ozawa, Sh. 1984-94. *Gencho-hishi-zenshaku* I-VI. Tokyo.
Yuan-chao-mi-shi. Si-bu-cong-kan third edition. Shanghai 1936.
Yuan-chao-mi-shi san-zhong. Taibei 1975.

EXCHANGE-MARRIAGE IN THE ROYAL FAMILIES OF NOMADIC STATES

Nobuhiro Uno

Preamble. My speciality is the history of nomadic states, but I am also endeavouring to incorporate the ideas of cultural anthropology into the study of history. Towards this end, in this article I propose to apply the alliance theory of cultural anthropology to an analysis of marriage in the royal families of the Mongol empire and the Liao. The Liao was a nomadic state of the Khitan people that extended its power from northern China to the Mongolian Plateau in the tenth to twelfth centuries, while the Mongol empire was a nomadic state of the Mongol people that spread far across the Eurasian continent in the thirteenth and fourteenth centuries. Detailed data on marriage in the royal families of these two nomadic states has been preserved in the Liao-shih in the case of the Liao and in the Yüan-shih and Jāmiʿ al-Tawārīkh in the case of the Mongol empire. While analyzing those data, I discovered some valuable instances of "exchange-marriage," and my findings have previously been published in four articles written in Japanese.[1] I shall give hereafter examples of exchange-marriage and also present my ideas on the role played by exchange-marriage in nomadic states.

1. *Characteristics of exchange-marriage in the royal families of nomadic states*. The Elementary Structures of Kinship by C. Lévi-Strauss was an epoch-making work that introduced the concept of "exchange" to the study of marriage, and it had an enormous influence not only on anthropology, but also on various fields in the humanities. However, it also became the target of harsh criticism, and today, in the wake of the decline of structuralism, its theories no longer attract much attention.

I have come to realise, however, that, when studying marriage in the royal families of nomadic states, it is most effective to introduce the concept of the "exchange of women" in order to analyze the complex marriage relationships of the royal houses of the Khitans and Mongols and elucidate the underlying marriage system. But it is inappropriate to apply to the Liao and the Mongol empire the models of exchange-marriage in the form educed from Lévi-Strauss's alliance theory, that is, "restricted

---

[1] Uno 1993, 1995, 1997, 1999.

exchange" and "generalised exchange." His models did not derive from actual examples of marriage, and were conceptual models deduced from kinship systems. Consequently, I have found when analyzing concrete examples of marriage in the royal families of nomadic states that, unless his models of exchange-marriage are modified with regard to some basic points, they do not conform to actual examples found in nomadic states.

Let me describe which points need to be modified. Lévi-Strauss considered that when specific forms of consanguineous marriage are repeated, this results in patterns of exchange of women between groups, and he called this "exchange-marriage." For example, in the case of a patrilateral cross-cousin marriage, when a male marries his father's sister's daughter, give-and-take exchange-marriages take place between the two groups (fig. 1). The exchange-marriages of the Mongol royal family considered in this article would seem at first sight to resemble this patrilateral cross-cousin marriage, and they are identical insofar that they represent reciprocal give-and-take exchange-marriages between two groups.

There is, however, also a fundamental difference. The royal houses of both the Liao dynasty and the Mongol empire practised polygyny, and therefore it was possible for patterns of give-and-take exchange to occur even in cases of non-consanguineous marriage. This happened, for instance, when the king gave to his chief wife's brother a daughter borne to him by one of his concubines (fig. 2). When seen from the husband's position, this was not a case of consanguineous marriage, for his wife was not related to him by blood. Even in such cases of non-consanguineous exchange-marriage, the royal families of nomadic states were able to maintain marriage relationships with affinal relatives if the marriages followed this pattern of give-and-take.

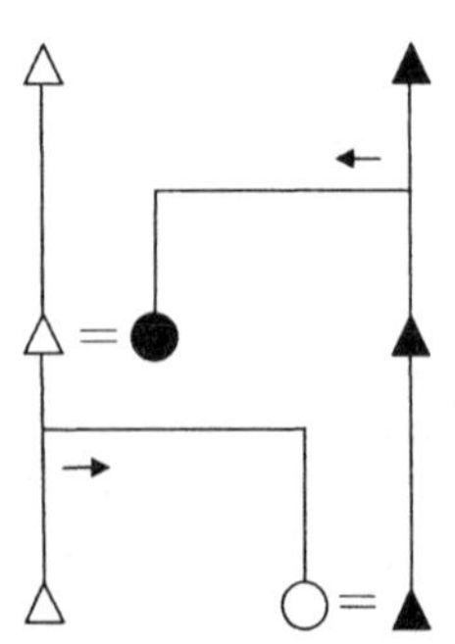

Fig. 1 *Patrilateral cross-cousin marriage*

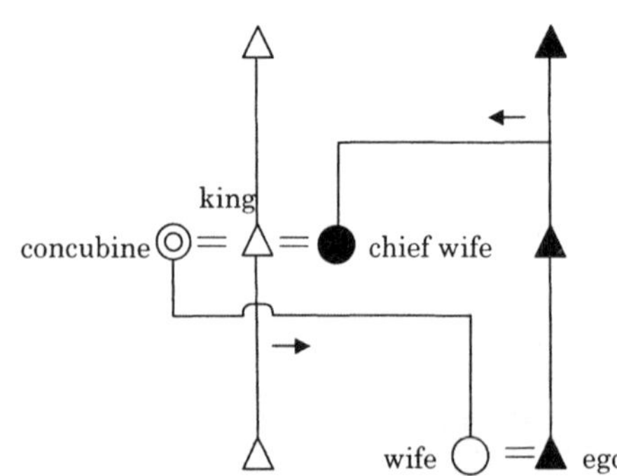

Fig. 2 *Non-consanguineous exchange-marriage*

One further important point is that it was not necessary for all males in the royal family to practise exchange-marriage. All that was required was that there take place a sufficient number of exchange-marriages to ensure the maintenance of marriage relationships with specific affinal relatives, and it usually sufficed if one or two exchange-marriages took place during a single generation. In other words, not all members of the royal family were required to practise exchange-marriage in accordance with a single marriage rule.

In the above, I have pointed out some basic characteristics of exchange-marriage in the royal families of nomadic states. Next, I wish to analyze the patterns of exchange with reference to some actual examples of exchange-marriage.

2. *Exchange-marriage in the royal family of the Liao*. In the Liao, founded by the Khitan Yeh-lü A-pao-chi when he ascended the throne in 907, the royal family bore the clan name of Yeh-lü, and many of its members took wives from the Hsiao clan. At the same time, women belonging to the royal family married men of the Hsiao clan, and intermarriage was practised between the two clans. A typical example is shown in fig. 3.[2]

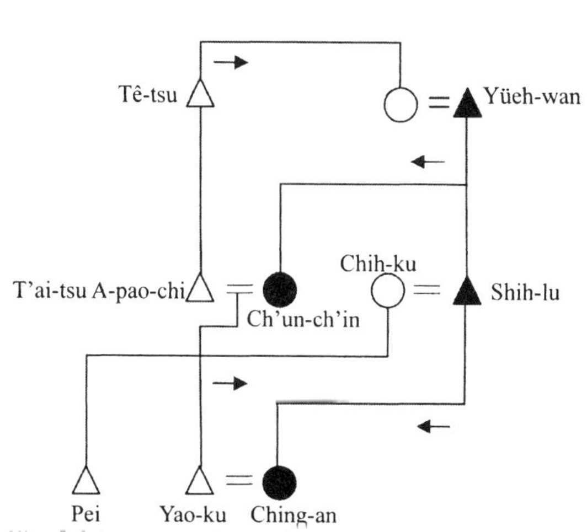

Fig. 3 *Marriage relationships between the Yeh-lü and Hsiao clans of Liao*

The dynastic founder Yeh-lü A-pao-chi (T'ai-tsu) married Empress Ch'un-ch'in of the Hsiao clan in the sec–ond half of the 890s, and in 899 their eldest son Pei was born. Ch'un-ch'in had a younger brother by the name of Shih-lu, who married T'ai-tsu's daughter Chih-

[2] Karl A. Wittfogel made the important observation that marriage between the Yeh-lü and Hsiao clans represented "reciprocal" marriage (Wittfogel & Fêng 1949, 206-212). But he did not go so far as to detect any pattern of exchange in these marriages. A detailed analysis of the marriage relationships of the Liao from the viewpoint of political history can be found in Holmgren 1986.

ku.[3] These two marriages were exchange-marriages. The important point about these exchange-marriages is that they were not simply based on the principle of give-and-take, but followed a specific pattern of exchange in which the husband, in return for having taken a woman in marriage, gave his daughter to his wife's brother.

These exchange-marriages continued, and in the first half of the 920s T'ai-tsu's second son Yao-ku (who became his eventual successor) married Shih-lu's daughter, and upon his accession to the throne she became Empress Ching-an.[4] When considered in conjunction with Shih-lu's marriage, this marriage was one in which Shih-lu, in return for having taken Chih-ku as wife, gave his daughter to Chih-ku's brother, the future emperor, and like the previous example, it followed a pattern of exchange in which the husband, in return for having taken a woman in marriage, gave his daughter to his wife's brother.

This pattern of exchange-marriages between the Yeh-lü and Hsiao clans was subsequently repeated, with some breaks, throughout the Liao dynasty. Although I cannot go into details here, detailed analyses can be found in my earlier articles published in Japanese.[5]

3. *Exchange-marriage in the royal family of the Mongol empire.* Činggis Qan's family members, representing the royal house of the Mongol empire, intermarried with a large number of tribes, and they practised reciprocal marriage with the Qonggirad and Oyirad tribes in particular, giving their women in marriage to one another over many generations. In the following, I shall present some typical examples of exchange-marriage from among their marriage relationships with the Qonggirad and Oyirad tribes.

In 1206 Temüǰin ascended the throne, became Činggis Qan, and founded the Mongol empire. At the time, he and his chief wife Börte had four sons — Jöči, Čaγadai, Ögödei and Tolui — and one daughter, Tomalun.[6] Around the time of his accession to the throne, Činggis Qan

---

[3] *Liao-shih* 3, "Pen-chi 3: T'ai-tsung"; *ibid.* 64, "Piao 2: Huang-tzu piao"; *ibid.* 65, "Piao 3: Kung-chu piao"; *ibid.* 67, "Piao 5: Wai-ch'i piao"; *ibid.* 71, "Lieh-chuan 1: Hou-fei"; *ibid.* 72, "Lieh-chuan 2: "I-tsung Pei."

[4] *Liao-shih* 67, "Piao 5: Wai-ch'i piao"; *ibid.* 71, "Lieh-chuan 1: Hou-fei"; *ibid.* 73, "Lieh-chuan 3: Hsiao Ti-lu."

[5] Uno 1995, 1997.

[6] Börte was the daughter of Dei Sečen of the Qonggirad tribe and the elder sister of Alči Noyan (*Yüan-shih* 118, "T'e-hsüeh-ch'an chuan"; Али-заде 1965, 394; Topkapı 1518, fol. 64b).

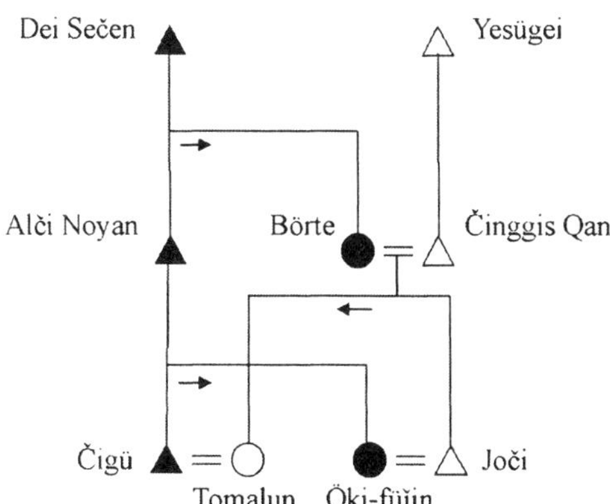

Fig. 4 *Marriage relationships between Činggis Qan's family and the Qonggirad tribe*

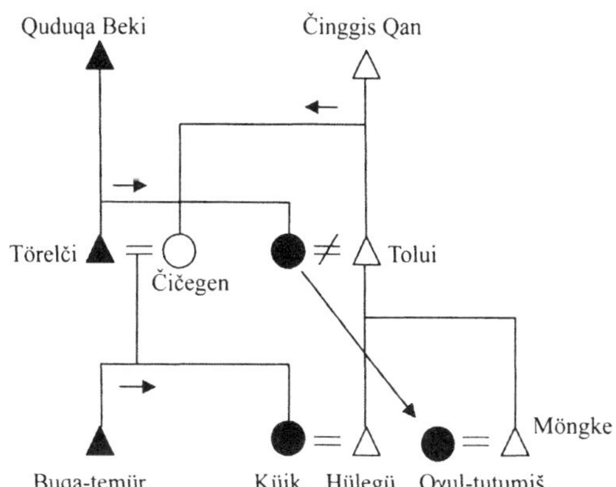

Fig. 5 *Marriage relationships between Činggis Qan's family and the Oyirad tribe*

married his daughter Tomalun to Čigü, the son of Börte's younger brother, Alči Noyan (fig. 4).[7] When considered in conjunction with Činggis Qan's own marriage, this marriage was one in which Činggis Qan, in return for having taken Börte as wife, gave his daughter to the son of his wife's younger brother, and it was thus an exchange-marriage following a pattern of give-and-take exchange in which the husband, in return for having taken a woman in marriage, gave his daughter to his wife's brother's son. When compared with the examples from the Liao dynasty, it differs in that the daughter was married not to the wife's brother, but to the wife's brother's son. This pattern of exchange-marriage appears repeatedly in the marriage relationships with the Qonggirad tribe, the most important affinal relatives of Činggis Qan's family, and it also appears frequently in the marriage relationships with the Oyirad tribe, their next most important affinal relatives. Fig. 5 illustrates an example of exchange-marriage of this pattern between Činggis Qan's family and the Oyirad tribe. In return for having taken in marriage Čičegen, the Oyirad

[7] The information about Tomalun's husband in the *Jāmi' al-Tawārīkh* is confused (Ализаде 1965, 396-397; Topkapı 1518, fol. 65a, 130a). On the basis of *Yüan-shih* 109, "Chu-kung-chu piao," I therefore consider Tomalun's husband to have been "Ch'ih-k'u" (= Čigü).

Törelči gave his daughter Küik to Hülegü, the son of Čičegen's brother Tolui.[8]

On the basis of the above analysis, it is to be surmised that marriages, in which the husband, in return for having taken a woman in marriage, gave his daughter to his wife's brother's son, represented one of the basic patterns of exchange-marriage in the Mongol empire.

I now wish to return to fig. 4, which illustrates the marriage relationships of Činggis Qan's family with the Qonggirad tribe. Around the time of the marriage of Čigü and Tomalun, Öki-fūǰin, the daughter of Börte's younger brother Alči Noyan, married Činggis Qan's eldest son, Jöči (fig. 4).[9] When considered in conjunction with the marriage of Čigü and Tomalun, this meant that Jöči of Činggis Qan's family and Čigü of the Qonggirad tribe had exchanged sisters. In cultural anthropology, this type of marriage is known as a "sister-exchange marriage." Because this sister-exchange marriage creates a double affinity, it makes possible the formation of strong bonds. In the marriage relationships of Činggis Qan's family with both the Qonggirad and Oyirad tribes, sister-exchange marriages took place at important junctures pivotal to political marriages. An example of a sister-exchange marriage with the Oyirad tribe is shown in fig. 5. The Oyirad Törelči and Činggis Qan's son Tolui decided to perform a sister-exchange marriage, and Törelči's sister Oγul-tutmiš became engaged to Tolui.[10] But for some reason the marriage did not go ahead, and she ended up marrying Möngke. Although the sister-exchange marriage did not eventuate, the fact remains that plans were made for it.

On the basis of the above analysis, it is to be surmised that sister-exchange marriage was also one of the basic patterns of exchange-marriage in the Mongol empire.

The basic patterns of the two kinds of exchange-marriage outlined above differ in respect to whether they involved members of the same generation or members of two successive generations, but nonetheless they are both forms of exchange-marriage based on the principle of a give-and-take exchange of women. In its principal marriage relationships, that is, its marriage relationships with the Qonggirad and Oyirad tribes, Činggis Qan's family used a combination of these two basic patterns of exchange-marriage to continue intermarrying with these two tribes, even though these marriage relationships were sometimes discontinued and

[8] Али-заде 1965, 222-229.

[9] Topkapı 1518, fol. 158a.

[10] Topkapı 1518, fol. 185b.

later resumed because of political upheavals or else alternated with the levirate on account of a husband's death.

4. *Exchange-marriage as a form of political marriage.* By analyzing the complex marriage relationships of the Mongol empire and the Liao in terms of exchange-marriage, I have been able to discover certain patterns of exchange in these relationships. But what do these patterns of exchange tell us?

In this article I have been able to present only a sampling of the exchange-marriages in nomadic states that I have analyzed to date, but these represent examples of exchange-marriage that continued in all for seven or more generations. It is not sufficient to analyze these examples only from the viewpoint of exchange-marriage, and they must also be analyzed as political marriages that were always closely linked to the political affairs of the royal house. Because the affinal relatives of one generation become the maternal relatives of the next generation, when a male belonging to the royal family took a wife from a distinguished family of affinal relatives, not only would this work to his own advantage in any dispute about succession to the throne, but his son's parentage on his mother's side would be enhanced and this would benefit the son too in any succession dispute. By analyzing the background to the exchange-marriage from the individual political vantage point of view, it becomes possible to bring to light the political motives behind these marriages. For instance, among the four sons born to Činggis Qan and Börte, it was the eldest son Jöči who married a woman related the most closely by blood to his mother. As can be seen in fig. 4, Jöči's wife Öki-füǰin was Börte's niece. Doubts are said to have been cast on Jöči's parentage on his father's side, but when one considers that, among all the brothers, it was he who was permitted to marry a woman related the most closely by blood to his mother, there is a possibility that he might in fact have been a contender for the position of Činggis Qan's successor. Other instances that I have examined in a similar manner must be omitted here because of a lack of space, but details can be found in my earlier articles published in Japanese.[11]

5. *The role of exchange-marriage in nomadic states.* As has been described in the above, the royal families of the Mongol empire and the Liao, both nomadic states, practised exchange-marriage, in which women were exchanged in accordance with patterns of give-and-take, over many

---

[11] Uno 1993, 1999.

generations. A male of the royal family who took a wife from affinal relatives would in the next generation give in return his own daughter in marriage. As a result, the affinal relationships of one generation would be reproduced across generations, and political ties that were to some degree stable would be formed between the royal family and its affinal relatives for several generations. This constituted one of the foundations for the maintenance of political power in a nomadic state, for in the case of the king of a nomadic state his paternal relatives were not only kinsmen, but also potential rivals against whom he might have to contend in a dispute about succession to the throne. The king's most trustworthy allies were not his paternal relatives, but rather his own affinal relatives or his father's affinal relatives, that is, his maternal relatives. For this reason, the kings of nomadic states practised exchange-marriage with their affinal relatives for successive generations in an attempt to build stable political ties with them that would last for several generations.

Bibliography and Abbreviations

Али-заде, А. А. (ed.) 1965. *Фазлаллах Рашид ад-Дин, Джами ат-Таварих*. Том 1, Часть 1. Москва.

Holmgren, J. 1986. 'Marriage, Kinship and Succession under the Ch'itan Rulers of the Liao Dynasty (907-1125)'. *T'oung Pao* LXXII, 44-91.

Lévi-Strauss, C. 1949. *Les Structures élémentaires de la Parenté*, Paris.

— 1969. *The Elementary Structures of Kinship*. (English version of rev. edition.) Boston.

Uno, N. 1993. 'Changes of Affinal Relationships of the Family of Činggis Qan'. *Tōyōshi Kenkyū* 52-3, 69-104 (in Japanese).

— 1995. 'Exchange Marriages Found in the Affinity of the Royal Family of the Liao Dynasty: From the Reign of T'ai-tsu to Sheng-tsung'. *Shiteki* 17, 34-54 (in Japanese).

— 1997. 'Exchange Marriage as Seen in the Marriage Relationships of the Liao Imperial House: From the Reign of Hsing-tsung to the Reign of Tao-tsung'. *Tōhōgaku Ronshū: Eastern Studies Fiftieth Anniversary Volume*. Tokyo, 193-208 (in Japanese).

— 1999. 'Symmetric Marriage Alliance in the Marriage Relationships of Chinggis Khan's Family'. *Bulletin of the National Museum of Ethnology*, Special Issue no. 20, 1-68 (in Japanese).

Wittfogel, K. A. & Fêng Chia-Shêng 1949. *History of Chinese Society: Liao (907-1125)*. Philadelphia.

Topkapı 1518: *Jāmi' al-Tawārīkh*. Topkapı Sarayı Müzesi, Kütüphanesi, MS. Rewān köşkü 1518.

DIE GEHEIME GESCHICHTE DER MONGOLEN AUS ETHNOLOGISCHER SICHT

Käthe Uray-Kőhalmi

Dem Jubilanten wurde es gegönnt ein Meisterwerk auf den Tisch zu legen. Wohl probierte sich fast jeder Mongolist an der Geheimen Geschichte der Mongolen, aber Rachewiltz's reich kommentierte Übersetzung übertrifft an Umfang und Inhalt alle bisherigen Übersetzungen und Kommentare. Diese Kommentare besprechen so ungefähr Alles was man bisher von einer gegebenen Frage weiss, aber, zum Glück, eben nur ungefähr. Manche Türen blieben noch offen, oder, was oft der Fall ist, fordert der Kommentar zum Weiterdenken auf. Dieses kann unter Umständen auch abweichende Meinungen bedeuten.

Die Geheime Geschichte der Mongolen ist nicht nur ein besonders interessantes, sondern auch merkwürdiges Werk. Als exakte Historiographie kann es nicht betrachtet werden, darin sind sich die Forscher schon einig geworden. Es ist aber ein Werk, das historisch auswertbar ist, es ist nur die Frage, aus welcher Sicht. Der Jubilant drückt das so aus, daß die Geheime Geschichte das Fleisch an dem Skelett der Geschichte der Mongolen ist, die anhand anderer, für exakter betrachtbarer historischer Werken, wie z.B. dem Yuan Shi oder Rašid ad Dins's Arbeit eruiert werden kann. Eben zu diesem Fleisch gehören die Berichte über das Alltagsleben der Mongolen des 13. Jh., das heißt, in erster Linie die ethnographisch auswertbaren Angaben. Igor de Rachewiltz beschäftigt sich in seinen weitläufigen Kommentaren recht ausführlich mit den bisherigen Forschungen zu ethnographischen Fragestellungen.[1] Die Ausführungen von Rachewiltz betreffen manchmal materielle Dinge, wie die Form und Anwendung von gewissen Pfeilen, oder gesellschaftliche Einrichtungen, wie die Form der Eheschliessung, z.B. die Dienzeit der Braut im Haushalt des Brautvaters wie es im Falle von Temüǰin und Börte geschah. Er billigt die Meinungen über die Kultstätte der mongolischen Sippen bei dem dichtbelaubten Baum (§§57, 117), und die Anwendung von blutloser Tötung in Falle von gesellschaftlich-kultisch wichtigen Personen, wie bei Büri bökö (§140), Kököčü (§245), J̌amuqa (§201) und Tolui (§272). Auch in der recht heiklen Frage der in 70 Kesseln gekochten Činos (§§128-129) bekennt er sich zur An-

[1] de Rachewiltz 2004, Einführung lxii-lxiv.

nahme, daß es sich hier um männliche Angehörige des Činos Klans handelt, die nach Rachewiltz sogar lebendig gekocht wurden.[2]

Selbstverständlich können, und werden auch sicher, weitere Einzelfragen ethnographisch auswertbar sein. So ist mir z.B. aufgefallen, daß in der Episode in §169, in der die zwei Pferdehirten des Yeke Čeren, Badai und Kišlik sich entschliessen zu Temüǰin zu reiten mit der Warnung, daß von Senggüm seine Umzinglung und Tötung geplant wird, eine interessante Angabe zu finden ist. Als Vorbereitung zur Flucht schlachten sie ein Lamm, das sie als Wegzehrung mitnehmen möchten, aber um nicht aufzufallen, holen sie das Brennmaterial zum Kochen nicht von draussen, sondern machen Feuer aus den Brettern des Bettes in der Jurte. Daraus ist zu entnehmen, daß die Mongolen, auch die nicht hochrangigen, schon zu Činggis Qans Zeiten auf hölzernen Bettgestellen ruhten. Ähnliche Beispiele können wir so manche finden, aber hier möchte ich mich nicht mit diesen Einzelheiten beschäftigen.

Denn die Geheime Geschichte birgt nicht nur in Einzelfragen, sondern auch als Werk, als Ganzes, wichtige Hinweise zur der Ethnologie im allgemeinen und der Kulturgeschichte der Mongolen. Im Vergleich zu den anderen Werken, die als Quellen für die Geschichte der Mongolen dienen, spiegelt die Geheime Geschichte die Denkweise und die ideologischen Werte der Mongolen zur Zeit Činggis Qans wieder. Und dieses unabhängig von der Exaktheit der historischen Angaben, und den verschiedenen Interessen, die bekanntlich in der Darstellung der Ereignisgeschichte zu finden sind. An einem Beispiel möchte ich zeigen, wie die verschiedenen Quellen ein gewisses Motiv, ihrer ideologischen Einstellung entsprechend, darstellen. Bekannt ist die Episode, in der nach dem Tod von Dobun Mergen seine Witwe, Alan goa, auf wunderbare Weise schwanger wird. In §21 der Geheimen Geschichte heißt es: *„sönit büri čeügen šira gü'ün gerün erüge dotorqa-yin gege'er oroǰu ke'eli minu biliǰü gege'en inu ke'elitür minu šinggegü büle'e qarurun naran sara-yin kili-iyer sira noqai metü šičabalǰuǰu qarqu büle'e"* 'Every night, a resplendent yellow man entered by the light of the smoke-hole or the door top of the tent, he rubbed my belly and his radiance penetrated my womb. When he departed, he crept out on a moonbeam or a ray of sun in the guise of a yellow dog.'[3] Diese

[2] Vgl. de Rachewitz 2004, 476-479. Bei den Ewenki und den südsibirischen Türken diente das Kochen des besiegten Feindes in erster Linie nicht der Tötung des Körpers, sondern der Lebensseele, das heißt, es sollte eine Wiedergeburt verhindern und konnte daher auch mit dem leblosen Körper geschehen (Uray-Kőhalmi 1970, 255-57).

[3] 'Nacht für Nacht kam ein goldglänzender Mann durch die Dachluke der Jurte herein. Er streichelte meinen Bauch, und sein Strahl senkte sich in meinen Leib. Wenn er

Erzählung ist die Erklärung der Alan goa für ihre, vorher von Dobun dem Klugen gezeugten Söhne, Belgünütei und Bügünütei, die es merkwürdig finden, daß ihre Mutter ohne Hausgenossen-Brüder und ohne einen Mann zu haben, Söhne geboren hat. Die Söhne schenken den Worten ihrer Mutter über den wunderlichen Hergang vollständigen Glauben. Diese Episode erscheint auch im Altan Tobči in ähnlicher Form, mit dem kleinen Unterschied, daß der Hund nicht gelb, sonderm schwarz ist.[4]

Eine völlig andere Einstellung zu diesem Ereignis finden wir in Werken mit buddhistischem Hintergrund und ganz besonders in solchen mit muslimischem. Im Geschichtswerk des Sagang Sečen über die Geschichte der Mongolen, empören sich nicht nur die Söhne über die Schwangerschaft der Witwe Alan goa, sondern auch „übelgesinnte Leute", das heißt ihre moralische Verurteilung ist breiter, und geht über den Rahmen der Familie hinaus. Noch interessanter ist die Erzählung der Fürstin Alan goa. Sie spricht von einem Traum, nach dem „in jeder Nacht ... ein Wesen in reizender Jünglingsgestalt erschien, welches das Kopfkissen mit mir teilend übernachtete und sich mit Anbruch des Tages entfernte".[5] Hier handelt es um einen Traum über einen hübschen Jüngling. Weder von gelbem Glanz, noch von Strahlen, geschweige denn von einem Hund ist die Rede. Die ganze mythische Athmosphere ist ausgeräumt. Doch es gelingt Alan goa auch so sich vor den Leuten zu rechtfertigen.

Noch deutlicher kommt die Tendenz zur Verschweigung von unerklärbaren oder unzumutbaren Ereignissen in der Beschreibung des Rašid ad Dins zum Vorschein. In einem langen Absatz erörtert er den von Menschen unbegreiflichen Willen Allahs, aus dessen Gebot Söhne auch ohne einem Vater entstehen können. Als Bestätigung und Bekräftigung dieses Gebotes diene der ungewöhnliche Vorfall und das bewunderungswerte Ereignis der Alan goa: aus derer reinem Leib, ohne Heirat, oder einer Verbindung mit einem Manne, drei mit göttlichem Glanz strahlende Söhne zur Welt kamen, was zu den ungewöhnlichsten Seltenheiten und wunderbarsten Erscheinungen gehört. Dann berichtet er von zwei Versionen des Empfängnisses, im ersten kommt ein Lichtstrahl durch die Dachluke und senkt sich in ihren Schoß (diese Begründung der Schwangerschaft ist bei den Türkvölkern Asiens über die Empfängnis des Činggis Qans verbreitet); im zweiten erscheint allnächtlich in ihrem Traum ein blonder, blauäugiger Mann, der sich ihr nähert. Mit letzterer Traumerzählung

hinausging, kroch er hinaus auf dem Sonnen- und Mondstrahl wie ein gelber Hund' (Taube 1989, 5).

[4] Bawden 1955, 115.

[5] Sagang Sečen 1985, 88.

beschwichtigt Alan goa die „männlichen Verwandten ihres Mannes" die von einer großen Schande redeten.[6] In dieser Darstellung sind selbstverständlich der Hund, als unreines Tier, und die dem Islam nicht entsprechenden mythischen Umstände ausgetilgt. Diese Beispiele bezeugen mit welcher Intoleranz und Taubheit einige historische Quellen den mythischen, animistischen Erscheinungen der Geheimen Geschichte begegnen.

Die Geheime Geschichte ist nämlich noch in einer Weltanschauung verfasst worden, die sich grundsätzlich von jener der großen Religionen unterscheidet, (und so auch von der exakten Betrachtungsweise der Chinesen und der aufgeklärten Europäer.) Die Einstellung zur Welt und ihren Werten, die sich in der Geheimen Geschichte wiederspiegelt, entspricht dem kulturellen Syndrom der Steppenhirten, zu denen auch die Mongolen der Zeit Čінggis Qans gehörten. Vieles davon stimmt auch mit der Denkweise der heutigen Mongolen und Türken überein, aber nicht alles. Wohl darum können wir, wie auch unsere mongolischen Zeitgenossen, in vielen Fällen nicht hinter den Sinn einiger Äußerungen in der Geheimen Geschichte kommen. Aber Zeit bringt Rat. Manchmal wird wahrscheinlich die Epik der Mongolen, die ja sehr vieles vom altertümlichem Gedankengut bewahrt hat weiterhelfen.

Bei eingehenderem Studium des Werkes fällt es auf, daß besonders in den ersten Kapiteln nicht nur die Züge einer Hirtenkultur auftauchen, sondern auch die einer Jägerkultur. Dic Werte und Anschauungen dieser beiden Kulturen überdecken sich in manchen Fällen, andersmal können sie gut unterschieden werden. Es hat den Anschein, als hätten die frühen Mongolen, oder wenigstens ein Teil von ihnen, ungefähr vier-fünf Generationen vor Temüǰins Geburt einen Kulturwandel durchgemacht, der von einem Waldjägerdasein zum Steppenhirtentum geführt hat.[7] Ein solcher Wandel vollzog sich in der Geschichte der Hirtennomaden Innerasiens öfters. Die Alttürken werden zuerst als die Bergwerker und Schmiede der Ruan-ruan erwähnt, die historischen Kirgisen kamen aus Sibirien; die Ahnen der Kitai und der Dschürtschen lebten früher in den Wäldern am Amur und im Khinggan Gebirge; die Solonen, oder Pferdetungusen wechselten im 16.-17. Jh. aus dem Wald am Onon auf die Steppe. Die Oiraten taten dieses bereits im 14. Jh., während ein Teil der Burjaten bis heute in den Wäldern Südsibiriens lebt.

Die Erscheinungen des Kultursyndroms der Waldjäger gehören zu den tiefsten Schichten der Kultur der Mongolen. In der Geheimen Geschichte zeugen hiervon die ersten, mythischen und vorgeschichtlichen Kapitel

[6] Rašid ad Din 1952, tom. I, 11-12.
[7] Uray-Kőhalmi 1981, 273.

(§§1-78, 97). Sehr auffallend ist, wie oft in diesen Kapiteln von der Jagd als Lebensunterhalt die Rede ist. Wegen dem Absperren ihrer Zobel-, Eichhörnchen-, und Großwild-Jagdgründe sucht der Klan des Qorilartai Mergen neue Jagdgründe am Burqan Qaldun. Diese Leute, die Qorilar, lebten in erster Linie von der *Jagd* auf Fleischwild und Pelztiere, was typisch ist für das südsibirische Jägersyndrom. Die Mutter der Alan goa, der Ahnfrau der Mongolen, war die Barγudai goa, Tochter des Barγudai Mergen, beide Träger von Eponimen, die sie von ihrem früheren Lebensort, der Senke Barγuǰin mitbrachten. Dieses Gebiet ist auch heute noch ein typisches Taigagebiet mit einer ursprünglichen Jägerbevölkerung. Von Dobun Mergen, dem Gatten der Alan goa wissen wir außer seiner Abstammung nur, daß er jagen gegangen ist und dabei nach altem Jägerbrauch den Beuteanteil eines Hirschen von einem Urianghai Mann verlangte und auch bekam (§§12-16); Alan goa's jüngster Sohn, Bodončar, lebte vom Jagen mit einem Beizvogel (§§25-27).

Von Viehbestand ist weniger zu lesen. Einer der Urväter, Toroqolǰin bayan besitzt (nur) *zwei* Pferde (§3); Alan goa kocht ihren Söhnen ein Lamm (§19); Bodončar besitzt ein Reitpferd (§24) und zusammen rauben die fünf Brüder den Viehbestand der Leute, die am Tünggelik Bach lebten (§§35-39). Darunter waren sicher Pferde, denn Bodočar trinkt bei ihnen gegorene Pferdemilch. Von anderem Vieh ist keine Rede. Jägergruppen mit wenigen Pferden leben seit vorchristlichen Zeiten bis heute in den Wäldern Südsibiriens und des Khinggan Gebirges. Diese Lebensweise kann auch als Vorstufe zum Umsteigen auf das Steppenleben betrachtet werden.[8]

Zum Kultursyndrom der südsibirischen Waldjäger gehört neben der Pelzjagd, in Innerasiens internationalem Handel seit Urzeiten ein wichtiger Aspekt, auch das Schmieden. An der Südgrenze Sibiriens ziehen sich Bergketten hin, vom Altai bis zum Jablonowoi Gebirge, die sehr reich an verschiedenen Erzen sind. Neben Gold, Silber und seltenen Erzen wie Wolfram und Molybden, bergen sie auch Eisenerz in solchen Mengen, daß bei den Ewenki praktisch alle erwachsenen Männer die Eisenbearbeitung verstanden. Alle hatten in ihrer konischen Hütte die nötigen Instrumente und Geräte, darunter auch den Blasebalg.[9] Das Schmieden gehörte ebenso eng zum Kultursyndrom der südsibirischen Taigajäger wie die Pelzjagd, das Fischen, die Renntierzucht und manchmal das Halten von wenigen

[8] Uray-Kőhalmi 2002, 260-261; Ravenstein 1861, 339, 343; Patkanov 1906, 233-234, 237; Lattimore 1935, 42-43; Vasilevič 1969, 86-90; Franke 1975, 126-138.

[9] Vasilevič 1969, 90-91; Tugolukov 1975, 99; Uray-Kőhalmi 1997, 125; 2002, 258; Birtalan 2001, 1034-1035; Pallas 1776, 171-172.

Pferden. J̌arči'udai, der den Namen seines Klans führte, gehörte auch zu dieser Taigakultur: er jagte Pelztiere und gelegentlich schmiedete er sich die Jagdwaffen (oder gar einen Wagen für Sübegetei), darum hatte er einen Blasebalg bei sich, außerdem schenkte er dem kleinen Temüǰin in §97 der Geheimen Geschichte eine selbstgejagte Zobelpelzdecke.

Ähnlich verhält es sich mit den Herrengeistern der Erde und der Berge. In den Übersetzungen der Geheimen Geschichte werden interessanterweise die Herrengeister der chinesischen Gebiete, die Ögödei Qan krank machen, allgemein akzeptiert. Vielleicht, weil es sich in dieser Episode, die mit dem Opfertod des Tolui endet, um etwas Mystisches handelt. Die Herrengeister der Naturerscheiungen war sowohl bei den Steppenvölkern Innerasiens, wie auch bei den Jägervölkern Sibiriens von großer Bedeutung. Die Naturerscheinungen von der Sonne bis zum Eichhörnchen waren Wesenheiten, ähnlich den Menschen. Sie alle hatten Seelen.[10] Besonders wichtig waren die Berge. Der Kult der Berge und ihrer Herrengeister, sowie der Berggottheiten ist in Asien vom Kaukasus bis Japan verbreitet. Überall glaubt man, daß der Herrengeist des Berges sich in menschlicher Form manifestieren kann, gelegentlich auch in tierischer, so als Wolf, bzw. Hund, Tiger, Bär oder gar Schlange. Weiterhin sind die Herrengeister der hohen Berge zugleich die Inhaber, Besitzer, und Herren der umliegenden Wälder und Weiden zusammen mit all dem Gewächs und Getier, das dort gedeiht und lebt. Die Menschen sind nur Nützer dieses Reichtums.[11]

Denn weder in Innerasien und Tibet, noch in Sibirien gab es ursprunglich ein Eigentum an Grund und Boden! Die Erde und die Berge sind in ihrer Wesenheit Gottheiten, wie auch der Ewige Himmel. Eine Gottheit kann nicht geteilt und besessen werden. Nur das Gebiet und seine Reichtümer an Pflanzen und Wild dürfen mit der Genehmigung der Herrengeister von den Menschengruppen benützt werden; bei der Verpflichtung von Opferungen.[12] Diese Auffassung ist für uns schwer fassbar, da wir seit der Römerzeit den Grundbesitz kennen. Für die Völker der Taiga und der Steppen, wie auch der Berghalden Innerasiens, aber auch den sich mit ihnen beschäftigenden Ethnografen, ist das so selbstverständlich, daß in meinen Arbeiten, die sich mit den Herrengeistern des Burqan Qaldun

[10] Zum Seelenglauben der Mongolen siehe: Birtalan 2001, 942 (Animismus), 1038-1039 (Seelenvorstellungen).

[11] Birtalan 2001, 949, 976-977; Uray-Kőhalmi 1997, 41; Taksami 1984, 450-457.

[12] Vgl. die Angaben in den Arbeiten von Diemberger 1998, 46; Schicklgruber 1998, 99; Tautscher 1998, 176, 178. Hier werden die Herrengeister der Berge explizit 'Landlords' genannt.

Berges beschäftigen, die Frage des Besitzers nicht entsprechend herausgehoben wurde.[13] Die Existenz eines menschlichen Inhabers, Landbesitzers 'Landlords', ist in diesen Gegenden und Zeiten ein Absurdum.

Im Namen der Gruppe verhandelt mit den Herrengeist ein Bevollmächtigter, der Klanälteste, der 'Vater' in ihrer Terminologie, der Schamane, oder wenn es sich um eine Stammesfederation oder ein Reich handelt, der Herrscher, der Khan. Darum müssen auch die Schamanen der Ewenki und der Burjaten jedes Jahr vom Herrengeist des Gebietes und dem Artengeist des Wildes die Beutetiere des kommenden Jahres in einem Ritual erbeten und mit Opfergaben entgelten. Auch das Weiderecht wurde mit Opferungen entgeltet.[14] Dieses ist für jene Völker bis heute eine Tatsache geblieben, wie auch die Qing Kaiser den Erdherren am Erdaltar in Peking opferten. Das Wohlwollen der Herrengeister konnte für längere Zeiten auch so gesichert werden, indem der Herrengeist, oder die Geisterherrin im Abstammungsmythus zum Ahnen, bzw. Ahnfrau des Herrscherhauses gemacht wurde. Dafür gibt es viele Paralellen in Asien aus Tibet, Korea, Japan, usw.[15] In solchen Fällen entsteht ein sehr inniges Verhältnis zwischen dem Herrengeist des Berges und der vom Berg abstammenden Sippe. Die nächste Umgebung des heiligen Berges dient auch als ewige Ruhestätte für die Mitglieder der Sippe, sie kehren zum Berg heim. Da der heilige und vor Fremden streng gehütete Begräbnisort der Borǰigin Sippe, insbesonders der Čінggis-Tolui Linie am Burqan Qaldun lag, kann man vermuten, daß einer der Stammväter ein Berggeist gewesen ist, auch mit Hinsicht auf Alan goas wunderbare Schwangerschaft. Verdächtig ist in erster Linie Dobun Mergen und sein Bruder Duwa Soqor deren Name auch mit der Bedeutung Bergspitze, bzw. einäugiges Geisteswesen verstrickt ist.[16] Vielsagend ist, daß es in ganz Sibirien, besonders jedoch in den Gegenden der Burjaten, Ewenki, Jakuten und Jukagiren, bis heute viele Erzählungen und Legenden von einäugigen Berggeistern, die zugleich auch Stammväter von Sippen sind gibt.[17] Heilige Sachen sind für Eingeweihte aus Andeutungen klar, darum soll es uns nicht wundern, wenn die Verwandschaft mit dem Herrengeist des Burqan Qaldun nicht ausführlich niedergeschrieben worden ist. In den meisten der mit Berg-

[13] Uray-Kőhalmi 1987, 143-145; 2002, 255-256, besonders 255, wo ich mich auch auf Mostaert 1968, 230 berufe, der hier das Wort *eǰed* in der Bedeutung von Herrengeist behandelt.

[14] Birtalan 2001, 949, 998-999; Uray-Kőhalmi 1997, 38, 41, 87-88; Diemberger 1998, 48.

[15] Uray-Kőhalmi 1987, 144, 148; Birtalan 2001, 938; Kreiner 1990, 145, 150.

[16] Uray-Kőhalmi 2002, 256; 1987, 143-144; 1970, 250.

[17] Uray-Kőhalmi 1987, 141-144, 148; Birtalan 2007, 27.

gottheiten verbundenen Abstammungsmythen wird das Motiv der Zeugung verschleiert, traumhaft dargestellt.

In der Geheimen Geschichte erscheint als tierische Erscheinungform der Gottheit, die Alan goa besucht, ein gelber Hund. Dieses ist auffallend, da bei den Mongolen (und Türken) meistens Wölfe als göttliche Tiere agieren. Hunde kommen als Totemtier bei den Kirgisen vor und sehr oft auch bei den Ewenki. Der Hund war in Sibirien und Ostasien ein geehrtes Tier.[18]

Zum Jägersyndrom können wir auch die Verlobung des Temüǯin mit Börte zur Zeit als beide noch Kinder waren rechnen, da die Bedingung der Ehe die Dienstleistungen des jungen Temüǯin für die Familie des Dei Sečen waren (§§61-63). Die Abdienungsehe ist bei den Mongolen zwar nicht unbekannt, jedoch selten. In der Geheimen Geschichte kommt sie auch nur an dieser einzigen Stelle vor. In Sibirien aber ist es die am weitesten verbreitete Art der Eheschliessung. Der Freier arbeitet, manchmal Jahre, für die Familie der Braut, und auch nachdem er sich schon die Erlaubnis zum Sexualverkehr erdient hat, bleibt das junge Paar meistens bis zur Geburt des ersten Kindes bei den Brauteltern wohnen. Dieser Ablauf wird in der Geheimen Geschichte durch den Tod des Yesügei gestört; Temüǯin holt Börte nach Jahren einfach heim (§94).

Ich muß gestehen, daß mir gerade diese Zeit im Leben Temüǯins, zwischen dem Besuch bei Dei Sečen als die Ehe der Kinder abgemacht wurde, und die endliche Heimholung der Braut nach Jahren als Temüǯin schon ein junger Mann war, Gedanken gemacht hat. Nach der Beschreibung der Geheimen Geschichte verbringt die engste Familie Temüǯins, seine Mutter, die zweite Frau des Vaters und ihre insgesammt sechs Kinder diese Jahre im Wald, wo sie Wurzeln und Beeren sammeln, Tarbagane jagen und insgesammt neun Pferde haben. Sie waren nämlich nach dem Tod des Vaters, Yisügeis, von ihrer Sippe verstoßen worden. Es gibt aber keine Angabe dazu, daß ihnen auch all ihr Vieh genommen worden wäre; sie mußten ja vorher Herdentiere gehabt haben, da sie eine angesehene Familie waren. Während dieser Zeit wird Temüǯin von der verwandten Sippe Taiči'ut gefangen genommen, wahrscheinlich weil sie ihn aus irgendeinem Grund für gefährlich hielten; aber einen mittellosen Jungen, der von Beerensammeln und Fischen lebt? Bald nach seiner Flucht von den Taiči'ut wird die Ehe mit Börte ervollkommt. Abgesehen davon, daß die Braut weder abgedient worden ist, noch ein Brautpreis für sie gezahlt worden war, was in diesen Gesellschaften recht ungewohnt ist, bleibt noch

[18] Uray-Kőhalmi 1997, 83-84; 1987, 147-148; Tryjarski 1979, 137-153.

die Frage: von woher hatte die Familie Temüǰins auf einmal soviel Lebensunterhalt, daß die Braut heimgeholt werden konnte? Von nun an wird auch nichts mehr von ihrer Armut berichtet, aber auch nicht wie sie zu den Herden, usw. gekommen sind. Temüǰin hegt schon kühne Pläne und sucht ein Bündnis mit dem Anda seines Vaters, Ong Khan, zu schließen. Als die rachedürstigen Merkit Leute erscheinen erfahren wir, daß Börte von einer alten Dienerin in einem von Rindern gezogenen Wagen, der voll mit der geschorenen Wolle der Schafe war, versteckt wird.[19] Die alte Frau sagt, daß sie zur Hauptjurte gekommen sei, um die Schafe zu scheren, und nun auf dem Rückweg zu den ihren sei, anscheinend Dienstleuten oder Verwandten (§§98-101). Wohl bekommt Börte kein Reitpferd, aber in den Beschreibungen der Geheimen Geschichte reitet sie merkwürdiger Weise nie.[20] Also gab es Schafe und Rinder aber nur wenige Pferden in der Familie von Temüǰin. Ich habe den Eindruck gewonnen, daß das karge Waldleben entweder darum in die Lebensgeschichte des jungen Čingġis Qans eingewoben wurde, um seine Karriere noch steiler, noch ansehnlicher erscheinen zu lassen, oder hatte die Einwebung des Waldlebens irgendwelche mythischen Gründe, wurde es von einer gewissen Heiligkeit, Ursprünglichkeit umwoben?[21]

Schon mehrere Wissenschaftler, zuerst P. Pelliot[22], machten auf das merkwürdige Verhältnis der Borǰigin und der Uriangqai Sippen aufmerksam. Es scheint eine Art Abhängigkeit der letzteren bestanden zu haben. Von ihnen wissen wir auch durch Rašid ad Din, daß sie teilweise noch ein Waldjägerleben führten und sogar Renntiere hatten.[23] In der Nähe der Borǰigin lebte noch ein anderes Volk, das wenigstens teilweise aus Waldjägern bestand, ihre schärfsten Rivalen, die Merkit. Ein Teil von ihnen bestand aus Jäger-Fischern (§109), ein anderer Teil, die Uduyit-Merkit, ziehen sich nach Niederlagen in die Wälder von Barquǰin zurück (§157). Von den beiden rivalisierenden Völkerschaften, die unlängst den Wandel zum Steppenleben durchgemacht hatten, den Merkit und den Mongolen,

[19] Börte hätte auf dem Handpferd wegreiten können, aber sie zieht den Wagen vor. Schon Dei Sečen spricht nur von Wagen mit denen sie ihre Töchter zu den hochrangigen Bräutigamen schicken. Es ist mir aufgefallen, daß Börte kein einziges Mal in der Geheimen Geschichte zu Pferde erscheint, immer nur im Wagen. Konnte sie nicht reiten? War ihr Volk ein Wagenvolk, wo höchstens die Männer ritten?

[20] Vgl. Geheime Geschichte §§64-65; Rachewiltz 2004, 14-15, 331-332.

[21] In der Geheimen Geschichte finden wir Paralellen dazu, z.B. Tolus Tod, dessen hier beschriebene Umstände nicht der historische Wahrheit entsprechen, sondern die Erwartung, wie es hätte sein sollen ausdrücken.

[22] Pelliot 1959, 336.

[23] Rašid ad Din 1952, 123-124.

gewannen letztere, allerdings erst nach vielen und schweren Kämpfen, das Rennen und die Merkit verschwanden.

Die meisten Züge, die die frühen Mongolen mit dem Waldleben verbinden, finden sich in den ersten Kapiteln der Geheimen Geschichte. Die späteren zeugen von einem Steppenleben, aber auch noch gegen Mitte der Geheimen Geschichte findet man einen Gedanken, der mit den Weltvorstellungen der sibirischen Völker harmonisiert. In §245 werden der ungestüme Kököčü Tebtenggeri und Temüge Otčigin von Činggis Qan aufgefordert, außerhalb der Jurte ihre Kräfte zu messen. Der Vater Kököčüs, Mönglik ahnt böses, er nimmt die Kappe seines Sohnes an sich, riecht an ihr und sagt dann unter Tränen: 'I have been your companion / Since the brown earth / Was only the size of a clod, / Since the sea and rivers / Were only the size of a rivulet'[24]; das heißt seit die Welt besteht. In den Mythen der Ewenki über die Schaffung (oder Entstehung) der Erde ist diese anfangs ein kleines Hügelchen oder nur so groß wie ein Renntierfell und die Gewässer sind nur eine Pfütze. Dann wächst sie an, bis sie die heutige Größe erreicht. Die Vorstellung von der ursprünglich kleinen, dann aber anwachsenden Welt gehört ebenfalls in das Syndrom der Jägervölker Sibiriens. Aber, wie dieser Passus zeigt, war sie auch den Mongolen nicht fremd.[25]

Mit diesem kurzen Aufsatz habe ich versucht, auf die Zusammenhänge zwischen der Geheimen Geschichte der Mongolen und dem Syndrom des sibirischen Waldjägertum aufmerksam zu machen. Besonders in den ersten Kapiteln, aber auch später, z.B. in der Kököčü Episode, oder dem Opfertod des Tolui zeigt sich das Bestreben der Autoren die Ereignisse ihren kulturellen Erwartungen anzupassen, also zu beschreiben, wie es sein müsste und nicht so wie es war. Solche Tendenzen habe ich auch in der Beschreibung von Temüǰins Jugend erahnt. Wenn man aber den Text der Geheimen Geschichte im ganzen als Kulturerscheinung wertet und nicht als schriftliche Fixierung mehr oder minder wahrheitsgemäßer historischer Ereignisse, dann sind solche Tendenzen vollständig am Platz.

Bibliographie

Bawden, C. 1955. *The Mongol Chronicle Altan Tobči*. Wiesbaden.

Birtalan, Á. 2001. *Die Mythologie der mongolischen Volksreligion*. (Wörterbuch der Mythologie Bd. VII/2, Abt. I/34.) Stuttgart.

[24] Rachewiltz 2004, 173, 884-886.

[25] Uray-Kőhalmi 1997, 125; Vasilevič-Alkor 1936, 215; Vasilevič 1966, 178, 179, 213-218, 221, 241, 250.

Birtalan, Á. 2007. '*Ada*: A Harmful Female Spirit in the Mongolian Mythology and Folk Belief'. In: V. Veit (Hrsg.), *The Role of Women in the Altaic World*. (Asiatische Forschungen 152.) Wiesbaden, 19-33.

Franke, H.1975 'Chinese Texts on the Jurchen'. *Zentralasiatische Studien* 9, 119-186.

de Rachewiltz, I. 2004. *The Secret History of the Mongols* I-II. Leiden · Boston.

Diemberger, H. 1998. 'The Horseman in Red'. In: A.-M. Blondeau (Hrsg.), *Tibetan Mountain Deities, Their Cults and Representations*. Wien, 43-55.

Kőhalmi, K. U., siehe: Uray-Kőhalmi, K.

Kreiner, J. 1990. 'Heilige Berge Japans, Miwa und Fuji'. In: K. Gratzl (Hrsg.), *Die Heiligsten Berge der Welt*. Graz, 145-152.

Lattimore, O. 1935. *The Mongols of Manchuria*. London.

Mostaert, A. 1968. *Dictionnaire Ordos*. New York · London.

Pallas, P. S. 1776. *Reise durch verschiedene Provinzen des Russischen Reichs*. Teil III vom Jahr 1772-1773. St. Peterburg.

Patkanov, S. 1906. *Opyt geografii i statistiki tunguzskix plemen' Sibiri* I. St. Petersburg.

Pelliot, P. 1959. *Notes on Marco Polo* I. Paris.

Rašid-ad-Din 1952. *Sbornik letopisej*, I/1. Übersetzt von L. A. Xetagurov. Moskau · Leningrad.

Ravenstein, E. G. 1861. *The Russians on the Amur*. London.

Sagang Sečen 1985. *Geschichte der Mongolen und ihres Fürstenhauses*. Hrsg. W. Heissig. Zürich.

Schicklgruber, C. 1998. 'Race, Win and Please. The Gods: Horse-Race and Yul Lha Worship in Dolpo'. In: A.-M. Blondeau (Hrsg.), *Tibetan Mountain Deities, Their Cults and Representations*. Wien, 43-55.

Taksami, A. M. 1984. 'Survivals of Early Forms of Religion in Siberia'. In: M. Hoppal (Hrsg.), *Shamanism in Eurasia*, Part 2. Göttingen, 450-457.

Taube, M. 1989. *Geheime Geschichte der Mongolen*. Leipzig · Weimar.

Tautscher, G. 1998. 'Kalingchok and Sailung: a «Female» and a «Male» Mountain in Tamang Tradition'. In: A.-M. Blondeau (Hrsg.), *Tibetan Mountain Deities, Their Cults and Representations*. Wien, 169-180.

Tryjarsky, E. 1979. 'The Dog in the Turkic Area: An Ethnolinguistic Study'. *Central Asiatic Journal* 23, 297-319.

Tugolukov, V. A. 1975. 'Konnye tungusy'. In: *Etnogenez i ětničeskaja istorija narodov severa*. Moskau, 78-110.

Uray-Kőhalmi, K. 1970. 'Sibirische Parallelen zur Ethnographie der Geheimen Geschichte der Mongolen'. In: L. Ligeti (Hrsg.), *Mongolian Studies*. Budapest, 247-264.

— 1978. 'Synkretismus im Staatskult der frühen Dschingisiden'. In: W. Heissig & H.-J. Klimkeit (Hrsg.), *Synkretismus in den Religionen Zentralasien*. Wiesbaden, 136-158.

— 1981. 'Daurien: das Keimen und Absterben eines Nomadenreiches'. *Acta Orientalia Hungarica* 35, 255-273.

— 1997. *Die Mythologie der Mandschu-Tungusischen Völker*. (Wörterbuch der Mythologie Bd. VII, Abt. I/27.) Stuttgart.

Uray-Kőhalmi, K. 2002. 'Tungusen in der Geheimen Geschichte der Mongolen?'. *Acta Orientalia Hungarica* 55, 253-262.

Vasilevič, G. M. 1966. *Istoričeskoj fol'klor ěvenkov*. Moskau · Leningrad.

Vasilevič, G. M. & Ja. P. Alkor 1936. *Sbornik Materialov po êvenkijskomu (tungusskomu) fol'kloru*. Leningrad.

MONGOL OR TURKIC? NOTES ON *bökevül*, A MILITARY AND COURT OFFICIAL OF THE TURCO-MONGOLIAN POLITICS

István Vásáry

When Chinggis Khan brought to allegiance 'the people of the felt-walled tents' (*sisgei to'urqatu ulus*) at the sources of the Onon river in the *quriltai* of 1206, he appointed ninety-five colonels and rewarded his faithful men by conferring different ranks on them (de Rachewiltz 2006, 133, 758). This date signifies the real birth of the Great Mongol Empire (*Yeke Mongqol ulus*), a polity that initially encompassed only the tribes of the steppe and forest regions. The institution and appellation of the new dignitaries and title-holders of the empire were moulded according to the patterns and traditions of the Mongol and Turco-Mongol tribal world, so most of them bore former and/or newly invented Turkic or Mongolian titles. Names of Chinese and Arabo-Persian office-holders appeared only later, after the conquest of China and the Muslim world of Central Asia and Iran, and even then, only in a negligible quantity. Obviously enough, most terms concerning the army and military administration have ever since remained of Turco-Mongolian origin. Among the numerous terms pertaining to the domestic administration of the khan's court, many have become with time mere titles, the bearers of which fulfilled important military and administrative functions in the state's administration. One of those dignitaries that played an important role in the administration of the Turco-Mongolian polities of Asia from the 13th century onward until the 20th century, was the *bökevül*. Hereafter I will try to elucidate a few points concerning the function, meaning and especially the origins of the Turco-Mongol institutions covered by the aforementioned term.

To begin with, *bökevül* originally belonged to the basic office-holders of the khan's court, always connected to and mentioned together with other officials of the royal household, such as *ba'urči* 'cook', *čerbi* 'quartermaster', *e'üteči* 'doorkeeper', *aqtači* 'groom, equerry', *šiba'uči* 'falconer', etc. Among these terms, all figuring in the *SHM*[1], *bökevül* had

---

[1] de Rachewiltz 2006, 462-463 (*ba'urči*); 445, 462 (*čerbi*); 693 (*e'ütenči, e'üdečin*); 465, 483, 677 (*aqtači*); 305 (*šiba'uči*). Cf. also *bāvurči* 'Koch' ← W-Mo. *ba'urči* id. (TMEN No. 82); *čerbi* 'Höflinge, die für den kaiserlichen Haushalt sorgten, später Quartiermacher' ← W-Mo. *čerbi* 'Höflinge' (TMEN No. 176); *eyūdǟčī* 'Türhüter' ←

the closest link to *ba'urči* in the company of which it often occurs in Rashīd al-Dīn's *Jāmi' al-tavārīkh*[2]. Before delving into the intricate question of origins, let me enumerate, for a preliminary information's sake, the translations, or rather interpretations, of the word *bökevül* that have come up to this day in the secondary literature. The first group of meanings can be related to an official in charge of kitchen activities and serving meals: 'cook, chef, overseer of the kitchen, table-decker, carver, taster, cup-bearer, chief of protocol', while a second group of meanings, though evidently connected with food and provisions, refers to a broader scale of household activities and a higher level of responsibilities: 'warden, steward, chamberlain, superintendant'. Both groups of functions are inherent in the term, which can clearly be demonstrated from the sources.

It is striking, however, that, in contrast with other terms mentioned above, *böke'ül* does not appear in the *SHM*, although a great number of Mongol technical terms ending in *-'Ul* (= Mo. *-gUl*) occurs therein, e.g. *čayda'ul* ~ *čaydu'ul*, *hire'ül*, *qara'ul*, *kebte'ül*, *šiya'ul*, *todqa'ul.*[3] On the other hand, it seems reasonable to assume that *böke'ül* existed already in Chinggis Khan's time since Rashīd al-Dīn's monumental historical work on the Mongols, a most reliable source on the whole, often makes mention of the *bökevül*s, the office of which must have been instituted already during Chinggis's lifetime. But the undisputed lack of *böke'ül*s in the *SHM* may have lead many to claim Turkish origin to the term *bökevül*, although G. Doerfer himself, proponent of a Turkic etymology, remarked that "Wegen der für das Wmmo. typischen Endung *-vül* (nomen agentis collectivum, z.B. *qara-* 'spähen', *qara-vul* 'Spähtrupp') sollte man

---

W-Mo. *e'üdäči* id. (TMEN No. 74); *aḫtačī* 'Hofstallmeister' ← W-Mo. *aχtači* id. (TMEN No. 9).

[2] E.g. initially Güchügür noyan of the Besüt tribe was a *böke'ül* and *ba'urči*, but when he became old and weak, Boroghul noyan of the Hushin tribe (in the *SHM*: the Jürkin tribe) became *böke'ül* and *ba'urči* in his place. When Boroghul noyan became commander of ten thousand, Önggür noyan of the Baya'ut tribe became *böke'ül* and *ba'urči*. All these persons stood in Genghis Khan's service. (Ravshan & Mūsavī 1994-5:I, 172, 180; Thackston 1998-99, 93, 96).

[3] For these terms see *čaġdāvul* 'Nachhut, Kommandant der Nachhut' ← W-Mo. *čaġda'ul, čaġdu'ul* id. (TMEN No. 178); *hirǟvül* 'Vorausabteilung' ← W-Mo. *hirä'ül* 'Duellanten, Vorkämpfer' (TMEN No. 394); *qarāvul* 'Spähtrupp, berittene Patrouille' ← W-Mo. *qara'ul* id. (TMEN No. 276); *kebtǟvül* 'Nachtwache' ← W-Mo. *kebtä'ül* id. (TMEN No. 322); *šiqāvul* 'Gastbegleiter' ← W-Mo. *šiġā'ul* id. (TMEN No. 232); *totqāvul* 'Straßenwächter, Feldgendarm' ← W-Mo. *totqa'ul* id., actually 'der Hinderer' (TMEN No. 124).

zunächst an eine mo. Herkunft des Ausdrucks denken. Jedoch findet sich kein passender Vergleich"[4]. Doerfer's suggestion that the basis of *bökevül* is a rare Turkic verb *bök-* 'to be disgusted / surfeited, to overeat oneself,' (attested only in Kāšġarī, and in Bashkir and Uzbek) lacks any probability[5]. Anyhow, the idea of Turkic origin has had deep roots, it goes back to W. Bang who in his classical work "Vom Köktürkischen zum Osmanischen" devoted a separate chapter to the formant *-aul*, within which he deals also with the word *bökevül*[6]. Unfortunately, the basic idea of this chapter, notwithstanding the keen observations in the details, belongs to those thoughts of the brilliant Bang which are erroneous, namely he tried to explain the formant *-vUl* on Turkic ground from an *-(A)gU+l*. Doerfer clearly pointed to the failure of Bang's explanation.[7] The view that the formant *-vUl* is of Mongol origin which later spread also to Middle Eastern Turkic after the Mongol period, is by now generally accepted. In Turkic the suffix was taken over as *-AvUl* and added to both verbal and nominal stems, as e.g. *čapavul* 'raid, inroad; participants of a raid' (< *čap-*), *tapavul* 'servant; scout(?)' (< *tap-*), *yortavul* 'galloping warrior(s)' (< *yort-*), *sözevül* 'recruiter' (< *söz*), etc.[8] After Bang's and Doerfer's attempts, Rybatzki has recently also suggested a Turkic derivation. In his view *bökegül* is a denominal noun from *böke* 'warrior, wrestler' (> Middle Mo. *bökö* id.)[9], but this derivation cannot be accepted owing to the semantic discrepancy between *böke* and *bökegül*.

I think that F.W. Cleaves made the first step in the right direction to answer the question concerning the origin of *bökevül*, and I wonder why most scholars did not realize that after Cleaves' findings one must search the origin of *bökevül* primarily within Mongolian, and not Turkic. Cleaves pointed out the existence of a Mongol vocable in the Chinese sources of the thirteenth and fourteenth centuries (most of his data are from the *Yuan shi*, official annals of the Mongol dynasty in China)[10]. The word in question is *bokesun* 孛可孫 which is the evident Chinese rendering of a

---

[4] TMEN I, 302.

[5] First, this meaning is only a secondary development from the Tu. verb *bük-* 'to bend, bow' having a low stylistic value (something like English *gobble*), and its usage is limited only to Bashkir and Uzbek; secondly, the supposition that a Mongol court official's name (*bökevül*) meant 'Fresser [gobbler]', as Doerfer interprets it, is nonsensical (TMEN II, 302).

[6] Bang 1919, 61-62.

[7] "Völlig verfehlt is die Darstellung dieses Suffixes bei Bang …" (TMEN I, 33).

[8] TMEN I, 33-34; Özönder 1996, 43-44.

[9] Rybatzki 2006, 236.

[10] Cleaves 1964, and 1967.

Mongol *bökesün*. According to the Chinese data, the office of *bökesün* was established at the beginning of the Yuan dynasty, and these officials had sole charge of fodder, i.e. their main duty was to furnish fodder for the horses and camels of the imperial court and other institutions[11]. Although the word *bökesün* has not yet been attested in any Mongolian source of the age, its existence in China in the Yuan period is unquestionable. If so, it goes without saying that it must have direct connection with *bökegül* ~ *böke'ül* used mainly in the western half of the Mongol Empire. Cleaves was absolutely right in drawing the following conclusion: "That these words – *bökesün* and *bökegül* – were alternate forms of a single word signifying basically 'steward' seems indisputable. The form *bökegül* seems to have been that used in the western part of the Mongolian empire and *bökesün*, that used in the eastern. A perfect analogy is afforded by the words *todqaγul* and *todqosun* (< **todqasun*), derivatives in *-γul* and *-sun* respectively of an unattested verb **todqa-*, each signifying 'postal relay inspector', the former used in the western half of the Mongolian empire and the latter, in the eastern"[12].

The relevant Chinese data relating to *bökesün*, unearthed by Cleaves, passed largely unnoticed by further research. The fact that the preponderant majority of data concerning *bökevül* derive from Turkic and Persian sources and languages, and that the term has survived in a number of Turco-Mongol polities in Western Asia (even in Mughal India), may have blurred the memory that it was originally an institution of Chinggis' Mongol state, and its origins also must be searched there. Indeed, since A. Temir's publication in 1959 of the Mongol appendix to Jaǰa oğlu Nūr al-Dīn's *waqf* written in 1272, the word *bökegül* has been known also from an early Mongolian text: *Nabči-yin bökegül Toγtoγ-a* 'Nabči's *bökegül* Toγtoγ-a'; *Möngkegür-bökegül* 'Möngkegür, the *bökevül*'[13]. But even these Mongol data did not seem to have convinced Cleaves himself who, under the spell of the Turkic origin, insisted that "It seems virtually certain, moreover, that *bökegül* in Mongolian is a borrowing from the Turkish **bökägül* > *bökäül*"[14]. Moreover, Cleaves inclined to think that probably *todqa'ul* and *qara'ul* in Mongolian were also borrowings from Turkic[15]. But once *bökesün* has been accepted as a Mongol word derived

[11] Cleaves 1964, 384, 385-386, 390.

[12] Cleaves 1964, 392-393.

[13] Temir 1989, 160, ll. 34-35; 161, ll. 57-58.

[14] Cleaves 1964, 392.

[15] Cleaves 1964, 393. — For the correct Mongol etymologies of these words, see TMEN No. 124, and No. 276.

from an unattested verb **böke-* (as Cleaves himself established), how can *bökevül*, another derivative of the same verb referring to the same function, be a Turkic derivation? We are compelled to search for a Mongol etymology.

In doing so, an attentive reading of those passages of Rashīd al-Dīn's *Jāmi' al-tavārīkh*, that relate to the office and persons of *bökevül*s, unexpectedly comes to our assistance. Three passages will be analysed in this respect.

Speaking of Önggür-noyan, who was chronologically the third *bökevül* in Chinggis' Khan's service, Rashīd al-Dīn says: "He was called Önggür Qisat (in the Naiman language a *bökä'ül* is called *qisat*, which means to bend over) ["*bi-zabān-i Nāimān bukāvul-rā qīsāt gūyand ya'nī qīsmīshī kardan*"]. This Önggür was of the Kähärün Baya'ut"[16].

Essentially the same statement is repeated later, also in the narrative about Önggür-noyan: "The *hazara* of [Önggür] Noyan of the Baya'ut, a branch of the Dürlükin. Chingis Khan's chief *bökä'ül* and *ba'urchi* was Güchü[gür] Noyan of the Besüt clan. (Among the Naiman the name Qisat means a *bökä'ül* [taster], i.e. he does [service]) ["*va laqab-i ū qīchāt bi-lughat-i Nāimān bukāvul bāshad ya'nī tadqīq kunad*"]"[17]. Thackston's translation "he does [service]" was based on a text قديق‌كند the first word of which was amended by him to خدمت . The Persian text-edition reads *tadqīq kunad*, which accordingly translates 'he investigates'. But either 'doing service' or 'investigating' seem to be very different from 'bending over', as Thackston also remarks: "where *qisat* is defined before ... it is said to be because the *qisat* "bends over" (*qismishi*), presumably while serving"[18].

In a third instance, Jamuqa and his followers want to trap Chinggis Khan by inviting him to a feast where they want to capture him. The invitation was sent by a certain Bundai Qijat [r: Buqadai Qičat — بوقدای قیچات]. "In the Naiman language and that of some other Mongols a *bökä'ül* is called *qisat*, which the Mongols call *qijat* [r: Qičat — قیچات] [*va būkāvul-rā dar aṣl bi-zabān-i Nāimān va ba'ḍī Moghūlān qisat mī-gufta and va Moghūlān qīchāt mī-gūyand.*]"[19].

The quoted passages clearly reveal that in the Naiman language and that of some other Mongols a *bökevül* was called *qisat* which word was pronounced as *qıčat* by the Mongols. Rashīd al-Dīn connects the meaning of the Naiman term once with the notion of "bending, bowing", and once

16 Thackston 1998-99, 96; Ravshan & Mūsavī 1994-95/I, 180_8.

17 Thackston 1998-99, 277; Ravshan & Mūsavī 1994-95/I, 602_6.

18 Thackston 1998-99, 277, n. 9.

19 Thackston 1988-99, 185; Ravshan & Mūsavī 1994-95/I, 383_{11-12}.

with that of "investigating, controlling". In the wake of Howorth, Poucha and others, Doerfer was absolutely right in calling attention to the fact that the Naiman must have originally spoken a Turkic language, consequently the term *qisat* must be interpreted on Turkic ground. He amended the Naiman word to *qišat* and the basis of the Persian phrase *qīšmīšī kardan* to *qiš-*.[20] The verb *qïš-* can uninterruptedly be attested in East Middle Turkic from the 11th century onward.

The following data are at hand: Kāš. *qïšmaq* 'sich neigen, abweichen'[21]; Qarshi Tafsir *qïš-* 'ukloniat'sia [to diverge, deviate, digress, swerve]; otkloniat'sia', (one of the three examples given: *nätäk qïštïlar ya'nï mäyl qïlurlar ḥaqdïn batïl taba* [r: *tapa*][22]; Rylands Tafsir *qïš-* 1. 'to swerve away, turn from (Ar. *ḍalla* to lose one's way, Pe. *gum kardan* to lose [one's way])', derivatives: *qïšmaq, qïšur-, qïštur-*[23]. Kāšġarī's data as the earliest ones are extremely important, so let us refer to them here again: *er yoldïn qïšdï* 'the man deviated (*māla*) from the road', and 'also used of the sun when it declines from the zenith (*zālat 'an kabidi'l-samā'*)'[24].

Returning to the Naiman term *qišat* it must have been the name of a court official or servant who was named after the most characteristic gesture of serving, i.e. bowing or stooping. Consequently, *qišat* meant '[a servant] who bows / bends / stoops (as a sign of homage)'. The tasks and functions of these court servants have not been included in the designation itself, the name referred solely to their status as servants, similarly to Pe.

---

[20] TMEN No. 1604. — In addition to *qīsāt, qīčāt* and *qīsmīšī* both terms have a lot of variants in the MSS of the *Jāmi' al-tavārīkh*: *qīšāt, qnsāt, qyāt, qnčāt, ftčāt, qbḥāq* and *qnīšmīšī, qšmšī.* For these see the notes to pp. 180_8, $383_{11\text{-}12}$, 602_6 in Ravshan & Mūsavī 1994-95/III; TMEN III, 571-573. — Ravshan and Mūsavī, without referring to Doerfer's study, erroneously deny the existence of a Turkic verb *qïš-*, and return to an old explanation of Pelliot which tried to connect the word with the Turkic word *qïs-* 'to compress, squeeze' (Ravshan & Mūsavī 1994-95/III, 2150-2151, 2397).

[21] Brockelmann 1928, 156.

[22] Borovkov 1963, 210.

[23] Eckmann 1976, 228-229. — In Radloff's *Wörterbuch* there is an Ottoman word *qïš-* 'gnut'sia, nakloniat'sia [bend, stoop, incline, decline]; sich krümmen, sich neigen', taken from Zenker's Dictionary (Radloff II, 835). Even Doerfer referred to this word (TMEN III, 573) but such an Ottoman word is non-existent, as noted already by Atalay (Atalay III, 182, n.), since Zenker designates the word as Eastern Turkic, i.e. Chagatay.

[24] Clauson 1972, 670. — Dankoff (Kāšġarī, *Dīwān* 244) put a question mark to the word: *qïš-*(?), probably because of the graphs QA̱IYI̱ŠDI̱Y, i.e. it is written in the MS with three superfluous *harekes*. Dankoff's doubts are baseless since the existence of the word *qïš-* is perfectly documented in the aforecited Middle Turkic *Tafsirs*.

(hence Tu.) *ḫidmatkār* 'servant'. At this juncture comes in *bökevül*. Once Naiman *qišat* meant 'one who bows, i.e. a servant' and the Mongols used the term *böke'ül* in its stead, *böke'ül* must have the same semantic field as *qišat* has, so it must similarly mean '[a servant] who bows'. And really, the Mo. verb *bököyi-* ~ *bökeyi-* seems to be the right solution, the data for which are as follows: *bökü̈i-* ~ *bökei-* v.i. 'to bend down, bow one's head, salute by bowing, stoop, incline; to lean'. Derivatives: *bökü̈ilge-* v.caus. of *bökü̈i-*; *bökülǰe-* v.i. 'to bend or bow repeatedly'; *bögtür* ~ *bögetür* n. and adj. 'stooping, bent; hunchback'; *bögčü̈i-* ~ *bögčei-* ~ *bökücei-* v.i. 'to shrivel, shrink; to bend forward'; *bögčü̈ilge-* v.caus. of *bögčü̈i-*; *bögčügür* 'stooped, hunchbacked; convex'; *bögtü̈i-* ~ *bökütü̈i-* v.i. 'to bend, stoop over, bow; to be stopped, bent, curved'; *bögtü̈ilge-* v.caus. of *bögtü̈i-*; *bögtürde-* v.i. 'to be excessively stooped', *bögtüre-* v.i. 'to bend down; to bow; to fold'[25]. — The Mo. and Tu. data of the *Muqaddimat al-adab* are very insrustive: Mo. *bökeibe öbügen,* Chag. *büküldi* [r: *büküldi*] *qarï* 'starik stal sogbennym [the old man became bent]'; Mo. *bökeibe erüdü,* Chag. *egildi yazuqqa* 'sklonilsia k grekhu [he was inclined to sins]'; Mo. *böketür bolba ötegü,* Chag. *bögri* [r: *bükri*] *boldï qarï* 'starik stal gorbatym [the old man became huntchbacked]'; Mo. *bökeyıksen,* Chag. *egilgen* 'sognuvshiisia [bent, stooping]'[26].

From those data one may present the development of the Mongolian terms in the following manner: **bökeyi-sün* > **bökē-sün* > *bökesün* (in the eastern *ulus*es) and **bökeyi-gül* > **bökē-'ül* > *böke'ül* (in the western *ulus*es). The fact that *bökesün* and *böke'ül* are two different derivatives of one and the same verbal root, displaying difference only in their territorial distribution (similarly to the aforementioned *todqasun* and *todqa'ul*), may indicate that these terms came about in the early, formative period of the Chingisian empire, when the establishment of an administrative hierarchy was in the making and the names and functions of dignitaries exhibited some sort of elasticity. But whereas the use of *bökesün* in Yuan China proved ephemeral, and it fell out of use toward the end of the Mongol dynasty, *böke'ül* in the west was borrowed into the Turkic languages as *bökevül* and into Persian as *bukāvul* (either directly from Mongolian or via Turkic), and made a phantastic career. It was used from the earliest times in Ilkhanid Persia and the Golden Horde, it survived all dynasties in Iran, it flourished during the Timurids, a branch of whom carried it to Mughal India. The Shaibanids and Safavids knew the *bukāvul*s, and in the Central

[25] Lessing 123, 126, 127.
[26] Poppe 1938, 123.

Asian Khanates they were office-holder as late as the twentieth century. In sum, practically all Turco-Mongolian polities of Asia, the Iranian world and Mughal India knew the office of the *bökevül*s (*bukāvul*s). The delineation of their changing functions and duties falls outside the scope of this short article which primarily aims at elucidating the problems of origins. In the rest of this article I will attempt shortly to present the spread and survival of this technical term in the Turkic-speaking world of Inner Asia.

From its very beginnings, the Turks formed an integral part of the Mongol Empire. They actively participated in and contributed essentially to establishing the empire's institutions. In many parts of the empire the Turco-Mongolian elite was bilingual, hence they used and understood both the Mongol and the Turkic idioms. The official Mongolian terminology of the new empire was intensely permeated with older and newer Turkic layers, and conversely, the Turks, when necessary, borrowed the new Mongolian words, or sometimes they only Turkicized the new terms. The latter case occurred when the Mongol word was homonymous with or cognate to the Turkic one. This happened also to the Mongolian term *böke'ül* which, from the first moment of its existence, must have been used also by the Turks as *bökevül.* Its integration in Turkic was facilitated by the simple fact that the verb *bökeyi-* (*bökē-*, *böke-*) that lay basis for the term *böke'ül*, sounded *bük-* and meant 'to bend, bow (both intr. and tr.)' in Turkic, a word that has survived in most Turkic languages[27]. One may only put forward the conjecture that the *-ü-* of the Turkic word *bük-* may have influenced the pronunciation of the new term as *bükevül.*

The Turkic term was first attested in the first half of the 14th century, in the *Codex Cumanicus* (45v 15): Latin *Placerius,* Persian *Tataul,* Cuman *Bogaul*[28]; the Cuman word must be read as *böge(v)ül*[29]; the voiced *-g-* in place of *-k-* is typical of the Kipchak languages of the age. The same Kipchak form found its way into Old Russian where the word is several times attested in the sources of the 14th-16th centuries; Old Russian *begeul* meant also 'bailiff'[30].

---

[27] Clauson 1972, 324.

[28] Drimba 2000, 95.

[29] Grønbech's reading (1942, p. 62) of »bogaul« with velar vowels as *boɣavul* 'Gerichtsdiener, 'placerius'' is erroneous. The meaning 'bailiff' of the word is assured by Medieval Latin *placerius* which meant in Medieval Ligurian 'greffier, officier de police chargé de porter les ordres du consul', 'custode della pubblica loggia' (Drimba 2000, 95).

[30] *Begeulъ* 'pristav', its first occurrence is in a grant to the Spasskii Monastery in Yaroslav before 1345 (Sreznevskii I, 47). For further data on *běgaulъ*, *běgaulь*

That both Cuman *bögevül* and Russian *begeul,* borrowed therefrom, mean 'bailiff', a meaning which deviates from the two basic meanings 'taster' and 'steward', is a bit perplexing and I cannot find a really satisfactory explanation to that. My conjecture is that the meaning of *tutqavul* 'bailiff' somehow radiated to *bögevül*, since they are often mentioned together in the sources. The Persian equivalent *tataul* in the CC which must be some distorted rendering of Mo. *totqa'ul* / Tu. *tutqavul* seems to corroborate this supposition[31]. G. Doerfer's idea, which *mutatis mutandis* goes back to an old idea of L. Budagov that the word *bögevül* 'bailiff' must be separated from *bökevül* 'taster; steward', and can be derived from another verbal stem, seems to me too far-fetched to be acceptable[32].

The term was regularly used in the immunity charters of the Golden Horde, although we have data only from Kazan and the early Crimean Khanate in the 15th-16th centuries. In these documents *bökevül*s were always mentioned together with the quartermasters (*čerbi*), in the *promulgatio* of the documents as follows: ... *bökevül čerbileringe* ... 'to the stewards and quartermasters'[33].

During the Ilkhans and post-Ilkhanid dynasties of Iran, such as the Jalairids, the *bökevül*s (Pe. *bukāvul*s) were important officials of the army, second in rank to emirs. Not only the troops of a ten thousand (Mo., Tu. *tümen*, Pe. *tūmān*), but also those of a thousand (Mo. *mingqan*, Tu. *ming*, Pe. *hazāra*) had their 'superintendents' in charge of the provisions and fodder. In Ghāzān Khan's time we hear of corrupt *bökevül*s who accepted bribes[34]. Muḥammad ibn Hindūshāh Nakhchivānī, in his *Dastūr al-kātib*, a

(*bĕgoulь, bĕgulъ*) 'pristav' see (*SRIa* I, 87). — Cf. also Fasmer I, 142. In Shipova (1976) the word is not attested.

[31] On the other hand, there is a suspicious Chagatay word deriving from Vámbéry (1867, 248): *bögeöl* 'der Nachtrab; l'arrière-garde' which was taken over by Radloff's dictionary (IV, 1694): *bökäül* 'der Nachtrab'. Since the meaning 'rear-guard' of the Chagatay word is not attested elsewhere, one must be very cautious, as always, with Vámbéry's data.

[32] TMEN II, 305-307; Budagov I, 262-263.

[33] These terms occur in *six* documents: Uluġ Muḥammad (1420), Ḥājjī Girey (1453), Mengli Girey (1467 and 1468), Muḥammad Girey sulṭān (1502), Sa'ādet Girey (1524). Suffice is here to refer to one of the best constructed and nicely preserved diploma issued by Ḥājjī Girey in 1453 (Kurat 1940, 64, 176). — In several cases the second word was misread as *čerileringe* (instead of *čerbileringe*), and Samoilovich even fabricated a false interpretation for the non-existent *bökevül čerileri* with the meaning 'okhrannye voiska [defence army]' (Samoilovich 1918, 1115-1116).

[34] Herrmann 2004, 119, 122; Ravshan & Mūsavī 1994-5/II, 1477, Thackston 1998-99, 730, 731.

wonderful handbook of Jalairid administration accomplished in the 1360s, gave a detailed description of the functions of a military *bökevül* in three letters of appointment[35]. In the Timurid and Aqqoyunlu states the institution of *bökevül*s survived and their activities are well documented in the sources[36]. It is interesting to see that in the late Timurid period there were special *bökevül*s at schools and colleges (*madrasa*), whose task was the procurement of provisions for the *madrasa*s[37].

At the beginning of the 16th century, Prince Bābur and his court transplanted the Timurid institutions, among others that of *bökevül*, on Indian soil where it survived throughout the Mughal period. The *Bāburnāma* contains remarkable data concerning the *bökevül*s. It was a high court rank, one grade higher than that of *bavurči* 'cook'[38]. In describing the ill-omened event when an attempt was made to poison Bābur, he remarks that *Hindūstān ili bökevülni čāšnīgīr dirler*[39], i.e. 'The people of Hindustan call the *bökevül* »čāšnīgīr«'. Since the latter Persian term refers to a 'taster', the primary meaning of *bökevül* was evidently 'taster'. The word *bökevül* was often used after personal names as an expression of rank[40].

All the Chagatay dictionaries of the 16th-19th centuries carefully register the word, mainly with the meaning 'taster'[41]. Especially noteworthy is the entry in the *Sanglakh*, the best Chagatay dictionary: 'A taster (*khvānsālār*) is called *bökevül* ... The author of the Farhang-i Jihāngīrī, in explaining the meaning of taster, says that it is a *chāshnīgīr*; the Turks call it *tüshimel*

---

[35] *Dar tafvīḍ-i būkāvulī-yi lashkar*: Ali-zade II, 53-57.

[36] Cf. Manz 1989, 172; Woods 1999, 17.

[37] As Marwarīd reports, their main task was the distribution of victuals (*qismat-i ma'qūlāt*) which consisted of beverage (*mudāmat*), soup (*āsh*) and food (*ṭa'ām*) (Roemer 1952, 61-63, 155-156).

[38] When Bābur rewarded one of his loyal servants Qul Bayazid for a valiant deed in 1505, he "promoted him from the rank of cook to that of royal taster, ..." (Thackston 1996, 193) = *bāvurčiliq martabasidin ḫāṣṣe bökevülluq martabasiġa yitkürüb irdim* (Mano 2006, $233_{8\text{-}9}$).

[39] Mano 2006, 492_{18}.

[40] 1496: Ḥājji Pīr *Bökevül*; 1507: Šayḫ Muḥammad 'Abdullāh *Bökevül*; 1519: Yūsuf 'Alī *Bökevül*; 1519: Mīr Ḫurd *Bökevül*; 1528: Ašïq *Bökevül* (Mano 2006, 53_5, 322_{54}, 347_{17}, 379_{21}, 533_{10}).

[41] Abušqa *bakavul* [r: *bekevül*] 'ételkóstoló [taster]' (Vámbéry 1862, 31); بکاول 'çeşnigir' (Véliaminov-Zernoff 1869, 131); Badā'i' al-luġat بکاول *bäkäwul* [r: *bekevül*] 'dvoreckii' (Borovkov 1961, 135). — Cf. also بکاول 'officier dégustateur' (PdC 158); Özönder 1996, 41.

and the Hindis say *bökevül*'[42]. At another place *bökevül* is defined simply as 'table-decker [*sufrachī*]'[43]. So *bökevül* was so well naturalised in the Mughal court that contemporaries of the 17th century, as e.g. the author of the Persian dictionary *Farhang-i Jihāngīrī*, considered it a native Indian word[44].

Finally, *bökevül* survived as an archaic word used on a dialectal level in Uzbek and Modern Uyghur, two major Turkic languages of Central Asia: Uzb. (dial. of Khiva) *bekevil* 'ashpag, ashpaglarbashligi [cook, chef]'[45] and Turki *bɛk'aul* 'cook, chef de cuisine, taster'[46].

Bibliography and Abbreviations

Abdullaev, F. & Ishaev, A. 1966. *Ŭzbek shevalari leksikasi*. Tashkent.

Ali-zade: Ali-zade, A. A. (ed.). Muḥammad ibn Hindūshāh Nakhchivānī, *Dastūr al-kātib fī ta'yīn al-marātib*. (Rukovodstvo dlia pisca pri opredelenii stepenei I:1/1964, I:2/1971, II/1976.) Moscow.

Atalay, B. 1941. *Divanü Lûgat-it-türk tercümesi* I-III. Ankara.

Bang, W. 1919. *Vom Köktürkischen zum Osmanischen. Vorarbeiten zu einer vergleichenden Grammatik des Türkischen*. Anhang: *Über die Abstrakta auf* -aul (Abhandlungen der Preussischen Akademie der Wissenschaften, Phil-hist. Klasse, Jahrgang 1919, Nr. 5.) Berlin, 56-66.

Borovkov, A. K. 1961. *"Badā'i' al-luġat". Slovar' Ṭāli' Īmānī Geratskogo k sochineniiam Alishera Navoi*. Moscow.

— 1963. *Leksika sredneaziatskogo tefsira XII–XIII vv*. Moscow.

Brockelmann, C. 1928. *Mitteltürkischer Wortschatz nach Maḥmūd al-Kāšyarīs Dīvān luyāt at-turk*. (Bibliotheca Orientalis Hungarica 1.) Budapest · Leipzig.

Budagov, L. 1869-71. *Sravnitel'nyi slovar' turecko-tatarskikh narechii* I-II. St. Petersbourg.

Clauson, Sir G. 1960. *Sanglax. A Persian Guide to the Turkish Language by Muhammad Mahdî Xân*. Facsimile text with an introduction and indices by Sir Gerard Clauson. (E. J. W. Gibb Memorial New Series XX.) London.

— *An Etymological Dictionary of Pre-Thirteenth-Century Turkish*. Oxford.

---

[42] '*bökevül* (بکاول) khvānsālār-rā gūyand … Va mu'allif-i Farhang-i Jihāngīrī dar bayān-i ma'nīyi sālārkhvān gufta ki *chāshnīgīr* bāshad ki ān-rā bi-turkī *tüšimel* (تشمال) va hindī *bökevül* gūyand' (Clauson 1960, 126r:27-29). Otherwise Clauson (1960, 45) reads the word as *bekewül* [r: *bekevül*] which possibly evolved from *bökevül*.

[43] Clauson 1960, 8r:22.

[44] For *tüšimel*, also a word of Mongolian origin which later became a substitute for *bökevül*, see توشمال (*tūšimāl*), originally 'ein Beamter unteren Ranges', appr. 'Polizeiinspektor', later 'Küchenchef' ← W-Mo. *tüšimel* 'Beauftragter, Beamter' (TMEN No. 138).

[45] Abdullaev & Ishaev 1966, 69.

[46] Jarring 1964, 51.

Cleaves, F. W. 1964. 'Bökesün ~ bökegül'. *Ural-Altaische Jahrbücher* 35, 384-93.

— 1967. 'Addendum to «Bökesün ~ Bökegül»'. *Ural-Altaische Jahrbücher* 39, 49-52.

de Rachewiltz, I. 2006. *The Secret History of the Mongols. A Mongolian Epic Chronicle of the Thirteenth Century*. Translated with a historical and philological commentary by Igor de Rachewiltz . (Brill's Inner Asian Library 7/1-2.) Leiden · Boston.

Kāšġarī, *Dīwān*: Maḥmūd al-Kāšγarī, *Compendium of the Turkic Dialects (Dīwān Luγāt at-Turk)*. Edited and translated by Robert Dankoff in collaboration with James Kelly. Parts I-III. Harvard 1982/1984/1985.

Drimba, V. 2000. *Codex Comanicus. Edition diplomatique avec fac-similés*. Bucarest.

Eckmann, J. 1976. *Middle Turkic Glosses of the Rylands Interlinear Koran Translation*. (Bibliotheca Orientalis Hungarica 21.) Budapest.

Fasmer: Fasmer, M., *Ėtimologicheskii slovar' russkogo iazyka* I-IV, 2nd edition. Moscow 1986-87.

Grønbech, K. 1942. *Komanisches Wörterbuch*. (Monumenta Linguarum Asiæ Maioris.) Kopenhagen.

Herrmann, G. 2004. *Persische Urkunden der Mongolenzeit*. (Documenta Iranica et Islamica 2.) Wiesbaden.

Jarring, G. 1964. *An Eastern Turki-English Dialect Dictionary*. Lund.

Kurat, A. N. 1940. *Topkapı Sarayı Müzesi Arşivindeki Altın Ordu, Kırım ve Türkistan hanlarına ait yarlık ve bitikler*. Istanbul.

Lessing, F. D. 1995. *Mongolian-English dictionary*. Bloomington.

Mano, Eiji 2006. Ẓahīr al-dīn Muḥammad Bābur, *Bābur-nāma. Vaqāyi'*. Critical edition based on four Chagatay texts with introduction and notes; second edition. Kyoto.

Manz, B. F. 1989. *The Rise and Rule of Tamerlane*. Cambridge.

Özönder, F. Sema Barutçu 1996. 'Alî Şîr Nevâyî *Muḥâkemetü'l-lugateyn. İki Dilin Muhakemesi*. Ankara.

PdC: Pavet de Courteille, A., *Dictionnaire turc-oriental*. Paris 1870.

Poppe, N. N. 1938. *Mongol'skii slovar' Mukaddimat al-adab* I-II. Moscow · Leningrad.

Radloff: Radloff, W., *Versuch eines Wörterbuches der Türk-Dialecte* I-IV. St. Petersburg 1893-1911.

Ravshan, M. & M. Mūsavī (eds) 1994-95. *Jāmi' at-tawārīkh-i Rashīd ad-Dīn Faḍlullāh Hamadānī* I-IV. Tehran 1373.

Roemer, H. R. 1952. *Staatsschreiben der Timuridenzeit*. (Veröffentlichungen der Orientalischen Komission 3.) Wiesbaden.

Rybatzki, V. 2006. *Die Personennamen und Titel der mittelmongolischen Dokumente · Eine lexikalische Untersuchung*. (Publications of the Institute for Asian and African Studies 8.) Helsinki.

Samoilovich, A. N. 1918. 'Neskol'ko popravok k iarlyku Timur-Kutluga.' *Izvestiia Rossiiskoi akademii nauk* 1918, 1109-1124.

Shipova, E. N. 1976. *Slovar' tjurkizmov v russkom jazyke*. Alma-Ata.

SHM: *Secret History of the Mongols*

SRIa: *Slovar' russkogo iazyka XI-XVII vv*. Moscow 1975–. 25 vols. until now.

Sreznevskii: Sreznevskii, I. I., *Materialy dlia slovaria drevnerusskogo iazyka po pis'mennym pamiatnikam* I-III. St. Petersbourg 1893-1903; *Dopolneniia*. St. Petersbourg 1912.

Steingass, F. 1977[7]. *A Persian-English Dictionary*. London. (1st edition: 1892)

Temir, A. 1989[2]. *Kırşehir emiri Caca oğlu Nur el-Din'in 1271 tarihli Arapça-Moğolca vakfiyesi*. Ankara. (1st edition: 1959)

Thackston, W. M. 1996. *The Baburnama. Memoirs of Babur, Prince and Emperor*. Translated, edited, and annotated by W. M. Thackston. Washington, D.C. · New York · Oxford.

— 1998-99. (English translation & annotation of) Rashiduddin Fazlullah, *Jami'u't-tawarikh · A History of the Mongols* I-III. (Sources of Oriental Languages & Literatures 45. Central Asian Sources IV.) Harvard.

TMEN: Doerfer, G. 1963/1965/1967/1975. *Türkische und mongolische Elemente im Neupersischen* I-IV. Wiesbaden.

Vámbéry, H. 1867. *Ćagataische Sprachmonumente*. Leipzig.

— 1862. *Csagatajtörök szógyüjtemény*. Budapest.

Véliaminov-Zernoff, V.V. 1869. *Dictionnaire djaghataï-turc*. St. Petersbourg.

Woods, J. E. 1999. *The Aqquyunlu. Clan, Confederation, Empire*. Revised and expanded. Salt Lake City.

DIE MONGOLEN UND DER KORAN

Michael Weiers

Die Übersetzung der *Geheimen Geschichte der Mongolen* sowie die zahlreichen Arbeiten über die Mongolen im 13. und 14. Jahrhundert im Bannkreis Chinas machen leicht vergessen, daß Igor de Rachewiltz seine Aufmerksamkeit auch Themen gewidmet hat, mit denen er territorial weit über das damalige China hinausreichende Verbindungen des Mongolischen Weltreichs sowie der mongolischen Teilreiche u.a. zu Europa einer breiten Leserschaft vorgestellt hat[1]. Die dabei immer wieder berücksichtigten Persönlichkeiten und Ländereien, die dem muslimischen Kulturkreis verbunden waren oder ihm angehörten, sind Anlaß genug, Igor de Rachewiltz auch mit dem muslimischen Teil der mongolischen Geschichte verbunden zu sehen, und ihm zu seinem achtzigsten Geburtstag vorliegenden Beitrag zu widmen.

Zu den frühesten Darstellungen der Geschichte der Mongolen gehört das in persischer Sprache abgefaßte Werk *ta'rīḫ-i ǧahān-gušā* „Geschichte des Welteroberers"[2]. Verfasser dieses Werkes war *'Alā ad-Dīn 'Aiā Malik-i Ǧuwainī.* Er stammte aus dem von Tschinggis Khan und seinen Söhnen auf ihrem Westfeldzug 1219-1225 ausgelöschten Reich der Choresm (Ḫwārizm)-Šāhs und wurde geboren als Sproß einer der vornehmsten dortigen Familien wahrscheinlich 1226 im Bezirk Ǧuwain, Provinz Chorasan (Ḫurāsān). Ǧuwainī, verstorben am 5. März 1283, begann seine „Geschichte des Welteroberers" während eines Aufenthaltes in Qaraqorum, der damaligen Hauptstadt des Mongolischen Weltreichs, zwischen Mai 1252 und September 1253. Er stand in mongolischen Diensten und war unter Hülegü (reg. als erster Ilqan 1260-65) Statthalter von Irak ('Irāq-i 'Arab mit der Hauptstadt Bagdad) und der Provinz Ḫūzistān (Südwesten des heutigen Iran)[3].

Ǧuwainī war Muslim, und zwar, wie wohl die meisten der Bewohner von Ǧuwain, Angehöriger der šāfi'ītischen Rechtsschule[4]. Diese Rechtsschule führt sich zurück auf Abū 'Abd Allāh Muḥammad ibn Idrīs aš-

---

[1] Rachewiltz 1971.
[2] Textausgabe: Qazvini 1912/-16/-37. Übersetzung: Boyle 1958.
[3] Krawulsky 1978, 36, 88.
[4] Halm 1974, 77.

Šāfi'ī (767-820), der u.a. aufgrund des *Kitāb al-Umm* und durch sein Werk *Risāla* „Traktat" als eigentlicher Begründer und Theoretiker der muslimischen Rechtswissenschaft gilt. Er suchte nach festen Grundsätzen für die Anwendung der vier „Wurzeln des Rechts" (*uṣūl al-fiqh*), zu denen neben dem Koran auch der *ḥadīṯ* „Überlieferung von Propheten" gehört[5].

Ǧuwainī dürfte natürlich, auch wenn er die Ereignisse selber nicht miterlebt hatte, über die Invasion der Mongolen, die seine Heimat verödet hatte, und ihre Folgen, die das Land gut ein Jahrzehnt brach hatten daniederliegen lassen, bescheid gewußt haben. Selber erlebt mochte er dann die mongolische Kontrolle durch Čormaqan und seine Tammači-Einheiten haben. Auch als Muslim konnte er das Vorgehen der Mongolen nicht völlig befürwortet haben. Dennoch trat Ǧuwainī in mongolische Dienste, wohl mit der Überlegung, daß es ihm in der Position einer mit Entscheidungsgewalt und Einfluß ausgestatteten Persönlichkeit möglich sein könnte, seiner Heimat mehr zu nützen, als durch Resignation oder gar offene Auflehnung.

Ǧuwainī war bekanntlich nicht die einzige Persönlichkeit iranischer oder mittelasiatischer Herkunft, die damals als Muslim unter den jeweils herrschenden mongolischen Machthabern eine einflußreiche Stellung innehatte. Muslime gab es ja auch unter den Mongolen, und im 14. Jahrhundert gab es unter den im Westen gelegenen mongolischen Teilreichen sogar kein Reich mehr, in dem die Mongolen nicht zu Muslimen geworden wären. Der Islam war im größten Teil der von Mongolen beherrschten Territorien auch für die dortigen Mongolen selber zur alleinigen Staatsreligion, Staatsnorm sowie Rechtsnorm geworden. Islam und Mongolen waren im 14. Jh. gleichsam identisch. Lediglich im Yuan Reich hingen die in ihrem Ursprungsgebiet verbliebenen Mongolen wohl noch mehrheitlich ihrem indigenen Schamanismus an, während die herrschenden Tschinggisiden aus dem Hause Qubilai sowie die Inhaber hoher Regierungsposten in der fernen Hauptstadt Daidu (Qanbalyq) im Stadtgebiet des heutigen Peking zwar als Staatsideologie der ursprünglich aus Indien stammenden Idee des Cakravartin Herrschers folgten, persönlich jedoch verschiedenen Glaubenrichtungen angehörten, darunter auch dem Islam.

Als Statthalter im Ilqanat unter Hülegü dürfte für Ǧuwainī als Sohn eines Landes, dessen von ihm geliebte Šāh-Dynastie von den Mongolen vernichtet worden war, das Bewußtsein, nun in Diensten eben dieser Macht zu stehen, die er zwar wegen ihrer militärischen Fähigkeiten bewundert, jedoch nicht hochgeschätzt oder gar geliebt haben konnte, eine

[5] Hartmann 1944, 53. Gibb & Kramers 1961, 512b-515b.

schwere Last gewesen sein[6]. Nicht weniger dürfte ihn als Muslim auch belastet haben, daß Hülegü, der Herrscher, dem er zu dienen sich bereit gefunden hatte, im Ilqanat das Christentum derart förderte, daß die christlichen syrischen Nestorianer ihn geradezu als den „Neuen Konstantin" priesen[7].

Ǧuwainī hat in seiner „Geschichte des Welteroberers" viele mit solchen Belastungen eng verknüpfte Ereignisse und Zustände, die er als Sohn seines Landes und als Muslim eigentlich gar nicht gut geheißen haben konnte, bekanntlich mit großer Zustimmung geschildert. Spiegelt diese Zustimmung nun seine wirkliche Einstellung wider, oder hatte er sie nur vordergründig zum Ausdruck gebracht, weil er in mongolischen Diensten stand? Vielleicht offenbaren die zahlreichen Zitate aus dem Koran, die er in seinen Text eingestreut hat, zumindest mittelbar seine wirkliche Einstellung, wenn man diese Zitate im Zusammenhang mit den Ereignissen, auf die sie sich beziehen, zu interpretieren versucht. Man könnte so vielleicht auf indirektem Wege wenigstens in Ansätzen ein Bild davon gewinnen, wie ein gesellschaftlich hochstehender Muslim, der darüber hinaus mit seiner eigenen iranischen Geschichte und Literatur bestens vertraut war, mit der weitgreifenden politischen Macht aus der Steppe, aus der Hülegü ja direkt in den Iran gezogen war, umgegangen ist und den „Kampf der Kulturen" zu bestehen versucht hat.

Den folgend diskutierten einschlägigen Stellen aus der „Geschichte des Welteroberers", die auf den Koran verweisen, werden jeweils die arabischen Entsprechungen aus dem Koran nebst ihren Übersetzungen gegenübergestellt[8].

Die Einleitung des Werkes spricht in Fol. [11] unter Bezug auf die Mongolen und die Yasas über die Mißachtung des Willens Gottes und zitiert als Beispiel für diesen Willen die Empfehlung Gottes im Koran, Sure 2:190: „Und stürzt euch nicht selber mit euren eigenen Händen in den Ruin". Bekanntlich ist der Koran (ar. *qur'ān* < ar. *qara'a* „lesen") für die Muslime sowohl ein Lektionar für die Rezitation, als auch ein Lesebuch, das von Gott gegebene absolute Entscheidungsnormen enthält. Wird etwas aus dem Koran zitiert, gilt das Zitierte als unfehlbarer und unumstößlicher Wille Gottes, hinter den man als Muslim nicht zurückgehen kann. Dem hier gegebenen Befehl Gottes, der dazu rät, sich den Mongolen, deren Yasas als vorbildlich gelobt werden, zu fügen, um sich nicht

[6] Vgl. Boyle 1958, vol. 1, xxix-xxxv.
[7] Fiey 1975, 18-32.
[8] Die Transliteration der Koranstellen wird ihrer typographisch einfacheren Handhabung wegen nach Zirker 2007 durchgeführt.

selber mit den eigenen Händen in den Ruin zu stürzen, findet nun aber gar keine Entsprechung in Sure 2: 190 oder in vorausgehenden bzw. folgenden Versen. Es wird hier vielmehr ein angebliches Zitat aufgeführt, das sich mit Sure 2: 190, aber auch mit Teilen in den folgenden Versen bestenfalls dahingehend lose verbinden läßt, daß man darauf achten soll, sich nicht selber in den Ruin zu stürzen. Der Verweis auf Sure 2:190 dürfte jedoch nicht zufällig gewählt sein, denn Vers 190 lautet: *wa-qātilū fī sabīli llāhi llaḏīna yuqātilūnakum wa-lā ta'tadū inna llāha lā yuḥibbu l-mu'tadīn*[a] „Bekämpft auf Gottes Weg, die euch bekämpfen; aber begeht keine Übertretungen! Wahrlich Gott liebt nicht diejenigen, die übertreten." Vers 191 fährt dann unmittelbar bezogen auf Vers 190 fort: *wa-qtulūhum ḥaiṯu ṯaqiftumūhum wa-aḫriǧūhum min ḥaiṯu aḫraǧūkum...* „Und tötet sie, wo ihr sie trefft, und vertreibt sie, von wo sie euch vertrieben haben!..". Vers 193 fügt mit gleichem Bezug dann noch hinzu: *wa-qātilūhum ḥattā lā takūna fitnatun wa-yakūna d-dīnu li-llāhi* „Und bekämpft sie, bis es keinen Aufruhr mehr gibt und die Religion Gott zukommt..." Das angebliche Zitat, das Ǧuwainī als Befehl Gottes im Koran anführt, nämlich den Mongolen und ihren Yasas zu willfahren, um sich nicht selber in den Ruin zu stürzen, vermittelt also gar kein Zitat, sondern führt einen gewissenhaften Muslim lediglich hin zu den einschlägigen Stellen im Koran, wo dann zu lesen ist, wie man sich entsprechend dem Willen Gottes gegenüber solchen, die einem zu Unrecht bekämpfen, zu verhalten hat.

Der gleiche Abschnitt bringt aber auch unter Hinweis auf die zahlreichen Prinzen aus der Familie Tschinggis Khans und ihre Nachkommen, deren weltlicher Macht die Würde des Islams hinzugefügt worden sei, sowie mit Hinweis auf ihre schier unzählbare Gefolgschaft, die mit dem Ruhm des muslimischen Glaubens ausgezeichnet und geschmückt worden sei, ein Zitat, das einen Teil von Sure 8:61 wortwörtlich wiedergibt: *wa-in ǧanaḥū li-s-salmi fa-ǧnaḥ lahā...* „Und wenn sie sich zum Frieden neigen, dann neige (auch du) dich ihm zu...!" Im Koran verbinden sich mit diesem Befehl natürlich nicht wie hier in der Darstellung des Ǧuwainī die muslimisch gewordenen Tschinggisiden und ihr Gefolge, sondern entsprechend Vers 55 der gleichen Sure *...llaḏīna kafarū...* „...diejenigen, die ungläubig sind..." Als Ǧuwainī seine Geschichte verfaßte, und das war zwischen 1252 und 1260, waren aber noch keineswegs so viele Mongolen zu Muslimen geworden, daß ihre Mehrzahl nicht mehr als Ungläubige und damit nicht mehr als Feinde hätte gelten können. Mit den als so zahlreich angegebenen mongolischen Muslimen mochte Ǧuwainī unter seinen muslimischen Mitbürgern im Iran die Leser davon zu überzeugen versucht haben, daß man die Mongolen bereits als Muslime ansehen könne, die dem Frieden zuneigen. Berufen konnte er sich dabei auf die ihm sicher bekannte Neigung des damaligen Großkhans Möngke (reg. 1251-59) in Qaraqorum, der vorzugsweise Muslime aus Mittelasien an seinen Hof berief, weswegen Ǧuwainī die Muslime unter den Mongolen als schon so zahlreich ausweisen zu dürfen glaubte. Mit der damaligen historischen Wirklichkeit hat Ǧuwainīs Darstellung allerdings nichts zu tun.

Das Kapitel über die Gesetze und die Yasas Tschinggis Khans stellt Tschinggis Khans Macht und seine Siege mit einem angeblichen Koranzitat heraus (Fol. [17]), in dem Ǧuwainī offensichtlich Tschinggis Khan selber als Herren angesprochen sehen will: „Wahrlich die Macht des Herrn ist wirklich groß". Ǧuwainī hat hier wohl aus dem Gedächtnis zitiert, denn wörtlich findet sich ein solches Zitat im Koran nicht[9]. Vielleicht hat er dabei an eine ähnliche Textstelle gedacht wie z.B. die in Sure 29:42: *inna llāha.....l-'azīzu...*"Wahrlich Gott....ist der Mächtige..." Passend dürfte solch ein „Zitat" für Ǧuwainī allemal gewesen sein, denn von Tschinggis Khan, dem Herrn, dessen Macht wirklich groß ist, leitet er ab, daß alle diejenigen, die sich Tschinggis Khan vor allem in den Ländern des Islams von den Grenzen Turkistans bis zum äußersten Syrien widersetzt hatten, gescheitert und vernichtet worden seien. Solches Scheitern und solche Vernichtung hat sich nach Ǧuwainī also schon im Koran, dem von Gott offenbarten und zu lesen bestimmten Buch, vorangekündigt, und war dementsprechend von Gott gewollt und gleichsam als unabänderliches Übel hinzunehmen.

Das Kapitel über die Gesetze und die Yasas Tschinggis Khans handelt auch über die Jagd bei den Mongolen (Foll. [19] und [20]). Fol. [20] beschreibt, wie die von den Jägern eingekreisten und in die Enge getriebenen Tiere sich gebärden, und daß die gesamte Jagdgesellschaft nunmehr an die festgesetzte Stunde dächte, in der die Tiere erlegt werden sollten. Diese Momente auf einer mongolischen Treibjagd sucht Ǧuwainī durch ein wortwörtliches Zitat aus dem Koran, Sure 81:5, zu vergegenwärtigen: *wa-iḏā l-wuḥūšu ḥuširat* „Und wenn die wilden Tiere versammelt werden." Sure 81 trägt die zum geschilderten Vorgang scheinbar passende, auf den ersten Vers der Sure Bezug nehmende Bezeichnung *at-takwīr* „Das Umwickeln", womit sich aber im Text der Sure nicht ein Jagdgeschehen verbindet, sondern eine feierliche Ankündigung des Gerichtstages am Ende der Zeit. Die Verwendung des Koranzitats macht deutlich, daß Ǧuwainī daran gelegen war, in seiner „Geschichte des Welteroberers" alle Belange

[9] Flügel 1898.

Tschinggis Khans und der Mongolen, wenn sich dafür nur irgend eine Möglichkeit bot, mit dem Koran in Verbindung zu bringen.

Ganz ähnlich verfährt das Kapitel über die Gesetze und die Yasas Tschinggis Khans auch mit der mongolischen Vorschrift für das Militär, genau am verabredeten Treffpunkt sowie pünktlich zum verabredeten Zeitpunkt zu erscheinen. Ǧuwainī zitiert hierfür einen Teil des Verses 34 von Sure 7. Der gesamte Vers 34 lautet (der von Ǧuwainī zitierte Teil zwischen { }): *wa-li-kulli ummatin aǧalun fa-iḏā ǧā'a aǧaluhum* {*lā yasta'ḫirūna sā'atan wa-lā yastaqdimūn*[a]} „Und jede Gemeinschaft hat einen Termin. Wenn der dann kommt, {bleiben sie nicht eine Stunde zurück und kommen nicht (eine) davor}."

Welch unterschiedlichen Lebensumständen die von Ǧuwainī aus dem Koran herangezogenen oder auf ihn verweisenden Zitate entstammen können, um mit ihnen Gepflogenheiten der Mongolen als mit dem Islam vereinbar erscheinen zu lassen, belegt das auf Fol. [24] berichtete Verfahren bei der Auswahl schöner Mädchen, die vor den mongolischen Herrscher oder vor mongolische Prinzen gebracht worden waren. Waren Mädchen ansehnlich, sollen laut Ǧuwainī Herrscher und Prinzen gesagt haben: „Behaltet sie in Ehren", während über die anderen beschlossen wurde: „Schickt sie freundlich weg". Für beide Urteile bezieht sich Ǧuwainī auf Sure 2:229, wo über die Ehescheidung gesprochen wird. Der einschlägige Teil des Verses 229 lautet: [a]*-ṭṭalāqu marratāni fa-imsākun bi-ma'rūfin aw tasrīḥun bi-iḥsānin* „Die Entlassung gibt es zweimal. Dann muß man entweder rechtmäßig behalten oder im Guten freigeben...".

Im Kapitel, das u.a. über den Aufstieg Tschinggis Khans zur Macht berichtet, läßt Ǧuwainī den Beginn der Machtausübung Tschinggis Khans (Fol. [26]) entstanden sein in Übereinstimmung mit der in Sure 2:117 zum Ausdruck gebrachten Befehlsgewalt Gottes als Schöpfer der Welt. Der Vers 117 lautet (die von Ǧuwainī zitierte Stelle zwischen { }): *badī'u samāwāti wa-l-arḍi wa-iḏā qaḍā amran fa innamā yaqūlu lahū* {*kun fa-yakūn*[u]} „Der Schöpfer der Himmel und der Erde – wenn er eine Sache beschließt, dann sagt er nur zu ihr {»Sei!«, und dann ist sie"}. Tschinggis Khans Macht hat Ǧuwainī hier durch das Zitat aus dem Koran, dessen Inhalt den Muslimen als unmittelbar von Gott offenbart gilt, als mit der Schöpfermacht Gottes verbunden vorgestellt.

Der Koran diente Ǧuwainī auch als Vorlage bei der Schilderung von Begebenheiten, die nicht unmittelbar mit den Mongolen verbunden waren. Im Rahmen der Geschichte der Uighuren beispielsweise (Kapitel IV, Folio [37]) berichtet er über Verschwörer und deren Verhör, das sich auf ihre Machenschaften bezog. Als Wortlaut des Verhörs zitiert Ǧuwainī die in

Sure 46:34 wiedergegebene Befragung von Ungläubigen, die beim Letzten Gericht dem Feuer vorgeführt werden. Der gesamte Vers lautet (Ǧuwainīs Zitat zwischen { }): *wa yawma yu'raḍu llaḏīna kafarū 'alā-n-nāri a-laysa hāḏā bi-l-ḥaqqi* {*qālū balā wa-rabbinā qāla fa-ḏūqū l-'aḏāba bi-mā kuntum takfurūn*[a]} „Und am Tag, an dem die, die ungläubig gewesen sind, dem Feuer vorgeführt werden (sagt Gott zu ihnen:) »Ist das nicht die Wahrheit?« {Sie sagen: »Ja doch! Bei unserem Herrn!« Er sagt: »Dann kostet die Strafe dafür, daß ihr dauernd ungläubig gewesen seid.«"} Hieran schließt sich dann die Nachricht an, daß die Verschwörer, die ihre Machenschaften mit dem Zitat „Ja doch! Bei unserem Herrn!" zugegeben hatten, hingerichtet worden seien.

Die vorstehend gebrachten Beispiele für Koranzitate in Ǧuwainīs Werk ließen sich noch buchfüllend vermehren. Die „Geschichte des Welteroberers" ist mit Koranzitaten geradezu durchwirkt. Der Leser dieser Geschichte stößt unausweichlich immer wieder auf Zitate aus diesem Heiligen Buch des Islams, das für die Muslime als universale Botschaft und endgültige Schrift, die von jeder irdischen Verderbnis geschützt und für alle Zeiten gegenwärtig, von Gott dem Mohammed, dem „Gesandten Gottes und Siegel der Propheten" (*...rasūla llāhi wa-ḫātama n-nabiyyīna...* Sure 33:40), offenbart worden ist.

Im Blickfeld dieser Zitate wird, wie einige der hier vorgeführten Beispiele zeigen, Tschinggis Khan und sein Heer, das zusammen mit seinen Söhnen Vernichtung und Tod brachte, als von Gott gewollt und in seine Pläne eingebunden vorgestellt. Ǧuwainīs Geschichtswerk bringt Tschinggis Khans Machtausübung mit Hilfe von Koranzitaten sogar in Einklang und Übereinstimmung mit Gottes schöpferischer Befehlsgewalt. Kein Wunder, daß auch die mehr profanen Seiten mongolischer Lebensgestaltung durch ihre Verbindungen zum Koran in muslimischen Augen aufgewertet werden konnten. Genau das nun dürfte Ǧuwainī mit seiner Geschichte neben einer Unterrichtung seiner Leser über historische Begebenheiten auch beabsichtigt haben. Die in den verschiedensten Bereichen und Vorgängen der Geschichte Tschinggis Khans und der Mongolen von Ǧuwainī immer wieder durch Zitate hergestellten Verbindungen zum Koran lassen das Heilige Buch des Islams zu einem Teil der „Geschichte des Welteroberers" und seiner Mongolen werden. Ǧuwainī hat den Koran in seiner Darstellung geradezu verankert, und damit die von ihm erzählte Geschichte Tschinggis Khans und der Mongolen „koranisiert" und damit muslimisiert. Der Koran erscheint oftmals schon gleichsam als Vorgänger und Modell für die Machtausübung Tschinggis Khans und seiner Mongolen.

Betrachtet man die „Geschichte des Welteroberers“ unter dem Aspekt der für die Darstellung vom Autor herangezogenen Quellen, so fällt der Nachweis nicht schwer, daß Ǧuwainī mit der Benutzung des Korans etwas unternommen hat, was man als breit angelegten Versuch einer Inkulturation bezeichnen kann. Ǧuwainī hat sich bemüht, Tschinggis Khan und die Mongolen dem Koran und damit auch automatisch dem Islam anzunähern. Der Versuch ist sicherlich nicht überall erfolgreich und überzeugend gelungen. Einiges wirkt eher gezwungen und nicht gerade „glücklich“, wie man so sagt. Dennoch dürfte Ǧuwainīs „Geschichte des Welteroberers“ nicht wenig dazu beigetragen haben, daß sich die Mongolen, wie oben schon erwähnt, zur Zeit der Teilreiche im 14. Jahrhundert in den von ihnen beherrschten Gebieten im Westen Eurasiens dem Islam zugewandt haben.

Geht man davon aus, daß der Religionswechsel zum Islam und der damit verbundene tiefgreifende Kulturwandel bei den Mongolen im Iran tatsächlich auch von Ǧuwainīs „Geschichte des Welteroberers“ profitiert haben, und zwar auch angesichts der Tatsache, daß die dortigen Mongolen in der Mitte des 13. Jahrhunderts demographisch eine nur hauchdünne, zunächst noch nichtmuslimische Minderheit bildeten, die von einer erdrückenden Mehrheit von Muslimen umgeben war, darf man Ǧuwainī als erfolgreichen Verfasser eines Werkes ansehen, das vor allem auch kulturpolitisch nachhaltig gewirkt hat. Die in diesem Werk enthaltenen zahlreichen Versuche, die Geschichte Tschinggis Khans und der Mongolen, gestützt durch zahllose Zitate aus dem Koran, unter muslimischem Blickwinkel darzustellen, dürfen dann durchaus als herausragende Beispiele für Versuche muslimischer Inkulturation gelten. Solchen Versuchen auch weiterhin Aufmerksamkeit zu schenken und ihre Mechanismen herauszuarbeiten, könnte die derzeit weltweit geführte Diskussion um die Globalisierung sowie um den sogenannten „Kampf der Kulturen“[10] mit vielen einschlägigen Beispielen bereichern.

Bibliographie

Boyle, J. A. 1958. *The History of the World-Conqueror* by ʿAla-ad-Din ʿAta-Malik Juvaini. Translated from the Text of Mirza Muhammad Qazvini by John Andrew Boyle, Ph.D., 2 vols. Manchester.

de Rachewiltz, I. 1971. *Papal Envoys to the Great Khans*. London.

Fiey, J. M. 1975. *Chrétiens Syriaques sous les Mongols (Il-Khanat de Perse, XIIIe-XIVe s.)*. (Corpus Scriptorum Christianorum Orientalium Vol. 362, Subsidia Tomus 44.) Louvain.

Flügel, G. 1898. *Concordantiae Corani Arabicae*. Lipsiae.

[10] Huntington 1996 (1998).

Gibb, H. A. R. & J. H. Kramers†. *Shorter Encyclopaedia of Islam*, Photomechanical Reprint. Leiden · London.

Halm, H. 1974. *Die Ausbreitung der šāfiʿītischen Rechtsschule von den Anfängen bis zum 8./14. Jahrhundert*. Wiesbaden.

Hartmann, R. 1944. *Die Religion des Islam. Eine Einführung*. Berlin.

Huntington, S. Ph. 1996 (1998). *The Clash of Civilizations and the Remaking of World Order*. New York. (deutsch: *Kampf der Kulturen – Die Neuordnung der Welt im 21. Jahrhundert*. München).

Krawulsky, D. 1978. *Īrān – Das Reich der Īlḫāne. Eine topographisch-historische Studie*. Wiesbaden.

Qazvini, Mirza Muḥammad (Hrsg.) 1912/-16/-37. *The Ta'ríkh-i-Jahán-Gushá of 'Alá'u d-Dín 'Aṭâ-Malik-i-Juwayní*. (= E. J. W. Gibb Memorial Series, Old Series, 3 Bände.) London.

Zirker, H. 2007. *Transliteration des gesamten Heiligen Qur'an*. Unter Weltnetz http://eslam.de/begriffe/t/transliteration_des_quran.htm.